ADVANCED TEXTS IN ECONOMETRICS

General Editors

C. W. J. GRANGER   G. E. MIZON

BAYESIAN INFERENCE IN DYNAMIC ECONOMETRIC MODELS

LUC BAUWENS, MICHEL LUBRANO,
AND JEAN-FRANÇOIS RICHARD

OXFORD

UNIVERSITY PRESS

OXFORD

UNIVERSITY PRESS

Great Clarendon Street, Oxford OX2 6DP

Oxford University Press is a department of the University of Oxford.
It furthers the University's objective of excellence in research, scholarship,
and education by publishing worldwide in

Oxford New York

Athens Auckland Bangkok Bogotá Buenos Aires Calcutta
Cape Town Chennai Dar es Salaam Delhi Florence Hong Kong Istanbul
Karachi Kuala Lumpur Madrid Melbourne Mexico City Mumbai
Nairobi Paris São Paulo Singapore Taipei Tokyo Toronto Warsaw

and associated companies in Berlin Ibadan

Oxford is a registered trade mark of Oxford University Press
in the UK and certain other countries

Published in the United States
by Oxford University Press Inc., New York

British Library Cataloguing in Publication Data

Data available

Library of Congress Cataloging in Publication Data

Data available

ISBN 0–19–877312–9 (hbk)
ISBN 0–19–877313–7 (pbk)

Typeset by the authors
Printed by Biddles Ltd., Guildford and King's Lynn

FOREWORD

The purpose of a foreword is to augment the prior information of decision-makers like librarians (should I order this book?), potential readers or users (what may I expect to learn from this book?), teachers (should I assign this book as a text or reference?), journal editors (should I commission a review of this book?), etc. It gives me pleasure to recommend unambiguously this volume to all such decision-makers. Comprehensive works on Bayesian econometrics are not numerous. This one is very well done. It has the further advantage of combining a thoughtful general introduction to Bayesian inference in econometrics (chapters 1–4) with a comprehensive treatment of a class of models that have been the subject of extensive research over the past twenty years, namely dynamic models (chapters 5–9).

Compared with first-generation works on Bayesian econometrics (my generation), the introductory part of this book is enriched with an up-to-date chapter on numerical integration (chapter 3). The value of that chapter is enhanced by its coverage of both deterministic and Monte Carlo methods, with illustrations of how combining both approaches may enhance overall effectiveness.

The second part of the book covers a vast territory. The dynamics may affect exogenous variables, endogenous variables or error processes; they may be linear or non-linear; they may concern a single equation or a system of equations. The organization of this volume fits most relevant cases into five solid and logically separated chapters. One of these is devoted to the special topic of unit roots, a topic to which the Bayesian approach makes a distinct contribution. Readers eager to discover the state of Bayesian arts in a specific area will find the answer here. They will also find serious applications to substantive problems, going well beyond mere numerical examples.

Dynamic econometric models have received sustained attention in recent years in part because they have received much attention in economic theory, both micro and macro. The participation of Bayesian econometricians in this effort reflects the progress made with implementation of the Bayesian approach in general, as summarized in the first part of the book. Without the versatility attained in such areas as numerical integration or the specification of prior densities, the extensions to dynamic models would not have been possible. The continuity of the research effort is apparent here, reflecting in part the immanence of basic concepts (like exogeneity) or problems (like identification), but also the pervasiveness of Bayesian methods. The fact that the combined research experience of the authors spans most of the short history of Bayesian econometrics has no doubt contributed to this quality of continuity.

The scope and depth of the more recent contributions is rewarding for all those who were associated with earlier developments. It also holds promise for further extensions. Bayesian techniques of statistical inference are naturally oriented towards pooling in a rigorous way information coming from separate sources. When applied to temporal data, they lend themselves to complementing the information extracted from streamlined dynamic models with specific information about unique historical events—whether they introduce breaks in time trends or more simply non-centred disturbances. The possibility of introducing such specific information in a probabilistic rather than deterministic way adds an important element of flexibility. I would hope that researchers will be attentive to this prospect. Similarly, the integration of time-series and cross-section data is a natural challenge for Bayesian econometricians. The availability of increasingly general and sophisticated methods of analysis for dynamic models should permit further progress along that rewarding avenue. I hope, and trust, that the authors of this monograph will contribute to such developments.

In their preface, the authors acknowledge an intellectual debt to 'the Bayesian school of Louvain' (CORE). I claim the right to acknowledge gratefully how much each of them individually, and all three of them collectively, have contributed to the research effort in Bayesian econometrics at CORE and more generally in Europe. They have played a significant role in extending early ideas into the solid developments to which this book bears testimony. For instance, they brought numerical integration and dynamic modelling to Louvain. From a human angle, they have been instrumental in maintaining the atmosphere of friendly exchanges and interactive stimulation which enriches the life of a research centre. Reading them today evokes many pleasant memories. I wish them similar experiences in the future and look forward to the further developments for which this book provides inspiring foundations.

Jacques H. Drèze
CORE, Louvain-la-Neuve
May 1999

PREFACE

This book originates from different lecture notes of courses on Bayesian econometrics which the three authors individually taught at Duke, Louvain, Marseille, and Toulouse in the 1980s. During a visit to Marseille, Clive Granger suggested that these lecture notes could be elaborated into a book for a new series that he had started to edit with Grayham Mizon. Our first idea, after making up a team, was to write a book that would reflect the state of the art until 1990, and, given our personal scientific trajectories, with an emphasis on all the work done at CORE in the previous 25 years, mainly in the areas of decision theory and of the Bayesian treatment of simultaneous equation models. Bayesian inference was still a rather confidential area of econometrics, but at the end of the 1980s there were already signs of change. Indeed, the field evolved at a fast rate during the 1990s. So we gradually changed our conception of the book from a backward looking view to a forward one. We wanted to pick up 'hot' topics like unit roots, cointegration, ARCH, non-linear time series. This required the development of new research and slowed down our writing (probably drawing too much on the patience of Andrew Schuller, who was in charge of the series at OUP). But we are convinced that the result is much more exciting than what it would have been otherwise.

We would all like to underline the debt we owe to what could be called 'the Bayesian school of Louvain'. We have all been, or even still are, connected with the University of Louvain and more precisely to CORE. This had a considerable influence on our vision of Bayesian econometrics and our book reflects that influence. This is the reason why a first chapter is entirely devoted to decision theory, why we consider Bayesian cuts and Bayesian reduction of models, why priors are desired to be informative, and also why there is so little material on posterior odds and none about model averaging. Some readers may be upset by that last aspect. Having recalled this context and influence, the reader is entitled to look for a large amount of material devoted to simultaneous equation models, a domain to which the Louvain school contributed a lot. But we have preferred not to enlarge the length of this book too much as the Bayesian treatment of the simultaneous equation model is already extensively covered in Chapter 9 of the *Handbook of Econometrics* which was written by one of the coauthors in collaboration with Jacques Drèze. We do not want to say that nothing has been written since then on this topic. Chapter 9 gives extensive references on the topic and its last section constitutes a guide for further reading. We have tried in this book to give as many empirical illustrations as possible. This required a huge effort of programming and is a reason for us to evoke the memory of Hans Tompa. Hans arrived at CORE in the early 1970s and brought both rigour and competence to numerical analysis and programming. At that time all the computations were done in Fortran, but nowadays macro languages like GAUSS, Matlab, or Ox are widely used. Nevertheless, algorithms still have to be precise and well written. The influence of Hans is still alive.

The book is structured so that it can be used in different ways, depending on the background of the reader. It can be viewed as consisting of two parts that are relatively autonomous. The first four chapters explain mainly the basic concepts and tools of Bayesian inference. This part starts with a synthesis of the foundations of Bayesian inference and its relation to decision theory, and continues with the implied principles of Bayesian inference. A few essential ingredients are then reviewed: reduction of models, inference on the linear regression model, numerical techniques including Markov chain methods, and the building of prior densities for the regression model (covering elicitation methods for informative priors and general principles for building non-informative priors). The remaining chapters, and in fact the second part of the book, are devoted to Bayesian inference in a set of particular dynamic econometric models. They cover autoregressive regression models, including moving average errors and the well-known error correction model. Then the much debated topic of unit root inference is introduced in a separate chapter. The book continues with heteroscedastic models, giving a detailed treatment of the functional heteroscedastic model and of the famous ARCH/GARCH class of models, with a special emphasis on the statistical properties of this model. Non-linear time series models have become an important topic in the 1990s and receive their own treatment, showing how the Bayesian approach can nicely solve some problems. Up to this point, the book deals exclusively with single-equation regression models. Systems of equations are introduced in the last chapter, starting with VAR models and proceeding with the cointegrated case. The simultaneous equation model, as already said, is only covered briefly. A detailed appendix gives the properties of all the probability distributions used, and another gives simulation algorithms.

A reader already familiar with the basics of Bayesian inference can thus in principle directly select the chapter(s) he is interested in among Chapters 5 to 9. A 'novice' reader should at least read Chapters 1, 2, and 4 before other chapters.

We could not have written this book without the support of several institutions that provided funds to help us to meet regularly in Marseille or Louvain-La-Neuve. Let us mention: Commissariat Général aux Relations Internationales, Center for Operations Research and Econometrics, Fonds National de la Recherche Scientifique, Université catholique de Louvain (in Belgium); Centre National de la Recherche Scientifique, Ecole des Hautes Etudes en Sciences Sociales, Groupe de Recherche en Economie Quantitative et Econométrie, Ministère des Affaires Etrangères (in France), and the European Commission through the Human Capital and Mobility Programme network 'Simulation Methods in Econometrics'. We warmly thank all of them. The scientific responsibility for the contents of the book is exclusively ours.

We prepared the manuscript using LaTeX. Most of the illustrations were produced with Gnuplot, a few with GAUSS. Since a book cannot be free of mistakes, we hope to get feedback from readers, who can email us at bauwens@core.ucl.ac.be. We shall put any corrections on the website of Luc Bauwens, which can be reached at http://www.core.ucl.ac.be/econometrics/index.htm. This site also provides the data sets used in this book, and several GAUSS programs.

Luc Bauwens, Michel Lubrano, Jean-François Richard
Louvain-la-Neuve
May 1999

CONTENTS

DECISION THEORY AND BAYESIAN INFERENCE

1.1 Introduction

Mathematical statistics and decision theory are closely connected. This is especially true for the school of thought which is at the core of our book: the Bayesian approach to econometrics. Though the viewpoint adopted in this book is more one of scientific reporting than of decision making, it is useful to begin our presentation with a brief survey of the Bayesian approach to decision making under uncertainty. We believe this approach provides a strong rationale for the use of Bayesian techniques in econometrics, a critical requirement in light of the fact that the majority of econometricians belong to the classical school of thought, whereby parameters are treated as unknown constants and inference procedures are evaluated in terms of their performance across hypothetical repeated samples. In particular, the most publicized area of disagreement between classical and Bayesian econometricians (and statisticians!) has to do with the nature of probability itself. Bayesians argue that probability need not be restricted to its frequentist interpretation, since it fundamentally represents uncertainty (typically expressed in the form of willingness to bet on uncertain outcomes) and is, therefore, largely subjective.

This chapter is organized as follows. In Section 1.2 we introduce a baseline decision model which will serve as the point of reference for much of the discussion that follows. Section 1.3 briefly introduces a set of simple axioms which are meant to formalize a concept of 'rational behaviour' in the face of uncertainty. Alternative interpretations of the concept of probability are discussed in Section 1.4. Bayes' theorem, which is the cornerstone of Bayesian inference procedures, is introduced in Section 1.5. The 'extensive' and 'normal' modes of analysis are defined in Sections 1.6 and 1.7, respectively. Section 1.8 discusses the related concepts of statistical inference and scientific reporting, setting the scene for much of our book. Estimation and hypothesis testing are presented, both from a classical and Bayesian perspective, in Sections 1.9 and 1.10, respectively.

1.2 The Baseline Decision Problem

One of the primary objects of statistical analysis is that of assisting agents in making rational decisions in a situation of uncertainty. Rational decisions do not mean that the decision taken proves to be the right one *ex post* but simply that the agent making the decision is coherent, in the sense of a set of axioms detailed in Section 1.3.

Consider the following baseline decision problem:

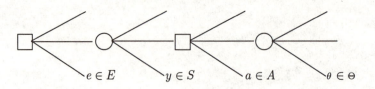

$$e \in E \qquad y \in S \qquad a \in A \qquad \theta \in \Theta$$

FIG. 1.1. Decision tree

1) The decision maker has to select a decision a in a set of decisions A, whose consequences depend upon an unknown quantity θ in a set Θ, commonly called the state of nature.

2) In order to reduce uncertainty on θ the decision maker may select a preliminary experiment e among a set of experiments E and observe an outcome y in a sample space S. E typically includes a null experiment e_0 which consists of skipping the experimentation stage and directly proceeding to the final decision stage.

It is convenient to represent that sequence in the form of a game tree, as given in Fig. 1.1, where decision nodes are represented by squares and chance nodes by circles. In fact the decision sequence just described corresponds to a game against nature, where nature selects experimental (sample) outcomes and states of nature. Note that nature has no hidden agenda and, in particular, is not playing strategically against decision makers.

Our baseline description of the game tree calls for additional technical details:

1) The parameter θ, the state of nature, is meant to include a full description of the environment relevant to the decision problem under consideration. The set Θ contains all relevant states of nature. Throughout this textbook Θ is restricted to be a subset of R^p, so that θ is a p-dimensional vector of numerical characteristics, commonly called parameters, meant to describe the relevant aspects of states of nature. Furthermore, θ will generally be of fixed dimensionality relative to the dimensionality of y (i.e. loosely speaking, relative to sample size), though exceptions will be considered. All together the above restrictions imply that we are essentially focusing our attention on parametric techniques of Bayesian inference.

2) To each branch of the game tree in Fig. 1.1 we associate a consequence c which is meant to characterize the decision maker's payoff (monetary or other), which results from that specific game sequence. Let $c(e, y, a, \theta)$ denote the consequence associated with the sequence (e, y, a, θ).

3) Decisions are actions which the decision maker can choose in accordance with the rules of the game. In the context described by Fig. 1.1, decisions are sequential and include two components: the immediate choice of an experiment e in E and, once a sample outcome y obtains, the choice of a final action a in A. Largely for notational convenience, we assume that

$(e, a) \in E \times A$. Formally a decision (e, a) attaches a consequence $c(e, y, a, \theta)$ to each pair (y, θ). Accounting for the sequential nature of the game requires the introduction of the concept of decision rules. Specifically a decision rule d is a mapping from $E \times S$ into A which associates a decision a to each pair (e, y). It accounts for the fact that the rules of the game allow the decision maker to postpone the final decision until the outcome y which obtains from the initial choice e is observed. A strategy σ is a complete game plan which, in the present context, consists in an immediate choice of experiment e together with a decision rule d. Clearly once the decision maker is committed to a strategy σ, his or her presence is no longer required in order to play the game, since by definition σ covers all potential outcomes generated by nature's moves.

4) The only experiments worthy of consideration in the present context are those which 'convey information' on the unknown state of nature θ. Specifically and somewhat anticipating the axiomatic analysis which follows, we assume that to each pair (e, θ) there corresponds a probability distribution for the sample outcome y. Our reason for mentioning sampling distribution at this early stage of the discussion lies in the fact that it helps to flesh out the concept of experiments. Furthermore, the need to assess sampling distributions is recognized by both Bayesian and classical statisticians and is, therefore, largely uncontroversial.

We assume further that the probability distribution of y, given the pair (e, θ), is dominated by a σ-finite measure and may, therefore, be represented by a (nonnegative) density function f such that the sampling probability of an arbitrary measurable event B in S is given by

$$\Pr(B|\theta, e) = \int_B f(y|\theta, e)\, d\nu(y). \tag{1.1}$$

It is generally the case in econometrics that E includes a single (often 'sequential') experiment e. In such cases we shall delete explicit reference to it. Also, unless otherwise indicated, ν is the conventional Lebesgue measure on the sample space and $d\nu(y)$ is then replaced by dy. Hence we shall commonly use the following shorthand notation for (1.1):

$$\Pr(B|\theta) = \int_B f(y|\theta)\, dy. \tag{1.2}$$

Note that within our decisional framework θ has been introduced primarily to characterize the states of the world. There is no logical implication, especially in the context of real life applications, that θ may equally serve unambiguously to index sampling distributions. Hence it might well be the case that there exists pairs of distinct states of the world θ and θ' such that the corresponding sampling distributions are identical, i.e. that

$$f(y|\theta) = f(y|\theta'), \qquad y \text{ almost surely.} \tag{1.3}$$

In such a case θ and θ' are said to be observationally equivalent. Observational equivalence is discussed at greater length in Subsection 2.2.4, in so far as Bayesian techniques are ideally suited to deal with such situations, which are generally perceived to be pathologies within a classical framework.

1.3   The Moral Expectation Theorem

The issue we now address is that of characterizing 'coherent decision making' within the context of the sequential game we have just outlined. Conventional practices within the vast literature devoted to the topic consist in postulating a (minimal) set of axioms, which are meant to capture the salient features of coherency and lead to a mathematically convenient formulation of the decision maker's objective function.

Different routes are available to generate such sets of axioms. DeGroot (1970), for example, sequentially introduces the concepts of subjective probability and utility. In contrast Drèze (1975) aims at axiomatizing coherent behaviour *per se* and, in so doing, derives a joint characterization of probabilities and utilities. A detailed discussion of the various approaches goes way beyond the objectives of our book, notwithstanding the fact that excellent discussions and surveys are available elsewhere, a number of which are included in our list of references.

We limit ourselves to outlining the key components of one such axiomatic setup which appears to be well suited to the object of our discussion, drawing heavily on Drèze's contribution. Essentially Drèze assumes the existence of a simple ordering which is successively applied to acts, acts conditionally upon events, consequences, and finally events. In the present context events are defined as (measurable) subsets of $S \times \Theta$ and acts are pairs consisting of an experiment e and a final decision a.

Four axioms are introduced in succession (refer to Drèze 1975, for details regarding the successive refinements of the initial ordering):

1) Acts: A simple preference ordering among acts is postulated. Using the symbol $\succeq$ to mean 'preferred or indifferent', we postulate that for all pairs (e, a), (e', a') and (e'', a''):

   - either $(e, a) \succeq (e', a')$ or $(e', a') \succeq (e, a)$;
   - $(e, a) \succeq (e', a')$ and $(e', a') \succeq (e'', a'') \Rightarrow (e, a) \succeq (e'', a'')$.

2) Acts conditionally upon events (strong independence): If two acts have identical consequences under a certain event E, then the choice between them should proceed as if E did not exist as a possibility.

3) Consequences: The consequences are so defined that preferences among them are never modified by knowledge of the event that obtains.

4) Events: Which one of two events the decision maker prefers to stake a wager on does not depend upon the nature of the price.

All together these four axioms generate a remarkable result, known as the 'moral expectation theorem' which establishes that under suitable technical refinements:

Theorem 1.1   *1) There exists a (countably additive) probability distribution* Π *on* $S \times \Theta$.

2) There exists a real-valued 'utility function' U defined up to a linear transformation on $E \times S \times A \times \Theta$ *such that the ordering among acts is fully representable by an expected utility function, which is given by*

$$U(e,a) = \int_{S \times \Theta} U(e,y,a,\theta)\, \Pi(y,\theta)\, dy\, d\theta. \tag{1.4}$$

The decision maker's problem is then reduced to that of selecting the decision(s) which maximize(s) expected utility. In order to reformulate the decision maker's optimization problem in a way which accounts for its sequential nature, we introduce appropriate factorizations of the joint density Π in Section 1.5.

We ought to mention the fact that the theory we have just outlined is far from being uncontroversial. There now exists a large body of economic experiments that seem to suggest that economic agents (mostly students) when confronted with experimental scenarios often behave in ways that appear to contradict theory prescriptions. Whether or not such experimental evidence actually contradicts theory is often a matter of interpreting the agents' perceptions of the situation they are confronted with; this comment applies *a fortiori* to real life situations—see e.g. the debate relative to belt wearing in Marshall, Richard, and Zarkin (1992). The main attraction of the axioms we have just introduced lies in the fact that it provides a complete formal and logical framework to initiate normative research in a broad range of situations requiring decisions under uncertainty, even though specific applications might require additional qualifications (see the discussion in Drèze 1975).

We also ought to emphasize that all the axiomatic validations of decision making under uncertainty we are aware of share the characteristic of relying on the concept of wagers which naturally requires that wagers can be settled unambiguously at some point in time. That requirement may often be satisfied in a broad range of real life applications but does raise conceptual problems in econometrics when θ corresponds to theoretical constructs such as elasticities. We shall reassess this issue in the context of Section 1.8 where we discuss the more operational notion of scientific reporting as a natural complement to that of decision making.

1.4   The Interpretation of Probabilities

Even though the moral expectation theorem provides an essential conceptual framework for analysing decision making under uncertainty, practitioners generally ignore its axiomatic basis and immediately focus their attention on (direct) probability and utility assessments—notwithstanding the deeper issue of whether probability and utility assessments can be separated from each other. This latter issue will not be addressed here, but useful references are DeGroot (1970) and Winkler (1972).

Furthermore, utility assessment is often reduced to the bare minimum, e.g. by the (implicit) selection of a quadratic loss function. No such short cut exists when it comes to discussing probability assessment on parameter spaces. The interpretation of such probability measures has been and still is the object of most lively debates between classical and Bayesian statisticians and also among Bayesians themselves. The key issue is that of establishing a link between formal definitions of probabilities as additive functions on sets, valued on the interval $[0, 1]$ on one hand, and one's perception of the surrounding physical world on the other hand.

We first comment on formal definitions of probability. Let us consider a set Ω of (random) outcomes. Subsets of Ω are called (random) events. Events have to be defined in such a way that their collection forms a Boolean algebra. Let $\mathcal{E}$ denote a collection of events from Ω. $\mathcal{E}$ is said to form a Boolean algebra if and only if the following three conditions are verified:

1) $\Omega \in \mathcal{E}$;
2) if $F \in \Omega$, then $\overline{F} \in \Omega$ (where $\overline{F}$ denotes the complement of F in Ω);
3) if $F_1 \in \Omega$ and $F_2 \in \Omega$, then $F_1 \cup F_2 \in \Omega$.

A probability defined on the pair $(\Omega, \mathcal{E})$ is an additive function verifying the three axioms of Kolmogorov:

1) $\forall F \in \Omega, \Pr(F) \geq 0$;
2) $\Pr(\Omega) = 1$;
3) If $F_1 \in \Omega$, $F_2 \in \Omega$, $F_1 \cap F_2 = \emptyset$, then $\Pr(F_1 \cup F_2) = \Pr(F_1) + \Pr(F_2)$.

The concept of probability just defined is largely uncontroversial. In contrast, the more practical issue of settling which sets can be extended into probability spaces is highly controversial. In particular, can we define a probability on the parameter space? There is no objective reason why we could not. But the question lies in the domain of the interpretation of probabilities, and directly relates to the assumed links between the formal system and the physical world. Three types of links have been proposed in the literature: the empirical link, the logical link, and the subjective link.

The 'empirical' interpretation of probability which has long been the most widely used is that of the limit of an empirical frequency. As a consequence one can speak of probability only for physical events that can be reproduced, for instance, by casting a die or a coin, whence a probability statement represents an assertion that can only be accepted or rejected after an empirical experience. Probability only exists as a physical phenomenon. It is associated with a parameter in an experiment. Well-known tenants of this interpretation are Venn (1886), Von Mises (1928), and later the classical school represented by Fisher (1956) and Neyman (1952).

An alternative viewpoint denies the fact that a probability statement has to be associated with an empirical statement. Probability does not exist as a physical phenomenon. It simply represents a logical relation between a proposition and a corpus of knowledge. This viewpoint goes back to Keynes (1921) and has been advocated further by Carnap (1962) among others. Consensus regarding the logical link between the underlying corpus of knowledge and the resulting propositions produces a unique system of probabilities. The system of invariant prior probability distributions of Jeffreys (1961) belongs to this system. Prior probabilities are formally introduced in Section 1.5. They are meant to represent uncertainty about parameters prior to the observation of experimental outcomes and constitute the main area of contention between classical and Bayesian econometricians.

The subjective interpretation of probability differs somewhat from the logical one. Probability still represents a degree of belief about a proposition confronted by a set of facts, but it is no longer based on a universal logical system. It is personal and thus can vary from one person to the other. Probability is simply a personal system of representation of degrees of beliefs.

Rejecting both the logical and the subjective interpretations implies that it is not possible to represent by probabilities the uncertainty about propositions relative, in particular, to parameter spaces, whence the observation of events cannot be used to update such probabilities (see Savage 1962).

Econometricians display a wide range of attitudes towards these polar interpretations of probability. In particular there are classical econometricians who are nevertheless willing to depart from the strict frequentist definition of probability, but accept only the logical interpretation and consequently use prior densities which can be qualified as 'objective'. In this stream of literature, it is valuable to quote the contribution of Phillips (1991a). The idea of a prior density that could summarize the personal opinion of an expert is rejected, as based on a subjective interpretation of probability. An objective prior has to reflect a consensus, the only one possible being a consensus on ignorance. The prior probability has to reflect this ignorance and (ideally) should not distort the inference process (the learning mechanism).

We, the authors of this book, share the subjective viewpoint, but its adoption by the reader is by no means required. The prior densities which are used below can serve to reflect a decision maker's personal beliefs in a specific decision context. More fundamentally, we use prior densities as essential devices for interpreting sample evidence. Bayes' theorem provides us with a coherent learning mechanism whereby a prior density is transformed into a posterior density. Explicit comparisons between prior and posterior densities constitute an invaluable device for calibrating and interpreting sample information, especially when the latter is deficient in some ways, e.g. in small-sample situations.

Two important issues naturally arise in this context. One is the use of so-called 'non-informative', typically non-finite, prior measures which aim at minimizing the contribution of prior information to the overall posterior density. Such priors are often used as 'reference priors' in the context of a broader sensitivity analysis. They are also instrumental in providing a range of classical techniques with Bayesian reinterpretations, a viewpoint which has been widely used by Zellner (1971). Difficulties arise from the fact that there does not exist a unique and widely accepted concept of non-informative prior measures and, relatedly, that if we except simple classes of models, the (lack of) informational content of a prior measure is by no means trivial to assess. See e.g. the recent discussion on the selection of non-informative priors in the context of unit root inference (Phillips 1991a).

Secondly, we give priority in this book to the obtention of analytically tractable posterior densities, often at the cost of imposing (severe) limitations on the choice of prior densities. Not only are such results often more easily interpretable than results based on numerical integration techniques but, more importantly, they are essential components of the efficient design of numerical procedures under more general prior densities. In practice, the use of analytically tractable prior densities raises the obvious issue of whether or not they can truly reflect one's subjective prior opinions. Chapter 4 bears on the issue of eliciting prior densities, especially in the context of the linear regression model.

1.5   Factorizations of Π: Bayes' Theorem

Assuming for the moment that the probability measure Π is 'proper', in the sense that its integral on $S \times \Theta$ is equal to one, two of its factorizations will play an essential role throughout our analysis.

Π can be factorized into the product of a marginal probability density φ on Θ and a (family of) conditional probability densities $f(.|\theta)$ on S:

$$\Pi(y,\theta) = \varphi(\theta) f(y|\theta) \qquad (1.5)$$

for all (y,θ) in $S \times \Theta$, such that $\varphi(\theta) > 0$.

The conditional density $f(y|\theta)$ corresponds to the concept of sampling probability which was introduced in Section 1.2. Note that within a Bayesian framework, where both sample outcomes and parameters (states of the world) are treated as random variables, $f(y|\theta)$ is meant to characterize a genuine conditional distribution. In contrast classical statisticians generally treat θ as an unknown fixed quantity which fundamentally serves the purpose of indexing sampling distributions (which by no means precludes the selection of an index that has an interesting economic interpretation). This being said, a cursory look through the relevant literature indicates that sampling distributions *per se* rarely constitute an object of controversy between Bayesian and classical econometricians. Econometricians may disagree strongly among themselves about the formulation of specific sampling probabilities, but we believe that such disagreements come from different perceptions of the salient features of the real life problem under scrutiny rather than from 'philosophical' differences.

The same cannot be said about the marginal distribution φ on Θ commonly called 'prior density' of θ. That terminology emphasizes the fact that φ is meant to capture whichever (often subjective) information was available to the decision maker, prior to the observation of y. Disagreements upon the issues of whether or not prior distributions are relevant for the purpose of statistical inference are among the most widely publicized aspects of the controversies that often separate Bayesian statisticians from classical ones. In this book, we intend to present a more constructive version of that debate and set the emphasis on complementarities between the two approaches, beyond their basic philosophical differences.

Π can also be factorized into the product of a marginal density f on y and (a family of) conditional densities $\varphi(.|y)$ on Θ:

$$\Pi(y, \theta) = f(y)\,\varphi(\theta|y) \tag{1.6}$$

for all (y, θ) in $S \times \Theta$ such that $f(y) > 0$.

The conditional density $\varphi(\theta|y)$ is called the posterior density. It is meant to capture all relevant (prior plus sample) information regarding θ, posterior to the observation of y. The marginal density f is called the (*ex ante*) predictive density of y.

From eqns (1.5) and (1.6) we can deduce that

$$\varphi(\theta|y) = \varphi(\theta)\,\frac{f(y|\theta)}{f(y)}, \tag{1.7}$$

which corresponds to a density version of the famous Bayes' theorem. It plays a central role in the Bayesian approach to statistical inference, in that it characterizes how a prior density is coherently revised into a posterior density in the light of the observation of a sampling result y.

Note that the distinction between prior and posterior probabilities is inherently relative to a given sampling experiment. Under sequential sampling, the posterior density relative to one sample serves as the prior density relative to the next sample. Let $y = (y_1, y_2)$ denote a sequence of two samples. Let $\varphi(\theta)$ denote the initial prior density. In all generality let the joint sampling density be factorized as follows:

$$f(y|\theta) = f_1(y_1|\theta)\,f_2(y_2|y_1, \theta). \tag{1.8}$$

The posterior density relative to y_1 is given by

$$\varphi(\theta|y_1) = \varphi(\theta)\,\frac{f_1(y_1|\theta)}{f_1(y_1)}, \tag{1.9}$$

where

$$f_1(y_1) = \int_\Theta f_1(y_1|\theta)\,\varphi(\theta)\,d\theta. \tag{1.10}$$

It serves as the prior density relative to y_2 and the corresponding posterior density is given by

$$\varphi(\theta|y_1, y_2) = \varphi(\theta|y_1)\,\frac{f_2(y_2|y_1, \theta)}{f_2(y_2|y_1)}, \tag{1.11}$$

where

$$f_2(y_2|y_1) = \int_\Theta f_2(y_2|y_1, \theta)\, \varphi(\theta|y_1)\, d\theta. \tag{1.12}$$

Note that $\varphi(\theta|y_1, y_2)$ can also be derived by application of Bayes' theorem to the joint sample:

$$\varphi(\theta|y) = \varphi(\theta)\, \frac{f(y|\theta)}{f(y)}, \tag{1.13}$$

where

$$\begin{aligned}
f(y) &= \int_\Theta f(y|\theta)\, \varphi(\theta)\, d\theta \\
&= \int_\Theta f_2(y_2|y_1, \theta)\, f_1(y_1|\theta)\, \varphi(\theta)\, d\theta \\
&= \int_\Theta f_2(y_2|y_1, \theta)\, \varphi(\theta|y_1)\, f_1(y_1)\, d\theta \\
&= f_1(y_1)\, f_2(y_2|y_1).
\end{aligned} \tag{1.14}$$

The last equality indicates that (1.13) also obtains from formulae (1.9) to (1.12) which ensures the coherency of sequential learning.

We are now in a position to formalize the decision maker's optimization problem. Two (equivalent) forms of analysis are available: the *extensive* form analysis, which is solution oriented and proceeds by backwards induction on the game tree; and the *normal* form (or strategic) analysis, which sets the emphasis on strategies and thereby provides useful insights on the nature of the game itself.

1.6   Extensive Form Analysis

An extensive form analysis refers to a standard backwards optimization algorithm commonly used in dynamic programming whereby the game tree is solved recursively starting from its terminal nodes. The relevant operators are the expectation operator at any chance node and the maximization operator at any decision node in accordance with the prescription of the moral expectation theorem.

According to the game tree represented in Fig. 1.1, the decision maker has to evaluate sequentially the following functionals:

1) Each sequence (e, y, a) is evaluated by means of the following *posterior* expected utility:

$$U_1(e, y, a) = E_{\theta|y} U(e, y, a, \theta). \tag{1.15}$$

2) One step backward in the game tree, each sequence (e, y) requires the solution of the following optimization problem:

$$U_2(e, y) = \max_{a \in A} U_1(e, y, a). \tag{1.16}$$

Note that this optimization problem has to be solved for all possible sequences (e, y) before we can proceed to the next step. Hence the outcome of this terminal analysis is an optimal decision rule d_* of the form

$$d_* = E \times S \to A; \; (e, y) \to d_*(e, y), \tag{1.17}$$

where $d_*(e, y)$ denotes a decision for which (1.16) obtains (unicity need not be assumed at this stage of the discussion).

3) Next, each experiment e is evaluated by means of the following predictive expectation:

$$U_3(e) = \mathrm{E}_y \, U_2(e, y). \qquad (1.18)$$

4) Finally, the decision maker ought to select an experience e_* which maximizes $U_3(e)$. Let

$$U_* = \max_{e \in E} U_3(e), \text{ and } e_* = \arg \max_{e \in E} U_3(e). \qquad (1.19)$$

In summary an extensive form analysis is characterized by the following sequence of operations:

$$e_* = \arg \max_{e \in E} \mathrm{E}_y \max_{a \in A} \mathrm{E}_{\theta|y} U(e, y, a, \theta). \qquad (1.20)$$

Its outcome consists of one (or several equivalent) immediate decision(s) e_* and of one (or several equivalent) optimal decision rule(s) d_*, where $d_*(e_*, y)$ describes how the decision maker plans to react to the observation of y, which obtains under e_*. An extensive form analysis prescribes that the decision maker ought to commit him- or herself to d_* even before y is observed, since it would be suboptimal to deviate from d_* once y is observed. It is in that sense that game theorists emphasize the point that once optimal strategies, or 'mutual best responses', in a game with several strategic players have been evaluated, the participants' presence is no longer required in order to 'play' the resulting game. Note also that, in the terminology of game theorists, an extensive form analysis generates pure (non-random) optimal strategies, in the sense that the decision maker has nothing to gain by randomizing his or her actions in so far as the decision maker faces a non-strategic opponent, such as nature. The same does not necessarily apply when several strategic players compete against each other. Full predictability of one's action might provide opponents with an edge. Under such circumstances, randomization among sets of equivalent pure strategies becomes a key component of mutual best response strategies.

The extensive form of analysis is solution oriented. However, it suffers from a number of conceptual drawbacks. It does require, in particular, a preliminary application of Bayes' theorem to the effect that the respective contributions of prior and sample information to the optimal solution are difficult to assess, except possibly by means of a 'sensitivity' analysis, a topic that will be addressed later (we shall frequently discuss classes of prior densities rather than focus on a single subjective prior density; the examination of how key characteristics of the posterior densities vary accordingly is an essential component of a sensitivity analysis). Such an assessment is critical when it comes to evaluating the respective merits of Bayesian and classical inference techniques. Furthermore, classical statisticians often set the emphasis on evaluating specific inference strategies rather than computing optimal decisions. The normal (or strategic) form of analysis which we discuss next offers greater conceptual appeal, though it is computationally far more demanding than the extensive form analysis.

1.7 Normal or Strategic Form Analysis

As already mentioned, a strategy σ is a complete game plan which, in the present context, consists in an immediate decision e and a decision rule $d : E \times S \to A$. Clearly the cardinality of the set of all strategies is such that a scanning of all possible strategies is downright impossible (except for the most simplest illustrations). Nevertheless large sets of strategies can easily be eliminated either because they are blatantly suboptimal, such as those which are constant on A, or because they are dominated by others, in a sense to be clarified later. This being said, the normal form of analysis consists in evaluating individual strategies by means of the corresponding expected utilities:

$$U(\sigma) = \mathrm{E}_{y,\theta} U(e, y, d(e, y), \theta). \tag{1.21}$$

An optimal strategy σ_* is one which maximizes $U(\sigma)$. Not surprisingly both the extensive and the normal forms of analysis ought to produce the same set of optimal strategies. One advantage of the strategic formulation in eqn (1.21), as opposed to that in eqn (1.20), lies in the fact that the evaluation of $U(\sigma)$ can be conducted under either one of the two factorizations of the joint density Π, as given in formulae (1.5) and (1.6). If, in particular, we rely upon the factorization into the product of prior and sampling densities, (1.21) can be written as

$$U(\sigma) = \mathrm{E}_\theta \left[\mathrm{E}_{y|\theta} U(e, y, d(e, y), \theta) \right]. \tag{1.22}$$

Since the inner integral on the right hand side does not depend on the choice of the prior density, formula (1.22) provides us with an obvious way of evaluating the contribution of $\varphi(\theta)$ in the evaluation of $U(\sigma)$. Even more importantly, the factorization in (1.22) constitutes a key component of our evaluation of the respective merits of the Bayesian and classical approaches in econometrics. However, in order to address that issue, we first have to simplify somewhat the general decisional framework considered until now and, in particular, introduce the concept of statistical inference which is markedly narrower than that of (statistical) decision making.

1.8 Statistical Inference and Scientific Reporting

Decision making *per se* is not the object of our book, though the decisional framework we have just outlined will serve as our constant guideline. A cursory look at the current applied econometric literature quickly reveals that the primary motivation of most applied econometricians is not one of solving real life decision problems. We do not mean to imply that the problems they address have no real life implications, but we have to acknowledge the fact that the functions of scientific investigation and decision making are widely separated. Empirical research generally aims at producing and interpreting statistical evidence. Whether or not such research influences policy makers has little to do with its coherency (in the sense in which this notion is used in the previous discussion).

If we restrict our attention to scientific reporting, the alleged superiority of Bayesian techniques—on the grounds that they are decision oriented—is somewhat more debatable. Though this book includes several examples where Bayesian and classical procedures for scientific reporting may produce markedly different results, communicability with potential users is critical for scientific reporting. On that account Bayesian statisticians have to concede the fact that many practitioners are more familiar with classical inference techniques than with their Bayesian analogues. Furthermore, they themselves ought to be able to derive useful information from a set of classical results—which often constitutes a set of 'sufficient statistics'—even though they might interpret them differently from their classical colleagues.

This being said, one of the primary objectives of the present book is that of proposing a range of Bayesian scientific reporting procedures which are easily interpretable and which, relative to their classical counterparts, provide additional decision-oriented insights, especially when the models under consideration are informationally deficient.

In the meantime let us focus our attention on two commonly used forms of statistical inference that constitute the bulk of scientific reporting in the econometric literature, namely estimation and hypothesis testing.

Estimation and hypothesis testing are commonly discussed within a decisional framework which is simpler than that which corresponds to Fig. 1.1, on several accounts. First, we shall assume separability between the consequences (typically costs) associated with the experimentation stage (e, y) and those resulting from the final decision stage (a, θ). Specifically the utility function is assumed to be additively separable:

$$U(e, y, a, \theta) = U_1(e, y) + U_2(a, \theta). \tag{1.23}$$

Furthermore econometricians often deal with samples that are already available—such as national accounts time series—in which case they are solely concerned with the final decision stage, i.e. with the U_2 component in (1.23).

It is common practice to replace U_2 by an equivalent loss function. Let $a(\theta)$ denote an optimal decision for known θ, i.e.

$$a(\theta) = \arg \max_{a \in A} U_2(a, \theta). \tag{1.24}$$

The loss (or regret) function $l(a, \theta)$ is then defined as

$$l(a, \theta) = U_2(a(\theta), \theta) - U_2(a, \theta) \tag{1.25}$$

and is a non-negative real-valued function. Maximizing the posterior expectation of U_2 is equivalent to minimizing the posterior expected loss.

Within a pure decisional framework, once a sample y has been observed, one ought to select a decision which minimizes posterior expected loss. Assuming unicity for the ease of presentation, let

$$a_* = \arg \min_{a \in A} E_{\theta|y}[l(a, \theta)]. \tag{1.26}$$

If, for example, one selects a quadratic loss function (typically on the grounds of tractability), then an explicit solution is available for a_*. Let

$$l(a, \theta) = [a - a(\theta)]' Q [a - a(\theta)] = \text{tr } Q [a - a(\theta)] [a - a(\theta)]', \tag{1.27}$$

where Q is a positive definite symmetric (PDS) matrix. The posterior expected loss is then given by

$$E_{\theta|y}[l(a, \theta)] = \text{tr } [Q\Sigma(y)] + [a - \bar{a}(y)]' Q [a - \bar{a}(y)], \tag{1.28}$$

where $\bar{a}(y)$ and $\Sigma(y)$ represent the posterior expectation and the posterior co-variance matrix of $a(\theta)$ respectively (assuming existence). The optimal decision is then given by $a_* = \bar{a}(y)$ and the corresponding (minimal) posterior expected loss by

$$l_*(y) = \text{tr } [Q\Sigma(y)]. \tag{1.29}$$

The ease with which these results can be derived justifies the predominant use of quadratic loss functions in statistics and econometrics. Note, however, that quadratic loss functions offer disadvantages that cannot be underestimated. First, they are symmetric in the difference $[a - a(\theta)]$ while there are many instances where one might not be indifferent between 'missing' $a(\theta)$ from below or from above. Even more importantly, quadratic loss functions are unbounded, which may preclude the existence of the posterior expectation in formula (1.28). The use of asymmetric or bounded functions has occasionally been advocated on these grounds, but typically necessitates numerical integration, see e.g. Zellner (1986a).

As discussed in Section 1.7, the Bayesian principle whereby optimal point decisions are those which minimize posterior expected loss can easily be construed into a decision rule. Let

$$\delta_* : S \rightarrow A : y \rightarrow a_* = \delta_*(y) \tag{1.30}$$

denote the decision rule which to each sample $y \in S$ associates the corresponding optimal decision in A as defined in eqn (1.26). It follows from the equivalence between the extensive and normal forms of analysis that δ_* is also a solution of the following functional optimization problem:

$$\delta_* = \arg \min_{\delta \in \Delta} E_{\theta, y} [l(\delta(y), \theta)], \tag{1.31}$$

where Δ denotes the set of all applications from S to A. The concept of risk can usefully be introduced at this stage.

Definition 1.2 *The risk function R of a decision rule δ is given by*

$$R : \Theta \times \Delta \to \mathbb{R}; \quad \theta \to R(\theta, \delta) = E_{y|\theta}[l(\delta(y), \theta)]. \tag{1.32}$$

Definition 1.3 *The Bayes risk of a decision rule δ, relative to a prior φ, is given by*

$$R_\varphi : \Delta \to \mathbb{R}; \quad \delta \to R_\varphi(\delta) = E_\theta[R(\theta, \delta)]. \tag{1.33}$$

Let us emphasize that the risk function of a decision rule is a *function* of θ, while the Bayes risk of a decision rule is a real *number*. Formula (1.31) can be rewritten as

$$\delta_* = \arg \min_{\delta \in \Delta} R_\varphi(\delta). \tag{1.34}$$

In the sequel of this discussion, decision rules which satisfy eqn (1.34) are called *Bayes rules*. Bayesian inference principles can now be summarized as follows for the ease of later reference.

1) *Actions:*
   - A decision a_1 is strictly preferred to a decision a_2 if and only if

$$E_{\theta|y}[l(a_1, \theta)] < E_{\theta|y}[l(a_2, \theta)]. \tag{1.35}$$

   - An optimal decision is one which minimizes the posterior expected loss.
2) *Decision rules:*
   - A decision rule δ_1 is strictly preferred to a decision rule δ_2 under a prior φ if and only if

$$R_\varphi(\delta_1) < R_\varphi(\delta_2). \tag{1.36}$$

   - An optimal decision rule, relative to a prior φ, is one which minimizes the corresponding Bayes risk.
3) *Correspondence theorem:* An optimal decision rule δ_* can be obtained by choosing for each y, with predictive probability $p(y) > 0$, a decision which minimizes posterior expected loss. The optimal decision δ_* can be assigned arbitrarily for those y for which $p(y) = 0$.

The above theorem essentially follows from the equivalence between the extensive and normal forms of analysis.

Classical statisticians aim at ranking decision rules without reference to a prior density φ and to that effect use the risk function $R(\theta, \delta)$. It is clearly desirable for them to select decision rules which have low risk. Note, however, that while the Bayes risk of a decision rule δ is a number, the risk of δ is a function of θ. The key issue now is whether or not there exists decision rules that are *uniformly* 'best' on Θ. In order to address progressively that issue we can first eliminate the decision rules that are uniformly worse than some other.

Definition 1.4 *A decision rule δ_1 dominates a decision rule δ_2 if and only if*

$$R(\theta, \delta_1) \leq R(\theta, \delta_2) \text{ for all } \theta \in \Theta \tag{1.37}$$

with the strict inequality holding for some θ.

Note that the formulation of Definition 1.4 is definitely classical. Bayesians draw no distinction between decision rules that differ only on subsets of Θ with zero prior probabilities. Hence, from a Bayesian perspective, Definition 1.4 is rephrased with the requirement that a strict inequality holds on a non-zero prior probability subset of Θ.

Definition 1.5 *A decision rule δ_1 is inadmissible if there exists a decision δ_2 which dominates δ_1. It is admissible otherwise.*

Clearly dominance defines only a partial ordering among decision rules and, moreover, the set of admissible rules generally remains hopelessly large. In particular Bayes rules are essentially admissible. A heuristic proof of that important assertion runs as follows: let δ denote a Bayes rule relative to a prior density φ. If δ were inadmissible, there would exist a rule δ_1 such that $R(\theta, \delta_1) \leq R(\theta, \delta)$, with strict inequality on a subset Δ of Θ. If the prior probability of Δ is positive, and the Bayes risk is finite, then $R_\varphi(\delta_1) < R_\varphi(\delta)$, which contradicts the initial claim that δ is a Bayes rule.

The previous result provides support for the use of Bayes rules even within a classical framework. Moreover, it fundamentally illustrates the fact that in all generality there does not exist a decision rule δ that is uniformly best in θ. Classical statisticians have addressed that non-existence issue by imposing additional constraints on the set of decision rules under consideration (e.g. by requiring that they be linear, unbiased, etc.). Under some circumstances these constraints may suffice to produce a (uniformly) best rule (such as ordinary least squares estimators). Note, however, that these additional constraints are introduced for mathematical convenience and have hardly any justification from a decisional perspective. In fact, as Example 1.6 in Section 1.9 illustrates, they may spuriously contribute to eliminating all Bayes rules from consideration.

The general framework we have introduced is used next to compare the classical and Bayesian approaches to estimation and hypothesis testing.

1.9 Estimation

Estimation problems are characterized by the property that the set of actions A coincides with the parameter space Θ (or with subsets of interest thereof). Providing point estimates for parameters of interest, i.e. assigning them a numerical value, constitutes a convenient form of scientific reporting which is easily accessible to a broad range of practitioners. Since, however, point estimates are derived under streamlined loss functions, such as quadratic ones, they might be rather poor substitutes for optimal decisions in real life decision problems, notwithstanding the fact that the parameters are rarely the actual decision variables.

Following eqn (1.26), a 'Bayes' (point) estimate' of θ is one which minimizes the posterior expectation of an appropriate loss function:

$$\theta_* = \arg \max_{a \in \Theta} \mathrm{E}_{\theta|y}\left[l(a, \theta)\right]. \tag{1.38}$$

If, in particular, the loss function is quadratic as in (1.27), then a Bayes estimate of θ is given by its posterior expectation. Within this context, a Bayes estimate of a function $g(\theta)$ is obtained by computing the posterior expectation of $g(\theta)$ itself (whether analytically if possible, or by numerical integration using the techniques described in Chapter 3).

Other loss functions would lead to different Bayes estimates of θ. Consider, for example, a case where θ is a scalar and a piecewise linear loss function is used in order to capture asymmetries between losses from overestimation ($a > \theta$) and losses from underestimation ($a < \theta$). Let

$$l(a, \theta) = \begin{cases} c_1(a - \theta) & \text{if } a \geq \theta \\ c_2(\theta - a) & \text{if } a < \theta. \end{cases} \tag{1.39}$$

Then

$$E_{\theta|y}[l(a, \theta)] = c_1 \int_{-\infty}^{a} (a - \theta)\, \varphi(\theta|y)\, d\theta + c_2 \int_{a}^{\infty} (\theta - a)\, \varphi(\theta|y)\, d\theta \tag{1.40}$$

and

$$\frac{\partial}{\partial a} E_{\theta|y}[l(a, \theta)] = (c_1 + c_2) \int_{-\infty}^{a} \varphi(\theta|y)\, d\theta - c_2. \tag{1.41}$$

The corresponding Bayes estimate of θ is given by the $c_2/(c_1 + c_2)$-fractile of its posterior distribution. If $c_1 = c_2$, i.e. the loss is proportional to the absolute difference between a and θ, then the Bayes estimate of θ coincides with the median of its posterior distribution.

As mentioned earlier, classical econometricians select estimators on the basis of their sampling properties. Maximum likelihood estimators in particular are shown to have 'optimal' sampling properties asymptotically at least, and to be invariant to transformations of θ. A natural Bayesian analogue would consist of using the mode of the posterior distribution of θ as an estimate. Obviously, if the posterior distribution of θ is symmetric around its mode, then the posterior mode and the posterior expectation coincide, provided the latter exists. Otherwise there does not exist a standard loss function which validates the use of posterior modes as Bayes estimates, except for discrete parametric spaces. Let $\Theta = \{\theta_1, \ldots, \theta_n\}$, with

$$p_i = \Pr(\theta = \theta_i|y) > 0 \text{ and } \sum_{i=1}^{n} p_i = 1. \tag{1.42}$$

Consider the 'all or nothing' loss function:

$$l(a, \theta) = \begin{cases} 0 & \text{if } a = \theta \\ 1 & \text{elsewhere,} \end{cases} \tag{1.43}$$

whose posterior expectation is given by

$$E_{\theta|y}l(a,\theta) = \begin{cases} 1 - p_i & \text{if } a = \theta_i \\ 1 & \text{elsewhere.} \end{cases} \tag{1.44}$$

The corresponding Bayes estimate of θ is that θ_i which has the highest posterior probability p_i, i.e. the posterior mode. If, however, the posterior distribution of θ is continuous, then the posterior probability of a subset of Θ with zero Lebesgue measure is itself zero and the previous argument does not carry over. A natural extension would consist of replacing a by $N_\epsilon(a)$, an ϵ-neighbourhood of a defined for example with reference to the Euclidean metric with matrix $Q > 0$:

$$N_\epsilon(a) = \{\theta | (a - \theta)'Q(a - \theta) < \epsilon\}. \tag{1.45}$$

Following the same logic as in the discrete case, we find that an 'all or nothing' Bayes estimate of θ is one which maximizes the posterior probability that $\theta \in N_\epsilon(a)$:

$$\theta_* = \arg\max_{a \in \Theta} \Pr(\theta \in N_\epsilon(a)|y). \tag{1.46}$$

It follows that θ_* should be located in such a way that $N_\epsilon(\theta_*)$ is a 'highest posterior density' region and contains, in particular, the posterior mode. It does not follow that the latter would coincide with θ_*, unless the posterior distribution is symmetric around its mode.

This being said, to the extent that posterior distributions are typically increasingly well behaved (symmetric, etc.) as sample size increases, it may be quite sensible to use posterior modes as Bayes estimates for large enough sample sizes. Relative to the evaluation of posterior means, which often requires tedious numerical integration, the computation of a posterior mode can be done with the optimization algorithms used for maximum likelihood estimation (after multiplication of the likelihood function by the prior density).

A systematic comparison of the classical and Bayesian approaches to estimation, and, in particular, of the classical admissibility of Bayes estimators, requires additional technical qualifications and goes beyond the objectives of our presentation. The interested reader can usefully consult DeGroot (1970) or, at a more technical level, Berger (1985a). We limit ourselves to discussing some of the key issues at hand in a simple example.

Example 1.6 Let $y' = (y_1, \ldots, y_n)$ where the y_i are identically independently distributed (IID) univariate normal random variables with unknown mean μ and known variance equal to one:

$$y_i|\mu \sim IN(\mu, 1) \qquad \mu \in R. \tag{1.47}$$

Let us consider the problem of estimating μ under a quadratic loss function:

$$l(a, \mu) = c(a - \mu)^2 \qquad c > 0. \tag{1.48}$$

Let δ_1 denote the conventional maximum likelihood estimator

$$\delta_1 : R^n \to R : y \to \bar{y} = \frac{1}{n} \sum_{i=1}^{n} y_i. \tag{1.49}$$

The sampling distribution of $\bar{y}$ given μ is itself normal:

$$\bar{y}|\mu \sim N\left(\mu, \frac{1}{n}\right). \tag{1.50}$$

Note, in particular, that its sampling expectation is μ ($\forall \mu \in R$), i.e. that $\bar{y}$ is an unbiased estimator according to the classical terminology. Its risk function is given by

$$R(\mu, \delta_1) = \frac{c}{n} \qquad \forall \mu \in R \tag{1.51}$$

which happens to be constant in μ. A well-known result is that, *if* we restrict our attention to the class of all *unbiased* estimators of μ, then δ_1 is a *best* estimator, in the sense that if we select any other unbiased estimator δ, then

$$R(\mu, \delta_1) \leq R(\mu, \delta). \tag{1.52}$$

Suppose we now remove the condition that the estimator be unbiased. Consider first the myopic decision rule δ_2 which consists of estimating μ by an arbitrary value μ_0, independently of y. That estimator is clearly operational. It is biased with sampling mean μ_0 and sampling variance 0. Its risk function is given by

$$R(\mu, \delta_2) = c\,(\mu - \mu_0)^2. \tag{1.53}$$

Hence

$$R(\mu, \delta_2) \leq R(\mu, \delta_1) \Leftrightarrow \mu_0 - \sqrt{\frac{1}{n}} \leq \mu \leq \mu_0 + \sqrt{\frac{1}{n}} \tag{1.54}$$

and neither rule dominates the other. Though δ_2 usefully serves to illustrate that unbiasedness is a rather arbitrary requirement, neither classical nor Bayesian statisticians would seriously consider using it, though for quite different reasons. A classical statistician might eliminate δ_2 on the grounds of its unbounded risk, e.g. by application of the rather conservative minimax principle (whereby estimators are ranked by the minimal values of their maximum risk). A Bayesian would prefer treating μ as a random variable with prior mean μ_0 and *non-zero* prior variance, reflecting prior uncertainty.

It is, however, trivial to make the comparison more interesting by introducing biased estimators that consist of a mix of δ_1 and δ_2. Two such estimators are briefly discussed here; they have similar structures though one is classical and the other one is Bayesian.

The first such decision rule aims at selecting $\delta_2(y) = \mu_0$ when μ is thought to be close enough to μ_0 and $\delta_1(y) = \bar{y}$ otherwise. For example, the issue can be settled by means of a preliminary test of the point hypothesis $H_0 : \mu = \mu_0$,

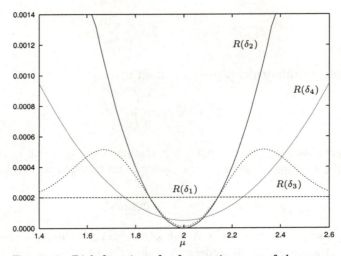

FIG. 1.2. Risk functions for four estimators of the mean

which leads to the concept of a pretest estimator. A classical test of H_0 with size $\alpha = 0.05$ is provided by the following rejection region:

$$C = \left\{ \bar{y} : |\bar{y} - \mu_0| > \frac{1.96}{\sqrt{n}} \right\} \tag{1.55}$$

and the corresponding pretest estimator is given by

$$\begin{cases} \delta_3(y) = \bar{y} & \text{if } \bar{y} \in C \\ \delta_3(y) = \mu_0 & \text{otherwise.} \end{cases} \tag{1.56}$$

Its risk function is given by

$$R(\mu, \delta_3) = c \left[\frac{1}{n} \Pr(\bar{y} \in C | \mu) + (\mu - \mu_0)^2 \Pr(\bar{y} \notin C | \mu) \right]. \tag{1.57}$$

In particular

$$R(\mu_0, \delta_3) = 0.05 \frac{c}{n} \quad \text{and} \quad \lim_{|\mu| \to \infty} R(\mu, \delta_3) = \frac{c}{n}. \tag{1.58}$$

The graph of $R(\mu_0, \delta_3)$ is shown in Fig. 1.2. The sampling properties of δ_3 ought to be quite attractive to a classical statistician who has good (objective?) reasons to believe that μ ought to be close to μ_0, especially when the same size n is small. Furthermore a remarkable result due to Stein (1956) establishes that, as soon as the y_i are of dimension greater than three, there exist pretest-type estimators that dominate $\bar{y}$, which is then inadmissible! This result does illustrate strikingly the arbitrariness of the unbiasedness requirement.

Finally, a typical Bayes estimator of μ is of the form (see Subsection 2.5.2)

$$\delta_4(y) = \lambda \overline{y} + (1 - \lambda)\mu_0, \qquad (1.59)$$

where μ_0 now denotes the prior mean of μ and

$$\lambda = \frac{n}{n + h_0} \in (0, 1), \qquad (1.60)$$

where h_0 is the inverse of μ's prior variance. From a sampling perspective δ_4 is biased since

$$E_{\overline{y}|\mu}[\delta_4(y)] = \lambda \mu + (1 - \lambda)\mu_0. \qquad (1.61)$$

Its sampling variance is given by

$$V_{\overline{y}|\mu}[\delta_4(y)] = \frac{\lambda^2}{n}. \qquad (1.62)$$

Hence

$$R(\mu, \delta_4) = c \left[\frac{\lambda^2}{n} + (1 - \lambda)^2 (\mu - \mu_0)^2 \right]. \qquad (1.63)$$

Being a Bayesian rule, δ_4 is admissible. In particular, the fact that it is not dominated by δ_3 originates from the inequality $\lambda^2 + (1 - \lambda)^2 < 1$. Note, however, that δ_4 does not dominate δ_1 (since, in particular, its risk function (1.53) is unbounded, though that unboundedness is an artefact of using a mathematically convenient quadratic loss function).

1.10 Hypothesis Testing

1.10.1 *Introduction*

An hypothesis H_i relative to a parameter $\theta \in \Theta$ consists of the (tentative) assertion that θ belongs to a subset Θ_i of Θ. 'Pure' hypothesis testing can be interpreted as a decision problem in which one considers a (finite) family of hypotheses $H = \{H_1, H_2, \ldots, H_m\}$ paired with a set of actions $A = \{a_1, a_2, \ldots, a_m\}$, where a_i denotes acceptance of H_i. In other words, it amounts to selecting one and only one hypothesis within H. No restrictions are imposed upon H at this stage of the discussion though, as we discuss below, the validation of some commonly used testing procedures, especially within the classical framework, may require imposing severe restrictions on H.

Within a strict decisional framework, hypothesis testing requires the introduction of a loss function $l(a_i, \theta)$ defined on $A \times \Theta$. Since, however, problems of hypothesis testing are rarely accompanied by an explicit selection of what follows the selection of a specific hypothesis, loss functions are often selected on the basis of largely heuristic considerations, mainly for the purpose of validating commonly used testing procedures. Furthermore, as we shall see below, scientific reporting versions of hypothesis testing generally do not require the specification of an explicit loss function. Naturally, Bayesian hypothesis testing procedures depend upon an assumed prior probability (sometimes measure) on Θ.

The H_i may correspond to economic 'theories' of particular interest to the analyst and whose 'validity' then has to be assessed in the light of available sample evidence (such as the hypothesis of a unit root, which, as discussed in Chapter 6, plays a central role in the analysis of numerous time series). They may also correspond to simplified and more operational versions of a baseline model or may loosely reflect the notion that parsimony in the parameterization of a model might be desirable in a situation of limited sample evidence. Though these different viewpoints may lead to different implementations of testing procedures, they nevertheless share many of the characteristics which are discussed below.

These comments also contribute to explaining why it is often the case that some (if not all) of the competing hypotheses in H are zero (Lebesgue) measure subsets of Θ. The Bayesian and classical viewpoints fundamentally differ in their treatment of zero measure hypotheses in relation to hypothesis testing. Within a Bayesian framework zero measure hypotheses matter only if they are assigned non-zero prior, and therefore posterior, probabilities. This immediately implies that, in order to give weight to zero measure hypotheses we have to rely upon mixed prior probabilities. As we discuss below, the assessment of such mixed probabilities and, in particular, of (conditionally) non-informative versions thereof can easily lead to ambiguities or occasional paradoxes, often resulting in the inadvertent production of extreme and patently unreasonable empirical conclusions. Within a classical framework, zero measure hypotheses play a more critical role in that they have a central role in the derivation of 'optimal' testing strategies.

In what follows, we first discuss the classical approach to hypothesis testing, mainly to set the scene where Bayesian procedures are introduced, and, occasionally, compared with their classical counterparts. Both viewpoints are then applied to a simple example and compared with each other.

1.10.2 *Classical Hypothesis Testing*

As discussed earlier, classical decision rules are evaluated without reference to a prior probability on Θ, the relevant concept being that of the risk function introduced in Definition 1.2. Within the pure hypothesis framework we have just introduced, a decision rule δ, which is an application from S to A, can usefully be characterized by a partitioning $\{S_i(\delta)\}$ of S, where $S_i(\delta)$ denotes the acceptance region of H_i and is defined in such a way that

$$y \in S_i(\delta) \Leftrightarrow \delta(y) = a_i. \tag{1.64}$$

Occasional indeterminacies which occur when some y can be transferred from one region to another without affecting the risk calculations are resolved by the adoption of an arbitrary (deterministic or stochastic) tie-breaking rule and will not be discussed further. Since $\delta(y)$ is constant on $S_i(\delta)$ where it equals a_i, the risk function introduced in eqn (1.32) can be rewritten as

$$R(\theta, \delta) = \sum_{i=1}^{m} l(a_i, \theta) \Pr\left[S_i(\delta)|\theta\right]. \tag{1.65}$$

A special case of interest is that of an 'all or nothing' loss function which takes the following form:

$$l(a_i, \theta) = \begin{cases} 0 & \text{if } \theta \in H_i \\ K_i & \text{otherwise.} \end{cases} \tag{1.66}$$

It is important to keep in mind that all probabilities in expressions such as that of the risk function in (1.65) are sampling probabilities conditional on θ.

We cannot expect to be able to find dominant strategies at a high level of generality. In fact, it is well known that one has to impose severe restrictions on H in order to secure the existence of a classical dominant test strategy. The simplest case for which such a result obtains is that where $m = 2$ and the two competing hypotheses, which for reasons explained below are traditionally labelled H_0 (the null hypothesis) and H_1 (the alternative hypothesis), are 'simple', i.e. consist of a singleton $(H_i = \{\theta_i\}, i = 0, 1)$. Under a '0–$K_i$' loss function, as defined in (1.66), the risk function associated with this special case is given by

$$\begin{aligned} R(\theta_0, \delta) &= K_0 \, \pi_\delta(\theta_0), \\ R(\theta_1, \delta) &= K_1 \left[1 - \pi_\delta(\theta_1)\right], \end{aligned} \tag{1.67}$$

where $\pi_\delta(\theta)$ denotes the probability of rejecting H_0, which is commonly referred to as the 'power function' (associated with the test strategy δ) and is defined as

$$\pi_\delta(\theta) = \int_{S_1(\delta)} f(y|\theta) \, dy. \tag{1.68}$$

An equivalent notation commonly used in classical statistics reads as

$$\begin{aligned} \alpha_\delta(\theta_0) &= \pi_\delta(\theta_0): & \text{Probability of a 'type I' error,} \\ \beta_\delta(\theta_1) &= 1 - \pi_\delta(\theta_1): & \text{Probability of a 'type II' error,} \end{aligned} \tag{1.69}$$

(a type I error consists in rejecting H_0 when it is 'true', while a type II error consists in rejecting H_1 when it is 'true'). Even for this simplest case it remains impossible to find a dominant strategy without additional qualifications. Consider, for example, the two extreme strategies

$$\begin{aligned} \delta_0 &: \text{always accept } H_0 \text{ with } S_0(\delta_0) = S, \\ \delta_1 &: \text{always reject } H_0 \text{ with } S_0(\delta_0) = \emptyset, \end{aligned} \tag{1.70}$$

for which we have

$$\begin{aligned} R(\theta_0, \delta_0) &= 0 & < R(\theta_0, \delta_1) = K_1, \\ R(\theta_1, \delta_0) &= K_0 > R(\theta_1, \delta_1) = 0. \end{aligned} \tag{1.71}$$

Clearly, there exists no strategy δ which can dominate both δ_0 and δ_1. A classical solution to that conundrum consists of minimizing $\beta_\delta(\theta_1)$ under the constraint that $\alpha_\delta(\theta_0)$ does not exceed a preassigned value $\alpha \in (0, 1)$ which is referred to as the 'size (or level)' of the test.

Theorem 1.7 *(Neyman and Pearson). Let Y denote a random variable with density function $f(y|\theta)$. Let $H_0 = \{\theta_0\}$ and $H_1 = \{\theta_1\}$ denote two simple hypotheses. Let $\alpha \in (0,1)$ denote the preset size of the test and R the risk function defined in (1.67). The strategy δ_* with acceptance region*

$$S_0(\delta_*) = \left\{ y \mid \frac{f(y|\theta_0)}{f(y|\theta_1)} \geq k_\alpha \right\}, \tag{1.72}$$

where k_α is chosen in such a way that $\Pr\left[S_0(\delta_*)|\theta_0\right] = 1 - \alpha$, is a dominant strategy of size α.

Proof We have to maximize $\pi_\delta(\theta_1) = 1 - \beta_\delta(\theta_1)$, subject to $\alpha_\delta(\theta_0) = \alpha$. Clearly $S_1(\delta_*)$ ought to include all sample points for which $f(y|\theta_0) = 0$ while $f(y|\theta_1) > 0$. For all other points in $S_1(\delta)$ we combine formulae (1.68) and (1.69) into the following expression:

$$\frac{1}{\alpha}\pi_\delta(\theta_1) = \mathrm{E}_{Y|\theta_0}\left[\frac{f(y|\theta_1)}{f(y|\theta_0)} \mid Y \in S_1(\delta_1)\right]$$

to be maximized by our choice of $S_1(\delta_1)$. Clearly $S_1(\delta_*)$ should consist of any fraction α of S containing the largest values of the ratio $f(y|\theta_1)/f(y|\theta_0)$. The result follows from the fact that $S_0(\delta_*)$ is the complement of $S_1(\delta_*)$. □

This remarkable result is nevertheless highly restrictive and essentially of no direct interest for empirical work in econometrics. Its generalization to empirically relevant scenarios requires additional qualifications. For the sake of later comparisons, this generalization is now briefly discussed at a heuristic level for 'one-parameter' models ($\theta \in \mathbb{R}$) and is illustrated in the example in Subsection 1.10.4.

As one solves eqn (1.72) in order to express $S_0(\delta_*)$ in the form of an explicit subset of S, it is often the case that $S_0(\delta_*)$ turns out to take one of the following forms:

$$\begin{aligned}
S_0(\delta_a^*) &= \{y \mid t(y) \leq a(\theta_0, \theta_1, \alpha)\}, \quad \text{for } \theta_1 > \theta_0, \\
S_0(\delta_b^*) &= \{y \mid t(y) \geq b(\theta_0, \theta_1, \alpha)\}, \quad \text{for } \theta_1 < \theta_0,
\end{aligned} \tag{1.73}$$

where $t(y)$ is a 'sufficient' statistic for y (see Section 2.3), while $a(.)$ and $b(.)$ are suitable bounds. If, furthermore, the ratio $f(y|\theta_0)/f(y|\theta_1)$ is monotone in θ_1 on either side of θ_0, it can be shown that neither $a(.)$ nor $b(.)$ depend on θ_1. In such a case it immediately follows that, for the one-sided test $H_0 : \theta = \theta_0$ versus $H_1^+ : \theta > \theta_0$, the strategy δ_a^* is optimal, or uniformly most powerful (hereafter UMP) in the classical terminology which is linked to the concept of power function defined by (1.68). Similarly, δ_b^* is UMP for the one-sided test $H_0 : \theta = \theta_0$ versus $H_1^- : \theta < \theta_0$. It turns out that the monotone likelihood ratio (hereafter MLR) property holds for a few one-parameter distributions in the exponential family (see Subsection 2.3.2), including such common distributions as the normal (either mean or variance fixed), the Poisson, the binomial, and the gamma (either parameter fixed).

However, except for very special cases, the MLR property does not hold on Θ, in which case we cannot expect to find a UMP strategy for the two-sided test $H_0 : \theta = \theta_0$ versus $H_1 : \theta \neq \theta_0$. In fact it can be shown (see e.g. Kendall and Stuart 1967: Chap. 23) that, if the MLR property holds on either side of θ_0, then

$$R(\theta_1, \delta_a^*) < R(\theta_1, \delta) < R(\theta_1, \delta_b^*) \text{ for } \theta_1 > \theta_0,$$
$$R(\theta_1, \delta_a^*) > R(\theta_1, \delta) > R(\theta_1, \delta_b^*) \text{ for } \theta_1 < \theta_0, \tag{1.74}$$

for $\delta \in \Delta$. It follows that 'good' testing strategies ought to achieve some sort of compromise between δ_a^* and δ_b^*. One obvious candidate is the strategy with acceptance region

$$S_0(\delta) = \{y \mid b(\theta_0, 0.5\alpha) \leq t(y) \leq a(\theta_0, 0.5\alpha)\}. \tag{1.75}$$

One additional qualification which rationalizes such a compromise is that of unbiasedness of a test statistic, which leads to the concept of uniformly most powerful unbiased (UMPU) test strategy. Under suitable technical conditions, a UMPU test strategy for general 'composite' hypotheses of the form H_0 and $H_1 = \Theta \setminus H_0$ is based upon the likelihood ratio (hereafter LR) test statistic

$$t(y) = -2\ln\left\{\frac{f(y|\hat{\theta}_0)}{f(y|\hat{\theta})}\right\}, \tag{1.76}$$

where

$$\hat{\theta}_0 = \arg\max_{\theta \in H_0} f(y|\theta), \text{ and } \hat{\theta} = \arg\max_{\theta \in \Theta} f(y|\theta). \tag{1.77}$$

For large enough sample sizes, $t(y)$ is often approximately distributed as a chi-squared random variable with a number of degrees of freedom equal to the number of (non-redundant) exact restrictions imposed upon θ by the definition of H_0, in which case an approximate size α obtains by using acceptance regions derived from chi-squared tables.

An important caveat applies to the testing strategies we have just described. Note that by controlling the size α of a test, we have effectively eliminated the loss function parameters K_0 and K_1 from consideration. It follows that the classical approach to hypothesis testing offers little guidance to the choice of α, despite its critical role in determining the acceptance region of a test. Conventional practice sets α at fairly low values (like 0.01, 0.05, or 0.10) under the implicit justification that the consequences of a type-I error are more severe than those of a type-II error. This precisely explains why the classical approach treats H_0 as the 'preferred' hypothesis and, more generally, why the null and the alternative hypotheses are asymmetrically treated. The previous argument, which is tantamount to setting $K_0 > K_1$ in the risk function (1.67), lacks rigour since we are lacking a formal link between the selection of (K_0, K_1) and that of α.

Neither does the classical framework offer clear guidance as to how to link α to the sample size. Since an increase in the sample size generally translates into informational gains, it is conceptually desirable to take advantage of such gains by lowering α as the sample size increases.

Attempts at removing the inherent indeterminacy in the selection of α have led to the concept of p-value which is commonly used for scientific reporting. Loosely speaking, the p-value of a test strategy δ (H_0 versus H_1) for a *given* sample y is defined as the size which places y on the boundary which separates $S_0(\delta)$ from $S_1(\delta)$, i.e. which is such that the analyst is 'indifferent' between accepting or rejecting H_0. A reader who selects a size which is lower (greater) than the reported p-value, knows immediately that he or she should accept (reject) H_0.

The concept of p-value has been frequently criticized by Bayesian statisticians for its lack of decision-oriented justification or, at a related level, for the fact that it can produce empirical results which differ sharply from 'similar' results derived under Bayesian procedures and are therefore labelled as being potentially misleading. We refer the interested reader to the literature related to the Lindley's paradox (see the remark at the end of Subsection 1.10.3), which applies to situations where p-values are claimed to overestimate the evidence against a simple hypothesis. See in particular Lindley (1957), Jeffreys (1961), and Berger and Delampedy (1987).

1.10.2.1 *Classical Confidence Regions* We conclude this section on classical testing procedures by introducing another important classical concept which is often used for scientific reporting, namely that of a confidence region (for which a Bayesian counterpart is presented in Subsection 1.10.3). Instead of selecting a specific null hypothesis of the form $H_0 : \theta = \theta_0$, the analyst reports a region which regroups all the hypotheses which would be 'accepted' in view of the observed sample result (or more appropriately, 'not rejected' since these null hypotheses are mutually exclusive). In order to provide a more formal definition, we consider the case of a test procedure which is based upon a statistic $t(y)$ and whose acceptance region for a specific null $H_0 : \theta = \theta_0$ (versus the alternative $H_1 : \theta \neq \theta_0$) and for a preset size α is denoted $S_0(\theta_0; \alpha) \subset S$; see formula (1.75) for an example.

Definition 1.8 *A* $100(1-\alpha)$ *per cent confidence region associated with a testing procedure based upon a statistic* $t(y)$ *with acceptance region* $S_0(\theta_0; \alpha) \subset S$ *is the subset* $C(y; \alpha) \subset \Theta$ *defined via the identity*

$$\theta \in C(y; \alpha) \Leftrightarrow t(y) \in S_0(\theta_0; \alpha). \tag{1.78}$$

An example is provided in Subsection 1.10.4. In order to avoid any confusion with related Bayesian concepts introduced in Subsection 1.10.3, it is essential to keep in mind that, even though $C(y; \alpha)$ is a subset of Θ, all underlying probability statements are relative to the sampling density $f(y|\theta)$. Statements like 'the true

θ lies in $C(y; \alpha)$ with probability $1 - \alpha$' make no sense in the classical framework despite their occasional occurrence in empirical studies.

1.10.3 Bayesian Hypothesis Testing

The Bayesian analysis of the general testing problem introduced in Subsection 1.10.1 is conceptually straightforward. It necessitates the introduction of a prior density $\varphi(\theta)$ on Θ. Following the correspondence theorem introduced in relation to formulae (1.35) and (1.36), the Bayesian optimal testing rule assigns the following acceptance region to H_i:

$$S_i(\delta_*) = \{y \mid l_\varphi(a_i; y) \leq l_\varphi(a_j; y) \text{ for } j = 1 \ldots m\}, \quad (1.79)$$

where $l_\varphi(a; y)$ is the posterior expected loss associated with a decision $a \in A$:

$$l_\varphi(a; y) = \mathrm{E}_{\theta|y} \left[l(a; \theta) \right]. \quad (1.80)$$

A (stochastic) tie-breaking rule can be imposed without loss of generality in the case of a tie for specific values of y in S. Additional simplifications obtain when the loss function is of the '0–K_i' type introduced in formula (1.66), in which case

$$l_\varphi(a_i; y) = K_i \left[1 - \mathrm{Pr}(H_i|y) \right], \quad (1.81)$$

where $\mathrm{Pr}(H_i|y)$ is the posterior probability of the hypothesis $H_i : \theta \in \Theta_i$.

This Bayesian procedure applies to a broad range of testing situations ($m > 2$, overlapping hypotheses, etc.) for which there exists no optimal classical procedures. On the other hand, the Bayesian treatment of hypotheses with zero (Lebesgue) measure in Θ raises potential problems related to 'conditioning paradoxes' of various sorts, in particular when the prior density φ is meant to be non-informative within hypotheses. See e.g. Kiefer and Richard (1979) for a detailed discussion of these problems within a general Bayesian testing framework.

In what follows, we consider mainly the case of a simple null hypothesis $H_0 : \theta = \theta_0$ versus the alternative $H_1 : \theta \neq \theta_0$ for which we can draw explicit comparisons between the classical and Bayesian procedures.

If one uses a continuous prior density φ on Θ, then both the prior and posterior probabilities of the simple hypothesis H_0 are zero, in which case H_0 is always rejected against H_1 on the posterior expected loss criterion. This is precisely why Bayesian statisticians have often expressed reservations about the notion of testing simple null hypotheses; see e.g. the discussion in Berger (1985a: 148–156).

In order to give 'weight' to H_0 we have to use a mixed prior density, assigning a non-zero prior probability p to θ_0. On H_1 we keep using a continuous density φ which can be usefully written as

$$\varphi(\theta) = (1 - p)\, \varphi(\theta|H_1), \quad \theta \in H_1, \quad (1.82)$$

where $\varphi(\theta|H_1)$ denotes a *proper* prior density on θ, conditional on $\theta \in H_1$. Attempting to use a non-informative version of $\varphi(\theta|H_1)$ muddles the interpretation of p and φ and can easily produce non-sensible results. The application of Bayes' theorem to our mixed prior density produces the following results:

$$p_* = \Pr(\theta = \theta_0|y) = p\,\frac{f(y|\theta_0)}{f(y)}, \tag{1.83}$$

$$\varphi(\theta|y) = (1-p)\,\frac{f(y|\theta)\,\varphi(\theta|H_1)}{f(y)}, \quad \theta \in H_1, \tag{1.84}$$

where

$$f(y) = p\,f(y|\theta_0) + (1-p)\,f(y|H_1), \tag{1.85}$$

and

$$f(y|H_1) = \int_{H_1} f(y|\theta)\,\varphi(\theta|H_1)\,d\theta. \tag{1.86}$$

The posterior density of θ, given that $\theta \in H_1$, is given by

$$\varphi(\theta|y, H_1) = \frac{f(y|\theta)\,\varphi(\theta|H_1)}{f(y|H_1)} = \frac{\varphi(\theta|y)}{1-p_*}, \quad \theta \in H_1. \tag{1.87}$$

The posterior probability p_* can usefully be rewritten as

$$p_* = \left[1 + \frac{1-p}{p}\,\frac{f(y|H_1)}{f(y|\theta_0)}\right]^{-1}. \tag{1.88}$$

Under a '0–K_i' loss function the posterior expected losses to be compared are given by

$$l_\varphi(a_0; y) = K_0\,(1-p_*) \quad \text{and} \quad l_\varphi(a_1; y) = K_1\,p_*, \tag{1.89}$$

in which case the acceptance region of the Bayesian optimal testing strategy is

$$S_0(\delta_*) = \left\{y \mid p_* \geq \frac{K_0}{K_0 + K_1}\right\}. \tag{1.90}$$

In the one-parameter example which is discussed in Subsection 1.10.4, and in other similar examples (some of which are discussed in the context of the regression model in Chapter 2), the Bayesian and classical acceptance regions share a common functional form. In such cases, the Bayesian formulation produces an implicit classical size which depends on K_0, K_1, and the sample size.

Remarks:

1) The terminology of 'posterior odds' is often used. In the case of two hypotheses, the posterior odds ratio (in favour of H_0) is the ratio of posterior probabilities $\Pr(H_0|y)/\Pr(H_1|y)$. Obviously, knowing this ratio is equivalent to knowing the posterior probabilities (since they add to one). The Bayesian optimal testing rule amounts to choose a_0 ('accept H_0') if $l_\varphi(a_0; y) < l_\varphi(a_1; y)$. In the case of a loss function of the '0–K_i' type, which is symmetric ($K_0 = K_1$), it is easy to verify that H_0 is accepted if the posterior odds ratio is larger than one. In a scientific reporting context (as opposed to a genuine decision one), this is often a convenient rule, as it 'avoids' the need to specify a loss function.

   From (1.88), it is easy to see that the posterior odds ratio can be expressed as

$$\frac{\Pr(H_0|y)}{\Pr(H_1|y)} = \frac{\Pr(H_0)}{\Pr(H_1)} K_{01}(y), \tag{1.91}$$

   where

$$K_{01}(y) = \frac{f(y|H_0)}{f(y|H_1)} = \frac{\displaystyle\int_{H_0} f(y|\theta)\,\varphi(\theta|H_0)\,d\theta}{\displaystyle\int_{H_1} f(y|\theta)\,\varphi(\theta|H_1)\,d\theta} \tag{1.92}$$

   is called the 'Bayes factor' (in favour of H_0). Notice that we have written the formula of the Bayes factor for a more general hypothesis H_0 than the simple hypothesis $\theta = \theta_0$ considered above, as it is generally valid. Formula (1.91) shows that the posterior odds ratio is equal to the prior odds one times the Bayes factor. If H_0 and H_1 are simple hypotheses, say $H_0 : \theta = \theta_0$ and $H_1 : \theta = \theta_1$, $K_{01}(y)$ is nothing more than the likelihood ratio $f(y|\theta_0)/f(y|\theta_1)$ which is used in the Neyman–Pearson lemma (Theorem 1.1). More generally, if H_i specifies $\theta \in \Theta_i$, $f(y|H_i)$ is the predictive density of the sample when H_i is taken to be the correct hypothesis. In the Bayesian approach to hypothesis testing, one uses the sample through $K_{01}(y)$, which is the ratio of *marginalized* likelihoods. In contrast, the classical generalized likelihood ratio procedure uses the ratio of *maximized* likelihoods, see (1.76).

2) As should be obvious from the previous remark, testing a composite null hypothesis is not fundamentally different from testing a simple null hypothesis. One must be careful that the integrals that appear in (1.92) are finite, otherwise the posterior odds ratio and probabilities are not defined. This typically precludes the use of non-informative prior measures on the parameters which are constrained under the null hypothesis. From

a computational point of view, testing a composite null hypothesis requires of course marginalization of the nuisance parameters (i.e. the parameters which are not constrained by the null hypothesis). For example, if $\theta = (\alpha, \beta)$, $H_0 : \alpha \in H_0$, and $H_1 : \alpha$ not in H_0, the Bayes factor is

$$\frac{\displaystyle\int_{H_0}\int_B f(y|\alpha,\beta)\,\varphi(\alpha,\beta|H_0)\,d\beta\,d\alpha}{\displaystyle\int_{H_1}\int_B f(y|\alpha,\beta)\,\varphi(\alpha,\beta|H_1)\,d\beta\,d\alpha}, \tag{1.93}$$

where B is the parameter space for β. When H_0 takes the more simple form $\alpha = \alpha_0$, the Bayes factor simplifies to

$$\frac{\displaystyle\int_B f(y|\alpha_0,\beta)\,\varphi(\beta|\alpha_0)\,d\beta}{\displaystyle\int_{H_1}\int_B f(y|\alpha,\beta)\,\varphi(\alpha,\beta|H_1)\,d\beta\,d\alpha}, \tag{1.94}$$

where $\varphi(\beta|\alpha_0)$ is the prior under the null hypothesis. This form of the Bayes factor is used in Chapter 6.

1.10.3.1 *Bayesian Confidence Regions* The notion of confidence region can be used to provide a Bayesian analogue to the classical concept. Since, however, confidence regions are collections of point hypotheses, we have to interpret the probability mass p attached to a null H_0 being tested as an intrinsic parameter of the Bayesian testing rule (exactly as the size α is an intrinsic parameter of the corresponding classical rule). Let us therefore consider a single prior density $\psi(\theta)$ on Θ and redefine the implicit prior associated with each specific null being tested according to formula (1.82), where $\varphi(\theta|H_1)$ is replaced by $\psi(\theta)$. It immediately follows from (1.88) and (1.89) that a Bayesian p-confidence region for θ is given by

$$C(y;p) = \left\{ \theta \,\Big|\, \frac{\psi(\theta|y)}{\psi(\theta)} \geq \frac{1-p}{p}\frac{K_0}{K_1} \right\}, \tag{1.95}$$

where, in accordance with (1.87),

$$\psi(\theta|y) = \frac{f(y|\theta)\,\psi(\theta)}{\displaystyle\int_\Theta f(y|\theta)\,\psi(\theta)\,d\theta}. \tag{1.96}$$

In other words, $\psi(\theta|y)$ coincides with the 'usual' posterior density of θ (with no probability mass being attached to any point) and the Bayesian confidence region includes all the points for which the ratio between the posterior and the prior density exceeds a threshold value $K = (1-p)K_0/pK_1$. Again, the classical and Bayesian confidence regions may share a common functional form, in which case to each threshold value K there corresponds an implicit size α.

An alternative concept which is commonly used by Bayesians for scientific reporting but which is not directly related to testing *per se* is that of credible region.

Definition 1.9 *A* $100(1-a)$ *per cent credible set for* θ *is a subset* C *of* Θ *such that*

$$\Pr(\theta \in C|y) \geq 1 - a. \tag{1.97}$$

The inequality sign is introduced in order to account for situations where the posterior distribution of θ contains 'atoms' (i.e. points of non-zero probability), in which case there may not exist a region C with posterior probability exactly equal to $1 - a$ for any $a \in [0,1]$. Typically there are (infinitely) many sets C satisfying condition (1.97). It is often desirable to choose a credible set which is as small as possible, which is tantamount to including in C points with the largest possible values of the posterior density $\varphi(\theta|y)$.

Definition 1.10 *A* $100(1-a)$ *per cent highest posterior density (HPD) credible set for* θ *is a subset* C *of* Θ *of the form*

$$C = \{\theta \mid \varphi(\theta|y) \geq k_a\}, \tag{1.98}$$

where k_a *is the largest constant such that* $\Pr(C|y) \geq 1 - a$.

1.10.4   An Example

Consider a univariate random variable $y|\mu \sim N(\mu, \sigma^2)$, as defined in Subsection A.1.3. We assume that σ^2 is known so that $\theta = \mu$. We could set σ^2 equal to one without loss of generality, since it amounts to dividing y and μ by σ. We do not do so, as several formulae derived below remain valid in the case where σ^2 is unknown. Assume a sample of n IID observations $(y_1, \ldots, y_n)$ is available. It is well known—see also Section 2.4—that the sample mean $\bar{y} = \sum_{i=1}^{n} y_i/n$ is a sufficient statistic for μ (i.e. it contains all the sample information relative to μ). Since $\bar{y}$ is linear in the y_i, it follows that $\bar{y}|\mu \sim N(\mu, \sigma^2/n)$. Let us apply the various test strategies introduced in Subsections 1.10.2 and 1.10.3 to this example.

1.10.4.1   Classical Procedures

(i) $H_0 : \mu = \mu_0$. The expression of the normal density $f_N(\bar{y}|\mu, \sigma^2/n)$ is given in (A.25). It follows that the acceptance region of the test as defined in (1.72) is characterized by the inequality

$$\bar{y}(\mu_1 - \mu_0) \leq \frac{1}{2}(\mu_1^2 - \mu_0^2) - \frac{\sigma^2}{n} \ln k_\alpha. \tag{1.99}$$

Consider first the case where $\mu_1 > \mu_0$. The above inequality may then be rewritten as

$$\frac{\sqrt{n}}{\sigma}(\bar{y} - \mu_0) \leq \frac{\sqrt{n}}{2\sigma}(\mu_1 - \mu_0) - \frac{\sigma}{\sqrt{n}}\frac{\ln k_\alpha}{\mu_1 - \mu_0}, \tag{1.100}$$

where k_α has to be chosen in such a way that this inequality holds with probability $1 - \alpha$ on H_0. Since, however, $Z = \sqrt{n}(\bar{Y} - \mu_0)/\sigma \sim N(0,1)$ on H_0, it follows that

$$\frac{\sqrt{n}}{2\sigma}(\mu_1 - \mu_0) - \frac{\sigma}{\sqrt{n}}\frac{\ln k_\alpha}{\mu_1 - \mu_0} = z_\alpha, \tag{1.101}$$

where z_α is the 'α-critical value', defined by $\Pr(Z \geq z_\alpha) = \alpha$. Therefore, the acceptance region (for $\mu_1 > \mu_0$) is of the form introduced in (1.73) with $t(y) = \bar{y}$, and

$$a(\mu_0, \mu_1, \alpha) = \mu_0 + \frac{\sigma}{\sqrt{n}}z_\alpha. \tag{1.102}$$

A similar result holds for the case $\mu_1 < \mu_0$, for which we have

$$b(\mu_0, \mu_1, \alpha) = \mu_0 - \frac{\sigma}{\sqrt{n}}z_\alpha. \tag{1.103}$$

(ii) The bounds a and b we have just computed do not depend on μ_1. It follows that the test based upon formulae (1.102) and (1.103) are UMP for the corresponding one-sided tests ($H_1^+ : \mu > \mu_0$ and $H_1^- : \mu < \mu_0$, respectively).

(iii) The acceptance region for the two-sided test ($H_1 : \mu \neq \mu_0$), as defined in (1.75), is given by

$$\mu_0 - \frac{\sigma}{\sqrt{n}}z_{\alpha/2} \leq \bar{y} \leq \mu_0 + \frac{\sigma}{\sqrt{n}}z_{\alpha/2}. \tag{1.104}$$

The maximum likelihood estimates of μ on H_0 and Θ are given by μ_0 and $\bar{y}$, respectively. It follows that the acceptance region (1.99) is also that of the (UMPU) likelihood ratio test of (1.76).

(iv) A $100(1 - \alpha)$ per cent confidence region for μ is obtained by rewriting the condition (1.99) in terms of μ_0 for a given $\bar{y}$, whence

$$C(y; \alpha) = \left\{ \mu \,|\, \bar{y} - \frac{\sigma}{\sqrt{n}}z_{\alpha/2} \leq \mu \leq \bar{y} + \frac{\sigma}{\sqrt{n}}z_{\alpha/2} \right\}. \tag{1.105}$$

In light of the *sampling* interpretation of confidence regions we can conclude that if we were to generate a large number of independent draws $\bar{y}_1, \ldots, \bar{y}_R$ from the $N(\mu, \sigma^2/n)$ distribution for a fixed μ (and the given value of σ^2), we would find that approximately $100(1 - \alpha)$ per cent of the intervals in (1.105) contain the true value μ. This cannot be interpreted as a probabilistic statement on μ.

1.10.4.2 *Bayesian Procedures* By a direct application of Bayes' theorem (see Subsection 2.5.2 for a more general case), if the prior density of μ is

$$\mu \sim N(m_0, h_0^{-1}), \qquad h_0^{-1} = \sigma_0^2, \tag{1.106}$$

the corresponding posterior density is

$$\mu \sim N(m_*, h_*^{-1}), \qquad h_*^{-1} = \sigma_*^2, \tag{1.107}$$

with

$$h_* = nh + h_0, \qquad m_* = h_*^{-1}(nh\bar{y} + h_0 m_0), \tag{1.108}$$

and $h = \sigma^{-2}$ (it is often convenient to parameterize the normal distribution in terms of precision rather than variance).

Let us now assign a prior probability p to the null $H_0 : \mu = \mu_0$ (note that if we were interested only in testing a specific value μ_0, it might be reasonable in some contexts to set $m_0 = \mu_0$; however, as soon as we compute a Bayesian confidence region we have to consider the case where $m_0 \neq \mu_0$, since μ_0 then varies from one test to another). The density $f(y|H_1)$ in eqn (1.86) is directly obtained from Theorem A.14 and is given by

$$\bar{y}|H_1 \sim N\left(m_0, \sigma_0^2 + \frac{\sigma^2}{n}\right), \tag{1.109}$$

with

$$\sigma_0^2 + \frac{\sigma^2}{n} = h_0^{-1} + (nh)^{-1} = \frac{h_*}{nh_0 h}. \tag{1.110}$$

It follows that if $m_0 = \mu_0$, the posterior probability of H_0, given in formula (1.88), can be expressed as

$$p_* = \left[1 + \frac{1-p}{p}\sqrt{\frac{h_0}{h_*}}\exp\left(\frac{nh}{2h_*}z^2\right)\right]^{-1}, \tag{1.111}$$

where $z = \sqrt{nh}\,(\bar{y} - \mu_0)$. Finally, in view of (1.107), the $100(1 - \alpha)$ per cent Bayesian HPD interval for μ is

$$(m_* - z_{\alpha/2}\sigma_*, m_* + z_{\alpha/2}\sigma_*). \tag{1.112}$$

Remark (Lindley's paradox): The quantity z defined above is the classical test statistic for $\mu = \mu_0$. A classical two-tail test rejects at the size 0.05 if $|z| \geq 1.96$, whatever the sample size. If $z = 1.96$, p_* as given by (1.111) tends to one as n tends to infinity (provided that $p > 0$): for example, for $p = 0.5$, and $h_0 = h = 1$, $p_* = 0.37$ if $n = 10$, 0.60 for $n = 100$, and 0.82 for $n = 1000$; the corresponding values when $p = 0.1$ are 0.06, 0.14, and 0.34. It is not surprising that a given value of z, as n increases, provides increasing evidence in favour of H_0. The classical test does not account for this fact.

BAYESIAN STATISTICS AND LINEAR REGRESSION

2.1 Introduction

This chapter presents basic concepts and tools which are useful for modelling and for Bayesian inference. Section 2.2 explains the likelihood principle and its implications for the Bayesian treatment of nuisance parameters. It also introduces stopping rules to illustrate these notions. The question of identification is addressed. Section 2.3 defines density kernels, which are useful for simplifying notation and computations. Section 2.4 deals with sufficient statistics and the exponential family of probability distributions for which they are relevant. Section 2.5 introduces the notion of 'natural conjugate' inference, which is an important tool of Bayesian analysis in the case of the exponential family. An illustration of the tools is provided for the case of the multivariate normal sampling model. Section 2.6 deals with the issue of reduction of models, i.e. under which conditions a 'big' model can be reduced to a more simple one, without loss of information. This approach is illustrated in the case of the static linear regression model, for which Section 2.7 provides the details of the natural conjugate framework. Although we introduce natural conjugate prior densities in this chapter, the issues of the choice of prior densities are not considered in detail, since Chapter 4 deals almost entirely with this important aspect of Bayesian inference.

2.2 The Likelihood Principle

2.2.1 *Definition*

The Bayesian treatment of sample information is fully characterized by Bayes' theorem, as given in formula (1.7), which we repeat here for ease of reference:

$$\varphi(\theta|y) = \frac{f(y|\theta)\varphi(\theta)}{f(y)} \tag{2.1}$$

with

$$f(y) = \int_{\Theta} f(y|\theta)\varphi(\theta)d\theta. \tag{2.2}$$

Clearly, the shape of the posterior density $\varphi(\theta|y)$ is entirely determined by the product $f(y|\theta)\,\varphi(\theta)$ in its numerator. At this level of analysis, the predictive density $f(y)$ only serves as an integrating constant (see Section 2.2 below). It immediately follows that, from a Bayesian viewpoint at least, the functional $f(y|\theta)$ treated as a *function of θ for a given y* contains all the information relative to θ for that particular y.

Definition 2.1 *For any given* y, *the functional* $l(\theta; y) = f(y|\theta)$, *considered as a function of* θ, *is called the likelihood function.*

Formula (2.1) then leads to the following key concept:

Likelihood principle: In drawing inferences about θ after y is observed, all relevant sample information is contained in the likelihood function $l(\theta; y)$.

Or, to quote Savage (1954):

'The likelihood principle says this: [...] given the likelihood function in which an experiment has resulted, everything else about the experiment is irrelevant'.

The likelihood principle makes explicit the notion that *only* the observed y should be relevant to inference about θ, which is the cornerstone of Bayesian inference. Certain classical procedures, such as ML (Maximum Likelihood) estimation, do satisfy the likelihood principle, but most do not, essentially because their design is explicitly based upon sampling considerations that require paying attention not only to that y which obtains but also to all the other y in S that might have occurred (but did not). The following example adapted from Pratt (1965) illustrates this point.

Example 2.2 A physicist instructs a lab technician to run a one-hour experiment which consists of counting occurrences of a specific event. Occurrences are assumed to follow a Poisson process of unknown parameter λ. A null hypothesis of particular interest is that $\lambda = 85$, to be tested with size 0.05. A count of $y = 68$ is obtained. Using a normal approximation with mean and variance both equal to λ, the physicist concludes that H_0 cannot be rejected since $85 - 1.96 \times \sqrt{85} \leq 68 \leq 85 + 1.96 \times \sqrt{85}$.

A little later the technician casually informs the physicist that a standard post-experiment verification has shown the counter to be deficient in that it would not have recorded occurrences beyond the 99th (why should it matter since actually 68 occurrences were recorded?). Since, however, the probability that $Y > 99$ under H_0 turns out to be approximately equal to 0.065, a test of size 0.05 now has to include 99 in the acceptance region and is *de facto* transformed into a one-sided test which rejects H_0 since $68 < 85 - 1.645 \times \sqrt{85}$!

The technician is stunned by such a reversal and immediately adds that, had the counter registered 99, he would obviously have rerun the experiment after fixing the counter. To everyone's relief, the physicist reverts to her initial decision!

This brief story contradicts the likelihood principle which implies that values of y that could have occurred ($y \geq 99$) but did not should have no bearing on inferences on λ.

See Berger (1985b) for a more extensive discussion of the likelihood principle as well as its validation under a weaker set of axioms than that introduced in Chapter 1. Two important implications of the likelihood principle are discussed next.

2.2.2 *Nuisance Parameters*

The characterization of a data density often requires more parameters than those which are of specific interest to the decision maker or to the statistician.

Definition 2.3 *Let the data density be $f(y|\theta)$ with $\theta = (\alpha, \beta)$. The parameter β is a nuisance parameter if the utility function U of the decision maker can be expressed in the form of a function U_c which depends solely on α:*

$$U(\alpha, \beta) \equiv U_c(\alpha) \qquad \forall (\alpha, \beta) \in \Theta. \tag{2.3}$$

It follows that, except for special purposes such as a sensitivity analysis, we generally restrict our attention to the posterior density of the parameters of interest α. Let therefore the prior density of θ be factorized into the product of the marginal prior of α and the conditional prior of β given α:

$$\varphi(\alpha, \beta) = \varphi_1(\alpha)\, \varphi_2(\beta|\alpha). \tag{2.4}$$

The posterior density of α is obtained by integrating the posterior density of θ, as given by formula (2.1), with respect to β and can be rewritten as

$$\varphi(\alpha|y) = \varphi_1(\alpha)\, \frac{f_m(y|\alpha)}{f(y)} \tag{2.5}$$

with

$$f_m(y|\alpha) = \int_{B(\alpha)} f(y|\alpha, \beta)\, \varphi_2(\beta|\alpha)\, d\beta, \tag{2.6}$$

and

$$f(y) = \int_\Theta f(y|\theta)\, \varphi(\theta)\, d\theta = \int_A f_m(y|\alpha)\, \varphi_1(\alpha)\, d\alpha, \tag{2.7}$$

where $B(\alpha)$ denotes the support $\varphi_2(\beta|\alpha)$ and A that of $\varphi_1(\alpha)$. Treated as a function of α given y, the density $f_m(y|\alpha)$ is called a 'marginalized' (or 'marginal') likelihood and is denoted $l_m(\alpha; y)$. Formula (2.6) can usefully be rewritten in terms of likelihood functions:

$$l_m(\alpha; y) = \int_{B(\alpha)} l(\alpha, \beta; y)\, \varphi_2(\beta|\alpha)\, d\beta. \tag{2.8}$$

Hence the two key components of the Bayesian analysis of nuisance parameters are:

(i) A prior density for the nuisance parameters β, conditionally on the parameters of interest α.

(ii) A likelihood function which is then marginalized with respect to β.

An important concern in any application where nuisance parameters are present is that of the 'robustness' of the posterior density of the parameters of interest with respect to the selection of a prior density for the nuisance parameters.

A systematic analysis of Bayesian robustness would require a chapter by itself and goes beyond the objectives of this book. See e.g. Berger (1985a) for an in-depth analysis and for additional references.

In contrast with the Bayesian approach we just discussed, classical inference procedures generally eliminate nuisance parameters by (stepwise) optimization. For instance, the ML estimator of the parameters of interest α is given by

$$\hat{\alpha} = \arg \max_{\alpha \in A} \ln l_c(\alpha; y), \tag{2.9}$$

where

$$l_c(\alpha; y) = l(\alpha, \hat{\beta}(\alpha); y) \tag{2.10}$$

with

$$\hat{\beta}(\alpha) = \arg \max_{\beta \in B(\alpha)} \ln l(\alpha, \beta; y). \tag{2.11}$$

Relative to formula (2.10), the marginalization in (2.8) typically entails a loss of 'degrees of freedom' commensurate with the dimension of the vector β of nuisance parameters. This reduction in degrees of freedom may turn out to be critical in small-sample situations or when there are 'incidental' nuisance parameters (i.e. when the dimension of β increases proportionally to the sample size). The latter situation is characteristic of 'error-in-variables' models. See in particular Florens, Mouchart, and Richard (1974) for an in-depth analysis of such models. In addition, marginalization as opposed to optimization accounts for the global properties of the likelihood function and posterior density rather than for their local behaviour in the immediate vicinity of their modal values.

2.2.3 *Stopping Rules*

Example 2.2 illustrates the fact that the rules whereby an experiment is terminated and which actually are called 'stopping rules' may play a significant role in the evaluation of classical concepts such as probabilities of type I or II errors or confidence intervals. Classical procedures are evaluated on the basis of their sampling properties and depend, therefore, upon a precise characterization of the sampling process. In contrast, Bayesian procedures are often unaffected by stopping rules as we now briefly discuss.

Definition 2.4 *A stopping rule τ is a sequence of functions $\{\tau_j(y_{(j)}, \delta), j = 0, 1, \ldots, \infty\}$ valued in $[0, 1]$, where $\tau_j(.)$ denotes the probability that the sampling process will stop given that j observations $y_{(j)} = (y_1, y_2, \ldots, y_j)$ are already available. The function $\tau_0(\delta)$ gives the probability that no sampling will take place, and δ regroups all the parameters characterizing the stopping rule, typically nuisance parameters.*

The data 'density' of the pair (n, y_n) under a stopping rule τ is given by

$$f(n, y_{(n)}|\theta, \delta) = \psi(n|y_{(n)}, \delta)\, f_n(y_{(n)}|\theta), \qquad (2.12)$$

where

$$\psi(n|y_{(n)}, \delta) = t_n(y_{(n)}, \delta) \prod_{j=0}^{n-1} [1 - \tau_j(y_{(j)}, \delta)] \qquad (2.13)$$

and $f_n(.|.)$ denotes the data density of a sample of size n.

Definition 2.5 *If δ is a nuisance parameter and is a priori independent of θ (or if there is no δ at all), then the stopping rule τ is said to be non-informative for θ.*

Under the conditions of Definition 2.5 the marginalized likelihood of the pair $(n, y_{(n)})$ is proportional to

$$f_m(n, y_{(n)}|\theta) = \psi_m(n|y_{(n)})\, f_n(y_{(n)}|\theta) \qquad (2.14)$$

with

$$\psi_m(n|y_{(n)}) = \int_\Delta \psi(n|y_{(n)}, \delta)\, \varphi(\delta)\, d\delta \qquad (2.15)$$

and is, therefore, proportional to the likelihood of $y_{(n)}$ itself. It follows that the posterior density of θ does not depend on ψ_m, in which case the stopping rule is irrelevant for inference about θ. This does not imply that τ conveys no information at all on θ, it usually does, but rather it provides no information on θ *in addition* to that already contained in the likelihood function of $y_{(n)}$. Assume for a moment that only n were observed. The relevant likelihood would then be given by

$$\psi_1(n|\theta, \delta) = \int_{S_n} \psi(n|y_{(n)}, \delta)\, f_n(y_{(n)}|\theta)\, dy_{(n)}, \qquad (2.16)$$

which usually is informative on both δ and θ. There might also be cases where θ and δ are a priori dependent (including limiting cases where elements of δ are non-stochastic functions of θ):

$$\varphi(\theta, \delta) = \varphi_1(\theta)\, \varphi_2(\delta|\theta). \qquad (2.17)$$

The marginalized likelihood of $(n, y_{(n)})$ is then given by

$$f_m(n, y_{(n)}|\theta) = f_n(y_{(n)}|\theta)\, \psi_m(n|y_{(n)}, \theta) \qquad (2.18)$$

with

$$\psi_m(n|y_{(n)}, \theta) = \int_\Delta \psi(n|y_{(n)}, \delta)\, \varphi_2(\delta|\theta)\, d\delta, \qquad (2.19)$$

in which case the stopping rule δ clearly is informative on θ.

Example 2.6 Let us discuss two alternative stopping rules in the context of Example 2.2. Assume events occur at intervals of time drawn independently from one another and exponentially distributed:

$$f(y|\lambda) = \lambda \exp(-\lambda y). \tag{2.20}$$

Consider first the case where n is preassigned. The corresponding stopping rule is given by

$$\tau_j(y_{(j)}) = 0 \ (j = 0, 1, \ldots, n-1), \ \tau_n(y_{(n)}) = 1, \tag{2.21}$$

and is clearly non-informative relative to λ. The likelihood of $y_{(n)}$ is then given by

$$f(y_{(n)}|\lambda) = \lambda^n \exp(-\lambda t_n) \tag{2.22}$$

with $t_n = \sum_{i=1}^n y_i$. If instead the experience is interrupted after a preassigned period of time, which can be set equal to one unit of time at the cost of reinterpreting λ accordingly, then we have

$$\tau_0(\lambda) = \Pr(y_1 > \lambda|\lambda) = \exp(-\lambda), \tag{2.23}$$

$$\tau_j(y_{(j)}, \lambda) = \Pr(y_{j+1} > 1 - t_j|\lambda) = \exp[-\lambda(1 - t_j)], \tag{2.24}$$

which is clearly informative about λ. The likelihood of $(n, y_{(n)})$ for $n \geq 1$ is given by

$$\begin{aligned} f(n, y_{(n)}|\lambda) &= \tau_n(y_{(n)}, \lambda) \prod_{j=1}^n f(y_j|\lambda) \\ &= \lambda^n \exp(-\lambda) \text{ for } 0 \leq t_n < 1, \end{aligned} \tag{2.25}$$

and is zero otherwise. Finally if the technician is only required to count events, then the relevant likelihood is given by

$$\begin{aligned} \Pr(N = n|\lambda) &= \lambda^n \exp(-\lambda) \int_{\sum y_i \leq 1} dy_1 \, dy_2 \ldots dy_n \\ &= \frac{\lambda^n}{n!} \exp(-\lambda), \end{aligned} \tag{2.26}$$

which is the Poisson process that was used in Example 2.2.

2.2.4 *Identification*

In certain statistical or econometric models, there are parameters about which we cannot learn anything, even if we have as much data as we wish, unless we provide some extraneous information. These parameters are not identified. This kind of problem arises in both the classical and Bayesian inference paradigms. But the difference between the two paradigms, in this respect, lies in the type of information that must be brought in to identify the parameters: it can be probabilistic in the Bayesian approach, whereas it must be exact (or dogmatic) in the classical approach. Let us start with a definition, where we deal with a model defined by its density function $f(y|\theta)$.

Definition 2.7 *A value θ_a of the parameter is identified if there is no other value θ_b such that $f(y|\theta_a) = f(y|\theta_b), \forall y \in S$. The model is identified if all the parameter values are identified, in which case the parameter θ is said to be identified.*

The above definition is valid independently of any inference paradigm. Let us quote Kadane (1974: 175):

'identification is a property of the likelihood function, and is the same whether considered classically or from the Bayesian approach'.

When $f(y|\theta_a) = f(y|\theta_b)$, θ_a and θ_b are said to be observationally equivalent: it is not possible to know if a data set is a realization of $f(y|\theta_a)$ or of $f(y|\theta_b)$, using only the data. In terms of likelihood-based inference, if the parameter is not identified, the likelihood function $l(\theta; y)$ is flat with respect to θ.

Obviously, if the complete parameter vector θ is not identified, the statistical model is void of interest. In the multiparameter case, it may happen that some parameters are identified, while others are not. Or it may happen that some functions of the parameters are identified, as illustrated by the next example.

Example 2.8 Consider the bivariate regression model $y \sim N_T(x\alpha + z\beta, I_T)$, where y, x, and z are vectors of dimension T. If x and z are not collinear, α and β are identified. If there is a collinearity, e.g. $z = Kx$ with K a known constant, there is an infinity of values of α and β which are observationally equivalent: all the values that give the same value to $\gamma = \alpha + K\beta$. Indeed the model becomes $y \sim N_T(x\gamma, 1)$; γ is identified. Figure 2.1 shows the likelihood function as a function of α and β for an artificial sample of 50 observations, and $K = 1$. One sees that the function is flat over all the directions defined by $\beta = C - \alpha$ (whatever C). But the likelihood is not flat over any other direction. For example, fixing β, the likelihood is bell shaped in the direction of α, with its maximum at the least squares estimate $x'(y - x\beta)/x'x$. Or, as a function of γ, the likelihood is also bell shaped.

As the previous example illustrates, the issue of identification is relative to a parameterization. For some choice of parameters, there is no issue (γ in the previous example), but for another choice, there may be an issue (α and β in the example).

From the classical viewpoint, the consequence of unidentifiability of some parameters is that these parameters are not estimable: if the likelihood function is flat, the ML estimator is not defined. It can be shown also that the Fisher information matrix is singular. In the Bayesian approach, it should be noted that Bayes' theorem is operational, *whether θ is identified or not*. Hence the remark by Lindley (1972: 46):

'unidentifiability causes no real difficulties in the Bayesian approach'.

However, it should be obvious that if the full parameter is unidentified, the prior density is not revised by the sample: $\varphi(\theta|y) = \varphi(\theta)$. More interestingly, suppose that θ is partitioned into α and β, with β unidentified (note: this partitioning has nothing to do with that between parameters of interest and nuisance done in Subsection 2.2.2). Then we have the following set of results:

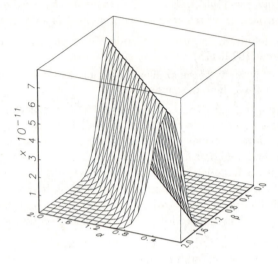

FIG. 2.1. Likelihood with globally unidentified parameter

Theorem 2.9 *Let $f(y|\alpha, \beta)$ be the data density, with β unidentified, and let $\varphi(\alpha, \beta)$ be the prior density. Then,*

(a) The marginal prior $\varphi(\alpha)$ is revised by the sample.

(b) The conditional prior $\varphi(\beta|\alpha)$ is not revised by the sample.

(c) The marginal prior $\varphi(\beta)$ is revised by the sample unless α and β are a priori independent.

Proof We leave the proof of (a) and (b) as an exercise. For (c),

$$\begin{aligned}
\varphi(\beta|y) &\propto \int f(y|\alpha, \beta)\, \varphi(\alpha, \beta)\, d\alpha \\
&= \int f(y|\alpha)\, \varphi(\beta)\, \varphi(\alpha|\beta)\, d\alpha \\
&= \varphi(\beta) f_m(y|\beta).
\end{aligned} \tag{2.27}$$

If $\varphi(\alpha|\beta) = \varphi(\alpha)$, the case of prior independence, the marginal 'likelihood' $f_m(y|\beta)$ does not depend on β, and in that case $\varphi(\beta|y) = \varphi(\beta)$.   □

In the classical approach, α is estimable, but β is not. The classical solution to an identification problem consists in fixing β to some preassigned value (sometimes a restricted set of values), or to a set of functions of α (obviously, as many functions as there are elements in β are necessary). In the Bayesian approach, the solution can be more flexible: it requires a prior density that links β to α through some form of probabilistic dependence. As we see directly in the proof above, this possibility comes from the fact that the Bayesian solution consists in integrating, rather than conditioning.

The above definition and theorem concern what is called the problem of 'global' identifiability. There can also be an issue of 'local' unidentifiability. When a parameter is globally unidentified, for any parameter value θ_a, one can find another parameter value that is observationally equivalent to it and is arbitrarily close to it. When a parameter is locally unidentified, for a parameter value θ_a, one can find another one which is observationally equivalent to it, but is at some distance from it. So any value in a neighbourhood of θ_a is not observationally equivalent to θ_a, but there may exist a value θ_b out of that neighbourhood such that $f(y|\theta_a) = f(y|\theta_b)$. Here is a simple example:

Example 2.10 Let $y \sim N(\theta^2, 1)$. The value 0 of θ is identified (in the sense of Definition 2.7), but any other value is not, since $f(y|\theta) = f(y|-\theta)$. But any value of θ is locally identified. Suppose that one observes an IID sample such that $\overline{y} = 1$. The likelihood function $l(\theta; \overline{y} = 1)$ is bimodal, with the two modes at 1 and -1, and $l(1; 1) = l(-1; 1)$. There are two ML estimators. Notice that unless the prior density is symmetrical around 0, the posterior has a global maximum, and it may have a local maximum. Anyway, the posterior is well defined and integrable.

Another example that is more relevant in econometrics is when a parameter is not identified when another one takes a particular value.

Example 2.11 Let $y \sim N_T(x\alpha + z\beta\alpha, I_T)$. When $\alpha = 0$, the parameter β is not identified, while for any other value of α there is no problem. Figure 2.2 shows the likelihood function for an artificial sample, over a portion of the parameter space. Clearly, the likelihood function is flat (but finite) in the direction of β when $\alpha = 0$ (we have sliced it at $\alpha = 0$ to show clearly that feature). In any other direction, it is curved. The posterior density is not integrable with a flat prior. With a non-flat prior that restores the usual bell shape of the posterior at $\alpha = 0$, the posterior becomes integrable. The situation is more difficult if the likelihood function is infinite at $\alpha = 0$ (i.e. flat but arbitrarily large in the direction of β). Clearly, there is a need in such a situation for a prior which restores the finiteness of the posterior. Such pathological cases occur in econometric models. See in particular Chapters 5, 6, and 8, where solutions are provided case by case.

2.3 Density and Likelihood Kernels

The notion of density kernels comes from Raiffa and Schlaifer (1961). Using kernels instead of densities simplifies the computations and saves a lot of notation. We start with a simple definition:

Definition 2.12 *A kernel of a density $D(y)$ is a function $K(y)$ such that*

$$D(y) = K(y)/\int K(y)\, dy. \tag{2.28}$$

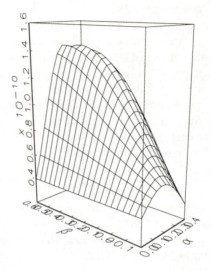

FIG. 2.2. Likelihood with locally unidentified parameter

A kernel includes all the factors of $D(y)$ that depend functionally on y. A direct implication of Definition 2.12 is that $K(y)/D(y)$ is constant with respect to y, which must be true since this ratio is the integration constant of $D(y)$. We shall use the convention to write

$$D(y) \propto K(y), \tag{2.29}$$

which reads '$D(y)$ is proportional to $K(y)$', when we wish to display the functional dependence of the density with respect to its argument and we do not care to show the constant of integration. A critical reader may have noticed that a kernel of a density is not unique since if $K(y)$ is multiplied by a constant, it also satisfies Definition 2.12. By taking the convention not to include any superfluous constant factor in $K(y)$, we can refer without ambiguity to *the* kernel of a density.

Let us again consider Bayes' theorem as given in (2.1). By definition, $f(y)$ is the integration constant of the posterior density; hence $\varphi(\theta) f(y|\theta)$ includes the kernel of the posterior density. As it also includes the integration constant of the prior density, it is clear that we can write

$$\varphi(\theta|y) \propto \kappa(\theta) f(y|\theta), \tag{2.30}$$

where $\kappa(\theta)$ is the kernel of the prior density. But we cannot replace $f(y|\theta)$ by its kernel because the latter does not include the factors of the integration constant of $f(y|\theta)$ that depend on θ. Since $f(y|\theta)$ defines the likelihood function $l(\theta; y)$, all we need to simplify (2.30) is the notion of likelihood kernel.

Definition 2.13 *The kernel of a likelihood function $l(\theta; y)$ is the function $k(\theta; y)$ such that $k(\theta; y)/l(\theta; y)$ is constant with respect to θ.*

Finally, we can write Bayes' theorem in the simplest form

$$\varphi(\theta|y) \propto \kappa(\theta)\, k(\theta; y). \tag{2.31}$$

The last formula is the most practical one to obtain the posterior density: after multiplying the prior kernel by the likelihood kernel, we try and recognize in the result a kernel of a known density in θ given y (using, for example, the definitions of probability densities in Appendix A). If this is possible, we have found the posterior density and we can use its properties (e.g. moments); if not, the posterior density kernel has to be treated by numerical integration.

We stress that the kernel of $f(y|\theta)$ is not equal to the likelihood kernel $k(\theta; y)$ because the former does not include the factors that depend only on θ and the latter does not include the factors that depend only on y. Before illustrating these differences by some examples, we introduce the notion of conditional kernel.

Definition 2.14 *The conditional kernel of a (conditional) density function $D(y|\theta)$ is the function $K(y|\theta)$ such that $K(y|\theta)/D(y|\theta)$ is constant with respect to both y and θ.*

This notion is useful for computing a marginal density. Assume we know analytically the densities $\varphi(\alpha|\beta)$ and $\varphi(\beta)$ but not $\varphi(\alpha)$ that we wish to compute by numerical integration, a rather usual situation in Bayesian inference (as we shall see in further chapters). Since

$$\varphi(\alpha) = \int \varphi(\alpha|\beta)\, \varphi(\beta)\, d\beta, \tag{2.32}$$

we can write

$$\varphi(\alpha) \propto \int \kappa(\alpha|\beta)\, \kappa(\beta)\, d\beta, \tag{2.33}$$

where $\kappa(\alpha|\beta)$ is the conditional kernel of $\varphi(\alpha|\beta)$ and $\kappa(\beta)$ is the kernel of $\varphi(\beta)$. This is quite important: in computing the integral in (2.33), the integrand must include all the factors of the conditional density that depend on α and β. We can now give examples.

Example 2.15 We assume a sample of one observation:

(i) If $Y \sim \text{Poisson}(\lambda)$, i.e. $f(y) = \exp(-\lambda)\, \lambda^y/y!$, $K(y) = \lambda^y/y!$, $k(\lambda; y) = \exp(-\lambda)\, \lambda^y$, and $K(y|\lambda) = f(y)$.
(ii) If $Y \sim N(\mu, \sigma^2)$, $K(y) = \exp[-(y-\mu)^2/2\sigma^2]$, $k(\mu, \sigma^2; y) = \sigma^{-1}.K(y) = K(y|\mu, \sigma^2)$; if σ^2 is known, $K(y|\mu) = K(y)$.

2.4 Sufficient Statistics

2.4.1 *Definition*

Data processing is simplified if it is possible to summarize the sample by a small number of characteristics. The summary of a sample for a parameter is defined by the function $t(y)$ from R^n to R^m where n is the sample size and m is fixed (it should not depend on n). This summary is a set of sufficient statistics for the parameter θ in the Bayesian sense if

$$\varphi(\theta|y) = \varphi[\theta|t(y)]. \tag{2.34}$$

This definition means that conditioning on $t(y)$ rather than on y does not change the inference results on the parameters.

How is it possible to know that sufficient statistics exist? Obviously, by the likelihood principle, the sufficient statistics should show up in the likelihood function. We have the following theorem:

Theorem 2.16 *A necessary and sufficient condition for $t(y)$ to be a sufficient statistic for θ is that it is possible to factorize the likelihood function as*

$$l(\theta; y) = h(y)\, k[\theta; t(y)]. \tag{2.35}$$

A proof of this result can be found in Raiffa and Schlaifer (1961: 33) or in DeGroot (1970: 156). The important aspect of the factorization is that the function $k(.)$ links θ to $t(y)$, not to y, i.e. the function $h(y)$ does not depend on θ (it may also not depend on y).

In (2.31) we see that the posterior density of θ can be obtained by using the kernel $k(\theta; y)$ of the likelihood function. It is natural to wonder what the link is between the likelihood kernel and the function $k[\theta; t(y)]$ of the above theorem. The answer is obvious: they are identical if we include in $h(y)$ all the factors of $l(\theta; y)$ that do not depend on y (i.e. constants). We can henceforth write a version of (2.31) that is valid when sufficient statistics exist:

$$\varphi(\theta|y) \propto \kappa(\theta)\, k[\theta; t(y)]. \tag{2.36}$$

The above formula justifies the definition of Bayesian sufficient statistics in (2.34). Examples are given in the next subsection.

2.4.2 *The Exponential Family*

The result of Theorem 2.16 is valid whatever the nature of the sampling process. If we stick to IID processes, we can wonder under which condition sufficient statistics exist. Roughly speaking it happens when the data density belongs to the exponential family, i.e. when the data density can be factorized in the following form:

$$f(y|\theta) = h(y)\, \exp\left(\sum_{j=1}^{m} u_j(y)\phi_j(\theta) \right), \tag{2.37}$$

where h, u_j, and ϕ_j are known functions. In this case the sufficient statistics of a sample of size n are given by the m following functions:

$$t_j(y) = \sum_{i=1}^{n} u_j(y_i) \qquad j = 1, 2, \ldots, m. \tag{2.38}$$

This result is valid if the support of the density $f(y|\theta)$ is independent of θ. Thus it is possible to find densities which admit sufficient statistics and do not belong to the exponential family, but the support of which is a function of θ. The most immediate case is that of the uniform density for which

$$l(\theta|y) = \begin{cases} 1/\theta & \text{if } y \in [0, \theta] \\ 0 & \text{otherwise,} \end{cases}$$

and a sufficient statistic is given by $\max(y_i)$ that is also the maximum likelihood estimator of θ.

Finally, whenever it is possible to express a probability density as a mixture of distributions, it is not a member of the exponential family and it has no sufficient statistics. This is particularly the case for the Student density which can be expressed as an infinite sum of normal densities mixed by an inverted gamma-2 gamma density (see Theorem A.7).

Example 2.17 We now give some examples of IID sampling models and derive the corresponding sufficient statistics.

(i) POISSON MODEL
For a sample of size n of the Poisson distribution with parameter λ—see Example 2.15(i)— the likelihood function is

$$l(\lambda; y) = \exp\left[-n\lambda + \sum_{i=1}^{n} y_i \log(\lambda)\right] / \prod_{i=1}^{n} y_i!,$$

and we see that n and $\sum_{i=1}^{n} y_i$ are sufficient statistics.

(ii) NORMAL MODEL
The likelihood function—see Example 2.15(ii)—for n data is

$$\begin{aligned} l(\mu, \sigma^2; y) &= \prod_{i=1}^{n} (2\pi)^{-1/2} \sigma^{-1} \exp[-\tfrac{1}{2\sigma^2}(y_i - \mu)^2] \\ &= (2\pi)^{-n/2} \exp[-(n\mu/2\sigma^2) - n\log\sigma \\ &\quad -(\sum_{i=1}^{n} y_i^2/2\sigma^2) - (\mu/\sigma^2)\sum_{i=1}^{n} y_i]. \end{aligned}$$

So n, $\sum_{i=1}^{n} y_i^2$, and $\sum_{i=1}^{n} y_i$ are sufficient statistics for μ and σ^2.

(iii) STUDENT MODEL
For a sample of size n of a Student random variable Y as defined by (A.31) with $m = 1$, the likelihood function is

$$\begin{aligned} l(\mu, s, \nu; y) &= \prod_{i=1}^{n} c_b^{-1}(\tfrac{1}{2}, \tfrac{\nu}{2}) s^{\nu/2} [s + (y_i - \mu)^2]^{-(\nu+1)/2} \\ &= c_b^{-n}(\tfrac{1}{2}, \tfrac{\nu}{2}) s^{n\nu/2} \exp\{-\tfrac{(\nu+1)}{2}\sum_{i=1}^{n} \log[s + (y_i - \mu)^2]\} \end{aligned}$$

which cannot be factorized because of the non-linearity of the log function. There are no sufficient statistics.

2.5   Natural Conjugate Inference

2.5.1   *General Principle*

When the probability density of an observation belongs to the exponential family and the sampling process is IID, the likelihood function of a sample of size n can be written as follows (using its kernel):

$$l(\theta; y) \propto \exp\left(\sum_{j=1}^{m} t_j(y)\,\phi_j(\theta)\right). \tag{2.39}$$

Let us consider a prior density of the following form:

$$\varphi(\theta) \propto \exp\left(\sum_{j=1}^{m} b_j\,\phi_j(\theta)\right). \tag{2.40}$$

By applying (2.36), we see that the posterior density has the same form as the prior and is given by

$$\varphi(\theta|y) \propto \exp\left(\sum_{j=1}^{m} [b_j + t_j(y)]\,\phi_j(\theta)\right). \tag{2.41}$$

The posterior parameters are the sum of the prior parameters and of the sufficient statistics. The prior density (2.40) is 'natural conjugate' to the sampling process $f(y|\theta)$; that is to say, the kernels of the prior density, the posterior density, and the likelihood function have the same functional form. The parameters of the posterior density are obtained by addition of the sufficient statistics of the sample and of the corresponding parameters of the prior density. The parameters b_j of the prior density (2.40) are not always the 'natural' parameters one is used to working with (e.g. the mean and the variance of a normal density), but it is always possible to combine the natural prior parameters with functions of the sufficient statistics in order to get the natural posterior parameters rather than the parameters $b_j + t_j(y)$. A complete example is provided in the next subsection.

In summary, the natural conjugate family is closed for inference and is a convenient tool to conduct inference if the prior information can be adequately represented by a member of this family (see Chapter 4 for a discussion of the representation of the prior information).

Natural conjugate families were disclosed by Raiffa and Schlaifer (1961) who gave a particular interpretation to them. They show that it is always possible in the exponential family to combine the sufficient statistics of two subsamples in order to get the sufficient statistics of the complete sample. The trick consists in interpreting the likelihood kernel of the first sample as a prior density for the second sample and then applying (2.41). As a consequence a natural conjugate prior density can be interpreted as the posterior density of an hypothetical previous sample analysed under a 'non-informative' prior density (this notion is explained in Chapter 4).

This interpretation did not lead to a consensus among Bayesian statisticians. For instance, De Finetti (1975: 238) thinks that the concept of natural conjugate family lacks sufficient theoretical foundations and constitutes a convenient framework for calculus, but nothing more.

2.5.2 *Inference in the Multivariate Normal Process*

The aim of this section is to analyse the multivariate normal model in the natural conjugate framework in order to illustrate the concepts introduced in the previous sections. This particular model has little practical interest in econometrics, but it gives rise to formulae that are useful for Bayesian inference in multivariate regression models (see Section 9.2).

Let us consider an IID sample of the random variable Y distributed as $N_k(\mu, \Sigma)$. The density of Y is given by (A.44), so that the likelihood function is given by

$$
\begin{aligned}
l(\mu, \Sigma; y) &= \prod_{i=1}^{n} f(y_i | \mu, \Sigma) \\
&\propto |\Sigma|^{-n/2} \exp[-\tfrac{1}{2} \sum_{i=1}^{n} (y_i - \mu)' \Sigma^{-1} (y_i - \mu)].
\end{aligned}
\tag{2.42}
$$

We can manipulate the sum in the exponential factor as follows:

$$
\begin{aligned}
&\sum_{i=1}^{n} (y_i - \mu)' \Sigma^{-1} (y_i - \mu) \\
&= \sum_{i=1}^{n} [(y_i - \overline{y}) - (\mu - \overline{y})]' \Sigma^{-1} [(y_i - \overline{y}) - (\mu - \overline{y})] \\
&= \sum_{i=1}^{n} (y_i - \overline{y})' \Sigma^{-1} (y_i - \overline{y}) + n(\mu - \overline{y})' \Sigma^{-1} (\mu - \overline{y}) \\
&= \operatorname{tr}(\Sigma^{-1} S) + n(\mu - \overline{y})' \Sigma^{-1} (\mu - \overline{y}),
\end{aligned}
\tag{2.43}
$$

where

$$
\overline{y} = \frac{1}{n} \sum_{i=1}^{n} y_i
\tag{2.44}
$$

and

$$
S = \sum_{i=1}^{n} (y_i - \overline{y})(y_i - \overline{y})'
\tag{2.45}
$$

are sufficient statistics (together with n). The likelihood can be written finally as

$$
\begin{aligned}
l(\mu, \Sigma; y) &\propto |\Sigma|^{-1/2} \exp[-\tfrac{n}{2} (\mu - \overline{y})' \Sigma^{-1} (\overline{y} - \mu)] \\
&\times |\Sigma|^{-(\nu+k+1)/2} \exp(-\tfrac{1}{2} \operatorname{tr} \Sigma^{-1} S),
\end{aligned}
\tag{2.46}
$$

where $\nu = n - k - 2$. We recognize in (2.46) the product of the conditional kernel of a normal density in $\mu | \Sigma$ with parameters $\overline{y}$ and Σ/n, and the conditional kernel of an inverted Wishart density in Σ with parameters S and ν. The natural conjugate prior density for the multivariate normal process is then defined by

$$
\mu | \Sigma \sim N_k(\mu_0, \Sigma/n_0),
\tag{2.47}
$$

and

$$\Sigma \sim IW_k(S_0, \nu_0). \tag{2.48}$$

We assume that the prior parameters satisfy the conditions that ensure that the prior densities are well defined, i.e.

$$n_0 > 0, \ \nu_0 > k - 1, \text{ and } S_0 \text{ PDS.} \tag{2.49}$$

Written explicitly, the kernel of the prior density is

$$\varphi(\mu, \Sigma) \propto |\Sigma|^{-(\nu_0+k+2)/2} \exp\left(-\frac{1}{2}\left[n_0(\mu - \mu_0)'\Sigma^{-1}(\mu - \mu_0) + \text{tr } \Sigma^{-1}S_0\right]\right). \tag{2.50}$$

Let us compute the posterior density of μ and Σ. Since we use a natural conjugate prior density, we know that the posterior density must be in the same family as the prior density, i.e.

$$\mu|\Sigma \sim N_k(\mu_*, \Sigma/n_*) \tag{2.51}$$

and

$$\Sigma \sim IW_k(S_*, \nu_*), \tag{2.52}$$

where μ_*, S_*, ν_*, and n_* are the posterior parameters. In order to define them as functions of the prior parameters and of the sufficient statistics of the sample, we must apply (2.36) and express the result as the kernel of an $N_k(\mu_*, \Sigma/n_*)$ density times an $IW_k(S_*, \nu_*)$ density. The product of (2.46) and (2.50) yields

$$\varphi(\mu, \Sigma|y) \propto |\Sigma|^{-(\nu_0+n+k+2)/2} \exp[-\tfrac{1}{2}\text{tr } \Sigma^{-1}(S_0 + S)] \\ \times \exp\left\{-\tfrac{1}{2}[n_0(\mu - \mu_0)'\Sigma^{-1}(\mu - \mu_0) + n(\mu - \overline{y})'\Sigma^{-1}(\mu - \overline{y})]\right\}. \tag{2.53}$$

This expression is not readily recognized as the kernel of a normal density times an inverted Wishart density. To arrive at it, we combine the sum of the two quadratic forms in μ of the exponential argument as follows:

$$\begin{aligned} &n_0(\mu - \mu_0)'\Sigma^{-1}(\mu - \mu_0) + n(\mu - \overline{y})'\Sigma^{-1}(\mu - \overline{y}) \\ &= n_*(\mu'\Sigma^{-1}\mu - 2\mu_*'\Sigma^{-1}\mu) + n_0\mu_0'\Sigma^{-1}\mu_0 + n\overline{y}'\Sigma^{-1}\overline{y} \\ &= n_*(\mu - \mu_*)'\Sigma^{-1}(\mu - \mu_*) - n_*\mu_*'\Sigma^{-1}\mu_* + n_0\mu_0'\Sigma^{-1}\mu_0 + n\overline{y}'\Sigma^{-1}\overline{y} \\ &= n_*(\mu - \mu_*)'\Sigma^{-1}(\mu - \mu_*) + (n_0 n)/n_*)(\mu_0 - \overline{y})'\Sigma^{-1}(\mu_0 - \overline{y}), \end{aligned} \tag{2.54}$$

where

$$n_* = n + n_0 \tag{2.55}$$

and

$$\mu_* = (n_0\mu_0 + n\overline{y})/n_*. \tag{2.56}$$

If we substitute the last line of (2.54) in (2.53) and define

$$S_* = S_0 + S + (n_0 n)/n_*)(\mu_0 - \overline{y})(\mu_0 - \overline{y})', \tag{2.57}$$

and

$$\nu_* = \nu_0 + n, \tag{2.58}$$

we can finally express the kernel of the posterior density as

$$\varphi(\mu, \Sigma | y) \propto |\Sigma|^{-(\nu_*+k+2)/2} \exp\left(-\frac{1}{2}\left[n_*(\mu - \mu_*)'\Sigma^{-1}(\mu - \mu_*) + \operatorname{tr} \Sigma^{-1}S_*\right]\right). \tag{2.59}$$

This is the result given in (2.51) and (2.52). The passage from the prior density to the posterior density is summarized by the four relations (2.55) to (2.58), which are the essential formulae of the natural conjugate inference in the multivariate normal model. Some comments can be made on these results. The posterior parameter n_* is the sum of the sample size n and the prior parameter n_0 that can be interpreted as the sample size of a hypothetical sample. The posterior expectation μ_* of μ is a weighted sum of the sample mean and of the prior mean (or the mean of the hypothetical sample), where the weights are the corresponding relative sample sizes. The scale parameter of the posterior density of the variance of the process Σ is given by the sum of the sample dispersion matrix S, the prior scale S_0 (dispersion of the hypothetical sample), and a term which is positive definite whenever the prior mean is different from the sample mean.

We can use the properties of matricvariate normal and inverted Wishart densities (see Theorem A.20) in order to give more detailed results. In particular, the marginal posterior density of the $1 \times k$ matrix μ' is matricvariate Student with parameters μ'_*, S_*, n_*, and ν_*, or equivalently the density of the vector μ is multivariate Student:

$$\mu | y \sim t_k(\mu_*, n_*^{-1}, S_*^{-1}, \nu_* + 1 - k) \tag{2.60}$$

(for the marginal prior density the same property holds if we replace the posterior parameters by the prior ones). It follows that $E(\mu | y) = \mu_*$ and

$$V(\mu | y) = \frac{1}{\nu_* - k - 1} \frac{S_*}{n_*}. \tag{2.61}$$

We can also compute predictive densities, like the predictive density of one observation y_i of the sample (or more generally of several observations), or the predictive density of the sample mean. Let us do this in detail for one observation. We use the prior (2.47) and multiply it by the conditional density of Y_i which is $N(\mu, \Sigma)$, considering Σ as fixed for a while. This gives the joint density of μ and Y_i, conditional on Σ, a multivariate normal density by Theorem A.14:

$$\begin{pmatrix} \mu \\ Y_i \end{pmatrix} \sim N_{k+k}\left[\begin{pmatrix} \mu_0 \\ \mu_0 \end{pmatrix}, \begin{pmatrix} \Sigma/n_0 & \Sigma/n_0 \\ \Sigma/n_0 & \Sigma/n_0 + \Sigma \end{pmatrix}\right]. \tag{2.62}$$

The marginal density of $Y_i | \Sigma$ is normal by Theorem A.12:

$$Y_i | \Sigma \sim N_k[\mu_0, \Sigma(n_0 + 1)/n_0]. \tag{2.63}$$

The joint density of Y_i and Σ is obviously the product of the conditional normal (2.63) and the prior inverted Wishart density (2.48). By the same argument as the one that gives (2.60) starting from (2.59) or from (2.51) and (2.52), we can conclude that the predictive density of Y_i is Student:

$$Y_i \sim t_k \left(\mu_0, \frac{n_0 + 1}{n_0}, S_0^{-1}, \nu_0 + 1 - k \right). \tag{2.64}$$

The predictive density of the sample mean is obtained in the same way, starting with the conditional density of the sample mean, which is $N_k(\mu, \Sigma/n)$. As an exercise, the reader should check that

$$\overline{Y} \sim t_k \left(\mu_0, \frac{n_0 + n}{n_0 n}, S_0^{-1}, \nu_0 + 1 - k \right). \tag{2.65}$$

Both (2.64) and (2.65) are proper densities under the conditions stated in (2.49).

2.6   Reductions of Models

A useful principle of modelling is to build a model that is both simple and adequate for the objective of the investigation. A too complex model would be a waste of resources, but a too simple one might imply that the available information has been used in an inefficient, or even misleading, way. A modeller has to make a compromise between the two requirements. An important notion in this respect concerns the reduction of a model, studied by Florens and Mouchart (1985a). Suppose that we have a random vector X and that we are interested in modelling only a subvector of X, or that we are interested in making inference only on some of the parameters that index the data density of X. How is it possible to reduce the big initial model? A reduction can be done by marginalization or by conditioning, either on the parameter space or on the sample space. Marginalization on the parameter space is possible only in a Bayesian framework and corresponds to the integration of nuisance parameters. Conditioning on the parameter space corresponds to parametric restrictions. Marginalization on the sample space corresponds to specifying the data generating process of only a part of the variables. In econometrics, we are often interested in conditioning on some of the variables, which are then treated as if there were not random; this corresponds to conditioning on the sample space. General concepts are presented in Subsection 2.6.1. They are applied in Subsection 2.6.2 to the multivariate normal process, in order to introduce the static regression model.

2.6.1   Reduction by Conditioning and Exogeneity

A Bayesian statistical model is defined by a joint probability density on the sample and the parameter spaces, say $\Pi(x, \theta)$. In order to make precise the notions alluded to above, we consider the following partitions of x and θ:

$$x = \begin{pmatrix} y \\ z \end{pmatrix} \qquad \theta = \begin{pmatrix} \alpha \\ \beta \end{pmatrix}. \tag{2.66}$$

A *marginal model* is obtained by integration of a part of x or of θ. For instance, if β is a nuisance parameter, we can get rid of it by working with the model

$$\Pi(x, \alpha) = \varphi(\alpha)\, f(x|\alpha), \tag{2.67}$$

where

$$f(x|\alpha) = \int f(x|\theta)\, \varphi(\beta|\alpha)\, d\beta. \tag{2.68}$$

Viewed as a function of α, the data density $f(x|\alpha)$ is the marginalized likelihood function—compare formula (2.6).

A *conditional model* is obtained by conditioning on a part of x or of θ. For instance, conditioning on z leads to

$$\Pi(y, \theta|z) = \varphi(\theta|z)\, f(y|\theta, z). \tag{2.69}$$

In general, $\varphi(\theta|z)$ cannot be replaced by $\varphi(\theta)$ in the previous formula: since $\Pi(y, z, \theta) = \Pi(y, \theta|z)\, f(z)$, we can write

$$\begin{aligned}
\Pi(y, \theta|z) &= \frac{\Pi(y, z, \theta)}{f(z)} = \frac{f(y, z|\theta)\, \varphi(\theta)}{f(z)} \\
&= f(y|z, \theta)\, \frac{f(z|\theta)\, \varphi(\theta)}{f(z)} \\
&= f(y|z, \theta)\, \varphi(\theta|z).
\end{aligned} \tag{2.70}$$

Another conditional model is obtained by conditioning on a part of the parameter space:

$$\Pi(x, \beta|\alpha) = \varphi(\beta|\alpha)\, f(x|\alpha, \beta), \tag{2.71}$$

which corresponds to a situation where α is considered to be known, i.e. to an exact restriction.

Under which conditions are such reductions admissible? Intuitively a reduction is admissible if it leads to inference results for the parameter of interest which are identical to those one would obtain with the complete model. More precisely let us consider two complementary reductions on the sample space, defined by

$$\Pi(z, \theta) \quad \text{(marginal model)},$$
$$\Pi(y, \theta|z) \quad \text{(conditional model)}.$$

We have the following definition:

Definition 2.18 *A reduction is admissible if its complementary reduction is not informative on the parameter of interest, i.e.*
(i) $\Pi(z, \theta)$ is admissible if $\varphi(\theta|z) = \varphi(\theta|y, z)$;
(ii) $\Pi(y, \theta|z)$ is admissible if $\varphi(\theta) = \varphi(\theta|z)$.

By using Bayes' theorem, it is easy to show that equivalent definitions are
that the marginal model $\Pi(z, \theta)$ is admissible if $f(y|z, \theta) = f(y|z)$, and that the
conditional model $\Pi(y, \theta|z)$ is admissible if $f(z|\theta) = f(z)$.

A very important notion is connected to the notion of reduction by conditioning. If a reduction by conditioning on z is admissible, then z is said to
be *exogenous for the parameter of interest*. Suppose that α is the parameter of
interest.

Definition 2.19 *z and α are mutually exogenous if the marginal model of z is
not informative on α:*

$$f(z|\alpha) = f(z),$$

and if the conditional model of $y|z$ is informative only on α:

$$f(y|z, \alpha, \beta) = f(y|z, \alpha).$$

Again, it can be shown that the first condition of the definition is equivalent to
the condition that $\varphi(\alpha|z)$ and $\varphi(\alpha)$ are equal. The second condition implies that
the nuisance parameter β need not be integrated out in the conditional process
in order to compute the posterior density of α.

The notion of exogeneity is closely linked to the notion of cut in a statistical
model. Here is the definition of a *Bayesian cut*:

Definition 2.20 *α, β, and z operate a Bayesian cut in $\Pi(x, \theta)$ if*

- *α and β are a priori independent;*
- *$f(x|\theta) = f(y|z, \alpha) f(z|\beta)$.*

Florens and Mouchart (1985a) give the following theorem:

Theorem 2.21 *If α, β, and z operate a Bayesian cut in $\Pi(x, \theta)$, then*

- *z and α are mutually exogenous;*
- *α and β are independent a posteriori.*

The proof is given by Florens and Mouchart (1985a). A Bayesian cut allows a
total separation of inference (on β) in the marginal model and of inference (on α)
in the conditional model. The notion of Bayesian cut has a classical counterpart.
In Definition 2.20, one has to replace the condition of *prior independence* between
α and β by the condition that α and β are *variation free*, i.e. are not subject to
cross-restrictions. Note that if two parameters are not variation free, they cannot
be independent in probability. For more details, the reader should refer to Section
2 of Florens and Mouchart (1985a). The notion of exogeneity in dynamic models
is discussed in Section 3 of their paper. Engle, Hendry, and Richard (1983)
give a treatment of the same issues, which is more oriented towards dynamic
econometric models. This topic is reviewed in Subsection 5.2.1.

2.6.2   *Conditioning and the Regression Model*

We write the static linear regression model at observation t as

$$y_t = \alpha + \beta' z_t + u_t, \tag{2.72}$$

where z_t and β are $k - 1 \times 1$ vectors. It is a tool to relate a random variable to other random variables (and possibly also deterministic ones) through its conditional expectation function (also called regression function), assumed linear (or linearized). We propose two ways to justify the regression model, based on an argument of reduction by conditioning in the multivariate normal sampling model.

For the first approach, we start from the multivariate normal vector

$$\begin{pmatrix} y_t \\ z_t \end{pmatrix} \sim N_k \left(\begin{pmatrix} \mu_y \\ \mu_z \end{pmatrix}, \Sigma \right), \qquad \Sigma = \begin{pmatrix} \Sigma_{yy} & \Sigma_{yz} \\ \Sigma_{zy} & \Sigma_{zz} \end{pmatrix}, \tag{2.73}$$

where y_t is a scalar and z_t a vector. We can decompose (2.73) into a marginal model of z_t and a conditional model of y_t given z_t according to Theorem A.12:

$$z_t \sim N_{k-1}(\mu_z, \Sigma_{zz}), \tag{2.74}$$

$$y_t | z_t \sim N(\alpha + \beta' z_t, \sigma^2), \tag{2.75}$$

where

$$\beta = \Sigma_{zz}^{-1} \Sigma_{zy}, \tag{2.76}$$

$$\alpha = \mu_y - \beta' \mu_z, \tag{2.77}$$

$$\sigma^2 = \Sigma_{yy} - \Sigma_{yz} \Sigma_{zz}^{-1} \Sigma_{zy}. \tag{2.78}$$

The parameters of the marginal model, μ_z and Σ_{zz}, and the parameters of the conditional model, namely α, β, and σ^2, are variation free. Therefore, if we define a prior which imposes independence between the two sets of parameters, the variable z_t operates a cut in the Bayesian model $\Pi(y_t, z_t, \mu_y, \mu_z, \Sigma)$. If the parameters of interest are functions only of the parameters of the conditional model, the cut implies that we can restrict our attention to the conditional sampling model (2.75) for inference. This model is equivalent to (2.72) if we define u_t to be the difference between y_t and its conditional expectation, and restrict it to have a normal distribution.

The reader may be a bit surprised by this approach of the regression model, as by construction the explanatory variables are exogenous for the parameters. Our second approach shows that a cut is not warranted even in the multivariate normal model.

For the second approach, we start from a multivariate normal process with a mean that changes with the index t:

$$\begin{pmatrix} y_t \\ z_t \end{pmatrix} \sim N_k \left(\begin{pmatrix} \mu_{yt} \\ \mu_{zt} \end{pmatrix}, \Sigma \right). \tag{2.79}$$

We assume that the *incidental* mean vector is constrained by the linear relationship

$$\mu_{yt} = \alpha + \beta'_* \mu_{zt}, \tag{2.80}$$

where α and β_* are parameters. This model can be interpreted as an error-in-variables model: the incidental means μ_{yt} and μ_{zt} are the unobservable exact values which are measured with errors by the corresponding variables y_t and z_t. It can also be interpreted as a non-stationary process, where the form of non-stationarity is not very precisely modelled. The decomposition into a marginal and a conditional model becomes

$$z_t \sim N_{k-1} \left(\mu_{zt}, \Sigma_{zz} \right), \tag{2.81}$$

$$y_t | z_t \sim N \left(\alpha + (\beta_* - \beta)' \mu_{zt} + \beta' z_t, \sigma^2 \right), \tag{2.82}$$

where β and σ^2 are defined by (2.76) and (2.78). For z_t to be exogenous for β, the parameters of the two complementary reductions must be variation free. This happens if the parameter β_* is equal to the regression coefficients β. This condition allows the operation of a cut in the model: the incidental parameters are all relegated in the marginal model, which can be ignored for inference on the parameters of the conditional model. Lubrano, Pierse, and Richard (1986) use this concept for testing the exogeneity of the interest rate in a UK money demand function. When the cut is valid, the conditional model (2.82) is equivalent to the static regression model (2.72) with normal error term.

It is of course not really necessary to justify the linear regression model (even with normal errors) by reduction of a large multivariate normal distribution. There is no need at all for the conditioning variables to be marginally distributed as a normal distribution. The previous reductions may be useful to show what is at stake when the 'exogeneity' of the conditioning variables is questioned.

Bayesian inference in the static regression model (2.72) is detailed in Section 2.7.

2.7   Inference in the Linear Regression Model

2.7.1   *Model and Likelihood Function*

In this section, we write the static linear regression model as

$$y_t = \beta' x_t + u_t \qquad t = 1 \ldots T \qquad u_t \sim IN(0, \sigma^2), \tag{2.83}$$

where x_t and β are $k \times 1$ vectors. The error terms are assumed to be independent and normal. The matrix version of (2.83) is the usual $y = X\beta + u$ with obvious definitions of X ($T \times k$ matrix), y, and u ($T \times 1$ vectors).

The variables x_t are assumed to be exogenous for the parameters β and σ^2 of the conditional model (see Subsection 2.6.2). The data density of the conditional model is then sufficient for (posterior and predictive) inference and serves to define the likelihood function of β and σ^2:

$$L(\beta, \sigma^2|d) \propto (\sigma^2)^{-T/2} \exp[-\tfrac{1}{2}\sigma^{-2}\textstyle\sum_{t=1}^{T}(y_t - \beta'x_t)^2]$$
$$\propto (\sigma^2)^{-T/2} \exp[-\tfrac{1}{2}\sigma^{-2}(y - X\beta)'(y - X\beta)], \tag{2.84}$$

where d denotes the data (y and X). We can show that (2.84) belongs to the class of normal–inverted gamma-2 density functions defined in Subsection A.2.4:

Theorem 2.22 *The likelihood function of the linear regression model (2.83) is proportional to a normal–inverted gamma-2 density in β, σ^2 defined as*

$$L(\beta, \sigma^2|d) \propto f_{NIg}(\beta, \sigma^2|\hat{\beta}, X'X, s, T - k - 2), \tag{2.85}$$

where

$$\hat{\beta} = (X'X)^{-1}X'y,$$

$$s = y'M_X y, \text{ with } M_X = I_T - X(X'X)^{-1}X'.$$

Proof

$$(y - X\beta)'(y - X\beta) = y'y + \beta'X'X\beta - 2\beta'X'y$$
$$= y'y - \hat{\beta}'X'X\hat{\beta} + (\beta - \hat{\beta})'X'X(\beta - \hat{\beta})$$
$$= s + (\beta - \hat{\beta})'X'X(\beta - \hat{\beta}),$$

which can be directly verified. Hence by substitution in (2.84), we get

$$L(\beta, \sigma^2|d) \propto (\sigma^2)^{-T/2} \exp\left(-\frac{1}{2}\sigma^{-2}[s + (\beta - \hat{\beta})'X'X(\beta - \hat{\beta})]\right), \tag{2.86}$$

which is the kernel of the normal–inverted gamma-2 density defined on the right hand side of (2.85), as can be checked from (A.71). □

It is obvious from (2.86) that the information of the sample that is relevant for inference on β and σ^2 is summarized by the statistics that define the parameters of the normal–inverted gamma-2 density in (2.85). They are the least squares formula, the sample precision matrix, the sum of squared residuals, and a degrees of freedom parameter ($T - k - 2$).

2.7.2 *Natural Conjugate Prior Density*

By a direct application of the principle defined in Section 2.5, we know that the natural conjugate prior density for β and σ^2 is in the class of densities to which the likelihood is proportional.

Definition 2.23 *The natural conjugate prior density for the linear regression model (2.83) belongs to the class of normal–inverted gamma-2 densities and can be defined as*

$$\varphi(\beta, \sigma^2) = f_{NIg}(\beta, \sigma^2 | \beta_0, M_0, s_0, \nu_0), \tag{2.87}$$

where the hyperparameters are subject to the restrictions $\beta_0 \in R^k$, $M_0 \in C_k$, $s_0 > 0$, *and* $\nu_0 > 0$.

If one is willing to represent prior information through such a density, one has to choose appropriate values for the hyperparameters. We therefore need an interpretation of these hyperparameters, and practical procedures to elicit or select their values. We also need to say what can be done if one has no prior information on some parameters or even on all of them, and if one has exact prior information on some parameters or on some functions of them. These issues are discussed in detail in Chapter 4.

2.7.3 *Posterior Densities*

We have seen that the likelihood function of the linear regression model is proportional to a normal–inverted gamma-2 density which is also the class of the prior density. Hence, as is always the case in a natural conjugate framework, the posterior density reproduces the form of the prior density.

Theorem 2.24 *The posterior density of* β *and* σ^2 *in the linear regression model (2.83), given the prior density (2.87), is a normal–inverted gamma-2 density defined by*

$$\varphi(\beta, \sigma^2 | d) = f_{NIg}(\beta, \sigma^2 | \beta_*, M_*, s_*, \nu_*), \tag{2.88}$$

where the hyperparameters are defined by

$$M_* = M_0 + X'X, \tag{2.89}$$

$$\beta_* = M_*^{-1}(M_0 \beta_0 + X'X\hat{\beta}), \tag{2.90}$$

$$s_* = s_0 + s + (\beta_0 - \hat{\beta})'[M_0^{-1} + (X'X)^{-1}]^{-1}(\beta_0 - \hat{\beta}), \tag{2.91}$$

$$\nu_* = \nu_0 + T. \tag{2.92}$$

Proof By Bayes' formula (2.31), the kernel of the posterior density is the product of the kernels of (2.85) and (2.87)—see also (2.86). This yields

$$\varphi(\beta, \sigma^2 | d) \propto (\sigma^2)^{-(\nu_0 + T + k + 2)/2} \exp\left(-\frac{1}{2}\sigma^{-2}[s_0 + s + Q_0(\beta) + \hat{Q}(\beta)]\right)$$

where

$$Q_0(\beta) = (\beta - \beta_0)'M_0(\beta - \beta_0)$$

and

$$\hat{Q}(\beta) = (\beta - \hat{\beta})'X'X(\beta - \hat{\beta}).$$

It can be checked directly that

$$Q_0(\beta) + \hat{Q}(\beta) = Q_*(\beta) + \beta_0' M_0 \beta_0 + \hat{\beta}' X' X \hat{\beta} - \beta_* M_* \beta_*,$$

where

$$Q_*(\beta) = (\beta - \beta_*)' M_* (\beta - \beta_*),$$

so that

$$\varphi(\beta, \sigma^2 | d) \propto (\sigma^2)^{-(\nu_0 + T + k + 2)/2} \exp\left(-\frac{1}{2}\sigma^{-2}[s_* + Q_*(\beta)]\right)$$

where

$$s_* = s_0 + s + \beta_0' M_0 \beta_0 + \hat{\beta}' X' X \hat{\beta} - \beta_* M_* \beta_*.$$

This is the kernel of a normal–inverted gamma-2 density with parameters β_*, M_*, ν_*, and s_*. It remains to check that the last expression of s_* is equal to that given in (2.91). Indeed

$$\begin{aligned}
&\beta_0' M_0 \beta_0 + \hat{\beta}' X' X \hat{\beta} - \beta_* M_* \beta_* \\
&= \beta_0' M_0 \beta_0 + \hat{\beta}' X' X \hat{\beta} - (\beta_0' M_0 + \hat{\beta}' X' X)(M_0 + X' X)^{-1}(\beta_0' M_0 + \hat{\beta}' X' X) \\
&= \hat{\beta}'[X'X - X'X(M_0 + X'X)^{-1}X'X]\hat{\beta} + \beta_0'[M_0 - M_0(M_0 + X'X)^{-1}M_0]\beta_0 \\
&\quad - 2\hat{\beta}'[X'X - X'X(M_0 + X'X)^{-1}M_0]\beta_0 \\
&= \hat{\beta}' M_0(M_0 + X'X)^{-1}X'X\hat{\beta} + \beta_0' M_0(M_0 + X'X)^{-1}X'X\beta_0 \\
&\quad - 2\hat{\beta}' M_0(M_0 + X'X)^{-1}X'X\beta_0 \\
&= (\hat{\beta} - \beta_0)' M_0(M_0 + X'X)^{-1}X'X(\hat{\beta} - \beta_0)'.
\end{aligned}$$

The last but one equality follows from the following matrix equalities:

$$X'X - X'X(M_0 + X'X)^{-1}X'X = M_0(M_0 + X'X)^{-1}X'X$$

(check by postmultiplying both sides by $X'X^{-1}(M_0 + X'X)$), and

$$M_0 - M_0(M_0 + X'X)^{-1}M_0 = M_0(M_0 + X'X)^{-1}X'X$$

(check by postmultiplying both sides by $M_0^{-1}(M_0 + X'X)$). Finally,

$$\begin{aligned}
M_0(M_0 + X'X)^{-1}X'X &= (M_0^{-1})^{-1}(M_0 + X'X)^{-1}[(X'X)^{-1}]^{-1} \\
&= [(X'X)^{-1}(M_0 + X'X)M_0^{-1}]^{-1} \\
&= [M_0^{-1} + (X'X)^{-1}]^{-1}
\end{aligned}$$

as in (2.91). □

By the properties of the normal–inverted gamma-2 density, we have the following results:

$$\beta | d \sim t_k(\beta_*, s_*, M_*, \nu_*) \tag{2.93}$$

(see formula (A.81) and what follows in Appendix A), so that

$$E(\beta | d) = \beta_*, \tag{2.94}$$

$$\text{Var}(\beta|d) = \frac{s_*}{\nu_* - 2} M_*^{-1}, \tag{2.95}$$

and

$$\sigma^2|d \sim IG_2(\nu_*, s_*), \tag{2.96}$$

so that

$$\text{E}(\sigma^2|d) = \frac{s_*}{\nu_* - 2}. \tag{2.97}$$

Formulae (2.93) to (2.97) have their counterparts in the prior densities. They provide in particular an interpretation of the posterior hyperparameters in terms of posterior moments. Formulae (2.89) to (2.92) are important because they show how the prior information is combined with the sample information. We can add several comments.

Remarks:

(i) From (2.89), we see that the posterior precision matrix M_* is equal to the sum of the prior precision M_0 and of the sample precision $X'X$.

(ii) From (2.90), we see that the posterior expectation β_* of β is a matrix-weighted average of the prior expectation β_0 and of the corresponding sample information $\hat{\beta}$ (the least squares formula); the weight of β_0 is $(M_0 + X'X)^{-1}M_0$, the share of M_0 in the total precision, and the weight of $\hat{\beta}$ is $(M_0 + X'X)^{-1}X'X$, the share of $X'X$ in the total precision. Hence, we see that each source of information counts in proportion to its precision. However, it is important to realize that β_{*j} is not necessarily between β_{0j} and $\hat{\beta}_j$ (the subscript j being used to denote the jth element of a vector), unless both M_0 and $X'X$ are diagonal matrices.

(iii) From (2.91), we see that s_* is the sum of the prior parameter s_0 and of the sample corresponding statistic s, plus a term measuring the distance between β_0 and $\hat{\beta}$. The distance is measured in the metric of the sum of the variances of the prior and of the sample, so that the difference $\beta_0 - \hat{\beta}$ is less important in s_* if the sum of the relative variances increases. Nevertheless s_* and $\text{E}(\sigma^2|d)$ (for given ν_*) increase with the distance between the prior expectation and the least squares estimate of β. Given (2.95), it is possible that the posterior variance matrix of β might be larger than the prior variance if the conflict of information between the prior and the sample is strong enough. It is straightforward to check that $M_*^{-1}/(\nu_* - 2)$ is smaller than $M_0^{-1}/(\nu_0 - 2)$; this effect will more than offset the increase of s_* with respect to s_0, unless the conflict of information is strong enough. A natural measure of this conflict could be precisely

$$CI = (\beta_0 - \hat{\beta})'[M_0^{-1} + (X'X)^{-1}]^{-1}(\beta_0 - \hat{\beta}). \tag{2.98}$$

This quantity is positive but not bounded; it could therefore be useful for comparing the degree of conflict with respect to a reference case: for example, for a given sample and prior mean, one can vary the precision M_0.

(iv) The interpretation of (2.92) is obvious: the prior degrees of freedom are added to the sample size to give the posterior degrees of freedom.

(v) Suppose the prior hyperparameters are in fact the sufficient statistics from a sample $(y_0 \, X_0)$, generated by the same model as $(y \, X)$ but independently, so that $M_0 = X_0'X_0$, $\beta_0 = (X_0'X_0)^{-1}X_0'y_0$, $s_0 = y_0'M_{X_0}y_0$, and $\nu_0 = T_0$; then (2.89) to (2.92) define the sufficient statistics of the union of the two samples.

2.7.4 Predictive Densities

We are going to compute the predictive density of a future sample

$$\tilde{y} = (y_{T+1} \, y_{T+2} \, \cdots \, y_{T+\tilde{T}})'$$

of size $\tilde{T}$, supposed to be generated by (2.83), independently of y. Let $\tilde{X}$ be the $\tilde{T} \times k$ matrix of observations of the future exogenous variables, to be conditioned on. The predictive density is the result of the following integration:

$$f(\tilde{y}|\tilde{X}, d) = \int \int \varphi(\beta, \sigma^2|d) f(\tilde{y}|\tilde{X}, d, \beta, \sigma^2) d\sigma^2 \, d\beta, \qquad (2.99)$$

where $\varphi(\beta, \sigma^2|d)$ is given by (2.88), and $f(\tilde{y}|\tilde{X}, d, \beta, \sigma^2) = f_N(\tilde{y}|\tilde{X}\beta, \sigma^2 I_{\tilde{T}})$. Since

- $E(\tilde{y}|\tilde{X}, d, \beta, \sigma^2)$ is linear in β,
- $\text{Var}(\tilde{y}|\tilde{X}, d, \beta, \sigma^2)$ does not depend on β and is linear in σ^2,
- $\tilde{y}|\tilde{X}, d, \beta, \sigma^2$ is normal,
- $E(\beta|d, \sigma^2)$ does not depend on σ^2,
- $\text{Var}(\beta|d, \sigma^2)$ is linear in σ^2,
- $\beta|d, \sigma^2$ is normal,

the joint density of β and $\tilde{y}$ conditionally on σ^2, $\tilde{X}$, and d is normal (see Theorem A.14) and defined by

$$\begin{pmatrix} \beta \\ \tilde{y} \end{pmatrix} | \tilde{X}, d, \sigma^2 \sim N_{k+\tilde{T}} \left(\begin{pmatrix} \beta_* \\ \tilde{X}\beta_* \end{pmatrix}, \sigma^2 \begin{pmatrix} M_*^{-1} & M_*^{-1}\tilde{X}' \\ \tilde{X}M_*^{-1} & I_{\tilde{T}} + \tilde{X}M_*^{-1}\tilde{X}' \end{pmatrix} \right). \qquad (2.100)$$

As $\sigma^2|d \sim IG_2(\nu_*, s_*)$, from (A.70) and (A.71) it follows that

$$\begin{pmatrix} \beta \\ \tilde{y} \end{pmatrix}, \sigma^2|\tilde{X}, d \sim NIG_{k+\tilde{T}+1} \left(\begin{pmatrix} \beta_* \\ \tilde{X}\beta_* \end{pmatrix}, \begin{pmatrix} M_* + \tilde{X}'\tilde{X} & -\tilde{X}' \\ -\tilde{X} & I_{\tilde{T}} \end{pmatrix}, s_*, \nu_* \right). \qquad (2.101)$$

Using Theorem (A.15), we can now easily state the following result:

Theorem 2.25 *The predictive density of $\tilde{y}$ is multivariate Student and defined by*

$$\tilde{y}|\tilde{X}, d \sim t_{\tilde{T}}(\tilde{X}\beta_*, s_*, (I_{\tilde{T}} + \tilde{X}M_*^{-1}\tilde{X}')^{-1}, \nu_*). \qquad (2.102)$$

The predictive expectation is

$$E(\tilde{y}|\tilde{X}, d) = \tilde{X}\beta_*, \qquad (2.103)$$

and the predictive variance

$$\text{Var}(\tilde{y}|\tilde{X}, d) = \frac{s_*}{\nu_* - 2}(I_{\tilde{T}} + \tilde{X}M_*^{-1}\tilde{X}'). \qquad (2.104)$$

The first term of the predictive variance reflects the genuine model variance, and the second term comes from the estimation of β.

We leave it as an exercise to obtain the posterior density of β_* given both d and $\tilde{d}$ (hint: start from (2.101), condition on $\tilde{y}$, and integrate out σ^2).

2.7.5   Tests of Linear Restrictions

Tests in the linear regression model can be done in two different perspectives: misspecification testing, and specification testing. Misspecification tests are central to modern model building. They are tools to check if the model under consideration is correctly specified. Are some variables omitted? Are the distributional assumptions in contradiction with the data set? Some tests of this type are discussed in Chapters 5 and 7. The second kind of test is based on an axiom of correct specification: the model under scrutiny does not suffer from major errors of specification that would invalidate any statistical procedure that relies on the maintained specification. Therefore, in practice, misspecification tests must precede specification tests.

The aim of a specification test is usually to test some economic hypotheses. For example, one can be interested in testing the hypothesis that a coefficient is equal to zero, that an elasticity is equal to one, that two regression coefficients have the same value, etc. If some restrictions pass the tests, one may decide to impose them in order to obtain a more parsimonious model. However, in a model simplification strategy, one may not desire to spend time eliciting a prior distribution on parameters that may be restricted later if the model under study is overparameterized. Therefore, we choose the test principles that can be based on a partially non-informative prior density. Such tests are derived from the posterior density of the regression coefficients.

Interesting hypotheses to be tested need not be linear equality restrictions of the type

$$H_0 : R\beta = r, \qquad (2.105)$$

where R is an $m \times k$ matrix of rank $m < k$ and r an m vector. H_0 represents a set of compatible linear constraints which are defined by R and r, which are known. Restrictions to be tested might be non-linear, or inequality restrictions. However for such types of restrictions, numerical procedures are required (see Chapter 3).

2.7.5.1   *HPD Regions: Bayesian F- and t-Tests*   An HPD region for H_0 as defined in (2.105) can be built analytically if the posterior density is Student as in (2.93). Let us define

$$\delta = R\beta - r. \tag{2.106}$$

By Theorems A.10 and A.15, a linear transformation of a Student random vector is also Student, and hence the posterior distribution of δ is Student:

$$\delta|d \sim t_m(R\beta_* - r, s_*, (RM_*^{-1}R')^{-1}, \nu_*). \tag{2.107}$$

The contours of the Student posterior density of δ are concentric ellipsoids defined by $(\delta - R\beta_* + r)'(RM_*^{-1}R')^{-1}(\delta - R\beta_* + r) = k$. An HPD region of level $1 - \alpha$ for δ is therefore the ellipsoid centred on $R\beta_* - r$ containing $1 - \alpha$ per cent of the probability. If the point $\delta = 0$ (the null hypothesis) lies inside this ellipsoid, H_0 is not rejected; otherwise, it is rejected. Unless m (the dimension of δ) is equal to one, it is not necessary to check if the point is in the ellipsoid or outside it. A simple transformation solves the problem. By a multivariate extension of Theorem A.8(ii), the quadratic form in δ defined by

$$\zeta = \nu_* \frac{(\delta - R\beta_* + r)'(RM_*^{-1}R')^{-1}(\delta - R\beta_* + r)}{ms_*} \tag{2.108}$$

is a Fisher random variable:

$$\zeta|d \sim F(m, \nu_*). \tag{2.109}$$

The point $\delta = 0$ (the null hypothesis) lies inside the $1 - \alpha$ HPD ellipsoid if the value ζ_o (the observed value of ζ),

$$\zeta_o = \nu_* \frac{(R\beta_* - r)'(RM_*^{-1}R')^{-1}(R\beta_* - r)}{ms_*}, \tag{2.110}$$

is smaller than the $1 - \alpha$ quantile of the $F(m, \nu_*)$ distribution. If this is the case, the null hypothesis is not rejected. One may also compute the Bayesian p-value, $P(\zeta > \zeta_o|d)$, and reject (not reject) H_0 if p is smaller (resp. larger) than α. The quantity ζ_o is the Bayesian equivalent of the classical F-statistic, to which it is equal if the prior is non-informative.

As a special case, let us choose $R = (1\,0\,\ldots\,0)$ and $r = 0$, so that the null hypothesis is $\beta_1 = 0$ (β_1 is δ). The posterior density of β_1 is univariate Student:

$$\beta_1|d \sim t(\beta_1^*, s_*, M_{11.2}^*, \nu_*), \tag{2.111}$$

where β_1^* is the first element of β_*, and

$$M_{11.2}^* = M_{11}^* - M_{12}^*(M_{22}^*)^{-1}M_{21}^*.$$

M_{11}^* is the first diagonal element of M_*, and M_{12}^*, M_{22}^*, and M_{21}^* are the complementary matrices obtained by partitioning M_*. The transformed variable

$$t = (\beta_1 - \beta_1^*) \sqrt{M_{11.2}^* \nu_*/s_*} \qquad (2.112)$$

has the standardized Student distribution $t(0, 1, 1, \nu_*)$. The HPD region of confidence level $1 - \alpha$ is the interval

$$\beta_1^* \pm t_{1-\alpha/2}/\sqrt{M_{11.2}^* \nu_*/s_*}, \qquad (2.113)$$

where $t_{1-\alpha/2}$ is the value of the standardized Student distribution with ν_* degrees of freedom such that $\Pr(-t_{1-\alpha/2} < t < t_{1-\alpha/2}) = 1-\alpha$. The value corresponding to the classical t-statistic for testing H_0 is

$$t_o = \beta_1^* \sqrt{M_{11.2}^* \nu_*/s_*}. \qquad (2.114)$$

In the univariate case, it is not necessary to use the transformation to a Fisher distribution.

Another application of the Bayesian F-test is in prediction evaluation. Suppose that we keep the last $\tilde{T}$ observations $\tilde{y}$ of a sample of size $T+\tilde{T}$ for prediction evaluation, i.e.

• we compute the posterior expectation (2.90) of β using the first T observations;
• we compute the predictive expectation (2.103) which is a Bayesian predictor for the future sample $\tilde{y}$ under a quadratic loss function;
• we evaluate the predictions by comparing them with the observations we have kept, i.e. we ask whether the prediction errors (observed $\tilde{y} - \tilde{X}\beta_*$) are different from a null vector, at a level of confidence $1 - \alpha$.

The question is: does the null vector (of size $\tilde{T}$) lie in the highest predictive region of level $1 - \alpha$ of the distribution of $\tilde{y} - \tilde{X}\beta_*$, which is Student by (2.102)? The answer is provided by a Bayesian F-test since

$$\eta = \nu_* \frac{(\tilde{y} - \tilde{X}\beta_*)'(I_{\tilde{T}} + \tilde{X}M_*^{-1}\tilde{X}')^{-1}(\tilde{y} - \tilde{X}\beta_*)}{\tilde{T}s_*} \sim F(\tilde{T}, \nu_*). \qquad (2.115)$$

For example, the answer is affirmative if η_o, i.e. η computed at the observed $\tilde{y}$, is smaller than the $1 - \alpha$ quantile of the F-distribution.

METHODS OF NUMERICAL INTEGRATION

3.1 Introduction

Numerical methods have progressively become an important tool in econometrics, whether in the Bayesian approach or in the classical one. This trend can
be explained by an increased use of complex models, for which analytical results
are not available, or even if they are, that require intensive computation. The
availability of powerful computers at low cost enables this kind of computation
to be performed.

Many interesting models require numerical computations, because they are
not in the exponential family, or even if they are, because the prior distribution
used is not in the natural conjugate family. In Section 3.2, we present the general
principle of the Bayesian analysis of models for which partly analytical results
are available, so that numerical computations are needed to obtain marginal
posterior results.

In the classical approach, the computations involve mainly the maximization
of a criterion function (e.g. a likelihood function). In the Bayesian framework,
we are interested in obtaining posterior densities, which can be summarized
by posterior expectations, variances, graphs of the marginals, etc. The typical
computational problem is to evaluate integrals that correspond to moments of
the posterior density. If $g(\theta)$ is an integrable function of θ, θ having the density
$\varphi(\theta)$, one is interested in computing

$$\mathrm{E}[g(\theta)] = \int g(\theta)\,\varphi(\theta)\,d\theta \qquad (3.1)$$

(where the integral is defined over the support of φ). Table 3.1 gives an example
list of functions $g(.)$ that are often useful for the scientific reporting of Bayesian
results; particular $g(.)$ functions can be defined for a specific decision problem.

When the integral in (3.1) has no known analytical solution, a method of numerical integration is needed to evaluate it. By nature, any numerical integration
method delivers an *approximation* of the integral. It is therefore important to
control as best as possible the numerical error of an integration procedure, and
we shall pay attention to this point in the sequel. Numerical integration methods are a branch of numerical analysis, which is itself a branch of mathematics.
The purpose of this chapter is not to survey the topic fully, but to present some
methods which we have found useful for Bayesian inference in econometrics. The
presentation is kept as simple as possible, and is oriented to help the reader in

Table 3.1 *Functions and corresponding expectations*

$g(\theta)$	$E[g(\theta)]$
θ	posterior mean
$[\theta - E(\theta)][\theta - E(\theta)]'$	posterior covariance matrix
$1_{\theta \in A}$	posterior probability of event A
$f(y_h^* \mid \theta)$	predictive density of y_h at value y_h^*
$E(y_h \mid \theta)$	predictive mean of y_h

the solution of practical problems. Software libraries for scientific computing generally include a bundle of procedures for numerical integration; useful references are Abramowitz and Stegun (1964) and Press (1992).

If we write (3.1) as the integral of $h(\theta) = g(\theta)\,\varphi(\theta)$, most numerical integration rules approximate the integral of h by a weighted average of values of h, i.e.

$$\int h(\theta)\,d\theta \simeq \sum_{j=1}^{n} w_j\,h(\theta_j), \qquad (3.2)$$

where w_j ($j = 1$ to n) are positive weights summing to 1. Remembering that an integral is a measure of a volume, the basic idea behind (3.2) is to split the integration space into small parts (by choosing n values of θ), to evaluate the volume of each part by $w_j\,h(\theta_j)$, and to sum the volumes of the small parts.

The differences between the methods come from the rules to choose the points and the weights. We can distinguish between *deterministic* rules (Section 3.3) and *stochastic* rules (Section 3.4). In the former case, the points are chosen so as to cover systematically the space of integration with a grid of points (although the points need not be equally spaced). In the latter case, the points, and sometimes the weights, are chosen randomly (according to some probability distribution)— hence the term 'Monte Carlo' methods. If a method is applied several times, in the deterministic case the points will always be the same for a given function and rule (thus always yielding identical results), while in the stochastic case the points will vary (thus providing slightly different results). Which type of methods to use for a given problem depends essentially on the dimension of θ: if it is larger than three (perhaps four), Monte Carlo methods are usually chosen. The reason is that deterministic rules typically require many functional evaluations if the dimension of θ is large: for example, in product rules whereby each coordinate is explored on G points, this number is equal to G^k, where k is the dimension of θ (if $G = 20$, $k = 9$, and one functional evaluation takes 10^{-6} seconds, the computing time is of the order of 6 days, but if $k = 10$, it is about 118 days).

In Bayesian computations, it is common to know only the kernel $\kappa(\theta)$ of the posterior density $\varphi(\theta)$. Then (3.1) is written as

$$E[g(\theta)] = \int g(\theta)\,\kappa(\theta)\,d\theta \,/\, \int \kappa(\theta)\,d\theta, \qquad (3.3)$$

showing that a ratio of integrals must be computed. This is done by approximating the numerator and the denominator and taking the ratio of the approximations. Instead of applying an integration rule to the numerator (with $h = g.\kappa$) and to the denominator separately (with $h = \kappa$), it is usually better practice to use for the numerator the points determined by the rule for the denominator. This strategy obviously saves computing time as there are often many g functions for which $E(g)$ is reported, and it can be argued that the error of this 'one-shot' method is smaller than the error of the alternative 'multiple shots' method.

3.2   General Principle for Partially Linear Models

The purpose of this section is to present the computing principles for the Bayesian analysis of models for which fully analytical posterior or predictive results are not available. We have especially in mind non-linear regression models which are partially linear in some parameters (such as linear regression models with heteroscedastic or autocorrelated errors). It is then possible to use the analytical results available for the linear model conditionally on the parameters that create the non-linearity, and to complete the analysis numerically. To proceed in this way, one must of course use a natural conjugate prior density that is conditional on the parameters that create the non-linearity. If this is considered too restrictive, there is usually no alternative other than to evaluate the posterior of all the parameters by numerical integration.

Let us pose the problem at a general level: we partition the parameter vector θ into

$$\theta = \begin{pmatrix} \alpha \\ \beta \end{pmatrix}, \tag{3.4}$$

and we assume that the density of the sample is such that, conditionally on α, the natural conjugate analysis applies to the model. The prior is thus naturally factorized as

$$\varphi(\alpha, \beta) = \varphi(\beta|\alpha)\,\varphi(\alpha), \tag{3.5}$$

with $\varphi(\beta|\alpha)$ the natural conjugate for the 'partial' likelihood $l(\beta|\alpha; y)$ (i.e. the likelihood function viewed as a function of β for a fixed value of α). Then the conditional posterior density $\varphi(\beta|\alpha, y)$ and its moments are known analytically. To obtain the marginal posterior results on β, we can proceed by marginalizing the conditional results:

$$\begin{aligned}
\varphi(\beta|y) &= E_{\alpha|y}\left[\varphi(\beta|\alpha, y)\right], \\
E(\beta|y) &= E_{\alpha|y}\left[E(\beta|\alpha, y)\right], \\
\operatorname{Var}(\beta|y) &= E_{\alpha|y}\left[\operatorname{Var}(\beta|\alpha, y)\right] + \operatorname{Var}_{\alpha|y}\left[E(\beta|\alpha, y)\right].
\end{aligned} \tag{3.6}$$

Every computation of the outside expectations $E_{\alpha|y}$ or $\operatorname{Var}_{\alpha|y}$ above is of the type

$$E[h(\alpha)] = \int h(\alpha)\,\varphi(\alpha|y)\,d\alpha, \tag{3.7}$$

where $h(\alpha)$ is one of the inner conditional moments (note that $\varphi(\beta|\alpha, y)$ is a function of α when β is fixed at the value at which $\varphi(\beta|y)$ is computed). We obviously need the posterior density of α to carry out these integrations. It is known through its kernel, since

$$
\begin{aligned}
\varphi(\alpha|y) &\propto \int \varphi(\beta, \alpha)\, f(y|\beta, \alpha)\, d\beta \\
&= \varphi(\alpha) \int \varphi(\beta|\alpha)\, f(y|\beta, \alpha)\, d\beta \\
&= \varphi(\alpha) \int \kappa(\beta|\alpha, y)\, d\beta \\
&= \varphi(\alpha)\, f(y|\alpha) = \kappa(\alpha|y).
\end{aligned}
\tag{3.8}
$$

The function $f(y|\alpha)$ is the predictive density of y conditional on α (it is the marginalized likelihood when considered as a function of α for a given y). The last but one equality of (3.8) shows that the posterior density of α is, apart from the prior, the inverse of the normalizing constant of the conditional posterior of β given α. The evaluation of the normalizing constant and of the moments of the posterior density of α has to be carried out by numerical integration, using one of the methods described in this chapter. This amounts to selecting $h(\alpha)$ in (3.7) as 1, α, $\alpha\alpha'$ ....

Marginal moments and densities of α and β are thus obtained by computing integrals like (3.7), with the appropriate choices of the function $h(\alpha)$. The only thing that is missing is the posterior covariance between α and β, but it is obtained by defining $h(\alpha)$ in (3.7) as $E(\beta|\alpha, y).\alpha'$ since

$$
\mathrm{Cov}(\alpha, \beta) = \mathrm{Cov}_{\alpha|y}\left[\alpha, E(\beta'|\alpha, y)\right].
\tag{3.9}
$$

Actually, the evaluation of (3.7) is performed as

$$
E[h(\alpha)] = \int h(\alpha)\kappa(\alpha|y)\, d\alpha \Big/ \int \kappa(\alpha|y)\, d\alpha,
\tag{3.10}
$$

since only the kernel of the posterior of α is known before carrying out the computations—compare (3.3). Note that the value of the predictive density $f(.)$ at y is nothing more than $1/\int \kappa(\alpha|y)\, d\alpha$.

Remark: To graph the univariate marginal density of β_1 (the first component of β), one defines a grid of points over β_1, and applies (3.7) with $h(\alpha) = \varphi(\beta_1|\alpha, y)$ for each value of β_1 in the grid. This obviously requires knowledge of $\varphi(\beta_1|\alpha, y)$ analytically (knowledge of its kernel is not sufficient, since in general its normalizing constant depends on α).

3.3 Deterministic Integration Methods

We present mainly Simpson's rules (Subsection 3.3.1) because we have found them to be efficient for a variety of problems. In Subsection 3.3.2, we give a brief overview of the trapezoidal rule, Gauss rules, and Laplace approximations. We refer to the book by Davis and Rabinowitz (1975) for more details. In this section θ is assumed to be a scalar, and the integration range the interval (0,1), since it is always possible to map another interval to (0,1), by a one-to-one transformation, as explained below.

3.3.1 *Simpson's Rules*

The *basic Simpson's rule* is a method based on an interpolation:

- $h(\theta)$ is approximated by a polynomial $P(\theta)$ of order 3 matching the values of h at the three points 0, 0.5, and 1;
- $\int h(\theta)\, d\theta$ is approximated by $\int P(\theta)\, d\theta$, i.e.

$$\int_0^1 h(\theta)\, d\theta \simeq [h(0) + 4h(0.5) + h(1)]/6. \tag{3.11}$$

One can easily check that (3.11) is exact if $h(\theta) = a\theta^2 + b\theta + c$, i.e. if h is a function of degree 2 at most, but it is not exact otherwise.

With formula (3.11), one can miss important regions of variation of h. To avoid this pitfall, one can split $(0, 1)$ into subintervals and apply Simpson's rule to each subinterval. With $2n$ intervals of equal length $d = \theta_j - \theta_{j-1} = 1/2n$ based on $2n+1$ points $\theta_0(= 0), \theta_1, \ldots, \theta_{2n}(= 1)$, one obtains the *extended Simpson rule*

$$\int_0^1 h(\theta)\, d\theta \simeq (d/3)\{h(\theta_0) + 4[h(\theta_1) + h(\theta_3) + \cdots + h(\theta_{2n-1})] \tag{3.12}$$
$$+ 2[h(\theta_2) + h(\theta_4) + \cdots + h(\theta_{2n-2})] + h(\theta_{2n})\}.$$

It is intuitively easy to understand that using more points increases the quality of the approximation. For functions having four continuous derivatives, the absolute error of the extended Simpson's rule is of order $(2n + 1)^4$ at worst, i.e. it goes to 0 as $2n + 1$ to the power -4, see Davis and Rabinowitz (1975: Section 2.2). Nonetheless, the error cannot be controlled beyond this statement. To do so, one can use the *iterative Simpson's method*, which works as follows:

- For a given interval of integration, say (θ_0, θ_4), apply the basic Simpson rule (3.11); call the result I_{04}.
- Split (θ_0, θ_4) into (θ_0, θ_2) and (θ_2, θ_4), and apply (3.11) to each of them; call the results I_{02} and I_{24}.
- If $|(I_{02} + I_{24}) - I_{04}| \leq \epsilon.I_{04}$ where ϵ is a small positive constant (called the maximum relative error), stop and present $I_{02} + I_{24}$ as the integral over (θ_0, θ_4); otherwise, subdivide (θ_0, θ_2) into (θ_0, θ_1) and (θ_1, θ_2), check if $|(I_{01} + I_{12}) - I_{02}| \leq \epsilon.I_{02}$, and go on as before; proceed likewise with (θ_2, θ_4).

Before starting this iterative process, it is wise to impose a minimum number of intervals, i.e. to start from an evaluation based on the extended Simpson rule with $2n$ subintervals (e.g. $n = 8$). It is obvious that the smaller ϵ is, the larger the selected number of points at which h is evaluated. More importantly, the points will not be equidistant as in the extended rule, rather they will be located intensively in the regions where the function varies a lot.

Remarks:

1) Commonly the integration range is of the type (a, b), $(-\infty, b)$, $(a, +\infty)$, or $(-\infty, +\infty)$. In such cases, rather than truncating the range of integration, it is safer to use a transformation of variable to compute the integral over $(0,1)$. By a theorem of calculus, if $\tau = F(\theta)$ and F is bijective and continuous from (a, b) to $(0,1)$, where a can be $-\infty$ and b can be $+\infty$,

$$\int_a^b h(\theta)\, d\theta = \int_0^1 h[F^{-1}(\tau)]\, (dF^{-1}/d\tau)\, d\tau, \qquad (3.13)$$

so that numerical integration over $(0,1)$ can be used. Useful transformations F^{-1} from $(0,1)$ to different types of intervals are listed in Table 3.2.

Table 3.2 *Transformations from $\tau \in (0,1)$ to θ*

Interval	Function $\theta = F^{-1}(\tau)$	Restrictions	Jacobian $dF^{-1}/d\tau$
(a, b)	$\theta = a + (b-a)\tau$		$b - a$
$(-\infty, b)$	$\theta = c\tau/(\tau - 1) + b$	$c > 0$	$-c/(\tau - 1)^2$
(a, ∞)	$\theta = c\tau/(1 - \tau) + a$	$c > 0$	$c/(1 - \tau)^2$
$(-\infty, \infty)$	$\theta = (c\tau - d)/[\tau(1 - \tau)] + e$	$c > d > 0$	$(d - c\tau^2)/[\tau^2(1 - \tau)^2]$

The constants c, d, and e of the transformations given in Table 3.2 can be chosen as follows: e = pseudo-mean (i.e. a guess of the mean) of θ, c = pseudo-standard deviation of θ, $d = c/2$ for a symmetric function. These constants determine the shrinking (or stretching) of a subinterval of the real line into a subinterval of $(0, 1)$ and should be chosen so that the subspace of the real line where the function takes significant values is mapped into almost all the unit interval.

2) It is worth noting that if the integrand $h(\theta)$ is a kernel of a density, the extended and iterative Simpson's rules provide as a by-product of the integrating constant a table of the distribution function of θ, i.e. $P(\theta \leq \theta_j)$ for the θ_j values used in (3.12) or selected by the iterative method. Probabilities (or quantiles) can be computed for other values of θ (or probabilities) by interpolation (or inverse interpolation).

3) Multi-dimensional integration: Simpson's rules can be applied to each coordinate of a multi-dimensional integral: for example, in dimension 2, since

$$\int_{\theta_a}^{\theta_b} \int_{\xi_a}^{\xi_b} h(\theta, \xi)\, d\theta\, d\xi = \int_{\theta_a}^{\theta_b} \left[\int_{\xi_a}^{\xi_b} h(\theta, \xi)\, d\xi \right] d\theta, \qquad (3.14)$$

the inner integral can be computed given any $\theta_* \in (\theta_a, \theta_b)$ by one of the rules for unidimensional integration. The result is some function $H(\theta_*)$ and the outer integral is of the form $\int H(\theta_*)\, d\theta_*$. The values of θ_* for which the inner integral must be computed are therefore simply determined by the integration rule chosen for the outer integral (e.g. iterative Simpson). Although such 'compound' rules are conceptually easy to generalize, their computing time explodes exponentially with the dimension of the integrand (see Section 3.1). In practice, for more than three coordinates, compound deterministic rules are seldom used (at least in econometrics), so that methods that use much less points (but well selected!) are required: this is the case of the Monte Carlo methods.

3.3.1.1 *Applications of Simpson's rules in econometrics* As explained in Subsection A.2.8, the computation of the integral, of the moments, and of the marginal densities of m-1 or m-0 poly-t densities in k variables requires a numerical integration over the unit cube in dimension m minus 1 (whatever the value of k). Section 4.5 gives details for the case of a 2-0 poly-t. Tompa (1973) found that the iterative Simpson's rule is very efficient for such functions because they can have very narrow peaks and be very skewed in one direction.

   Another application of deterministic integration is to regression models which are partially non-linear in the parameters, i.e. conditionally on one or two parameters the model is linear in the other parameters (see Section 3.2). Examples of the application of Simpson's rule in this context are provided in Chapter 5 (on an error correction dynamic model), in Chapter 6 (unit root inference), and in Chapter 8 (non-linear time series models).

3.3.2 Other Rules

3.3.2.1 *Trapezoidal Rule* The trapezoidal rule approximates the function to be integrated by a linear function through the endpoints and gives the area of the trapezium as the integral

$$\int_0^1 h(\theta)\, d\theta = \frac{h(0) + h(1)}{2}. \tag{3.15}$$

It is used in practice with $2n+1$ points $\theta_0(=0), \theta_1, \ldots, \theta_{2n}(=1)$, i.e. the function $h(.)$ is approximated by a piecewise linear function matching h at the selected points. With equidistant points $\theta_0(=0), \theta_1, \ldots, \theta_{2n}(=1)$, the integral is the sum of the trapezia:

$$\int_0^1 h(\theta)\, d\theta = \frac{d}{2}[h(\theta_0) + 2h(\theta_1) + 2h(\theta_2) + \cdots + 2h(\theta_{2n-1}) + h(\theta_{2n})] \tag{3.16}$$

(where d is the distance between two adjacent points). It converges as $(2n+1)^{-2}$, if the integrand has two continuous derivatives (so for integrands with four continuous derivatives, it is less efficient than Simpson's rule). An iterative trapezoidal rule can be defined (like the iterative Simpson's rule). The trapezoidal rule may be useful (with many points) if the integrand is very cheap to evaluate.

3.3.2.2 *Gauss Rules* In a Gauss rule, the points used in the right hand side of (3.2) are chosen as the zeros of some orthogonal polynomials and the weights are functions of these polynomials. For details, see Davis and Rabinowitz (1975: Chap. 2). Gauss rules are exact for polynomials of degree $2n - 1$, where n is the number of terms in (3.2). Contrary to the trapezoidal and Simpson's rules, Gauss rules do not use the endpoints of the interval of integration, which is an advantage for ill-behaved functions at the endpoints, and they cannot be made iterative since the points change as n increases, and they are actually irrational numbers. Richard (1973) used a compound Gauss rule to integrate the trivariate posterior of some parameters of a two-equation simultaneous equation model (the three parameters were the 'simultaneity' parameters: the coefficients of the endogenous variables, and the correlation coefficient between the two error terms).

3.3.2.3 *Laplace Approximations* The Laplace approximation of an integral is not a rule of the type (3.2). The method is described in detail in Tierney, Kass, and Kadane (1989a) (TKK hereafter). The Laplace approximation is an asymptotic expansion of an integral, where 'asymptotic' in this context means that the sample size T of the data (to which the posterior density is conditional) goes to infinity. We consider the computation of the ratio of integrals in (3.3). Defining

$$f(\theta) = -T^{-1} \log \kappa(\theta) \tag{3.17}$$

(i.e. minus the log of the posterior kernel divided by the sample size), we can write

$$\mathrm{E}[g(\theta)] = \frac{\displaystyle\int g(\theta)\,\kappa(\theta)\,d\theta}{\displaystyle\int \kappa(\theta)\,d\theta} = \frac{\displaystyle\int g(\theta)\,\exp[-Tf(\theta)]\,d\theta}{\displaystyle\int \exp[-Tf(\theta)]\,d\theta}. \tag{3.18}$$

Applying to both the numerator and the denominator the basic Laplace approximation of an integral of the type $\int g \exp(-Tf)$, after some simplifications (which amount to neglecting terms of order T^{-2}), TKK obtain

$$\mathrm{E}[g(\theta)] \simeq \hat{g} + \frac{\sigma^2 \hat{g}''}{2T} - \frac{\sigma^4 \hat{g}' \hat{f}'''}{2T}, \tag{3.19}$$

where $\hat{g} = g(\hat{\theta})$, $\hat{\theta}$ is the posterior mode, and $\sigma^2 = 1/f''(\hat{\theta})$ (i.e. the inverse Hessian of the log-posterior). The approximation uses the third derivative of the log-posterior. The error of the approximation goes to zero as T^{-2}. For example, the approximation to the posterior mean is

$$\mathrm{E}(\theta) \simeq \hat{\theta} - \frac{\sigma^4 \hat{f}'''}{2T}, \tag{3.20}$$

and the approximation to the posterior variance is

$$\text{Var}(\theta) = \text{E}(\theta^2) - [\text{E}(\theta)]^2 \simeq \frac{\sigma^2}{T} - \frac{\sigma^8(\hat{f}''')^2}{4T^2}. \tag{3.21}$$

The formulae extend to the multivariate case (see references in TKK). One should be careful in interpreting the results of Laplace approximations when the posterior is not 'well behaved' (in the sense that it is far from being approximately normal). The method should not be applied if the posterior is multimodal. See also Kass, Tierney, and Kadane (1990).

Phillips (1991a) has used the Laplace approximation to marginalize the posterior of the parameters of the model $y_t = \mu + \alpha t + \rho y_{t-1} + \sum_{i=1}^{k-1} \phi_i \Delta y_{t-i} + u_t$, $u_t \sim IN(0, \sigma^2)$ with respect to the parameters μ, α, and ϕ_i. Although the model is linear in the parameters, an analytical solution to this integration step is not feasible (as it would be with a flat prior) because Phillips's prior depends on the parameters in a complex way. He is then able to marginalize analytically the resulting approximate posterior of σ and ρ with respect to σ and is left with the marginal posterior of ρ, which must be integrated numerically (but he does not mention which method he used). This posterior is useful for inference on the unit root hypothesis ($\rho = 1$). The Laplace approximation of a marginal density in the case where θ is partitioned into $(\alpha' \ \beta')'$, where α has m elements, is (see Tierney and Kadane 1986)

$$\varphi(\alpha) \propto \int \kappa(\alpha, \beta) \, d\beta = \int \exp[-Tf(\alpha, \beta)] \, d\beta \\ \simeq |\Sigma|^{1/2} \exp[-Tf(\alpha, \hat{\beta}_\alpha)], \tag{3.22}$$

where $\hat{\beta}_\alpha$ is the mode of the log-posterior when α is fixed (i.e. maximized over β only), and Σ is minus the inverse of the Hessian of the log-posterior, evaluated at $\hat{\beta}_\alpha$. In the approximation, we have neglected an irrelevant constant. The resulting approximate kernel can be normalized to a density by the use of a deterministic rule (assuming that α is of dimension 1 or 2). As an alternative, Tierney and Kadane (1986) proposed to normalize the kernel by dividing the above approximation of the kernel by the Laplace approximation of $\int \kappa(\theta) d\theta$ (in doing so, the constant we have neglected above should be introduced). Tierney, Kass, and Kadane (1989b) mention that this kind of normalization does not always produce a proper density (in the sense that it integrates to 1), so that a renormalization by numerical integration may be necessary anyway. Note that in his calculations, Phillips used the approximation described in (3.22), since his objective was to get the kernel of the marginal posterior of σ and ρ (which were normalized afterwards). Another application of the Laplace approximation is found in Phillips (1998). He studies the simultaneous equations model, in a limited information setup, where a single structural equation is completed by a set of unrestricted reduced form equations for the endogenous variables included in the structural equation. The prior he uses is Jeffreys' prior. The posterior density of the parameters of the model is marginalized, by a Laplace approximation, with respect to all the parameters except the coefficients of the endogenous variables included in the structural equation. Finally, let us mention that Tierney, Kass, and Kadane (1989b) provide the Laplace approximation of the marginal of a non-linear function $g(\theta)$, as an extension of (3.22).

3.4 Monte Carlo Methods

Monte Carlo methods of integration overcome the curse of dimensionality of deterministic methods by selecting the grid of points at random but in a clever way, i.e. in areas where the integrand varies a lot. Exactly the same idea applies to iterative deterministic rules, which are, however, unfeasible for functions of many variables. The selection of points in the important regions of the integration space allows the use of much fewer points than with a blind deterministic grid that uses a large number of points. It is not exceptional to compute to a good precision an integral of a function of 10 variables with 10,000 points or less by Monte Carlo integration.

Any Monte Carlo method is a simulation method, in the sense that one has to generate random numbers according to some probability distribution. Techniques to do this are explained in Appendix B of this book. The general principle of a Monte Carlo method is:

(i) to express the solution of a problem as a parameter of a hypothetical population,
(ii) to use random numbers to build a sample of the population, and
(iii) to estimate the parameter of the population using the generated sample.

As in the case of deterministic methods, there is a variety of rules of Monte Carlo integration. Some methods like direct sampling (Subsection 3.4.1) and importance sampling (Subsection 3.4.2) are based on the simulation of independent samples. Other methods like Gibbs sampling and Metropolis–Hastings sampling (Subsection 3.4.3) are based on simulating dependent samples of a Markov chain type. We restrict our review to the most useful rules for Bayesian computing in econometrics.

3.4.1 *Direct Sampling*

In (3.1), let us take θ as our 'hypothetical population' characterized by the density $\varphi(\theta)$. Let us also assume that $\varphi(\theta)$ is a distribution for which an IID sample of values θ_j ($j = 1$ to n) can be generated directly in the sense that if n is large enough, the empirical distribution function of the sample is close to the population one. Then the sample mean

$$g_D = \sum_{j=1}^{n} g(\theta_j)/n \qquad (3.23)$$

is a 'good' estimator of $\mu_g \equiv E[g(\theta)]$, being best linear unbiased, consistent (by the law of large numbers), and asymptotically normal (by the central limit theorem). Such criteria are 'classical', but (3.23) can be interpreted also as the Bayesian estimator of the parameter μ_g under a quadratic loss function and a flat prior.

Let us define the relative error of (3.23) as

$$\epsilon = |(g_D/\mu_g) - 1| \qquad (\text{if } \mu_g \neq 0). \qquad (3.24)$$

The asymptotic normality result

$$n^{1/2}(g_D - \mu_g) \overset{a}{\sim} N(0, \sigma_g^2), \qquad (3.25)$$

where σ_g^2 is the population variance of $g(\theta)$, implies that for large n, with probability $1 - \alpha$, ϵ is smaller than a bound given by

$$\bar{\epsilon}_D = 2z_\alpha(\sigma_g/\mu_g)/n^{1/2} \qquad (3.26)$$

(where z_α is the $1 - \alpha$ quantile of the standard normal distribution). In practice, $\bar{\epsilon}_D$ is estimated by replacing σ_g/μ_g by s_g/g_D, s_g being the sample standard deviation of $g(\theta)$. It is good practice to report g_D and the corresponding estimate of $\bar{\epsilon}_D$ (for a given α), or the estimated confidence interval $g_D \pm z_\alpha(s_g/n^{1/2})$. The only factor that can be controlled in (3.26) is n, the sample size of the Monte Carlo simulation: increasing n reduces the error bound at the slow rate $\sqrt{n}$ (e.g. multiplying n by 100 divides $\bar{\epsilon}_D$ by only 10). It is remarkable that the rate of convergence of ϵ to zero is the same whatever the dimension of θ.

3.4.1.1 Antithetic Acceleration

A variant of direct simulation is antithetic sampling. Assume that $\varphi(\theta) = \varphi(2\mu - \theta) \; \forall \theta$, which means that the density φ is symmetric around μ. If $g(\theta)$ is linear in θ, say $g(\theta) = \theta$, then with a sample of size 1, say θ_+, one can estimate perfectly $\mu = E(\theta)$ (assumed to exist) by associating to θ_+ its 'antithesis' $2\mu - \theta_+$ and averaging. This is of course trivial since it is known at the outset that $E(\theta) = \mu$. For a non-linear function $g(\theta)$, the estimator

$$g_A = \sum_{j=1}^{n/2} [g(\theta_j) + g(2\mu - \theta_j)]/n \qquad (3.27)$$

is unbiased, consistent, and asymptotically normal. Its variance is

$$\text{Var}(g_A) = \{\sigma_g^2 + \text{Cov}[g(\theta), g(2\mu - \theta)]\}/n. \qquad (3.28)$$

Compared with $\text{Var}(g_D) = 2\sigma_g^2/n$, the variance of (3.23) for a sample of size $n/2$, $\text{Var}(g_A)$ is smaller if σ_g^2 is larger than $\text{Cov}[g(\theta), g(2\mu - \theta)]$, which is certainly the case if the covariance is negative. Note that if g is linear in θ, the correlation is equal to -1 and $\text{Var}(g_A) = 0$, so that if g is not too non-linear, the estimator based on antithetic sampling is expected to be more precise than the estimator based on direct sampling. Finally, if $\varphi(\theta)$ is not symmetric, the results above do not hold but one may still expect a gain from antithetic sampling for a linear g function, or even a slightly non-linear one, provided $\varphi(\theta)$ is moderately skewed; in this case, however, the choice of μ for computing (3.27) is not obvious a priori. See Geweke (1988a) for a review and an application of antithetic sampling.

3.4.1.2 *Applications of Direct Sampling in Econometrics* Even though the integrating constant and the moments of the posterior density of a parameter θ may be known analytically, if one is interested in the posterior density and moments of a non-linear function of θ, direct simulation (with antithetic sampling if possible) is a very easy method. A few examples follow.

- In a dynamic linear regression model (see Chapter 5): the interim and total multipliers and the mean lag of the effect of an explanatory variable on the dependent variable are ratios of linear functions of the regression coefficients (whose posterior density is often chosen in the Student or poly-t family). Note that the moments of these ratios do not exist since the denominator has a positive mass at zero, but the density exists and can be evaluated by Monte Carlo integration. Note that both the Student and the 2-0 poly-t densities are very easy to simulate, see Appendix B.
- In an $AR(p)$ $(p > 1)$ model, the roots of the characteristic equation are complicated non-linear functions of the parameters of the lag polynomial. Their posterior density could be used to infer the number of unit roots of the process and the type of convergence (cyclical or not) in the case of stationarity. See DeJong and Whiteman (1991a) for an example.
- Inequality restrictions on functions of parameters can be easily imposed in the Bayesian approach. During the simulation, one has just to discard the points θ_j (generated according to the non-truncated distribution) that do not pass the restrictions. This corresponds to using a prior imposing the inequality restrictions with probability 1. Examples of inequality restrictions are stationarity restrictions in dynamic models, sign restrictions on regression coefficients (Geweke 1986a; Bauwens, Fiebig, and Steel 1994) or on a total multiplier (Bauwens and Richard 1985). It is important to realize that equality restrictions cannot be imposed in the same way if they are of probability 0 as is the case if φ is continuous (no sampled value will ever pass the restriction).

3.4.2 *Importance Sampling*

For problem (3.3) rather than (3.1), direct simulation is not a solution since φ cannot be simulated. To circumvent the problem, the idea is to change the 'hypothetical population' from $\varphi(\theta)$ to $\iota(\theta)$, chosen as a distribution that can be simulated directly and is a 'good' approximation to $\varphi(\theta)$. Indeed, the right hand side of (3.3) can be written as

$$\mu_g = \int g(\theta)\, w(\theta)\, \iota(\theta)\, d\theta \, / \int w(\theta)\, d\theta = \mathrm{E}[g(\theta)\, w(\theta)]/\mathrm{E}(w(\theta)], \qquad (3.29)$$

where the expectations are taken with respect to $\iota(\theta)$ and

$$w(\theta) = \kappa(\theta)/\iota(\theta) \tag{3.30}$$

is called the weighting function, since it serves to weight $g(\theta)$ (in the numerator) and 1 (in the denominator) so that their expectations under φ are the same as under ι. Using ι, the method of direct simulation can be applied to approximate the numerator and the denominator. The same sample of θ_j can even be used for both to save computing time, and we explain below that this is likely to decrease the error of the approximation of the ratio. The estimator of μ_g by importance sampling is

$$g_I = \sum_{j=1}^{n} g(\theta_j)\, w(\theta_j)/\sum_{j=1}^{n} w(\theta_j) = \sum_{j=1}^{n} \omega_j\, g(\theta_j), \tag{3.31}$$

where

$$\omega_j = w(\theta_j)/\sum_{i=1}^{n} w(\theta_i).$$

In (3.31), the middle expression is useful in practice, but the last one shows that the estimator of μ_g is a weighted average of values $g(\theta_j)$, where the points θ_j are chosen randomly according to ι. The weights are random, and ω_j reflects the importance of the sampled value θ_j relative to the other sampled values. In comparison, the direct simulation estimator uses points chosen at random according to φ, but its weights $1/n$ are fixed, reflecting the use of the correct population φ.

3.4.2.1 *Properties of g_I as an Estimator of μ_g* The estimator g_I is consistent and asymptotically normal under suitable regularity conditions (see e.g. Geweke 1989a). Proving these results is not so obvious as for g_D since g_I is a ratio of estimators. For the same reason, it cannot be proved to be unbiased. The error analysis given for g_D applies to g_I, except that the asymptotic variance is different (again because of the ratio). Since it is usual to control the error bound of the estimation of $\mu = E(\theta)$ (i.e. g is the identity function), we derive the variance for this case, assuming θ to be a scalar to simplify the notation. The estimator of μ is

$$\theta_I = \mathbf{t}/\mathbf{u} = n^{-1}\sum_{j=1}^{n} \theta_j\, w(\theta_j)/n^{-1}\sum_{j=1}^{n} w(\theta_j) \tag{3.32}$$

(note that we use bold characters to denote random variables and the usual italics to denote generated values). Under regularity conditions, its asymptotic variance is obtained by the 'delta method', which states that if $\mathbf{s}$ is a consistent estimator with variance Σ, and $\mathbf{r} = h(\mathbf{s})$, then

$$\mathrm{Var}(\mathbf{r}) \simeq \frac{\partial h}{\partial x'}\Sigma\frac{\partial h}{\partial x},$$

the derivatives being evaluated at the estimate s. This estimator is a consistent estimator of $\text{Var}(\mathbf{r})$. With $\mathbf{s} = (\mathbf{t}, \mathbf{u})$, and $\mathbf{r} = \theta_{\mathbf{I}} = \mathbf{t}/\mathbf{u}$, we get

$$\text{Var}(\theta_{\mathbf{I}}) \overset{a}{\simeq} \text{Var}(\mathbf{t})/u^2 + t^2 \text{Var}(\mathbf{u})/u^4 - 2\,t\,\text{Cov}(\mathbf{t}, \mathbf{u})/u^3. \tag{3.33}$$

Let s^2 denote the consistent estimator of $\text{Var}(\theta_{\mathbf{I}})$ obtained by replacing in (3.33) the unknown quantities $\text{Var}(\mathbf{t})$, $\text{Var}(\mathbf{u})$, and $\text{Cov}(\mathbf{t}, \mathbf{u})$ by the corresponding sample moments:

$$n^{-1} \sum_1^n [\theta_j w(\theta_j)]^2 - t^2,$$
$$n^{-1} \sum_1^n [w(\theta_j)]^2 - u^2,$$
$$n^{-1} \sum_1^n \theta_j [w(\theta_j)]^2 - tu,$$

where t (resp. u) is the realized value of the random variable $\mathbf{t}$ (resp. $\mathbf{u}$), the numerator (resp. denominator) of (3.32). Finally, by the same argument as leading to (3.26), the relative error bound for the importance sampling estimator of μ is

$$\bar{e}_I = 2z_\alpha \left[\frac{\text{Var}(\theta_{\mathbf{I}})}{\theta_I^2} \frac{1}{n} \right]^{1/2}, \tag{3.34}$$

and is estimated by $2z_\alpha(s/\theta_I)/n^{1/2}$.

3.4.2.2 *Practical Hints about Convergence*

When applying importance sampling, one must take care in checking convergence of the estimates after n draws. It may seem that estimates have converged, while they are totally wrong. One should always monitor the behaviour of the weights as n increases. A good indication of convergence is given by a stable variation coefficient of the weights. From practical experience, we have found that if convergence has not occurred after 10–20000 draws, it is not worth increasing n (a better importance function must be sought). A stable variation coefficient smaller than one is an indication of the good quality of an importance function. One should also plot a histogram of the weights, and record the 10 or 20 largest weights to check that the estimates are not determined by a single draw having a relative weight almost equal to one. This happens for example with a draw far in the tails of the posterior, when the posterior has much thicker tails than the importance function. It is also advisable to compute the estimated error bounds of the posterior means, as defined above after (3.34): they should not exceed 5 to 10 per cent. This can be achieved by increasing n as needed if the variation coefficient of the weights is stable. A larger value of n is then useful for obtaining precise graphs of univariate and especially bivariate marginal densities.

3.4.2.3 *General Criteria for Choosing an Importance Function*

The choice of the importance function $\iota(\theta)$ should be guided by three recommendations:

1) ι must be amenable to direct simulation as already explained.

2) ι must be such that $E[w(\theta)]$ exists. In particular, ι must be different from zero for any θ in the support of φ, otherwise $w(\theta)$ is unbounded and $E[w(\theta)]$ does not exist. It is natural to choose ι as a density that has the same support as φ. If $w(\theta) \leq \overline{w} < \infty \; \forall \theta \in \Theta$ (the support of φ), $E[w(\theta)]$ exists.

3) ι must be as good an approximation of φ as possible. If $\iota = \varphi$, the weighting function is equal to one, its variance is zero, and $E[w(\theta)] = 1$, since we are back in the ideal case of direct simulation. If ι 'mimics' φ, we are close to this case, whereas if ι is totally unrelated to φ, we are in the worst situation for estimating $E[w(\theta)]$ precisely. The idea is to choose ι to reduce the variance of the weighting function: with a uniform importance function the variance will be larger than with a better approximation.

Although the motivation behind the third recommendation is to estimate the integrating constant $\int \kappa(\theta) \, d\theta$ of φ as precisely as possible, it can be argued that if ι is a good approximation of φ for this purpose, it will also do a good job in estimating $\int g(\theta) \kappa(\theta) \, d\theta$ and even better for the ratio, at least if $g(\theta) = \theta$. Indeed, from (3.32) and (3.33),

$$\mathrm{Var}(\theta_{\mathbf{I}})/\theta_I^2 \stackrel{a}{\simeq} \mathrm{Var}(\mathbf{t})/t^2 + \mathrm{Var}(\mathbf{u})/u^2 \\ - 2\rho_{\mathbf{tu}}[(\mathrm{Var}(\mathbf{t})/t^2)(\mathrm{Var}(\mathbf{u})/u^2)]^{1/2}. \tag{3.35}$$

The squared variation coefficient of θ_I, a crucial factor influencing $\overline{\epsilon}_I$, is equal (asymptotically in n) to the squared variation coefficient of the numerator $\mathbf{t}$, plus that of the denominator $\mathbf{u}$, minus a term that depends on the correlation between $\mathbf{t}$ and $\mathbf{u}$. If $\mathrm{Var}(\mathbf{t})/t^2 \simeq \mathrm{Var}(\mathbf{u})/u^2$, the closer $\rho_{\mathbf{tu}}$ is to one, the closer $\mathrm{Var}(\theta_{\mathbf{I}})/\theta_I^2$ is to zero. Since $\mathbf{t}$ and $\mathbf{u}$ are linear in weights, one expects $\rho_{\mathbf{tu}}$ to be close to one (or at least positive), if θ does not have a very large variance (with respect to φ): in this case $\theta \, w(\theta)$ indeed behaves almost as $w(\theta)$ and these two functions are positively correlated (with respect to ι).

3.4.2.4 *Methods for Choosing an Importance Function* For a given φ, the class of importance functions that satisfy the three recommendations stated above may be very broad. It is not sensible to believe that a general method can be given that ensures finding a good importance function in any situation. The single general recommendation we can provide is to try and use at best the information available about φ. This information can be theoretical (Ti) or empirical (Ei):

T1: conditions on the existence of moments;

T2: existence of one or several modes;

T3: characterization of some conditional densities of φ including their moments;

E1: mode and Hessian of $\log(\varphi)$ evaluated at the posterior mode (computed by numerical optimization);

E2: a first approximation of the moments of φ (computed, for example, by Laplace transform or by a normal approximation around the mode, or even by a first round of importance sampling using a crude importance function).

Bauwens (1984: 21) suggests trying to select ι so that it has the same location, covariance structure, and tail behaviour as φ. A correct location can be obtained if ι has the same mode(s) as φ (using T2, and E1 or E2). A correct tail behaviour can follow from choosing ι to have moments of order not higher than φ (using T1). Hesterberg (1991) even advocates that the importance function should have thicker tails than the posterior in some cases (this avoids extreme values of the weighting function in the tails). An approximation of the covariance matrix of φ is given by minus the Hessian inverse of $\log(\varphi)$ (using E1) or by E2. It is sometimes worth inflating the approximate covariance matrix a little. These suggestions may help to prevent the explosion of the weighting function in the tails of ι. We continue with a brief review of methods that have been used successfully in econometric applications to build importance functions.

1) **Normal or Student approximation around the mode:** a second-order Taylor expansion of the log-posterior around its mode θ_* gives

$$\log \varphi(\theta) \simeq \text{constant} - 0.5(\theta - \theta_*)'H(\theta - \theta_*), \qquad (3.36)$$

where $H = -\partial \log(\varphi)/\partial\theta\partial\theta'$, evaluated at θ_*. Hence one can approximate φ by an $N(\theta_*, H^{-1})$ density. If it is known that φ has moments of order ν at most, it is preferable to use the Student density $t(\theta_*, 1, H, \nu)$. Obviously, these kinds of importance functions are not appropriate for approximating very skewed or multimodal densities. In large enough samples (for the econometric model), the normal importance function is in principle a good approximation of φ under conditions required for asymptotic normality of the posterior density. Since the approximation is local (around the mode), the variance matrix may be too small in finite samples, and it can be inflated by a tuning constant (i.e. use cH^{-1} instead of H^{-1} with c larger than one).

2) **Importance functions incorporating exact conditional densities:** if $\theta' = (\alpha'\ \beta')$ and $\varphi(\beta|\alpha)$ can be simulated directly, this conditional density should be incorporated in the importance function, i.e. define

$$\iota(\theta) = \varphi(\beta|\alpha)\,\iota_m(\alpha), \qquad (3.37)$$

where $\iota_m(.)$ is the marginal importance function of α, an approximation of $\varphi(\alpha)$. If $\varphi(\alpha|\beta)$ is also known, $\iota_m(\alpha)$ can be defined as $\varphi(\alpha|\beta = \hat{\beta})$, where $\hat{\beta}$ is the posterior mode of β; otherwise, $\iota_m(\alpha)$ must be selected by another method. The simulation of (3.37) is done sequentially: a draw from $\iota_m(\alpha)$ is made, followed by a draw from $\varphi(\beta|\alpha)$ with α the previously drawn value. If this procedure is too intensive in computing time, one could use the importance function

$$\iota(\theta) = \varphi(\beta|\hat{\alpha})\,\iota_m(\alpha), \qquad (3.38)$$

which could be $\varphi(\beta|\hat{\alpha})\,\varphi(\alpha|\hat{\beta})$. Conditioning on $\hat{\beta}$ and $\hat{\alpha}$ often results in too small variances for the importance function. Examples of the application of this technique appear in Bauwens (1984) and in Bauwens and Lubrano (1996).

3) **Finite mixtures:** a finite mixture is a weighted average of several densities:

$$\iota(\theta) = \sum_{i=1}^{k} \pi_i \, \iota_i(\theta), \tag{3.39}$$

where the weights π_i are probabilities. The supports of the different components ι_i need not overlap to allow for efficient approximations in specific areas of the support of the posterior. Such importance functions can be useful to approximate posterior densities with several modes, or with different tail behaviour in different directions. Their main disadvantage is that they typically require a large number of parameters to be defined, and rather good knowledge of the shape of the posterior, which may be difficult to acquire, especially in a high-dimensional space. The 'split' Student importance function of Geweke (1989a) is an example. Mixtures were also used by van Dijk (1984) and Hesterberg (1991).

4) **Optimal choice of parameters of the importance function:** the choice of an importance function requires first the determination of a family of parametric densities to choose from, and secondly the selection of the parameters of the density within the class. If $\iota(\theta)$ is indexed by a parameter λ, the best choice of importance function within that class is given by the value of λ that minimizes the Monte Carlo variance of the quantity to be estimated. Choosing the latter as the variance of the weighting function (with respect to the importance function), one has to solve

$$\min_{\lambda} \int \frac{[\varphi(\theta)]^2}{\iota(\theta|\lambda)} d\theta. \tag{3.40}$$

This is often intractable analytically. However, Richard (1996) provides an algorithm to solve numerically an approximation of the original problem (3.40) when the importance function is in the exponential family, and finds that the procedure drastically improves the importance function compared with a naïve choice.

5) **Parameter transformations:** it may be possible to transform the parameter θ into a new parameter such that the transformed posterior is better behaved than the original one, e.g. it is closer to a symmetric distribution that can be well approximated by a normal or Student distribution. A useful reference is Smith, Skene, Shaw, and Naylor (1987). Although its motivation is slightly different, the 'mixed integration' method of van Dijk, Kloek, and Boender (1985) can be interpreted in this framework: it uses a parameter transformation and combines a deterministic integration rule on one (transformed) parameter with importance sampling on the other ones.

6) **Updating:** this has been alluded to above (see E2). If one has estimated some posterior characteristics using a first 'crude' importance function, one can update the parameters of the importance function within the chosen class, or even change the class of the importance function (e.g. to incorporate some skewness property of the posterior) and perform a second round of importance sampling.

Remark (Rao–Blackwellization): In conjunction with method 2, assuming (3.37) applies, it is more efficient to compute the posterior moments and densities of β by marginalizing the corresponding conditional quantities, than to use g_I—see (3.31). This works as follows for the posterior mean:

$$E(\beta) = E_\alpha[E(\beta|\alpha)] \simeq \sum_{j=1}^{n} E(\beta|\alpha_j)\, w(\alpha_j)/ \sum_{j=1}^{n} w(\alpha_j). \qquad (3.41)$$

Note that the weighting function depends only on α since the numerator and the denominator both include the factor $\varphi(\beta|\alpha)$. For the posterior variance matrix, we use

$$
\begin{aligned}
\mathrm{Var}(\beta) &= E_\alpha[\mathrm{Var}(\beta|\alpha)] + \mathrm{Var}_\alpha[E(\beta|\alpha)] \\
&\simeq \frac{\sum_{j=1}^{n} \mathrm{Var}(\beta|\alpha_j)\, w(\alpha_j)}{\sum_{j=1}^{n} w(\alpha_j)} + \frac{\sum_{j=1}^{n} E(\beta|\alpha_j)\, E(\beta'|\alpha_j)\, w(\alpha_j)}{\sum_{j=1}^{n} w(\alpha_j)} - E(\beta)\, E(\beta'),
\end{aligned}
$$

$$(3.42)$$

and for a marginal density (with scalar β):

$$\varphi(\beta) = E_\alpha[\varphi(\beta|\alpha)] \simeq \sum_{j=1}^{n} \varphi(\beta|\alpha_j)\, w(\alpha_j)/ \sum_{j=1}^{n} w(\alpha_j). \qquad (3.43)$$

This formula is applied to every value of β for which one wants to compute the posterior density (in order to plot its graph). That the Monte Carlo estimator (3.41) is more efficient than the estimator g_I follows from a relation like the first equality in (3.42) which shows that the variance of the conditional mean is not larger than the unconditional variance. The efficiency referred to in the previous statement is statistical efficiency; the method introduced in this remark is not necessarily more efficient than the alternative method in terms of computing time (in particular, it relies on the possibility of computing the required conditional quantities, which should be known analytically). This technique is used, for example, by Bauwens (1984), and Bauwens and Lubrano (1996).

3.4.2.5 *Rejection Sampling* A method related to importance sampling is rejection sampling. Instead of using $\iota(.)$ as an importance function to generate draws and to weight the draws, one can use a suitable criterion to check if a draw generated from the approximation ι is acceptable as a draw from the posterior. A candidate θ is accepted if

$$\frac{\kappa(\theta)}{c.\iota(\theta)} > u, \tag{3.44}$$

where $u \in (0,1)$ is a uniform random number, and c is given by

$$c = \sup_{\theta} \frac{\kappa(\theta)}{\iota(\theta)} < \infty \ \forall\theta. \tag{3.45}$$

The purpose of multiplying ι by c in (3.44) is to envelop κ. The volume between κ and the envelope is the rejection zone.

Once n draws have been accepted, they constitute an IID sample from the posterior, and they can be used as in the direct sampling method to estimate posterior moments. The percentage of accepted draws gives an estimate of $\int \kappa(\theta)d\theta$ divided by c. This percentage can be very low, and the method can be very inefficient in the sense that the average computing time to get one accepted draw is very large. With importance sampling, these rejected draws would be used with the appropriate weights. Since the rejection decision uses the value of the weight—see (3.44)—we advise the computation of the estimator g_I as a by-product, even if rejection sampling is used. Intuitively, a good importance function should provide a good envelope function and vice versa. It has been shown that for a given ι and g, the importance sampling estimator has a smaller Monte Carlo variance than the rejection sampling estimator; see Hammersley and Handscomb (1964: Section 5.2) for an easy proof in a simple case, and Richard (1996: Corollary 25-3) for a general proof.

3.4.2.6 *Applications of Importance Sampling in Econometrics* Importance sampling has been applied to posterior and predictive inference in a great variety of econometric models. To mention a few:

- Simultaneous equation, SURE, and VAR models: Kloek and van Dijk (1978); Bauwens (1984); van Dijk (1984); Richard and Steel (1988); Bauwens and Lubrano (1996); Kadiyala and Karlsson (1997).
- Disequilibrium models: Lubrano (1985).
- Poly-t densities: Bauwens and Richard (1985).
- ARCH models: Geweke (1989b); Kleibergen and van Dijk (1993); Bauwens and Lubrano (1998).

3.4.3 *Markov Chain Methods*

Markov chain Monte Carlo (MCMC) methods were introduced in econometrics around 1990, after being revived in statistics. Many papers have been written that apply these techniques to Bayesian inference on standard econometric models. One reason for their success is the relative ease with which they can be applied, compared with importance sampling. The latter method is often 'problem specific': one has to find a good enough approximation of a posterior density, and what may be a solution for one model or even one data set may not be for another. MCMC methods have been found to be somewhat easier to implement and to be less intensive in research time. The most useful MCMC methods are the Gibbs sampler and the Metropolis–Hastings algorithm. The latter is related to importance sampling. It can be used in combination with the Gibbs sampler when the latter is not fully feasible. What characterizes these two methods is that they generate samples from the exact posterior, which are, however, not independent samples. This is their relative weakness, since statistical estimation is generally more difficult with dependent observations than in the opposite situation. A key technical reference on MCMC methods is Tierney (1994). Surveys oriented towards econometrics are provided by Chib and Greenberg (1996), and by Geweke (1995). The book by Robert (1996) contains more details and is more oriented towards statistics.

3.4.3.1 *Gibbs Sampling* A simple presentation of the Gibbs sampler is given by Casella and George (1992). The Gibbs sampler is required to be able to simulate the 'full' conditional densities of $\varphi(\theta)$. This means that one must be able to partition θ into m 'blocks' (with $m \leq k$)

$$\theta = (\theta_1' \, \theta_2' \, \ldots \, \theta_m')' \tag{3.46}$$

such that, for all i,

$$\varphi(\theta_i | \theta_{-i}) \tag{3.47}$$

(where θ_{-i} is θ without θ_i) can be directly simulated. If there is just one block, we are in the case of direct sampling (see Subsection 3.4.1). At the other extreme, each block corresponds to a single parameter (which opens up the possibility of a useful variant known as the *griddy-Gibbs sampler* which is explained below). To ease exposition, we assume that we have only two blocks. Under some regularity conditions, the Gibbs sampler produces a sequence $\{\theta^n\}_{n=1}^N$ of dependent draws from the posterior. A sufficient condition, often true in econometric models, is that the full conditional densities are always striclty positive—see e.g. Geweke (1993). The next draw θ^n of the posterior is generated using the previous draw θ^{n-1} by the following cycle:

$$\begin{aligned} \theta_1^n &\sim \varphi(\theta_1 | \theta_2^{n-1}), \\ \theta_2^n &\sim \varphi(\theta_2 | \theta_1^n) \end{aligned} \tag{3.48}$$

($x^n \sim \varphi(x)$ means that x^n is a draw from the distribution $\varphi(x)$). The procedure is started using any value θ_2^a in the support of the posterior distribution. The influence of the starting conditions vanishes after a certain number of draws, say ns. If the algorithm converges, after ns draws it produces random draws of the posterior density of θ; the sample is, however, not independent because of the Markov chain structure.

There are two options for computing moments and marginal densities. In the first option, we can directly exploit the draws to compute sample moments and (smoothed) histograms. So for example $E(\theta_1)$ is estimated by

$$g_{Gu} = \frac{1}{N} \sum_{n=1}^{N} \theta_1^n. \tag{3.49}$$

This estimator is unbiased and converges at the usual slow speed $1/\sqrt{N}$, as in all Monte Carlo techniques. It is also asymptotically normal under suitable regularity conditions (see e.g. Tierney 1994). The Monte Carlo variance of this estimator is, however, not equal to $\mathrm{Var}(\theta_1)/N$ as when the draws are independent and from the exact posterior—see (3.25). When the draws are dependent, the numerator of the variance of the estimator has to take account of the autocorrelation structure of the sequence $\{\theta_1^n\}_{n=1}^N$. For example, if the observed sequence can be considered as a sample of a covariance stationary process, the variance of the sample mean (3.49) is equal to

$$\frac{1}{N} \left(\gamma_0 + 2 \sum_{n=1}^{N-1} \gamma_n \frac{N-n}{N} \right) \tag{3.50}$$

where γ_j is the jth-order autocovariance, which can be estimated by sample moments. In any case, variance reduction techniques should be used if possible. As discussed by Tierney (1994), conditioning (or 'Rao–Blackwellization') is one possibility. So in the second option, instead of averaging the θ_1^n sequence, we average the conditional means (if they are known) and define the estimator

$$g_{Gc} = \frac{1}{N} \sum_{n=1}^{N} E(\theta_1 | \theta_2^n) \tag{3.51}$$

of $E(\theta_1)$. The Monte Carlo variance of this estimator is again not equal to $\mathrm{Var}[E(\theta_1|\theta_2)]/N$, as in the case of an independent sample, where it is always smaller than $\mathrm{Var}(\theta_1)/N$. With a dependent sample, the numerator has to be adjusted for the autocorrelation structure of the conditional expectation. To quote Tierney:

'Whether this form of conditioning leads to a reduction in variance depends on the correlation structure'.

In particular, a sufficient condition is that the correlations of the conditional expectations $(E(\theta_1|\theta_2^n))$ are not larger than the correlations of the draws (θ_1^n).

Still in the second option, to compute the marginal variances by conditioning, we cumulate the conditional variances and the outer product of the conditional means as $\mathrm{Var}(\theta_1) = E[\mathrm{Var}(\theta_1|\theta_2)] + \mathrm{Var}[E(\theta_1|\theta_2)]$. For covariances, we can cumulate $E(\theta_1|\theta_2)\,\theta_2'$ instead of $\theta_1\theta_2'$, exploiting $\mathrm{Cov}(\theta_1,\theta_2) = \mathrm{Cov}[E(\theta_1|\theta_2),\theta_2]$. The graph of a marginal density requires a grid to be defined in advance. Each conditional, properly normalized, is evaluated over this grid, conditionally on the current draw of the other parameter. Conditional densities are then averaged. Suppose we want to compute $\varphi(\theta_{1*})$, where θ_{1*} denotes one point of the grid of values of θ_1. Since

$$\varphi(\theta_{1*}) = \int \varphi(\theta_{1*}|\theta_2, y)\, \varphi(\theta_2)\, d\theta_2, \tag{3.52}$$

the latter quantity is estimated by

$$\sum_{n=1}^{N} \varphi(\theta_{1*}|\theta_2^n, y)/N. \tag{3.53}$$

Generalizing the Gibbs sampler to m blocks implies that we consider a more general Markov chain. A draw θ^n of the posterior density is generated using the previous draw θ^{n-1} by the following cycle:

$$
\begin{aligned}
\theta_1^n &\sim \varphi(\theta_1|\theta_{-1}^{n-1}), \\
\theta_2^n &\sim \varphi(\theta_2|\theta_1^n,\, \theta_3^{n-1},\, \ldots, \theta_m^{n-1}), \\
&\ \vdots \\
\theta_i^n &\sim \varphi(\theta_i|\theta_1^n,\, \ldots,\, \theta_{i-1}^n, \theta_{i+1}^{n-1},\, \ldots,\, \theta_m^{n-1}), \\
&\ \vdots \\
\theta_m^n &\sim \varphi(\theta_m|\theta_{-m}^n).
\end{aligned}
\tag{3.54}
$$

The procedure is started using any value θ_{-1}^a in the support of the posterior distribution.

Remarks:

1) The way to partition θ into blocks—see (3.46)—is relevant for the efficiency of the Gibbs sampler. The ideal choice is a single block, as it brings us back to the direct sampling case. It is much preferable to have as few blocks as possible, and to have in the same block the parameters which are strongly dependent or correlated. If two parameters are strongly correlated and belong to different blocks, a complete 'exploration' of the posterior density will require many more draws than if they are independent. The choice of the blocks is often determined by the properties of the econometric model, as it determines the knowledge of some relevant conditional densities.

2) In order to compute posterior results, we have advocated the use of a 'long' sequence of draws produced by the Gibbs sampler, after discarding ns initial draws to achieve convergence (the so-called 'burn-in' phase). A variant of this procedure consists in subsampling the sequence in order to retain a subsequence which is approximately IID (e.g. by selecting every tenth observation). This is an inefficient procedure, both numerically as it wastes computing time, and statistically as it produces estimators with

larger variances than when the complete sequence is used (see MacEachern and Berliner 1994). Another procedure is to run a 'large' number (say K) of parallel chains, each starting from a different initial condition, and producing one draw after convergence (i.e. after ns draws in each sequence). In principle, the sample formed by the K final draws of the parallel sequences constitutes an IID sample from the posterior, whence posterior results can be computed in the same way as in direct sampling. This technique of parallel chains wastes a lot of draws. Moreover, it is not obvious how one should design the choice of the K different initial conditions. There is still some debate in the literature on the relative merits of the two approaches.

3.4.3.2 *Griddy-Gibbs Sampling*

With two blocks, Gibbs sampling can be applied if both conditional posterior densities can be directly simulated. In some cases the conditional posterior density of $\theta_1|\theta_2$ is known, but that of $\theta_2|\theta_1$ is not. So direct sampling from $\varphi(\theta_1|\theta_2, y)$ is easy, but sampling from $\varphi(\theta_2|\theta_1, y)$ is more complicated. A solution is then to use a rejection technique. Rejection sampling (see Subsection 3.4.2) is one possibility but its drawbacks have been outlined. Another rejection method is the Metropolis–Hastings algorithm (explained in the next subsection). An alternative solution is to use the griddy-Gibbs sampler (GGS), which is applicable even if no full conditional posterior density belongs to a class such that there exists an efficient algorithm to simulate it (like the normal family).

The kernel of the full conditional density of θ_i is simply given by the kernel of the joint posterior considered as a function of θ_i with θ_{-i} fixed. The kernel of $\varphi(\theta_i|\theta_{-i})$, conditionally on a previous draw of the conditioning parameter, can easily be evaluated over a grid of points when θ_i is a scalar. One can then compute the corresponding distribution function using a deterministic integration rule (see remark 2 in Subsection 3.3.1). Afterwards, one can generate a draw of θ_i by inversion of the distribution at a random value sampled uniformly in $(0, 1)$.

This technique is called the griddy-Gibbs sampler. It was first applied by Ritter and Tanner (1992) to bivariate posterior densities. It was also applied to a posterior of seven parameters by Bauwens and Lubrano (1998) in the context of GARCH models (see Chapter 7).

It is quite easy to incorporate in the griddy-Gibbs sampler the variance reduction techniques described above. This is especially useful to get accurate graphs of the univariate marginal densities with a relatively small number of draws. The algorithm works as follows for N draws and two scalar parameters called β and α (the generalization to k parameters is obvious):

1) Start the chain at a value β^0 for β.

2) Start a loop at $n = 1$.

3) Compute $\kappa(\alpha|\beta^{n-1}, y)$ over the grid $(\alpha_1, \alpha_2, \ldots, \alpha_G)$ to obtain the vector $G_\kappa = (\kappa_1, \kappa_2, \ldots, \kappa_G)$.

4) By a deterministic integration rule using G points, compute the values $G_\Phi = (0, \Phi_2, \ldots, \Phi_G)$ where

$$\Phi_i = \int_{\alpha_1}^{\alpha_i} \kappa(\alpha|\beta^{n-1}, y)\, d\alpha, \quad i = 2, \ldots, G.$$

Compute (and cumulate for the marginal) the normalized pdf values $G_\varphi = G_\kappa/\Phi_G$ of $\varphi(\alpha|\beta^{n-1}, y)$. Compute $\mathrm{E}(\alpha|\beta^{n-1}, y)$ and $\mathrm{Var}(\alpha|\beta^{n-1}, y)$ by the same type of integration rule as above, and store them in a table.

5) Generate $u \sim U[0, \Phi_G]$ and invert $\Phi(\alpha|\beta^{n-1}, y)$ by numerical interpolation to get a draw $\alpha^n \sim \varphi(\alpha|\beta^{n-1}, y)$. Store this draw in a table.

6) Repeat steps 3–6 for $\varphi(\beta^n|\alpha^n, y)$.

7) Increment n by 1 and go to step 3 unless $n > N$.

8) Compute the posterior moments of α and β from the tables where conditional moments are stored (by averaging). Likewise, plot the marginal densities (cumulated G_φ/N). With the table containing $\{\alpha^n, \beta^n\}_{n=1}^N$, one can compute posterior moments (as sample averages) and draw a histogram of any function of the parameters.

Remarks:

1) The choice of the grid of points has to be made carefully and constitutes the main difficulty in applying the method. One must have an idea of the bounds of integration. These may come from prior restrictions on the parameters, e.g. $0 < \beta < 1$. However, even in such cases we advise restricting the integration to the subset of the parameter space where the value of the posterior density is big enough to contribute to the integrals. Otherwise, too many points of the grids will be practically useless, at the expense of precision in the inversion of the cdf. It is worth exploring the shape of the conditional densities by varying the conditioning values enough, before fixing the integration ranges.

2) It is quite evident that a variable grid could be more efficient since more points could be used in the area where the posterior density varies a lot. A variable grid could be used, but it may be difficult to devise a way to adapt it at each iteration of the loop of draws (since the cdf varies because of the renewal of the conditioning values). An automatic way to adapt the grid is to use an iterative method of integration (but see the next remark).

3) Our description of the algorithm requires that the grid of points of each parameter remains constant throughout the N draws. Otherwise, we would have to interpolate the value of the conditional pdf over a fixed grid (using the values of the pdf over the variable grid of the current cycle) in order to apply (3.53). This is not recommended if the functional evaluation of the posterior density is expensive. For this reason, iterative integration methods (like the iterative Simpson's method) may be less attractive.

4) Bauwens and Lubrano (1998) used the trapezoidal rule of integration over fixed grids of 33 points, and linear interpolation between adjacent points to invert the cdf. The cost of the method being proportional to the number of points in the grids, a smaller number of points could be compensated by a more sophisticated interpolation method to invert the cdf.

3.4.3.3 *Metropolis–Hastings Algorithm* The Metropolis–Hastings (MH) algorithm was proposed by Metropolis, Rosenbluth, Rosenbluth, Teller, and Teller (1953) and extended by Hastings (1970). An introductory exposition is given by Chib and Greenberg (1995), see also Robert (1996: Chap. 4). It is a Markov chain algorithm which, when convergence is achieved, draws from the exact posterior density. It is related to the importance sampling method as it uses an approximation to the posterior to draw random numbers. But there is a rejection mechanism (instead of a weighting) to decide if a draw belongs to the exact posterior density or not. The algorithm uses an instrumental law $q(.)$ which serves to draw random numbers. A draw ζ is obtained from $q(\zeta|\theta_n)$. A probability of acceptance p for this draw is computed as a function of ζ and θ_n. This draw ζ is accepted as a draw from $\varphi(.)$ with probability p, otherwise the previous draw θ_n is kept with probability $1 - p$. This algorithm is very general because there is no restriction on the instrumental law $q(.)$. However, it produces a dependent sample because there are multiple occurrences of the same draw. A variant of this algorithm, known as the independent Metropolis, is very often used in econometrics. Its name comes from the fact that the instrumental law $q(.)$ is independent of the previous draw θ_n. By analogy with the importance sampling method, we shall use $q(.) = \iota(\zeta)$. The algorithm is as follows:

1) generate $\zeta \sim \iota(\zeta)$

2) compute $p = \min \left[\dfrac{\varphi(\zeta)}{\varphi(\theta^n)} \dfrac{\iota(\theta^n)}{\iota(\zeta)}, 1 \right]$

3) take $\theta^{n+1} = \begin{cases} \zeta & \text{with probability } p \\ \theta^n & \text{with probability } 1 - p. \end{cases}$

When $\varphi = \iota$, we are back to the case of direct sampling. Geweke (1995) has proposed this algorithm to make inference in the GARCH model. Bauwens, Bos, and van Dijk (1998) have used it inside their adaptive polar sampling algorithm.

Example 3.1 To illustrate very simply how the Metropolis–Hastings algorithm operates in the transition from θ to θ', suppose that we want to sample from an $N(0, 1)$ distribution, using as instrumental distribution an $N(0, 1/c)$ where c differs from 1. The acceptance probability is found to be

$$p = \min \left[\exp[\tfrac{1}{2}(c - 1)(\theta'^2 - \theta^2)], 1 \right].$$

Take for example $c = 3$ (the instrumental density is much too concentrated), $\theta' = 0$, $\theta = 2$. Then $p = \exp(-4) = 0.0183$: there is very little chance to move from 2 to 0 because 0 is too likely in the instrumental density compared with the target (the value 2 must be 'oversampled'). If one exchanges θ and θ', then $\beta = \exp(4) > 1$ so a move from 0 to 2 is accepted surely.

Among the many other possible implementations of the Metropolis–Hastings algorithm indicated for instance in Chib and Greenberg (1995) or Robert (1996), we have chosen the random walk variant. As in the Gibbs sampler, the convergence of the chain is obtained only when we manage to explore the complete domain of definition of $\varphi(.)$. So an attractive idea is to draw ζ according to a random walk. This means that $\zeta = \theta^n + \epsilon$, where ϵ is a white noise with zero mean. For the importance function $\iota(.)$, we have now just to select a matrix of variance–covariance Σ. If the instrumental law $\iota(.)$ is a symmetric function, the algorithm is as follows:

1) generate $\epsilon \sim \iota(\epsilon)$
2) compute $\zeta = \theta^n + \epsilon$
3) compute $p = \min\left[\dfrac{\varphi(\zeta)}{\varphi(\theta^n)}, 1\right]$
4) take $\theta^{n+1} = \begin{cases} \zeta & \text{with probability } p \\ \theta^n & \text{with probability } 1 - p. \end{cases}$

This algorithm was used for instance in Koop (1998). Robert (1996) does not seem to favour it very much because it fails to produce uniformly ergodic chains. But improvements are suggested for instance in Tierney (1994) in which ζ follows an autoregressive process which makes use of prior knowledge about the mean of $\varphi(\theta)$.

The calibration of a Metropolis–Hastings algorithm is not an easy task. In the independent Metropolis, the instrumental density must be chosen so as to maximize the acceptance rate p. This is the same strategy as in the importance sampling algorithm which is discussed in Subsection 3.4.2. With the random walk Metropolis, a high rate of acceptance is not desirable because p depends on the previous draw. A high rate may simply mean that the algorithm is stuck in one region of φ. The rate of acceptance can be monitored by inflating the variance–covariance matrix Σ.

It is not known at the time of writing for which cases each method (importance sampling or the Metropolis–Hastings algorithm, for a given model and given importance function) is more 'efficient' for Bayesian computing in econometrics. Bauwens and Lubrano (1998) report a case where importance sampling seems to provide more precise posterior results. Casella and Robert (1996) also report a case with a similar conclusion.

3.4.3.4 *Convergence Criteria for MCMC Methods*

A difficult but important practical issue is to assess if a Markov chain of draws has converged after N

draws. Several convergence criteria have been proposed in the literature. In the case of the Gibbs sampler, Gelman and Rubin (1994) have introduced a diagnostic based on multiple chains (with very dispersed starting values), in order to check if the posterior results are not too sensitive to the starting values. This criterion is not very attractive as it requires to run the Gibbs sampler many times, which may be numerically demanding.

Convergence criteria based on the examination of a single long run have also been devised. Zellner and Min (1995) put forward three simple criteria for the Gibbs sampler, which are useful only for the case of two blocks described in (3.48). Geweke (1992) provides a test statistic that compares the estimate of a posterior mean from the first N_A draws with the estimate from the last N_B draws of the chain. If the two subsamples (A and B) are well separated (i.e. there are many observations between them), they should be independent. The statistic is normally distributed if N is large and the chain has converged. It is

$$ Z = \frac{\bar{g}_A - \bar{g}_B}{(nse_A^2 + nse_B^2)^{1/2}}, \tag{3.55} $$

where $\bar{g}_i$ is the estimate of the posterior mean of g (a parameter), and nse_i is its numerical standard error, formed from subsample i with N_i observations (i = either A or B). So, $\bar{g}_i$ is just the sample average of the Monte Carlo draws. The squared numerical standard error nse_i^2 is an estimate of the variance of $\bar{g}_i$. The variance of the Monte Carlo estimator $\bar{g}_i$ is the variance of a mean. If the Monte Carlo sample is IID, as in direct or importance sampling, this variance is the population variance of g divided by the Monte Carlo sample size (N_i in our context); see the discussion around (3.25). If the Monte Carlo sample is a Markov chain, it is not an independent sample, and the variance of the sample mean is a function of the variance and the autocovariances of the process generating the draws, as discussed before (3.50). The variance of the sample mean can be expressed as the spectral density of the process at frequency zero, $S_g(0)$, divided by the Monte Carlo sample size. It can be estimated with a spectral estimator of $S_g(0)$. See Bauwens and Giot (1998) for an illustration.

Another convergence tool has been proposed by Yu and Mykland (1994). It is based on CUMSUM statistics, which are the partial sums of the draws or of the conditional expectations in the case of Rao–Blackwellization. Robert (1996) reports that this criterion works relatively well. Suppose we have N draws of a Monte Carlo Markov chain. A standardized version of the statistic proposed by Yu and Mykland is

$$ CS_t = \left(\frac{1}{t} \sum_{n=1}^{t} \theta^n - \mu_\theta \right) / \sigma_\theta, \tag{3.56} $$

where μ_θ and σ_θ are the empirical mean and standard deviation of the N draws. If the Monte Carlo Markov chain converges, the graph of CS_t against t should converge smoothly to zero. On the contrary, long and regular excursions away from zero are an indication of the absence of convergence. Standardizing the statistic is convenient if one wants to compare the convergence of different chains or parameters. A value of 0.05 for a CUMSUM after t draws means that the estimate of the posterior expectation diverges from the final estimate (after N draws) by 5 per cent in units of the final estimate of the posterior standard deviation; so a divergence of even 25 per cent is not a bad result. Bauwens and Lubrano (1998) declare that the sampler has converged after $N(\epsilon)$ draws *for the estimation of a certain quantity (like a posterior mean)* with a relative error of $100 \times \epsilon$ per cent, if CS_t remains within a band of $\pm\epsilon$ for all t larger than $N(\epsilon)$. The relative error should be fixed at a low value, such as 0.05.

3.4.3.5 *Applications of MCMC Methods in Econometrics* Numerous applications of MCMC methods have burgeoned in econometrics since about 1990. The techniques have been applied to standard econometric models which had been analysed previously using other numerical integration techniques. What is often missing in this type of research is a comparison of the efficiency of different techniques, an exception being the paper of Kadiyala and Karlsson (1997). They have also been applied to new models or to extend the analysis of old models which were too difficult to analyse by other integration techniques. Some examples follow:

- Regression models with normal errors following an AR or even an ARMA process: Chib (1993); Chib and Greenberg (1994).

- Regression models with normal or Student errors following a GARCH process: Bauwens and Lubrano (1998) use the griddy-Gibbs sampler, while Geweke (1994) uses the Metropolis–Hastings algorithm.

- Regression models with independent Student errors: Geweke (1993).

- Stochastic frontier models: Koop, Steel, and Osiewalski (1995b).

- Stochastic volatility models: Jacquier, Polson, and Rossi (1994); Geweke (1994); Steel (1998); Richard and Zhang (1997).

- Panel data models: Chib (1996).

- Curiously, not much has been done on simultaneous equation systems, although there are several possibilities: for example, the full conditional densities for the limited information analysis of a single equation are available from Bauwens and van Dijk (1990). Geweke (1994) analyses this model in the framework of reduced rank models (see also Geweke 1996 for computing a marginalized likelihood). Percy (1992) uses the Gibbs sampler to compute predictive results in SURE models. Kadiyala and Karlsson (1997) apply the Gibbs sampler to two VAR models analysed with an (extended) natural conjugate prior density (see Section 9.2 for details). Bauwens and Giot (1998) implement the Gibbs sampler in cointegrated VAR systems (see also Section 9.3 for details and an example).

3.5 Conclusion

We have reviewed the most useful methods (according to our experience) of numerical integration in Bayesian inference on econometric models. The presentation we have given may give the wrong impression that we think that the different methods are in competition. It is clear that for certain types of problems, some methods are more efficient than others (in a broad sense that is not reduced to statistical efficiency). But we do believe that for difficult problems, it is wise to try different methods, if possible, and to compare the results. Moreover, for a given problem, it may be possible to combine different methods. As an example, let us reconsider the presentation in Section 3.2: the partitioning of θ into its two components is dictated by the availability of partially analytical results. More generally, in the absence of such results, the procedures described in that section could be useful if the partitioning of θ were dictated by numerical considerations, e.g. one could combine a Monte Carlo technique for α with a Simpson rule over β conditionally on α, when β is of small dimension. This could be useful if β is a difficult parameter to deal with a Monte Carlo method (e.g. because it creates a lot of skewness). There is of course a price to pay, namely the numerical computation of conditional results (by Simpson's rule). Another method that combines different methods is the griddy-Gibbs sampler. Progress in numerical integration will come partly through the combination of different methods. An algorithm of this kind is proposed by Bauwens, Bos, and van Dijk (1998).

4

PRIOR DENSITIES FOR THE REGRESSION MODEL

4.1 Introduction

As was made clear in Chapter 1, the use of a prior distribution on the parameter space is one of the main differences between the classical and Bayesian schools of statistics. We explained how, in a decision framework, a simple set of axioms leads to the existence of a probability on the space of the 'states of nature', interpreted as the parameter space in problems of statistical inference. We also discussed what is commonly called the interpretation of probability; that is to say, what kind of link exists between the formal mathematical system of probabilities and the real physical world. From this debate we can retain that the subjective interpretation of probabilities is fully compatible with the idea of introducing subjective opinions concerning the parameters of a model by means of a prior density. But we must still tackle the question of how to specify precisely the shape and the contents of the prior density in an empirical application. This is the object of Section 4.2. In certain applications, one may not want to introduce precise prior information, or one may not feel like spending too much time eliciting a prior density. This is the case for instance in the phase of model building. We have thus to define the concept of non-informative (or diffuse) prior which is treated in Section 4.3. This idea is also compatible with the logical interpretation of the concept of probability (see Section 1.4). Defining a non-informative prior is far from trivial and uncontroversial, and it can produce some paradoxes. In Section 4.4, we explain the restrictive properties of the natural conjugate prior in the regression model. The natural conjugate prior embeds a probabilistic dependence between the regression coefficients and the error variance. This feature makes it unattractive when one wants to be non-informative on the error variance, while being informative on the regression coefficients. Moreover, when there is a conflict of information between the prior and the sample, it tends to be softened. In Section 4.5, we show how to avoid these difficulties with a convenient way of getting out of the natural conjugate framework, while retaining much of its analytical advantages. Section 4.6 is devoted to two special topics: the treatment of exact restrictions, and exchangeable prior densities. The examples in this chapter are built around the regression model which was introduced in Chapter 2.

4.2 The Elicitation of a Prior Density

This section gives hints on how to solve a problem which is often thought of as being very mysterious in empirical applications. From where does the value of the parameters of the prior density come? From which sources of information and through which method? We can distinguish two main groups of methods that differ by the source of the information used:

1) the aim of the first group of methods is to sum up by means of a prior density the information about some parameters that can be extracted from historical data;
2) the second group of methods relies on the quantification of personal or subjective opinions.

Let us review these two groups of methods, with a greater emphasis being given to the second one.

4.2.1 *Distributions Adjusted on Historical Data*

It is possible to interpret the parameters of a natural conjugate prior as the sufficient statistics of a previous hypothetical sample (see Subsection 2.5.1). In a certain number of cases this sample does exist either directly or indirectly. For instance, in a time series inference problem it may be possible to get data older than the sample considered; but these data are not complete, or the definitions of the variables have changed and so it is not possible to include them in the sample. Eliciting a prior density in this case is equivalent to simplifying the likelihood function of a set of data that would be too complicated to try to model directly.

Let us take an example which is drawn from Drèze (1980) and Drèze and Modigliani (1981). These authors present an interesting way of eliciting prior information. One of the questions they are interested in is to determine the effect of a working time reduction on employment in a small open economy like Belgium's. The idea is of work sharing, but sharing work induces extra costs (which can be borne by workers in a proportion α), and the cost increase has consequences, via the external constraint, on employment. So the final effect is not clear cut. One of the formulae they use for computing η_{NT}, the elasticity of employment to working time, is the following:

$$\eta_{NT} = \eta_{NY}\left[1 + (1 - \alpha)\,\eta_{NW}\right], \tag{4.1}$$

where η_{NY} is the elasticity of employment to production and η_{NW} is the elasticity of employment to wages (formula 9 in Drèze 1980). There is no information on α which is a parameter of economic policy. The result has to be given conditionally on a set of values of α. But there is a certain amount of information for determining the two elasticities η_{NY} and η_{NW}. The information concerning η_{NY} consists of classical estimates from four different macroeconometric models of the Belgian economy and is given in Table 4.1. Two prior densities for η_{NY} (short term and long term) are specified by means of two normal densities centred at the average values of these point estimates (0.3 and 0.9). But little indication is given by the data concerning a prior variance, except the standard errors of these estimates. The variance of each prior density is assessed so as to take this

Table 4.1 *Empirical data for η_{NY}*

Model	Short term	Long term
A	0.50	0.90
B	0.23	
C	0.30	
D	0.30	0.88

Table 4.2 *Prior information for η_{NY}*

	Expectation	Standard deviation
Short term	0.3	0.22
Long term	0.9	0.65

dispersion into account, but the result is fairly enlarged in order to stay on the conservative side. This information is summarized in Table 4.2.

The prior density on η_{NW} is somehow more complicated to elaborate, as this elasticity results from the combination of several other elasticities. Taking information from the SERENA model, and using normal approximations, Drèze and Modigliani obtained by numerical integration the prior moments given in Table 4.3.

Table 4.3 *Prior information for η_{NW}*

	Expectation	Standard deviation
Short term	−0.18	0.13
Long term	−1.82	0.80

Let us compute for different values of α the prior density of η_{NT} as defined by (4.1). The two normal prior densities for η_{NY} and η_{NW} are assumed to be independent. Obviously,

$$\eta'_{NW} = [1 + (1 - \alpha)\,\eta_{NW}] \tag{4.2}$$

is also normally distributed, and we must compute the distribution and the moments of the product of the following two normal independent variables:

$$\begin{aligned} \eta_{NY} &\sim N(\mu_y, \sigma_y^2), \\ \eta'_{NW} &\sim N(\mu_w, \sigma_w^2). \end{aligned} \tag{4.3}$$

The moments of η_{NT} are easily obtained because of the independence assumption. The mean is

$$\begin{aligned} \mathrm{E}(\eta_{NT}) &= \mathrm{E}(\eta_{NY})\,\mathrm{E}(\eta'_{NW}) \\ &= \mathrm{E}(\eta_{NY})\,\mathrm{E}[1 + (1 - \alpha)\,\eta_{NW}], \end{aligned} \tag{4.4}$$

and the variance is $\mathrm{Var}(\eta_{NT}) = \mathrm{E}(\eta_{NT}^2) - \mathrm{E}^2(\eta_{NT})$, where

$$\begin{aligned}
E(\eta_{NT}^2) &= E(\eta_{NY}^2)\, E[(\eta_{NW}')^2] = (\mu_y^2 + \sigma_y^2)(\mu_w^2 + \sigma_w^2) \\
&= [E^2(\eta_{NY}) + \text{Var}(\eta_{NY})] \\
&\quad \times \{[1 + (1-\alpha)\, E(\eta_{NW})]^2 + (1-\alpha)^2\, \text{Var}(\eta_{NW})\}.
\end{aligned} \tag{4.5}$$

Results are given in Table 4.4 for several values of α. The density of η_{NT} is obtained by marginalization:

Table 4.4 *Prior means and standard deviations of* η_{NT}

α	0.0	0.25	0.50	0.75	1.0
Short term	0.25	0.26	0.27	0.29	0.30
	(0.19)	(0.19)	(0.20)	(0.21)	(0.22)
Long term	−0.75	−0.33	0.08	0.49	0.90
	(1.04)	(0.71)	(0.45)	(0.42)	(0.65)

Standard deviations are given in parentheses

$$\begin{aligned}
f(\eta_{NT}) &= \int f(\eta_{NY}, \eta_{NT})\, d\eta_{NY} \\
&= \int f(\eta_{NT}|\eta_{NY})\, f(\eta_{NY})\, d\eta_{NY},
\end{aligned} \tag{4.6}$$

where, given (4.1)–(4.3), it is obvious that

$$\eta_{NT}|\eta_{NY} \sim N(\eta_{NY}\,\mu_w, \eta_{NY}^2\,\sigma_w^2). \tag{4.7}$$

The computation of the integral (4.6) cannot be done analytically. We used the iterative Simpson method with a relative error of 0.001—see Subsection 3.3.1. Graphs of the prior density $f(\eta_{NT})$ for various values of α are given in Fig. 4.1.

Drèze (1980) used this information as a device to summarize the available prior information. He had no specific empirical model. Suppose that we actually have a model for inference (using different data from those used to obtain the prior density displayed in Fig. 4.1) with η_{NT} as a direct parameter. We could use the results displayed in Table 4.4 to calibrate a normal or a beta prior density (depending on the value of α).

Other authors have used the approach of eliciting a prior density from data other than those entering into the likelihood function of the model. Morales (1971) builds a prior for the income elasticity of the demand for beef in the Belgian market, using a cross-section of data on consumer income and consumption. Schotman (1996) constructs a prior from cross-section data and uses it in a time series model concerning the valuation of bond options.

4.2.2 *Subjective Prior Information: a Discussion*

The second possible source of information is the personal knowledge of the decision maker, his or her personal degree of belief, and subjective opinions about an

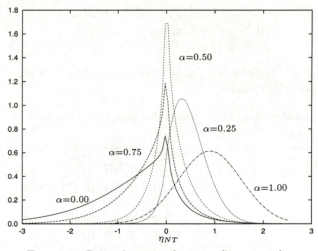

FIG. 4.1. Prior densities for η_{NT} (long term)

event. They result from day-to-day experience of the problem. More precisely, to determine the subjective probability of an event E, a person can compare the likelihood of E and of its complement $\overline{E}$. If E is felt to be twice as likely as $\overline{E}$, then the probability of E will be 2/3. This means that the person is ready to bet with odds of two against one in favour of E (a bet of k against 1 means that the underlying probability is $k/(k+1)$). Conversely a person who accepts a bet implicitly evaluates the probability of occurrence of the event on which he or she bets. De Finetti (1974: Chap. 5) describes practical procedures by which a rational person can quantify personal beliefs in a betting situation.

However, the question to be solved in econometrics is more complicated than that envisaged above: it is not to evaluate the probability of a single event, but to specify a complete probability density of a random variable (like the structural parameter of a regression equation). If the parameter for which we want to elicit a prior belongs to a discrete space, we can always assess the probabilities of each individual point of this space. For the continuous case, we have to elicit a histogram. This 'non-parametric' approach is of little use for the parameters of the regression model, since for computational convenience we impose an analytical form on the prior density (as illustrated for instance by the natural conjugate approach). The elicitation procedure then proceeds with the assignment of quantiles, either of the prior density or of the predictive density. By assigning for example the first and the third quartiles of a distribution, we can construct a situation where we are ready to bet at 1 against 1 that a value is inside or outside the interquartile range. This is known as the interval betting method.

A number of papers have been written on the subject of prior elicitation. We can quote Winkler (1967), Savage (1971), and Lindley, Tversky, and Brown

(1979). The main reference for the regression model is Kadane, Dickey, Winkler, Smith, and Peters (1980). Roughly speaking there are two strategies for eliciting a prior density representing subjective knowledge:

1) The first method proceeds by asking questions about the parameters of the model through the assessment of the quantiles of the prior distribution of the parameters in question. In a linear model the coefficients represent the partial derivatives of the conditional expectation of the endogenous variable with respect to the exogenous variables. If the variables of the model are transformed into logarithms, these coefficients represent elasticities. It seems quite possible for an economist to have prior ideas on these coefficients. This kind of prior information can come both from theoretical models and from past experience. It is also possible to assign directly the prior expectation and the prior standard deviation of a parameter (assuming they exist).

2) The second method is based on the predictive density of the model. The statistician questions the decision maker on the quantiles of the predictive density of the model for different values of the exogenous variables. From these quantiles it is possible to extrapolate to the values of the parameters of the prior density. The method is described in Kadane, Dickey, Winkler, Smith, and Peters (1980).

These methods each present some advantages and drawbacks. Kadane (1980) points out that the two methods can be combined. Zellner (1985) presents his own way to do that. Practical experience shows that the predictive method is rather difficult to implement even though it is certainly more appealing intellectually.

4.2.3 The Interval Betting Method for Regression Parameters

We present a method for the assignment of the parameters of a normal–inverted gamma-2 prior density. Its initial principles can be found in Raiffa and Schlaifer (1961: 60, 230, 292). This prior density is natural conjugate for the linear regression model with normal errors (see Subsection 2.7.2). This density is defined by

$$\begin{aligned}
\varphi(\beta, \sigma^2) &= \varphi(\sigma^2)\,\varphi(\beta|\sigma^2), \\
\varphi(\sigma^2) &= f_{Ig}(\sigma^2|s_0, \nu_0), \\
\varphi(\beta|\sigma^2) &= f_N(\beta|\beta_0, \sigma^2 M_0).
\end{aligned} \tag{4.8}$$

The marginal density of β is

$$\varphi(\beta) = f_t(\beta|\beta_0, s_0, M_0, \nu_0). \tag{4.9}$$

The above factorization shows that the elicitation process should begin with the parameters s_0 and ν_0 of the inverted gamma-2, and then proceed with the parameters β_0 and M_0 of the marginal Student. For ease of reference, we recall the moments of first and second order of σ^2 and β:

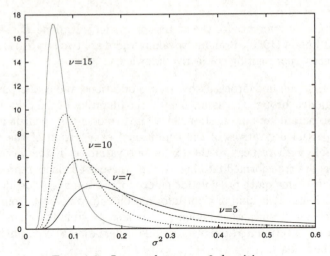

FIG. 4.2. Inverted gamma-2 densities

$$E(\sigma^2) = \frac{s_0}{\nu_0 - 2} \quad \text{if } \nu_0 > 2,$$

$$\text{Var}(\sigma^2) = \frac{2s_0^2}{(\nu_0 - 2)^2(\nu_0 - 4)} \quad \text{if } \nu_0 > 4,$$
(4.10)

$$E(\beta) = \beta_0 \quad \text{if } \nu_0 > 1,$$

$$\text{Var}(\beta) = \frac{s_0}{\nu_0 - 2} M_0^{-1} \quad \text{if } \nu_0 > 2.$$
(4.11)

4.2.3.1 *The Inverted Gamma-2 Prior* The method consists in assigning two quartiles of the prior distribution, for instance $\bar{q}_{.50}$ and $\bar{q}_{.25}$, which are defined by

$$\Pr(\sigma^2 < \bar{q}_{.50}) = 0.50,$$
$$\Pr(\sigma^2 < \bar{q}_{.25}) = 0.25.$$
(4.12)

Figure 4.2 shows the influence of the degrees of freedom ν on the shape and concentration of the inverted gamma-2 density and consequently on the quartiles. Table 4.5, which gives the quartiles of the inverted gamma-2 density for $s_0 = 1$, is very convenient to find the values of ν_0 and s_0 corresponding to the assigned quartiles.

Equating the theoretical ratio $q_{0.50}/q_{0.25}$ to the ratio $\bar{q}_{0.50}/\bar{q}_{0.25}$ of the elicited quartiles gives the value of ν_0 (found in the first column) as these ratios are independent of s_0. Once ν_0 is determined, s_0 is found as the solution of

$$q_{0.50} = \bar{q}_{0.50} \, s_0,$$
(4.13)

where $q_{0.50}$ is read in the table for $\nu = \nu_0$ and $\bar{q}_{0.50}$ is the elicited quartile.

Table 4.5 *Quartiles of inverted gamma-2 distributions*
$\Pr(\sigma^2 < q_\alpha) = \alpha \ (\alpha = 0.25, 0.50, 0.75)$

ν	0.25	0.50	0.75	0.75/0.25	0.50/0.25	0.75/0.50
1	0.756	2.198	9.849	13.02	2.91	4.48
2	0.361	0.719	1.738	4.81	1.99	2.42
3	0.243	0.422	0.825	3.40	1.74	1.95
4	0.186	0.298	0.520	2.80	1.60	1.75
5	0.151	0.231	0.374	2.48	1.53	1.62
6	0.128	0.187	0.289	2.26	1.46	1.55
7	0.111	0.157	0.235	2.12	1.41	1.50
8	0.098	0.136	0.197	2.01	1.39	1.45
9	0.088	0.120	0.169	1.92	1.36	1.41
10	0.080	0.107	0.148	1.85	1.34	1.38
11	0.073	0.097	0.132	1.81	1.33	1.36
12	0.067	0.088	0.119	1.78	1.31	1.35
15	0.055	0.070	0.091	1.65	1.27	1.30
20	0.042	0.052	0.065	1.55	1.24	1.25
30	0.029	0.034	0.041	1.41	1.17	1.21

This table is obtained from a χ^2 table—see e.g. Table 26.8 of Abramowitz and Stegun (1964). If $X \sim \chi^2(\nu)$, then $\sigma^2 = 1/X \sim IG_2(1, \nu)$, so that $\Pr(X > \chi_\alpha^2) = \alpha \Leftrightarrow \Pr(\sigma^2 < 1/\chi_\alpha^2) = \alpha$, and $q_\alpha = 1/\chi_\alpha^2$.

In a regression model it is not easy to have an idea about the quantiles of σ^2 as this parameter depends on the scale of the data. If the dependent variable is in logarithms, this scaling problem disappears provided the model includes a constant term: if

$$\log y = \log h(x) + u, \tag{4.14}$$

then

$$u = \log \frac{y}{h(x)} = \log \left(1 + \frac{y - h(x)}{h(x)} \right)$$
$$\cong \frac{y - h(x)}{h(x)}, \tag{4.15}$$

i.e. the error term and therefore its standard deviation (σ) is in percentage points (of the regression function).

If the dependent variable is not in logarithms, it is possible to get around the scaling problem of σ^2 by using another method. We know that σ^2 represents the conditional variance of y given the regressors. Let us denote σ_y^2 as the population unconditional (or marginal) variance of the dependent variable. The population multiple correlation coefficient is defined as $R^2 = 1 - \sigma^2/\sigma_y^2$. We define a pseudo-$R^2$ by replacing the unknown σ_y^2 by its empirical counterpart.

Definition 4.1 *The pseudo-R^2 denoted R_p^2 is defined as*

$$R_p^2 = 1 - \frac{\sigma^2}{s_y^2},$$

where s_y^2 is the empirical variance of y.

Instead of conducting the elicitation process on σ^2 we can proceed with the pseudo-R^2 which does not depend on the units of measurement of y. But we need its prior distribution, given by the following theorem.

Theorem 4.2 *If the prior density of σ^2 is an inverted gamma-2 with scale parameter s_0 and ν_0 degrees of freedom, then the prior density of $1 - R_p^2$ is also an inverted gamma-2 with ν_0 degrees of freedom, but with s_0/s_y^2 as a scale parameter. The range of R_p^2 is $]-\infty, 1]$.*

The proof of this theorem is quite simple and left to the reader (hint: write the inverted gamma-2 and the Jacobian of the transformation from σ^2 to $1 - R_p^2$).

We choose two quartiles for R_p^2, e.g. $\bar{r}_{0.25}$ and $\bar{r}_{0.50}$, and we transform them into the quartiles of $1 - R_p^2 = \sigma^2/s_y^2$:

$$\begin{aligned}
\Pr(R_p^2 < \bar{r}_{0.50}) = 0.50 &\Leftrightarrow \Pr(1 - R_p^2 < \bar{p}_{0.50}) = 0.50, \\
\Pr(R_p^2 < \bar{r}_{0.25}) = 0.25 &\Leftrightarrow \Pr(1 - R_p^2 < \bar{p}_{0.75}) = 1 - 0.25 = 0.75,
\end{aligned} \tag{4.16}$$

where

$$\bar{p}_\alpha = 1 - \bar{r}_{1-\alpha}. \tag{4.17}$$

For the ratio $\bar{p}_{0.75}/\bar{p}_{0.50} = \bar{r}_{0.25}/\bar{r}_{0.50}$, we can find in Table 4.5 the number of degrees of freedom of the prior of $1 - R_p^2$. For this value of ν_0 in the table, we read off the value of $p_{0.50}$ (for instance). As the scale parameter of the distribution of $1 - R_p^2$ is s_0/s_y^2, we have to solve $p_{0.50} = \bar{p}_{0.50} \, s_0/s_y^2$, which gives

$$s_0 = \frac{s_y^2}{1 - \bar{r}_{0.50}} \, p_{0.50}. \tag{4.18}$$

Example 4.3 Suppose we have $\Pr(R_p^2 < 0.40) = 0.25$ and $\Pr(R_p^2 < 0.60) = 0.50$. From the ratio $\bar{p}_{0.75}/\bar{p}_{0.50} = (1 - 0.40)/(1 - 0.60) = 1.50$, we get $\nu_0 = 5$ and $p_{0.50} = 0.231$. So if $s_y^2 = 50$, $s_0 = 50 \times 0.231/(1 - 0.60) = 6.93$.

4.2.3.2 *The Marginal Student Prior of β*   We turn to the elicitation of the parameters of the marginal Student prior of β, supposing that s_0 and ν_0 have been determined by one of the methods described for the prior on σ^2. Assuming that β is a scalar, it suffices to assign the first and the third quartiles of its distribution on the ground that whenever possible, it is easier to bet on events that are equiprobable. So we consider $\bar{q}_{0.25}$ and $\bar{q}_{0.75}$, such that $\Pr[\bar{q}_{0.25} < \beta < \bar{q}_{0.75}] = 0.5$, a 50 per cent highest prior density interval for β. In other words, we are ready to bet the same sum on the fact that β belongs to that interval or on the fact that it does not. The 50 per cent highest probability interval of the Student density is such that

$$\Pr\left[\beta_0 - t_{0.75}\sqrt{\frac{s_0}{\nu_0 M_0}} < \beta < \beta_0 + t_{0.75}\sqrt{\frac{s_0}{\nu_0 M_0}}\right] = 0.50, \qquad (4.19)$$

where $t_{0.75}$ is the third quartile of the standardized Student density with ν_0 degrees of freedom. Consequently, by equating $\bar{q}_{0.25}$ to the lower limit of the interval described in (4.19), and $\bar{q}_{0.75}$ to the upper limit, we get

$$\beta_0 = \frac{\bar{q}_{0.25} + \bar{q}_{0.75}}{2} \quad \text{and} \quad M_0 = \frac{s_0}{\nu_0}\left(\frac{2\,t_{0.75}}{\bar{q}_{0.75} - \bar{q}_{0.25}}\right)^2. \qquad (4.20)$$

and the prior on β is elicited.

When β is a vector of dimension k, we have to elicit k values for β_0 and $k(k+1)/2$ for M_0. For example, with $k = 10$, this is $10 + 55 = 65$, quite a large number. As underlined by Leamer (1982) it is not easy to elicit covariances in such a way that the prior variance matrix is positive definite. This entails of course restrictions in the elicitation process. If one decides to impose a diagonal prior variance matrix, the elicitation problem is highly simplified, as one can apply (4.20) for each element of β. What is the meaning of a diagonal M_0? Simply that one assumes a priori that the effect β_j of a change of any regressor x_{jt} on y_t is not correlated with the effect β_i of a change of any other regressor x_{it} on y_t. It is, however, not true that the two effects are independent in probability: if M_0 is diagonal, it is easy to check that the Student density (4.9) does not factorize into the product of k independent densities. This is a consequence of the dependence in probability between β and σ^2: although the elements of β are independent in probability conditionally on σ^2, they are not independent marginally, because they are 'mixed' by the integration of σ^2.

An indirect and sometimes convenient way to elicit prior covariances is to reason on some linear combinations of the elements of β. This idea is actually used in the predictive method (see the next subsection). A simple example illustrates the idea.

Example 4.4 Let us consider a two-variable regression equation

$$y_t = x_t\beta_1 + z_t\beta_2 + \epsilon_t,$$

with the usual normal–inverted gamma-2 density in the notation of (4.8). Suppose that $\nu_0 = 10$ and $s_0 = 10$. We have first prior information on β_1 which says that

$$\Pr[0.3 < \beta_1 < 0.7] = 0.95.$$

Secondly we know that $\beta_1 + \beta_2$ is very close to one, but almost certainly lower than this value. We translate this prior information into

$$\Pr[0.8 < \beta_1 + \beta_2 < 1) = 0.99.$$

Since the fractiles of the Student distribution with 10 degrees of freedom are $t_{0.95} = 2.23$ and $t_{0.99} = 3.17$, the application of formula (4.20) (adapted) and (4.11) gives the following prior moments for β_1 and $\beta_1 + \beta_2$:

$$E(\beta_1) = 0.5, \quad M_{11}^0 = 124.3, \quad \mathrm{Var}(\beta_1) = 0.01005,$$
$$E(\beta_1 + \beta_2) = 0.9, \quad \mathrm{Var}(\beta_1 + \beta_2) = 0.001244.$$

It follows that $E(\beta_2) = 0.4$. Since $\mathrm{Var}(\beta_1 + \beta_2) = \mathrm{Var}(\beta_1) + \mathrm{Var}(\beta_2) + 2\,\mathrm{Cov}(\beta_1, \beta_2)$, we have to fix $\mathrm{Var}(\beta_2)$ in order to get the covariance. Let us choose $\mathrm{Var}(\beta_2) = \mathrm{Var}(\beta_1) = 0.01005$. Then the prior covariance between the two parameters is equal to -0.0094. The correlation coefficient is equal to -0.94. It is close to -1 because β_2 has to be low (high) when β_1 is high (low).

A common practice consists in eliciting prior information only on a subset of the components of β and to remain non-informative on the other components. This happens because often one has prior information only on a subset of the parameters, such as the parameters of interest, or at least a part of them. So one wishes to be non-informative on the nuisance parameters. Or one has such vague information on some parameters that it is not worth eliciting an informative prior on them: a diffuse prior is a convenient simplification. The notion of non-informative or diffuse prior is discussed in detail in Section 4.3. Let us just indicate here how to be non-informative on a subset of β. For instance, let us partition β' into $(\beta_1'\ \beta_2')$, and the other vectors and matrices correspondingly. If we want to be non-informative on β_2 we set

$$\beta_0 = \begin{pmatrix} \beta_1^0 \\ 0 \end{pmatrix}, \qquad M_0 = \begin{pmatrix} M_{11}^0 & 0 \\ 0 & 0 \end{pmatrix}. \tag{4.21}$$

In operations where M_0 has to be inverted, the inverse of M_0 is formed by the inverse of the submatrix M_{11}^0 completed by rows and columns of zeros. Note that the posterior parameters given in (2.89)–(2.92) are well defined even in the case where M_0 is a singular matrix as in (4.21).

4.2.4 The Predictive Method

The direct assessment method just described is very appealing, but it has one serious drawback. It can lead to a low value of the predictive density of the observed sample or it may be in contradiction with the ideas one can have on the predictive density of the model. So there may be a problem of coherency. Kadane, Dickey, Winkler, Smith, and Peters (1980) introduced a method which is based on the predictive density of the model. It consists in asking questions about certain quantiles of the predictive density at various possible settings of the exogenous variables. The underlying parameters of the elicited predictive density are then recovered. The prior parameters can also be recovered, since the predictive density depends on them.

The predictive density of the linear regression model under a natural conjugate prior density is provided by Theorem 2.24 for a future sample. But the same result holds for the current sample by replacing the posterior parameters by the prior ones, and the future data by the current ones. This gives

$$p(y) = f_t(y|X\beta_0, s_0, (I_T + XM_0^{-1}X')^{-1}, \nu_0). \tag{4.22}$$

For a single observation, it is the univariate Student density

$$p(y_t) = f_t(y_t|x_t'\beta_0, s_0, (1 + x_t'M_0^{-1}x_t)^{-1}, \nu_0). \tag{4.23}$$

The method proposed by Kadane, Dickey, Winkler, Smith, and Peters (1980) consists in eliciting all the prior parameters β_0, M_0, s_0, and ν_0 by asking questions about the quantiles of $p(y)$ conditionally on different values for the exogenous variables. The method turns out to be rather clumsy for s_0 and ν_0. Therefore we present an adaptation of the method, supposing that values for s_0 and ν_0 result from an elicitation method presented previously. The problem is then to recover β_0 and M_0 from subjective assignments of the quantiles of the predictive distribution.

It is relatively easy to get an estimation of β_0. If x_t is of dimension k, we must be able to give $m \geq k$ assignments of the median of y_t. Let us call X_m an $m \times k$ matrix (of full rank) of values of the exogenous variables. For each row x_t of this matrix, a value of the median of y is required. Let us denote $y_{0.50}$ as the vector of these assigned medians. Then we can construct β_0 by least squares:

$$\beta_0 = (X_m'X_m)^{-1}X_m'y_{0.50}. \tag{4.24}$$

If we had a numerical value for the 'spread' matrix S_m of the predictive density of a sample y_m of size m, we could equate it to its theoretical counterpart given by

$$s_0(I_m + X_m'M_0^{-1}X_m) \tag{4.25}$$

(where s_0 and X_m are given), and solve for the value of M_0 (the reason for working with the spread rather than the variance matrix is to allow for a value of ν_0 smaller than two). The solution is

$$M_0 = s_0\left[(X_m'X_m)^{-1}X_m'(S_m - s_0I_m)X_m(X_m'X_m)^{-1}\right]^{-1}. \tag{4.26}$$

The difficulty resides in eliciting the numerical value of S_m. Let us give an idea of the method in the univariate case ($m = k = 1$). The spread of the predictive density for a single observation is

$$S(y_m|x_m) = s_0(1 + x_m^2 M_0^{-1}). \tag{4.27}$$

Using the same trick as from (4.19) to (4.20), we know that

$$S(y_m|x_m) = \nu_0\left[(y_{0.75} - y_{0.50})/(t_{0.75} - t_{0.50})\right]^2, \tag{4.28}$$

where t_α is the corresponding quantile of the standardized Student density with ν_0 degrees of freedom. Thus apart from the median $y_{0.50}$ of y_m that has been elicited to get β_0, the third quartile of the predictive distribution has to be elicited for the same value of x_m.

For eliciting a spread matrix of size m larger than k, independent questions about the predictive quantiles of $(y_1|x_1), (y_2|x_2), \dots$ are sufficient to build the diagonal elements of S_m, but not for the off-diagonal elements. We can stop here if we impose zero prior covariances. Questions about the quantiles of $(y_2|y_1, x_1, x_2)$ are necessary to obtain a PDS matrix of spreads. The least we can say is that it is rather awkward to answer such questions. See the paper by Kadane, Dickey, Winkler, Smith, and Peters (1980) for details.

4.2.5 *Simplifications for Assigning Prior Covariances*

The difficulty of the betting method and of the predictive method is the elicitation of covariances. The predictive method guarantees that the obtained matrices S_m and M_0 are PDS, but the necessary burden is quite heavy. Simpler methods are therefore welcome.

(i) One method which does not guarantee that the resulting M_0 is PDS has been proposed by Zellner (1985). Let us see how it works in the simple case of the bivariate regression model

$$y_t = x_t \alpha + z_t \beta + \epsilon_t. \tag{4.29}$$

The predictive variance of y_t can be obtained from one assignment of $(y_{0.50}, y_{0.75}|x, z)$. Two assignments are necessary to obtain the prior means and prior variances of α and β. The prior covariance of (α, β) can be obtained from the data and the three elicited variances:

$$\mathrm{Cov}(\alpha, \beta) = \frac{\mathrm{Var}(y_t) - \mathrm{Var}(\epsilon_t) - x_t^2 \, \mathrm{Var}(\alpha) - z_t^2 \, \mathrm{Var}(\beta)}{2\, x_t z_t}. \tag{4.30}$$

This can be repeated for several couples of values of (x, z), and if the results are not too different, an average of the covariances can be used. See Zellner's paper for a description of the method in the case of k exogenous variables.

To illustrate the difficulty of eliciting a positive definite matrix, suppose that we have three assignments of $(y_{0.50}, y_{0.75}|x_i, z_i)$ (for $i = 1, 2, 3$), from which we deduce three values V_i^2 of the predictive variance by using (4.28). Then we have to solve a system of three equations for $\mathrm{Var}(\alpha)$, $\mathrm{Var}(\beta)$, $\mathrm{Cov}(\alpha, \beta)$:

$$\begin{aligned}
V_1^2 &= x_1^2 \, \mathrm{Var}(\alpha) + z_1^2 \, \mathrm{Var}(\beta) + 2\, x_1 z_1 \, \mathrm{Cov}(\alpha, \beta) \\
V_2^2 &= x_2^2 \, \mathrm{Var}(\alpha) + z_2^2 \, \mathrm{Var}(\beta) + 2\, x_2 z_2 \, \mathrm{Cov}(\alpha, \beta) \\
V_3^2 &= x_3^2 \, \mathrm{Var}(\alpha) + z_3^2 \, \mathrm{Var}(\beta) + 2\, x_3 z_3 \, \mathrm{Cov}(\alpha, \beta)
\end{aligned} \tag{4.31}$$

under the constraints that

$$\mathrm{Var}(\alpha) \geq 0, \quad Var(\beta) \geq 0, \quad \mathrm{Var}(\alpha)\,\mathrm{Var}(\beta) - \mathrm{Cov}^2(\alpha, \beta) \geq 0. \tag{4.32}$$

The interesting question is: given the two assignments of $(y_{0.50}, y_{0.75})$ conditionally on (x_1, z_1) and (x_2, z_2), what is the admissible range for the assignment of $(y_{0.50}, y_{0.75})$ conditionally on (x_3, z_3)? The answer should be found from the conditions

$$\text{Var}(\alpha) \geq 0$$
$$\Leftrightarrow [K_1 z_2 z_3 V_1^2 - K_2 z_1 z_3 V_2^2 + K_3 z_1 z_2 V_3^2]/(K_1 K_2 K_3) \geq 0,$$

$$\text{Var}(\beta) \geq 0$$
$$\Leftrightarrow [K_1 x_2 x_3 V_1^2 - K_2 x_1 x_3 V_2^2 + K_3 x_1 x_2 V_3^2]/(K_1 K_2 K_3) \geq 0, \qquad (4.33)$$

$$\text{Var}(\alpha) \text{Var}(\beta) - \text{Cov}^2(\alpha, \beta) \geq 0$$
$$\Leftrightarrow 2 [K_1^2 K_2^2 V_1^2 V_2^2 + K_1^2 K_3^2 V_1^2 V_3^2 + K_2^2 K_3^2 V_2^2 V_3^2]$$
$$\geq K_1^4 V_1^4 + K_2^4 V_2^4 + K_3^4 V_3^4,$$

where $K_1 = x_2 z_3 - x_3 z_2$, $K_2 = x_1 z_3 - x_3 z_1$, and $K_3 = x_1 z_2 - x_2 z_1$. So the answer to the question is not trivial (since V_3 appears in all inequalities in a non-linear way). If the range obtained is not admissible, the assessments must be altered. The problem becomes more complex as the number of regressors increases.

(ii) Another method which delivers a prior covariance matrix very easily is Zellner's g prior distribution, see Zellner (1986b). We have up to now considered the regression model $y \sim N(X\beta, \sigma^2 I_T)$, for which a natural conjugate prior has been defined. Let us consider a hypothetical sample y_0 with the *same* design matrix X as observed:

$$y_0 \sim N(X\beta, g\sigma^2 I_T), \qquad (4.34)$$

where g is an unknown positive scalar. The natural conjugate argument tells us that the conditional prior density of β is

$$\varphi(\beta|\sigma^2) = f_N(\beta|\beta_0, g\sigma^2 (X'X)^{-1}), \qquad (4.35)$$

with $\beta_0 = (X'X)^{-1} X' y_0$; of course as y_0 is an hypothetical sample, we are free to select the prior mean of β as we like. But the prior precision matrix M_0 is equal to $g X'X$. Thus the prior covariance matrix is constrained to be proportional to the variance matrix of the least squares estimator, or the prior correlation matrix is completely determined by the observed data. This is convenient, but quite restrictive. We leave it as an exercise to check that under a g prior the posterior mean and variance of β are

$$E(\beta|y) = \frac{g\beta_0 + \hat{\beta}}{1 + g} \quad \text{and} \quad \text{Var}(\beta|\sigma^2, y) = (X'X)^{-1} \frac{\sigma^2}{1 + g}. \qquad (4.36)$$

The degree of precision is governed by a single number g. For $g = 0$, we get the ordinary least squares results as posterior mean. This remark directly introduces us to the next topic: non-informative priors.

4.3 The Quantification of Ignorance

In a certain number of cases, there is very little or just no prior information on the parameters and consequently one would like to avoid eliciting a prior. One may also desire to make inference without any prior information to study the sensitivity of the inference process to the prior density. In these cases the question is to find a convenient mathematical expression to replace $\varphi(\theta)$ in Bayes's formula for computing the posterior density. This mathematical expression should represent some form of prior 'ignorance'. This is especially the case when one has to integrate out nuisance parameters as explained in Subsection 2.2.2 in order to obtain the marginalized likelihood function.

4.3.1 Ancient Justifications for Ignorance Priors

Devising a non-informative prior is an old problem. The first principle, which can be found in the literature to justify a uniform prior, relates to the principle of insufficient reason (or of indifference). This principle was formalized by Pierre Simon de Laplace (1749–1827) in his book *A Philosophical Essay on Probabilities*. According to this principle, two events are equiprobable if there are no grounds for choosing between them. So with a fair die, the probability of getting a six is $1/6$. On a finite interval, say $[0, 1]$, if we have no grounds for choosing between two subintervals of equal length, we say that they are equiprobable. By choosing smaller and smaller intervals, we get a uniform density in the limit. However, things are not always as simple as shown for instance by Bertrand's paradox, which is as follows. Consider a circle and drop a rule at random over it. What is the probability that the length of the resulting chord is greater than the radius? We can reason on the angular distance or on the Cartesian distance to the centre. Applying the principle of insufficient reason to each case, we get two different answers: $2/3$ and $\sqrt{3}/2$; see Kyburg (1970: Chap. 3) for more details. For this reason, the principle is regarded with much suspicion nowadays.

Another historical justification for the uniform prior as a measure of indifference is found in Thomas Bayes' paper of 1763, *An Essay Toward Solving a Problem in the Doctrine of Chances*. Taking a binomial sampling process on X of parameter θ, Bayes justifies the use of a uniform prior on θ by considering the predictive density of X. If we know nothing before the trial, $\Pr(X = p)$ is constant, which implies that the prior on θ is uniform. See Stigler (1982) for more details on the interpretation of Bayes' paper.

4.3.2 Modern Justifications for Ignorance Priors

Bayes' argument was long forgotten and the principle of insufficient reason was regarded with much scepticism. The modern discussion on the definition and justification of non-informative priors can be classified as follows:

1) Arguments about the limiting behaviour of the posterior density when the sample size is increasing, with the idea that the prior information should have a decreasing weight compared with the sample information as the sample size increases. The first illustration of this idea was given by the principle of stable inference of Savage. The second illustration which is worth mentioning is that of the reference prior due to Bernardo (1979).

2) Arguments of invariance mainly to answer the critics addressed to the principle of insufficient reason. We have mainly under this rubric Jeffreys' invariance principle. But others also exist.

3) Arguments of scientific reporting. Suppose we have a natural conjugate prior density and we would like to report inference results and display their sensitivity to the prior information. We have to use a set of prior parameters which says that the prior information we introduce is less and less precise so as to reach a situation of absence of prior information. This is the concept of the limit of a natural conjugate prior density.

There are other principles used to define a non-informative prior density that we shall not review. Let us just mention the maximal entropy prior. In the discrete case, the entropy of a density φ defined over Θ is defined as

$$\mathcal{E}(\varphi) = -\sum_{i=1}^{n} \varphi(\theta_i) \log \varphi(\theta_i). \tag{4.37}$$

As the entropy is related to the information contained in φ, the density which contains the minimal information is that having the maximum entropy. If Θ has n elements, the maximum of (4.37) is obtained for $\varphi(\theta_i) = 1/n$. The discussion for the continuous case is very technical and the reader should refer for instance to Berger (1985a: 90) for more details. See also Bernardo (1979) for the notion of a reference prior which is based on the same type of idea.

4.3.3 Stable Inference

This point of view is a refinement of the old principle of insufficient reason. Since the posterior density is proportional to the product of the prior and the likelihood function, a uniform prior on a sufficiently large interval leads to a posterior density which is proportional to the likelihood function. As it is difficult to work with truncated distributions, the uniform prior over an interval will be approximated by an improper density (which does not integrate to unity), a uniform prior over the entire real line. Thus to express prior ignorance for a location parameter, such as a regression coefficient β in a linear regression model, we take

$$\varphi(\beta) \propto 1. \tag{4.38}$$

For a scale parameter, for instance the variance σ^2 of the error term in a regression model, the problem is a bit more complex as this parameter takes its values in $\mathbb{R}^+$. As a solution one takes a uniform prior on a convenient transformation of σ^2, such as the logarithm of σ^2, which takes its values on the real line. We have

$$\varphi(\log \sigma^2) \propto 1 \quad \Rightarrow \quad \varphi(\sigma^2) \propto 1/\sigma^2, \tag{4.39}$$

as the Jacobian of the transformation from $\log \sigma^2$ to σ^2 is $|\partial \log \sigma^2 / \partial \sigma^2| = 1/\sigma^2$.

Incidentally one can see that despite the fact that this type of prior is not a proper density, the posterior density is in general a proper density provided the number of observations is greater than the number of parameters.

The posterior density can be considered as the approximation of a posterior density evaluated under a proper prior density. Edwards, Lindman, and Savage (1963) give an upper bound to the absolute mean error which is committed when using an improper prior instead of a proper prior on a given interval; see also DeGroot (1970: 198–201).

4.3.4   *Jeffreys' Invariance Principle*

The view adopted by Jeffreys (1961) is different as it relies on a different interpretation of probability. Savage's principle is equivalent to considering the posterior density obtained under a diffuse prior as an approximation to the true posterior density obtained under an informative prior which is a summary of the subjective and personal prior information of the decision maker. On the contrary, Jeffreys considers probability from an objective point of view, that is to say the expression of the consensus existing among different persons, obtained on the basis of a set of observations. When there is no observation, what kind of consensus is it possible to obtain? Here the matter is to define a general principle formalizing ignorance.

Let us suppose that we have a likelihood function $l(\theta; y)$ and an 'objective' prior $\varphi_1(\theta)$. The likelihood function can equivalently be written as a function of η if $\eta = f(\theta)$ is in one-to-one correspondence with θ. Let us call $\varphi_2(\eta)$ the objective prior on η. Jeffreys' invariance principle requires that

$$\varphi_1(\theta)\, d\theta = \varphi_2(\eta)\, d\eta, \qquad (4.40)$$

or in other words the procedure for assigning the prior does not depend on the way the model is parameterized. Jeffreys shows that this principle implies that the prior be defined by

$$\varphi(\theta) \propto |I(\theta)|^{1/2}, \qquad (4.41)$$

where $|I(\theta)|$ denotes the determinant of the Fisher information matrix associated with the likelihood function of the model. For $\theta \in \mathbb{R}^k$ an element of this matrix is defined by

$$I_{ij} = -\mathrm{E}\, \frac{\partial^2 \log l(\theta; y)}{\partial \theta_i \partial \theta_j}, \qquad (4.42)$$

where the expectation is taken with respect to the sampling density of y. It should be stressed that Jeffreys' prior is not invariant for the functional form of the prior, which may actually change with the parameterization. This can easily be seen by an example.

Example 4.5 Let $y_t \sim N(\mu, 1)$. The information matrix is $I(\mu) = 1$, so that

$$\varphi_1(\mu) \propto 1,$$

which is constant with respect to the parameter. Consider the parameterization $\mu = 1/\eta$, i.e. $y_t \sim N(1/\eta, 1)$, assuming of course $\eta \neq 0$. The information matrix is $I(\eta) = 1/\eta^4$, so that

$$\varphi_2(\eta) \propto 1/\eta^2,$$

and the prior is proportional to the inverse of the square of the parameter. This prior is also obtained by transforming the prior $\varphi_1(\mu)$ with the usual technique for the transformation of densities:

$$\varphi_2(\eta) = \varphi_1(1/\eta) \left| \frac{\partial(1/\eta)}{\partial \eta} \right| \propto 1/\eta^2.$$

The last point of the previous example is the consequence of a general principle: if η is a reparameterization of θ, defined by $\theta = f(\eta)$, the transformation being one to one and differentiable, then

$$I(\eta) = J\,I(\theta)\,J', \tag{4.43}$$

where

$$J = \frac{\partial \theta}{\partial \eta'} = \left(\frac{\partial \theta_i}{\partial \eta_j} \right) \tag{4.44}$$

(the Jacobian matrix of the transformation), and all matrices on the right of the equality are evaluated at $\theta = f(\eta)$. Note that θ, η, and $f(.)$ are all vectors of dimension k. As a direct consequence, if we transform the posterior density of θ, obtained using Jeffreys' prior and the likelihood function $l(\theta; y)$, into the posterior of η, we find that the latter is exactly the posterior density of η that is obtained using Jeffreys' prior $I(\eta)^{1/2}$ with the likelihood function $l[f(\eta); y]$. In this sense, under Jeffreys' prior, the inference is invariant to reparameterizations. This is not the case with Savage's stable inference principle (which would lead to defining the prior of η as proportional to one in the previous example).

Jeffreys' invariance principle is very appealing in the case of a single parameter. In the case of several parameters, it is subject to problems as can be readily seen by an example.

Example 4.6 Consider $y_t \sim N(\mu, \sigma^2)$, with both parameters unknown. The information matrix is

$$I(\mu, \sigma^2) = \begin{pmatrix} \dfrac{1}{\sigma^2} & 0 \\ 0 & \dfrac{1}{2\sigma^4} \end{pmatrix}.$$

If we apply the invariance principle to both parameters we get

$$\varphi(\mu, \sigma^2) \propto \frac{1}{\sigma^3}.$$

In this prior, there is a factor $1/\sigma$ coming from the first diagonal element of the information matrix relative to μ. This factor is different from the result (a constant) we got in the previous example when σ^2 was assumed to be known. The above prior is also different from that given by the application of Savage's principle to μ and σ^2, which is proportional to $1/\sigma^2$. In the multi-dimensional case, Jeffreys recommends applying his principle to each parameter separately, i.e. to consider one parameter at a time, the others being fixed. In this example, this gives

$$\varphi(\mu) \propto 1,$$
$$\varphi(\sigma^2) \propto 1/\sigma^2.$$

The joint prior is then the product of the separate priors, in this case

$$\varphi(\mu, \sigma^2) \propto 1/\sigma^2.$$

Let us now give Jeffreys' prior for the parameters of the linear regression model. Its derivation is left to the reader (it is just an extension of the previous example).

Theorem 4.7 *For the linear regression model, Jeffreys' prior for the parameters* $\beta \in \mathbb{R}^k$ *and* $\sigma^2 > 0$ *is*

$$\varphi(\beta, \sigma^2) \propto 1/\sigma^2.$$

It can be factorized as

$$\varphi(\beta|\sigma^2) \propto 1,$$
$$\varphi(\sigma^2) \propto \sigma^{-2}, \tag{4.45}$$

but this kind of factorization is quite arbitrary because the joint prior is not a proper density: it does not integrate to a finite value. Non-informative or diffuse priors are thus not probability measures, but this is not a big deal for inference if the posterior is a probability measure. However, we follow the tradition of talking about prior 'densities' even if they are not integrable.

Jeffreys' prior of Theorem 4.7 is not computed as the square root of the determinant of the information matrix. The strict application of Jeffreys' principle would yield

$$\varphi(\beta, \sigma^2) \propto \sigma^{-(k+2)}. \tag{4.46}$$

Jeffreys' prior is obtained by application of the principle firstly to β as if σ^2 were known—this yields $\varphi(\beta) \propto 1$—and secondly to σ^2 as if β were known—this yields $\varphi(\sigma^2) \propto \sigma^{-2}$—and multiplying the two results. Since this way of defining the prior for the linear model was recommended by Jeffreys himself, in violation of his invariance principle, this prior is called Jeffreys' prior.

Jeffreys' invariance principle has been criticized in particular by Lindley (1972) on the basis of the following arguments:

1) In the multivariate case, in order to recover some similarity with the classical results (loss of a degree of freedom per parameter to estimate, see the next subsection), the basic principle has to be changed and thus it loses part of its appeal.

2) Jeffreys wants his prior to represent a consensus among people. However, this prior depends on the likelihood function and it will be different according to the sampling process which is considered. In a game of heads or tails, one can chose to sample according to a binomial process (number of successes for n drawings) or according to a Pascal process (number of drawings necessary to obtain r successes). The shape of Jeffreys' prior on the probability p of a success is different in each case. On the contrary, the natural conjugate prior is always the same (a beta density).

3) The blind use of Jeffreys' prior leads to an automatic practice of statistics which tends to hide certain traps and can lead to incoherencies. This practice gave birth to some strange results. An example is the treatment of the error-in-variables model by Zellner (1971) who finds the least squares estimator as a Bayesian estimator because he uses an ill-specified diffuse prior for an incidental parameter (see Florens, Mouchart, and Richard 1974). We can also quote the example of Jeffreys' prior for unit root models used by Phillips (1991a) and the controversy which resulted (see Chapter 6).

4.3.5 *Non-informative Limit of a Natural Conjugate Prior*

If the likelihood function of a model belongs to the exponential family, it is possible to find a prior density which is natural conjugate. This prior density is proper if its parameters take their values in the admissible domain of definition. Novick (1969) uses the natural conjugate family with values of its parameters chosen at a boundary of their domain, in order to define a non-informative prior. Then he wonders what quantity of information from the sample is necessary for the corresponding posterior parameters to lie in their admissible domain of variation; see also Raiffa and Schlaifer (1961: 66). This type of procedure presents two advantages.

1) The non-informative prior is viewed as the limit of a proper prior density the analytical form of which is specified. Consequently the temptation consisting in 'blindly' using a non-informative prior, which can be misleading in certain circumstances, is avoided. This issue is illustrated in Lubrano, Pierse, and Richard (1986) for the error-in-variables model. It sheds light on the traps that exist when one desires to specify a prior density on incidental parameters.

2) For reporting scientific information in a non-decisional framework, it is interesting to proceed to a sensitivity analysis which consists in observing how the posterior evolves in response to the prior information. This can be done by varying the precision of the prior information. At the limit where this precision is zero, this corresponds to a non-informative prior obtained as the limit of a natural conjugate prior.

Let us illustrate this approach for the linear regression model in the case of k regressors. The natural conjugate prior is a normal–inverted gamma-2 density, see (4.8). Its kernels are reproduced here for ease of reference:

$$\kappa(\beta|\sigma^2) = \sigma^{-k} \exp\left[-\frac{1}{2\sigma^2}(\beta - \beta_0)' M_0(\beta - \beta_0) \right],$$

$$\kappa(\sigma^2) = \sigma^{-(\nu_0+2)} \exp\left(-\frac{s_0}{2\sigma^2} \right). \tag{4.47}$$

The domain of variation of the parameters is

$$M_0 \in \mathcal{C}^k, \qquad \nu_0 > 0, \qquad s_0 > 0. \tag{4.48}$$

By letting the parameters M_0 and s_0 go to zero, we find the non-informative priors by computing the limits of the kernels (not the limit of the densities that are trivially equal to zero). Setting $M_0 = 0$, which corresponds to a zero precision, this gives for the conditional prior of β:

$$\kappa(\beta|\sigma^2) = \sigma^{-k}, \tag{4.49}$$

which is different from Jeffreys' prior on β.

Setting $s_0 = 0$, we find the non-informative limit of the kernel of the prior on σ^2 to be

$$\kappa(\sigma^2) = \sigma^{-(\nu_0+2)}, \tag{4.50}$$

which receives different interpretations according to the choice which is made for ν_0. To get at the boundary of the domain of ν_0, it is sufficient to take $\nu_0 = 0$. We then get a prior for σ^2 which is equivalent to Jeffreys' prior.

By combining the non-informative limits of the kernels of the conditional prior on β and of the marginal prior on σ^2, we get the kernel of the joint diffuse prior on (β, σ^2), which is

$$\kappa(\beta, \sigma^2) = \sigma^{-(\nu_0+k+2)}. \tag{4.51}$$

Let us discuss the choice of ν_0 and examine its influence on the behaviour of the Student posterior density of β which has $\nu_* = \nu_0 + T$ degrees of freedom—see (2.92):

1) For $\nu_0 = 0$, we get a prior which may look unusual as it is different from Jeffreys' prior for the regression model:

$$\kappa(\beta, \sigma^2) = \sigma^{-(k+2)} \tag{4.52}$$

(ironically, this is the prior which results from a strict application of Jeffreys' invariance principle). The posterior density of β is proper if $T \geq k$, being centred on the least squares estimate. There is no loss of degrees of freedom when there are more and more exogenous variables (until the point where $T < k$): the posterior variance is

$$\mathrm{Var}(\beta|d) = \frac{s}{T-2}(X'X)^{-1}, \tag{4.53}$$

where s is the sum of squared OLS residuals—see Theorem 2.21.

2) For $\nu_0 = -k$ we get Jeffreys' prior

$$\kappa(\beta, \sigma^2) = \sigma^{-2}. \tag{4.54}$$

The posterior density of β is proper if $T \geq k$ and the classical result of the loss of k degrees of freedom is recovered: the posterior variance is

$$\text{Var}(\beta | d) = \frac{s}{T - k - 2} (X'X)^{-1}. \tag{4.55}$$

Remark: The last formula reminds one of the *estimator* of the sampling variance of the OLS estimator, which is

$$\text{Var}(\hat{\beta}) = \frac{s}{T - k} (X'X)^{-1}.$$

Apart from the fundamental difference of interpretation between a posterior variance and an estimator of a sampling variance, there is a small numerical difference: in the Bayesian formula, there is a loss of two degrees of freedom in comparison with the classical formula. This arises because in the Bayesian approach, one integrates the nuisance parameter σ^2 in the joint posterior. In the classical approach, the sampling variance is $\sigma^2(X'X)^{-1}$, which is also the posterior conditional variance $\text{Var}(\beta | \sigma^2, d)$. The classical trick to get rid of the nuisance parameter is to substitute it with an estimator, in this case $s/(T - k)$.

4.3.6 *The Reference Prior*

Reference priors were introduced by Bernardo (1979) with the aim of finding a prior, specific for each inference problem and parameter of interest, which guarantees that we get the maximum information from the data, or in other terms that the distance between the prior and the posterior is maximum for a given type of experiment. Bernardo uses the Kullback–Leibler divergence as a measure of distance between two densities.

The ϕ-divergence between two densities f and g is defined by

$$D_\phi = \int \phi(f(x)/g(x)) \, g(x) \, dx.$$

For $\phi(z) = (\sqrt{z} - 1)^2$, we get the square of the Hellinger distance. We get the negative entropy for $\phi(z) = z \log(z)$ and the χ^2 distance for $\phi(z) = (z - 1)^2$. The Kullback–Leibler divergence is in fact the negative entropy and is expressed as

$$D_{KL} = \int \log(f(x)/g(x)) \, f(x) \, dx. \tag{4.56}$$

For a given experiment, the information is given by

$$\int \log \frac{\varphi(\theta|y)}{\varphi(\theta)} \, \varphi(\theta|y) d\theta. \tag{4.57}$$

Since the desired prior must be a reference for every type of outcome for y, the expected information of the experiment is considered, with

$$\int p(y) \int \log \frac{\varphi(\theta|y)}{\varphi(\theta)} \, \varphi(\theta|y) d\theta \, dy, \tag{4.58}$$

which actually measures the missing information about θ when the prior is $\varphi(\theta)$. The reference prior is defined to be the prior which maximizes the missing information. Under some mild regularity conditions, variational arguments lead to the following implicit equation:

$$\varphi(\theta) \propto \exp\left[\int l(\theta; y) \log \varphi(\theta|y) \, dy\right]. \tag{4.59}$$

The solution of this implicit equation is in general difficult, but interesting approximations can be obtained in the large-sample case. In particular, if the posterior density is asymptotically normal, then the reference prior is given by Jeffreys' prior. This argument extends to the multivariate case where the joint reference prior is the multivariate Jeffreys prior (obtained by applying Jeffreys argument to the whole parameter θ and not to each individual component of θ). However, when we are interested in making inference only on a subset of θ, say θ_1, which means that the other components of θ, say θ_2, are considered as nuisance parameters, this result no longer holds.

The principle used when there are nuisance parameters is relatively simple and natural. The expected information of the experiment is computed with the marginalized likelihood function, integrating out the nuisance parameters. Its application is on the contrary rather complex. The main problem lies in the choice of the prior with which the likelihood function is marginalized, that is to say $\varphi(\theta_2|\theta_1)$. Berger and Bernardo (1989) provide an algorithm. More details are given in Berger and Bernardo (1992) where the current status of the question is exposed. Berger and Yang (1994) have used a reference prior for the AR(1) model that is detailed and discussed in Chapter 6.

4.4 Restrictive Properties of the *NIG* Prior

In this section we deal with the natural conjugate prior for the regression model when one is informative on the regression coefficients and not informative on the error variance. In this case, the dependence between β and σ^2 may have unwanted consequences for the posterior moments. A solution to avoid these problems consists in imposing prior independence between σ^2 and β. Moreover, this type of prior helps to reveal more clearly a conflict of information between the prior information and the data than the natural conjugate prior.

4.4.1 *Diffuse Prior on σ^2 and Informative Prior on β*

In the regression model, it is tempting to use a diffuse prior on σ^2 since it is not usual to have prior information on this (nuisance) parameter. But a difficulty arises with the natural conjugate prior if we want to be non-informative on σ^2 and informative on β (or a subset of it).

Let us illustrate this problem in the simple case where there is one regressor and no constant term, to simplify the algebra. Let us note

$$\lambda_0 = \mathrm{E}(\sigma^2) = \frac{s_0}{\nu_0 - 2}, \tag{4.60}$$

so that

$$\mathrm{Var}(\beta) = \mathrm{E}(\sigma^2)\, M_0^{-1} = \lambda_0 / M_0. \tag{4.61}$$

A non-informative prior on σ^2 may be obtained in different ways. One way is to let both s_0 and ν_0 tend to 0, since the prior inverted gamma-2 kernel of σ^2 tends to Jeffreys' prior $1/\sigma^2$, see (4.47). Suppose that this is done in such a way that λ_0 tends to infinity. If one desires to keep the same marginal prior precision on β, one has to keep the ratio λ_0/M_0 constant, whatever the value of λ_0. Consequently M_0 has to go to infinity at the same speed as λ_0, which implies that we are more and more precise a priori on β. It is then not surprising to find that the posterior expectation of β becomes dominated by the prior information:

$$\lim_{M_0 \to \infty} \beta_* = \lim_{M_0 \to \infty} \frac{\beta_0 + x'y/M_0}{1 + x'x/M_0} = \beta_0. \tag{4.62}$$

For $M_0 \to \infty$, the posterior expectation of β converges to the prior expectation β_0, and the posterior variance of β converges to a null matrix; see Bauwens (1991), and Richard (1973: 180–182). This is a very undesirable feature of the learning mechanism. It comes from the prior dependence between β and σ^2, as revealed by the fact that the variance of β is proportional to the prior mean of σ^2.

This paradox illustrates that we cannot elicit prior information on β based on its marginal moments when we are not informative on σ^2. It does not imply that we cannot use the prior

$$\varphi(\beta, \sigma^2) = f_N(\beta|\beta_0, \sigma^2\, M_0^{-1})\, \sigma^{-2}. \tag{4.63}$$

Rather, it means that in using this prior it is quite difficult to choose M_0 since this cannot be done through prior ideas on the marginal distribution of β (which does not exist).

Two responses are possible in the face of this paradox:

1) The first consists in the affirmation that the quality of the information on β depends on the importance of the noise represented by σ^2. If one thinks that the process under observation presents an important noise, the probability judgements one can make on β will necessarily be relatively vague. This is equivalent to saying that β and σ^2 are a priori dependent and that one cannot be informative on β while being diffuse on σ^2.

2) The second attitude consists in making β and σ^2 a priori independent, arguing that the prior information one has on β comes from a previous or hypothetical sample which has a variance that is different from the variance of the observed sample.

The second attitude implies leaving the natural conjugate framework and factorizing the prior as

$$\varphi(\beta, \sigma^2) = \varphi(\beta)\,\varphi(\sigma^2). \qquad (4.64)$$

This approach is detailed in Section 4.5.

4.4.2   Conflicting Information

Bayes' theorem describes a learning mechanism: the revision of prior information by the observation of a sample. What happens when both prior and sample information deliver conflicting messages? What kind of behaviour can one expect from the learning mechanism? A desirable property would be that it warns us about the conflict. In the regression model, it turns out that a conflict tends to be masked when the prior is natural conjugate.

In the linear regression model, a conflict of information means that the prior expectation is very different from the least squares estimate, relatively to some norm (such as the prior precision or the sampling precision). But with a natural conjugate prior, the posterior density of β is unimodal. Its mode is equal to its posterior expectation which is a weighted average of the prior expectation β_0 and of the OLS estimator $\hat{\beta}$, the weights being given by the prior precision M_0 and the sample precision $X'X$; see Subsection 2.7.3 for a complete discussion. An information conflict cannot be revealed by the posterior mean. It can be detected through the posterior variance of β which is a function of the distance between β_0 and $\hat{\beta}$. As explained in Subsection 2.7.3, if this difference is big enough, the posterior variance of β may be greater than the prior variance. But the addition of the prior precision M_0 and the sampling precision $X'X$ is an opposite factor which masks the difference.

If the prior and the posterior densities do not belong to the same family, the conflict of information can be revealed more easily: for example, it may happen that the posterior density is bimodal, one mode coming from the prior and the other from the likelihood. Leaving the natural conjugate framework may be desirable.

4.5   Student Prior and Poly-t Densities

In the previous section, we concluded that it could be useful to define a prior for the regression model, where the variance of the error term is independent of the regression coefficients, i.e. a prior of the type (4.64). There are many possible ways of defining $\varphi(\beta)$ in this prior, assuming that we stick to an inverted gamma-2 density, or its diffuse version, on σ^2. We are of course free to choose the prior which reflects our prior opinions as best as possible. But there is a price to pay for this freedom: numerical integration of the posterior density. Although a lot of progress has been achieved, we do not believe that with the present state of technology, we can just say to researchers 'elicit your prior and do the required numerical integrations'. Moreover, it is not usual in econometrics to dispose of more information on a parameter than its prior location (or mean) and dispersion (or variance). Therefore, we are usually more or less indifferent between 'regular' prior densities which have the elicited mean and variance. If this is true, it is useful to choose the prior in order to minimize the burden of numerical integration of the posterior, provided it can incorporate the elicited prior moments.

In this section, we show that a convenient prior is the product of a Student density for β and an inverted gamma-2 density for σ^2. It is convenient because it can be elicited practically by the techniques described in Section 4.2 for the natural conjugate prior, and because the computational burden it implies for computing the posterior results is light: it consists of unidimensional numerical integration, whatever the dimension of β.

The problem of the natural conjugate prior is that the variance of the prior on β is not independent of the variance of the sampling process (σ^2). Recall that a natural conjugate prior can be interpreted as the posterior resulting from the combination of the likelihood of a previous (or hypothetical) sample and a diffuse prior. The dependence problem comes from the assumption that the variance of the sampling process is the same in the current sample as in the previous one. To break the dependence, one has just to assume that the variance changes. This situation is equivalent to the case where the sample can be split into two subsamples, each having a different variance. The model is

$$y_1|X_1 \sim N_{T_1}(X_1\beta, \sigma_1^2 I_{T_1}),$$
$$y_2|X_2 \sim N_{T_2}(X_2\beta, \sigma_2^2 I_{T_2}). \tag{4.65}$$

So let us first examine the linear regression model with unequal variances and then give some details on the Student prior.

4.5.1 *Pooling Two Independent Samples*

Applying Theorem 2.21 to each subsample, the likelihood function of the two subsamples (assumed to be independent) is

$$l(\beta, \sigma_1^2, \sigma_2^2; d) \propto \sigma_1^{-T_1} \sigma_2^{-T_2} \exp\left[-\frac{1}{2}\left(\frac{Q_1}{\sigma_1^2} + \frac{Q_2}{\sigma_2^2}\right)\right], \tag{4.66}$$

where d denotes the data of the two samples, and

$$\begin{aligned}
Q_i &= s_i + (\beta - b_i)'M_i(\beta - b_i), \\
M_i &= X_i'X_i, \\
b_i &= (X_i'X_i)^{-1}X_i'y_i, \\
s_i &= y_i'y_i - y_i'X_i(X_i'X_i)^{-1}X_i'y_i,
\end{aligned} \tag{4.67}$$

for $i = 1, 2$, assuming that $T_i > k$. Jeffreys' diffuse prior is

$$\varphi(\beta, \sigma_1^2, \sigma_2^2) \propto \frac{1}{\sigma_1^2} \frac{1}{\sigma_2^2}. \tag{4.68}$$

The marginal posterior density of β is obtained by multiplying (4.66) and (4.68) and integrating out the variances, which gives

$$\varphi(\beta|y) \propto [s_1 + (\beta - b_1)' M_1 (\beta - b_1)]^{-T_1/2} \\ \times [s_2 + (\beta - b_2)' M_2 (\beta - b_2)]^{-T_2/2}. \tag{4.69}$$

This density is composed of the product of two Student kernels, one for each sample. It was named *double-t* by Zellner (1971: 101). Later, Drèze (1978) called it a 2-0 *poly-t*, as it is a member of the *m-n* poly-t family, which is defined as a product of m Student kernels divided by another product of n Student kernels, see Subsection A.2.8. The 2-0 poly-t can be evaluated numerically by unidimensional integration. To see why, let us compute the integral of the joint posterior kernel as

$$\int_{\mathbb{R}^k} \int_0^\infty \int_0^\infty (\sigma_1^2)^{-\frac{T_1+2}{2}} (\sigma_2^2)^{-\frac{T_2+2}{2}} \exp\left[-\frac{1}{2}\left(\frac{Q_1}{\sigma_1^2} + \frac{Q_2}{\sigma_2^2}\right)\right] d\sigma_1^2 \, d\sigma_2^2 \, d\beta. \tag{4.70}$$

We make a transformation from σ_1^2, σ_2^2 to h and c with

$$h = \frac{\sigma_1^2 + \sigma_2^2}{\sigma_1^2 \sigma_2^2} \in (0, \infty),$$

$$c = \frac{\sigma_2^2}{\sigma_1^2 + \sigma_2^2} \in [0, 1]. \tag{4.71}$$

The Jacobian is $h^{-3} c^{-2} (1-c)^{-2}$. The inverse transformation is $\sigma_1^2 = 1/(ch)$ and $\sigma_2^2 = 1/[(1-c)h]$. Thereafter, the integral in (4.70) is equal to

$$\int_{\mathbb{R}^k} \int_0^\infty \int_0^1 c^{\frac{T_1-2}{2}} (1-c)^{\frac{T_2-2}{2}} h^{\frac{T-2}{2}} \exp\left[-\frac{1}{2}h\left(c Q_1 + (1-c) Q_2\right)\right] dc \, dh \, d\beta$$

$$\propto \int_{\mathbb{R}^k} \int_0^1 c^{\frac{T_1-2}{2}} (1-c)^{\frac{T_2-2}{2}} [c Q_1 + (1-c) Q_2]^{-T/2} \, dc \, d\beta, \tag{4.72}$$

where $T = T_1 + T_2$. The last result is obtained by the integrand property of the gamma density:

$$\int_0^\infty h^{\frac{T}{2}-1} \exp\left(-\frac{hQ}{2}\right) dh \propto Q^{-T/2}. \tag{4.73}$$

Next, we have

$$[c\,Q_1 + (1-c)\,Q_2]^{-T/2} = [s_c + (\beta - b_c)'\,M_c(\beta - b_c)]^{-T/2}$$
$$\propto f_t(\beta|b_c, s_c, M_c, T-k)\,|M_c|^{-1/2}\,s_c^{-\frac{T-k}{2}}, \tag{4.74}$$

where f_t denotes a Student density as defined by (A.81), and

$$\begin{aligned}
M_c &= c\,M_1 + (1-c)\,M_2, \\
b_c &= M_c^{-1}\,[c\,M_1 b_1 + (1-c)\,M_2 b_2], \\
s_c &= c\,(s_1 + b_1'\,M_1 b_1) + (1-c)\,(s_2 + b_2'\,M_2 b_2) - b_c'\,M_c b_c'.
\end{aligned} \tag{4.75}$$

Finally, we substitute (4.74) in (4.72), and we integrate β analytically, so that the integral of the posterior density is reduced to

$$K = \int_0^1 c^{\frac{T_1-2}{2}}(1-c)^{\frac{T_2-2}{2}}|M_c|^{-1/2}\,s_c^{-\frac{T-k}{2}}\,dc. \tag{4.76}$$

This is the integral to be computed numerically. The iterative Simpson rule (described in Section 3.3) has been found to be efficient for dealing with the integrand, which can have a very narrow peak and be very skewed. By construction, (4.76) is the integrating constant of the 2-0 poly-t posterior density (4.69). The posterior moments of β are obtained by marginalizing the conditional moments:

$$\begin{aligned}
\mathrm{E}(\beta|y) &= \mathrm{E}_{c|y}[\mathrm{E}(\beta|c,y)] = \mathrm{E}_{c|y}(b_c), \\
\mathrm{Var}(\beta|y) &= \mathrm{E}_{c|y}[\mathrm{Var}(\beta|c,y)] + \mathrm{Var}_{c|y}[\mathrm{E}(\beta|c,y)].
\end{aligned} \tag{4.77}$$

The outer moments are computed using the density of c given y, which is of course

$$\varphi(c|y) = K^{-1}\,c^{\frac{T_1-2}{2}}(1-c)^{\frac{T_2-2}{2}}|M_c|^{-1/2}\,s_c^{-\frac{T-k}{2}}. \tag{4.78}$$

More explicitly,

$$\mathrm{E}(\beta|y) = \int_0^1 b_c\,\varphi(c)\,dc,$$

$$\mathrm{Var}(\beta|y) = \int_0^1 M_c^{-1}\frac{s_c}{T-k-2}\,\varphi(c|y)\,dc \tag{4.79}$$
$$+ \int_0^1 [b_c - \mathrm{E}(\beta|y)]\,[b_c - \mathrm{E}(\beta|y)]'\,\varphi(c|y)dc.$$

Remarks:

1) The sampling model (4.65) can be extended to allow β to differ partly between the two subsamples, with $\mathrm{E}(y_i|X_i) = X_i\beta_i$ $(i = 1, 2)$, $\beta_1' = (\beta_{11}'\,\gamma')$, and $\beta_2' = (\beta_{21}'\,\gamma')$. Under Jeffreys' prior, the posterior density of β_1 and β_2 is then a 2-0 poly-t, but it can be factorized into three parts: $\varphi(\gamma|d)$ which is 2-0 poly-t, $\varphi(\beta_{11}|\gamma, d)$ which is Student, and $\varphi(\beta_{21}|\gamma, d)$ which is also Student. If β_1 and β_2 are completely different (so that γ does not exist), the posterior densities of β_1 and β_2 are Student and independent.

2) The results of this subsection can be extended to the analysis of three or more independent samples. With m samples, the posterior is an m-0 poly-t. Note that to write (4.67), we have assumed that each subsample size is larger than the number of exogenous variables ($T_i > k$).

3) The above algorithm is very useful for direct inference on the coefficients, but is of little help when one wants to make inference on non-linear functions of the parameters. In that case, it is more useful to sample directly from the posterior distribution as underlined in Section 3.4.1. As shown in Appendix B, it is relatively easy to sample from a 2-0 poly-t at low cost.

4.5.2 Student Prior

As should be clear from the previous analysis, a Student prior on β in the regression model can be interpreted as the posterior density of a hypothetical sample analysed under a non-informative prior, but having a different variance than the actual sample. In the natural conjugate framework, the prior for the linear regression model is written as in (4.8). In the case where the hypothetical prior sample has a variance ω^2 which is different from the variance σ^2 of the observed sample, we have

$$\begin{aligned}
\varphi(\omega^2) &= f_{Ig}(\omega^2|1, \tau_0), \\
\varphi(\beta|\omega^2) &= f_N(\beta|\beta_0, \omega^2 M_0^{-1}), \\
\varphi(\sigma^2) &= f_{Ig}(\sigma^2|s_0, \nu_0).
\end{aligned} \qquad (4.80)$$

The Student prior is obtained by integration of ω^2:

$$\begin{aligned}
\varphi(\beta) &= \int \varphi(\beta|\omega^2)\, \varphi(\omega^2)\, d\omega^2 \\
&= f_t(\beta|\beta_0, 1, M_0, \tau_0).
\end{aligned} \qquad (4.81)$$

Note that the scale parameter of the inverted gamma-2 prior on ω^2 has been set equal to 1, rather than a free parameter r_0. This is not restrictive, since the Student density (4.81) depends on the ratio M_0/r_0 (see Subsection A.2.5).

With the prior independence between β and σ^2, it is easy to be non-informative on σ^2, while being informative on β. Let us write this prior density as

$$\begin{aligned}
\varphi(\sigma^2) &\propto 1/\sigma^2, \\
\varphi(\beta) &\propto [1 + (\beta - \beta_0)' M_0 (\beta - \beta_0)]^{-(\tau_0 + k)/2}.
\end{aligned} \qquad (4.82)$$

The posterior density is obtained by combining the prior and the likelihood function as given in Theorem 2.21:

$$\begin{aligned}
\varphi(\beta, \sigma^2|d) \propto {}& [1 + (\beta - \beta_0)' M_0 (\beta - \beta_0)]^{(\tau_0 + k)/2} \\
& \times (\sigma^2)^{-(T+1)/2} \exp\left\{ -\frac{1}{2\sigma^2} \left[s + (\beta - \hat{\beta})' X'X(\beta - \hat{\beta}) \right] \right\}.
\end{aligned} \qquad (4.83)$$

The marginal posterior in β is obtained by integrating out σ^2, which gives

$$\varphi(\beta|d) \propto [1 + (\beta - \beta_0)'M_0(\beta - \beta_0)]^{-(\tau_0+k)/2}$$
$$\times [s + (\beta - \hat{\beta})'X'X(\beta - \hat{\beta})]^{-T/2}. \qquad (4.84)$$

This density is a 2-0 poly-t, and is composed of one Student kernel that comes from the prior and another that comes from the sample. As we have two Student kernels, each with its own location, the posterior density of β can be skewed in the case of conflicting information and even bimodal in extreme cases. Usually, the posterior variance of β is greater than that obtained with a natural conjugate prior (with the same prior parameters). Let us note finally that if we are non-informative on β by letting M_0 go to zero, $\varphi(\beta|d)$ is the Student density obtained with Jeffreys' prior.

It is of course also possible to be informative on σ^2, as in (4.80): in (4.84), s is replaced by $s + s_0$, and T by $T + \nu_0$.

4.5.3   A Wage Equation for Belgium

We consider a wage equation based on Phillips's curve which relates the growth rate of real wages $\Delta \log(W/P)$ to the growth rate of the consumption price index $\Delta \log P$, the lagged growth rate of labour productivity $\Delta \log Q_{-1}$, and the rate of unemployment UR:

$$\Delta \log(W/P) = \beta_0 + \beta_1 \Delta \log P + \beta_2 \Delta \log Q_{-1} + \beta_3 UR + \epsilon. \qquad (4.85)$$

The data consist of 22 annual observations for Belgium, covering the period 1954-1976. They were provided by the Belgian Planning Office.

We use this example to illustrate the elicitation of a prior density and to highlight the difference of behaviour in the face of conflicting information between the natural conjugate prior and the Student prior. Inference results with Jeffreys' diffuse prior are given in Table 4.6.

Let us begin by eliciting the inverted gamma-2 prior for σ^2. This type of Phillips's curve usually does not fit the data very well (in terms of R^2), as the variables are in first difference (except UR). We make the following assignments in term of pseudo-R^2:

$$\Pr(R_p^2 < 0.40) = 0.50,$$
$$\Pr(R_p^2 < 0.55) = 0.75,$$

which imply that $\overline{p}_{0.50}/\overline{p}_{0.25} = 0.60/0.45 = 1.33$, see (4.16). In Table 4.5, we find that the value of 1.33 in the penultimate column corresponds to $\nu_0 = 11$. By applying (4.18), we deduce a value of $0.00069 \times 0.097/(1-0.40) = 0.000112$ for s_0 (0.097 is the 0.50 quantile of the inverted gamma-2 with 11 degrees of freedom, see Table 4.5, and 0.00069 is the empirical variance of the dependent variable). Next, we want to introduce prior information on the regression coefficient of $\Delta \log P$, and to be non-informative on the other coefficients. We assign the 50 per cent highest probability interval for β_1 to be $[-0.10, 0.10]$, which implies $E(\beta_1) = 0$. This corresponds to Friedman's version of Phillips's curve, with no monetary illusion. As for $\nu_0 = 11$, the third quartile of the Student distribution is 0.697, the resulting value of the second diagonal element of M_0 is 0.000658, by

Table 4.6 *Prior and posterior moments for Belgian wage equation*

	σ^2	β_0	β_1	β_2	β_3
Jeffreys	0.000458	0.032	0.41	0.30	−0.54
	(0.000173)	(0.014)	(0.15)	(0.10)	(0.41)
Prior	0.0000166	0	0	0	0
	(0.778×10^{-8})	(∞)	(0.16)	(∞)	(∞)
NIG	0.000271	0.032	0.40	0.28	−0.53
	(0.0000752)	(0.011)	(0.11)	(0.08)	(0.32)
Student–IG	0.00290	0.033	0.28	0.28	−0.41
	(0.0000854)	(0.011)	(0.11)	(0.08)	(0.33)

Entries are posterior means and standard deviations (in parentheses) under Jeffreys' prior, a natural conjugate (NIG) prior, and a Student–inverted gamma-2 prior. Prior moments are given in the block labelled 'Prior'.

applying (4.20). This implies a prior standard deviation of 0.15, nearly the same value as the posterior standard deviation of β_1 obtained under Jeffreys' prior. Hence there is a certain degree of conflict about β_1: the difference between the posterior mean under a diffuse prior (or the OLS estimate), equal to 0.41, and the prior mean (0) represents about 2.7 prior standard deviations (and also 2.7 sampling standard errors). This conflict can be visualized in Fig. 4.3 (compare the prior density and the posterior under the diffuse prior).

Table 4.6 summarizes the prior moments and also gives the inference results obtained under a normal–inverted gamma-2 prior and under a Student–inverted gamma-2 prior.

Under the natural conjugate prior, this conflict is not at all reflected in the posterior which is located roughly in the same place as the sample information, but is more concentrated. With the Student prior, the corresponding posterior is pulled in the direction of the prior mean, reflecting a small conflict of information. However, the poly-t posterior is also more concentrated than the Student prior, as shown in Fig. 4.3. In the three posterior densities, zero is in the extreme left tail of the posterior density: there is clearly a degree of monetary illusion in the Belgian real wage rate. More details on this example can be found in Bauwens (1991).

4.6 Special Topics

This section covers two topics: exact restrictions on the parameters, which must be dealt with carefully to avoid a 'conditionalization paradox' exhibited by Kolmogorov (1950), and a special non-informative Student prior, based on the principle of exchangeability introduced by De Finetti (1937).

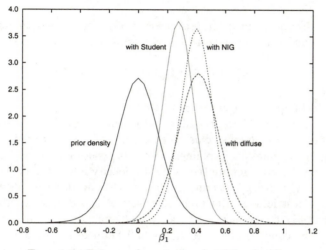

FIG. 4.3. Prior and posterior densities for β_1

4.6.1 *Exact Restrictions*

An exact restriction on the parameters is a function of the parameters which is assigned some numerical value with a probability equal to one. For example, the difference between two parameters is equal to zero—a linear restriction—or the product of two parameters is equal to one (a non-linear one).

The simplest and unequivocal way to conduct Bayesian inference in the presence of exact restrictions is to make explicit the restrictions, and reduce the dimension of the parameter space. Let us assume that the parameter vector θ can be split into α and β, and that $\alpha = f(\beta)$ are the functional restrictions. In the likelihood function $l(\theta; y)$, we can make the restrictions explicit, that is to say write the likelihood function only in terms of β:

$$l(\theta; y) = l(\alpha, \beta; y) = l[f(\beta), \beta; y] = l_r(\beta; y) \qquad (4.86)$$

(where the subscript r indicates that the restrictions have been taken into account). The prior density is then naturally defined on β, and Bayesian inference proceeds as usual. If prior or posterior probability statements on α are required, they can easily be made by transforming the prior or posterior density of β into that of α by the usual technique of transformation of random variables. Of course, the *joint* density function of α and β is degenerate.

Example 4.8 In the two-variable regression equation $y_t = x_t\beta_1 + z_t\beta_2 + \epsilon_t$, if we want to impose exactly the restriction $\beta_1 + \beta_2 = 1$, we can substitute $1 - \beta_1$ for β_2 and work with $y_t - z_t = (x_t - z_t)\beta_1 + \epsilon_t$.

In the ML approach, if the restricted likelihood function defined in (4.86) is maximized with respect to β, one gets the constrained ML estimator $\tilde{\beta}$, and

$\tilde{\alpha} = f(\tilde{\beta})$ is the constrained ML estimator of α. A second way to obtain the ML estimators $\tilde{\beta}$ and $\tilde{\alpha}$ is to perform the calculation

$$\max_{\alpha,\beta} l(\alpha, \beta; y) \text{ subject to } \alpha = f(\beta) \tag{4.87}$$

(using the technique of Lagrange multipliers).

Conceptually, there is a second way to conduct Bayesian inference in the presence of exact restrictions, which is somewhat analogous to the second way of performing ML estimation, explained above. It consists in acting as if there are no restrictions, i.e. to compute the posterior density in the full parameterization θ, so that $\varphi(\theta|y) \propto l(\theta; y)\varphi(\theta)$ and at the end to condition the posterior density by the exact restrictions. However, this way of proceeding is subject to two difficulties: firstly, the prior density has to be defined on the complete parameter θ; secondly, the conditioning operation is not defined in a unique way, because the conditioning event is of zero probability (or measure). It is well known that the conditional probability of an event, given another event of zero measure (such as a particular value of a continuous random vector), is defined by computing a limit—see e.g. Anderson (1984: 12). But there may be several ways to arrive at the limit, as illustrated by the following example taken from Drèze and Richard (1983: 522).

Example 4.9 Let $\varphi(\alpha,\beta) = 1$ for $0 < \alpha$, $\beta < 1$, i.e. a uniform density on the unit square, and let $D = \{\alpha, \beta \mid \alpha = \beta\}$ be a diagonal of that square. Obviously, $\Pr(D) = 0$. Suppose we are interested in the density of β given that $\alpha = \beta$. There are at least two ways to impose this equality:

1) Let $\delta = \beta - \alpha$. The joint density of β and δ is $\varphi(\beta, \delta) = 1/2$ for $0 < \beta < 1$ and $-1 < \delta < 1$, whence $\varphi(\delta) = 1/2$ and $\varphi(\beta|\delta = 0) = 1$.
2) Let $\rho = \beta/\alpha$. We get $\varphi(\beta, \rho) = \beta/\rho^2$ for $0 < \beta < 1$ and $\rho > 0$, $\varphi(\rho) = (2\rho^2)^{-1}$, and $\varphi(\beta|\rho = 1) = 2\beta$.

Both $\varphi(\beta|\delta = 0)$ and $\varphi(\beta|\rho = 1)$ are possible forms of $\varphi(\beta|D)$. But they are different. Which one to select depends on the parameterization which seems best suited for the purpose one has in mind.

The first approach described in this subsection to conduct Bayesian inference with exact restrictions requires an explicit choice of parameterization; this choice can be dictated by the fact that prior information is directly available on some parameters (β in our notation). It avoids the possible multiplicity of solutions of the second approach. The caveat of the first approach is that we must be able to make the restrictions explicit in one way or another. Implicit restrictions cannot be dealt with.

4.6.2 *Exchangeable Priors*

With this type of prior, we want to say that several parameters $\theta_1, \theta_2, \cdots, \theta_n$ have the same prior mean and variance and, moreover, that their order can be changed without changing the prior information. They can be exchanged. For instance, we have information on the rate of failure θ of a group of machines, but we have no information on the rate of failure θ_i of each individual machine. Here is another example: we are interested in estimating a system of seemingly unrelated equations, say consumption functions for similar countries. Their parameters should be alike, but not necessarily equal.

How can we build a prior density to reflect this type of prior information? Lindley and Smith (1972) have considered for this purpose the notion of exchangeability introduced by De Finetti (1937).

Definition 4.10 *A sequence of random events (or variables) $\{X_1, X_2, \ldots, X_n\}$ is said to be an exchangeable sequence if its probability does not depend on the order of appearance of the events (or variables):*

$$\Pr(X_1, X_2, \ldots, X_n) = \Pr(\text{any permutation of } \{X_1, X_2, \ldots, X_n\}).$$

The interest in exchangeability is that it implies the existence of a particular model for X and it associates a prior density to this model. This association is done via the 'representation' theorem first proved by De Finetti (1937):

Theorem 4.11 *Let us consider a sequence $(X_1, X_2, \ldots, X_n)$ of $\{0, 1\}$-valued random variables with probability measure $\Pr$. If this sequence is judged to be exchangeable, then there exists a probability density $\varphi(.)$ such that $\Pr$ can be represented by*

$$\Pr(x_1, x_2, \ldots, x_n) = \int_0^1 \prod_{i=1}^n \theta^{x_i} (1-\theta)^{1-x_i} \varphi(\theta) \, d\theta.$$

Thus in this case, $\prod_{i=1}^n \theta^{x_i}(1-\theta)^{1-x_i}$ is the likelihood function of the sample and $\varphi(\theta)$ is the prior density. This theorem is given here for the Bernouilli process, but it holds more generally for real-valued quantities; see Bernardo and Smith (1994: 177). Let us now try to devise an exchangeable prior for the coefficients of the regression model $y_t \sim N(x_t'\beta, \sigma^2)$. Assuming normality, the process generating the β_i is exchangeable if we have

$$\beta|\sigma^2 \sim N_k(\xi\iota, \sigma^2 R^{-1}), \tag{4.88}$$

with ι a $k \times 1$ vector of ones. The conditional mean ξ is common to all the β_i and the conditional variance matrix has the special structure

$$R^{-1} = \begin{pmatrix} 1 & \rho & \cdots & \rho \\ \rho & 1 & & \vdots \\ \vdots & & \ddots & \rho \\ \rho & & \cdots & 1 \end{pmatrix}, \qquad -1 \le \rho \le 1, \tag{4.89}$$

implying the same correlation coefficient for all pairs of parameters. From De Finetti's theorem, we know that in order to form a probability judgement on β, we have just to elicit a prior distribution on the hyperparameters ξ and σ^2 such that

$$\varphi(\beta) = \int \varphi(\beta|\xi,\sigma^2)\,\varphi(\xi|\sigma^2)\,\varphi(\sigma^2)\,d\xi\,d\sigma^2. \qquad (4.90)$$

We suppose that ρ is fixed and known a priori. Usually ρ is taken equal to zero. Let us consider a normal–inverted gamma-2 prior for ξ and σ^2:

$$\begin{aligned} \xi|\sigma^2 &\sim N(\xi_0, \sigma^2\psi_0^{-1}), \\ \sigma^2 &\sim IG_2(s_0, \nu_0). \end{aligned} \qquad (4.91)$$

Then by the usual properties of the normal density and formulae for the inversion of partitioned matrices,

$$\beta|\sigma^2 \sim N_k\left(\xi_0\iota, \sigma^2[R - R\iota(\psi_0 + \iota'R\iota)^{-1}\iota'R]^{-1}\right). \qquad (4.92)$$

Integrating out σ^2, we get the marginal Student prior of β:

$$\beta \sim t_k\left(\xi_0\iota, s_0, R - R\iota(\psi_0 + \iota'R\iota)^{-1}\iota'R, \nu_0\right). \qquad (4.93)$$

If we let ψ_0 go to zero, we get the non-informative limit of this exchangeable prior, which is still marginally Student, but with the singular precision matrix $(I_k - \iota\iota'/\iota'\iota)$ when $R = I_k$.

5

DYNAMIC REGRESSION MODELS

5.1 Introduction

The previous chapters have introduced all the essential tools of Bayesian analysis. Beyond this, our purpose in the rest of this book is to explain and illustrate how these tools can be used for inference and prediction with dynamic econometric models. This class of models is obviously very large, but stochastic difference equations that are linear in the variables (although not necessarily in the parameters) have been intensively used by econometricians for the last 20 years or so. Their justification, which is to a large extent due to their relative empirical success in economics, has even been grounded by the statistical theory of 'reduction of dynamic experiments' of Florens and Mouchart (1982, 1985a, 1985b) as explained in Section 5.2. We show how to extend to the dynamic case the notion of Bayesian cut seen in the static case to justify conditional inference, how to take account of non-stationarity in the Bayesian approach, and how to treat initial conditions which necessarily occur in dynamic models. In Section 5.3, we explain how Bayesian inference can be used for single-equation dynamic models and particularly a popular reparameterization known as the error correction model after Hendry and Richard (1982). In Section 5.4, we treat the particular case of models with autoregressive errors, and in Section 5.5, we discuss the specific issues of moving average errors. Finally, in Section 5.6, we illustrate the empirical use of the error correction model by an analysis of a money demand function for Belgium.

5.2 Statistical Issues Specific to Dynamic Models

Broadly speaking, a model is dynamic every time the variables are indexed by time and appear with different time lags. For instance, $y_t = \beta_0 x_t + \beta_1 x_{t-1} + u_t$ is a simple dynamic model, called a distributed lag model. Here the dynamic structure appears on the exogenous variables. It can also appear on the endogenous variables with for instance $y_t = \alpha y_{t-1} + u_t$ which is an autoregressive (AR) model. Finally the dynamic structure can also appear on the error process as considered in Sections 5.4 and 5.5. In Chapter 8, we consider models where the dynamic structure is non-linear in the lags of the dependent variable, whereas it is linear in the models of this chapter. In Chapter 7, we consider a different class of models, where the dynamic structure is put on the variance of the error process. In Chapter 9, we consider linear dynamic systems of equations.

5.2.1   *Reductions: Exogeneity and Causality*

Reductions by marginalization or by conditioning were introduced in Section 2.5 quite generally. No attention was paid to the issue of whether the model might be dynamic rather than static. The notions of cut and of exogeneity were defined relative to a sample of size T, i.e. they were global notions. In a static model (i.e. of independent observations), it does not make any difference if the cut is defined for the complete sample or for each observation. In the sequel of this book, we consider dynamic data generating processes, i.e. processes where the generated random variable is indexed by time. The function which associates t to x_t is called the trajectory of the process and the ordered collection of observations the history of the process. It is convenient to note

$$X_0^T = (x_0, x_1, \ldots, x_T). \qquad (5.1)$$

The first observation x_0 plays a specific role and is called the initial condition of the process. It represents presample information, the state of the system when it begins to be observable. The model can be characterized by its data density $f(X_1^T | x_0, \theta)$, by conditioning on the initial value x_0 (other approaches are discussed in Subsection 5.2.3). For model building, it is convenient to consider the data density from the point of view of sequential analysis which is based on the analysis of the generating process of an observation x_t conditional on the past and on the initial condition. This amounts to considering the following factorization:

$$f(X_1^T | x_0, \theta) = \prod_{t=1}^{T} f(x_t | X_0^{t-1}, \theta). \qquad (5.2)$$

In a sequential model like (5.2) it can be made apparent how prior information is revised by the arrival of a new observation. We can now introduce the definition of a sequential cut.

Definition 5.1 *Let us consider a reparameterization of θ in α and β and a partition of x_t in y_t and z_t. A Bayesian sequential cut is obtained if α and β are a priori independent and if*

$$f(X_1^T | x_0, \theta) = \prod_{t=1}^{T} f(y_t | z_t, X_0^{t-1}, \alpha) \prod_{t=1}^{T} f(z_t | X_0^{t-1}, \beta). \qquad (5.3)$$

An immediate consequence of a sequential cut is that the two members of the likelihood function (5.4) can be treated separately for inference as we shall see below. We have the following theorem given in Florens and Mouchart (1985a).

Theorem 5.2 *If α, β, and z_t operate a Bayesian sequential cut, then α and β are a posteriori independent.*

Engle, Hendry, and Richard (1983) call this type of exogeneity *weak exogeneity*. In a dynamic model, there are subtleties due to the occurrence of lagged variables. In (5.3), the first product does not represent the sampling density of $(Y_1^T|Z_1^T, x_0)$ and the second product is not the sampling density of $(Z_1^T|x_0)$. Therefore, at the phase of model building, a sequential cut is not a sufficient condition to separate the generating process into two subprocesses that could be specified separately. Because we are in a dynamic framework, we have to introduce a new definition, considering what we can call a *global cut* (called an initial cut by Florens and Mouchart 1985a).

Definition 5.3 *Let us consider a reparameterization of θ in α and β and a partition of x_t in y_t and z_t. A Bayesian global cut is obtained if α and β are a priori independent and if the data density can be factorized as*

$$f(X_1^T|x_0, \theta) = \prod_{t=1}^T f(y_t|z_t, X_1^{t-1}, x_0, \alpha) \prod_{t=1}^T f(z_t|Z_1^{t-1}, x_0, \beta). \qquad (5.4)$$

We must point out that the parameters α and β are not necessarily the same in the sequential and in the global cut. A global cut introduces a restriction on the marginal process of z_t, which is

$$f(z_t|X_0^{t-1}, \beta) = f(z_t|Z_1^{t-1}, x_0, \beta). \qquad (5.5)$$

This means that the past of y_t is of no use for predicting z_t. This is the notion of non-causality due to Granger (1969). When both a sequential and a global cut hold, we have the notion of strong exogeneity introduced by Engle, Hendry, and Richard (1983).

Definition 5.4 *Let us consider a stochastic process in x_t indexed by θ and a partition of x_t in y_t and z_t. The variable z_t is said to be strongly exogenous if the reparameterization of θ into α and β operates a sequential cut (z_t is weakly exogenous for inference on α) and y_t does not Granger-cause z_t.*

If there is weak exogeneity, the only part of the data density that is relevant for inference on α is the first product in (5.4), which is indeed the likelihood kernel of α. The posterior density of α is obtained by

$$\varphi(\alpha|X_0^T) \propto \varphi(\alpha) \prod_{t=1}^T f(y_t|z_t, X_0^{t-1}, \alpha). \qquad (5.6)$$

The important thing to notice in (5.6) is that we do not need the second product in (5.3) even though it depends on y. We do not need to specify the marginal density $f(z_t|X_0^{t-1}, \beta)$ for inference on α.

For predictive inference on y given z, weak exogeneity is not sufficient. Let us start from the predictive density of X_1^T which is

$$f(X_1^T|x_0) = \int f(X_1^T|x_0, \theta)\, \varphi(\theta)\, d\theta. \qquad (5.7)$$

If there is a global cut, this becomes

$$f(X_1^T|x_0) = \int f(Y_1^T|Z_1^T, x_0, \alpha)\, \varphi(\alpha)\, d\alpha \int f(Z_1^T|x_0, \beta)\, \varphi(\beta)\, d\beta \qquad (5.8)$$
$$= f(Y_1^T|Z_1^T, x_0)\, f(Z_1^T|x_0),$$

because

$$\prod_{t=1}^{T} f(y_t|z_t, X_1^{t-1}, x_0, \alpha) = f(Y_1^T|Z_1^T, x_0, \alpha). \qquad (5.9)$$

From (5.8) we see that we can forget $f(Z_1^T|x_0, \beta)$ and $\varphi(\beta)$ to compute the predictive density of y given z. However, if there is only weak exogeneity, the first product in (5.3) is not the conditional density $f(Y_1^T|Z_1^T, x_0, \alpha)$ that we need to compute $f(Y_1^T|Z_1^T, x_0)$, because the second product in (5.3) depends on y. So in dynamic models, weak exogeneity is necessary and sufficient for posterior inference as in static models, but strong exogeneity is necessary for prediction.

5.2.2   Reduction of a VAR Model to an ADL Equation

A VAR (Vector autoregressive) model with independent normal error terms is a commonly used representation for a dynamic multivariate stochastic process. Let us consider the k-dimensional random variable x_t. The VAR model is noted:

$$[I_k - A(L)]x_t = v_t, \qquad (5.10)$$

where $A(L)$ is a matrix of lag polynomials of order p (without a term of degree 0 in L):

$$A(L) = A_1 L + A_2 L^2 + \cdots + A_p L^p \qquad (5.11)$$

and $v_t \sim N_k(0, \Sigma)$. For simplicity, we do not introduce deterministic variables in (5.10). In what follows, we assume that the initial conditions $x_0 \ldots x_{-p}$ are known, but we do not write them explicitly as conditioning variables. So we note simply X_{t-1} for the past of x_t, including the initial conditions. The VAR model has gained important popularity with the work of Sims (1980). Because it requires many parameters and therefore observations, and it often lacks a 'structural' interpretation, econometricians are interested in admissible reductions of this model. We can partition x_t and Σ conformably in

$$x_t = \begin{pmatrix} y_t \\ z_t \end{pmatrix} \text{ and } \Sigma = \begin{pmatrix} \Sigma_{yy} & \Sigma_{yz} \\ \Sigma_{zy} & \Sigma_{zz} \end{pmatrix} \qquad (5.12)$$

where y_t is a scalar and z_t has $k-1$ elements. This partition is done because we wish to find a regression equation where y_t is the explained variable and z_t are the explicative variables. We continue by proposing the conformable partitioning of $A(L)$ in

$$A(L) = \begin{pmatrix} A_y(L) \\ A_z(L) \end{pmatrix} = \begin{pmatrix} A_{yy}(L) & A_{yz}(L) \\ A_{zy}(L) & A_{zz}(L) \end{pmatrix}. \qquad (5.13)$$

We can factorize the normal distribution of x_t

$$x_t | X_{t-1} \sim N_k(A(L)x_t, \Sigma) \tag{5.14}$$

into the marginal distribution of z_t

$$z_t | X_{t-1} \sim N_{k-1}(A_z(L)x_t, \Sigma_{zz}) \tag{5.15}$$

and the conditional distribution of $y_t | z_t$

$$y_t | z_t, X_{t-1} \sim N(c'z_t + b(L)'x_t, \sigma^2), \tag{5.16}$$

where

$$\begin{aligned} c &= \Sigma_{zz}^{-1}\Sigma_{zy}, \\ b(L) &= A_y(L) - c'A_z(L), \\ \sigma^2 &= \Sigma_{yy} - \Sigma_{yz}\Sigma_{zz}^{-1}\Sigma_{zy}. \end{aligned} \tag{5.17}$$

A sequential cut is obtained if we define the parameters α and β introduced in (5.3) as

$$\begin{aligned} \alpha &= [c,\, b(L),\, \sigma^2], \\ \beta &= [A_z(L),\, \Sigma_{zz}]. \end{aligned} \tag{5.18}$$

We assume prior independence between α and β. From (5.15) and (5.16), we see that z is weakly exogenous for α without further restrictions, because (5.3) holds automatically in the VAR model. For strong exogeneity, however, we need the restriction of Granger non-causality:

$$A_{zy}(L) = 0, \tag{5.19}$$

so that lagged values of y_t do not appear in the marginal model (5.15). As weak exogeneity is automatically satisfied, the conditional model (5.16) can be analysed independently of the marginal model (5.15). This leads to the regression equation

$$y_t = c'z_t + b(L)'x_t + u_t, \tag{5.20}$$

where $u_t \sim N(0, \sigma^2)$. Introducing the partition

$$b(L) = (b_y(L)\, b_z(L)') \tag{5.21}$$

we can express (5.20) as

$$y_t = b_y(L)y_t + c'z_t + b_z(L)'z_t + u_t. \tag{5.22}$$

Inference in this type of dynamic regression model, called the ADL (Autoregressive Distributed Lag) model is studied in the next section.

As in the static case, the (weak) exogeneity property in the dynamic case is a direct consequence of the properties of the multivariate normal distribution. Suppose now that we have incidental parameters, so that (5.10) becomes

$$[I_k - A(L)](x_t - \mu_t) = v_t. \tag{5.23}$$

Let us partition the incidental mean vector μ_t as x_t in (5.12) and let us assume that μ_t is constrained by the linear relation

$$\mu_{yt} = \bar{c}'\mu_{zt}. \tag{5.24}$$

We have the joint distribution of x_t

$$x_t|X_{t-1} \sim N_k(\mu_t + A(L)(x_t - \mu_t), \Sigma), \tag{5.25}$$

which factorizes into the marginal model

$$z_t|X_{t-1} \sim N_{k-1}(\mu_{zt} + A_z(L)(x_t - \mu_t), \Sigma_{zz}), \tag{5.26}$$

and, given (5.24), the conditional model

$$y_t|z_t, X_{t-1} \sim N((\bar{c} - c)'\mu_{zt} + c'z_t + b(L)'(x_t - \mu_t), \sigma^2). \tag{5.27}$$

The parameters of (5.27) are defined by (5.17). To obtain a conditional model without incidental parameters, we need the restriction

$$c = \bar{c} \tag{5.28}$$

to eliminate the term $(\bar{c} - c)'\mu_{zt}$, and, given (5.28) and (5.24),

$$A_{yz}(L) - \bar{c}'A_{zz}(L) = A_{yy}(L)\bar{c}' - \bar{c}'A_{zy}(L)\bar{c}' \tag{5.29}$$

to eliminate the term $b(L)'\mu_t$. With these restrictions, if we define the parameters α and β of (5.4) by

$$\begin{aligned} \alpha &= [\bar{c}, b(L), \sigma^2], \\ \beta &= [A_z(L), \Sigma_{zz}, \mu_1, \ldots, \mu_T], \end{aligned} \tag{5.30}$$

z is weakly exogenous for α. Imposing (5.19) also gives strong exogeneity.

5.2.3   Treatment of Initial Observations

In a dynamic model, the distribution of the initial observations (hereafter denoted y_0) plays a special role. We explain here how to treat this first observation, taking the autoregressive process of order 1—AR(1)—as an illustration. We write this model as

$$y_t = \alpha y_{t-1} + u_t, \tag{5.31}$$

where u_t is supposed to be normal with zero mean and variance σ^2. We suppose that the process is stationary ($|\alpha| < 1$). There are two approaches to treat the initial observation when y_0 is actually observable, and one solution when y_0 is not observable.

Conditional approach: one conditions on particular values, typically the first observations of the sample, in which case all the inference is conditional on the chosen values. In that case, the data density to be used to apply Bayes' theorem is $f(y_1, \ldots, y_T | y_0, \theta)$, which in the case of AR(1) is proportional to

$$\sigma^{-T} \exp\left[-\frac{1}{2\sigma^2} \sum_{t=1}^{T} (y_t - \alpha y_{t-1})^2\right]. \tag{5.32}$$

Clearly this likelihood function leads to a simple Bayesian analysis in the natural conjugate framework as it is the same as that produced by a static linear regression model. But no account is taken of the distribution of y_0. This is an approximate solution.

Exact approach: one has to take into account the marginal density of the initial observations, noted $f(y_0 | \theta)$. The complete likelihood function is formed by the product $f(y_0 | \theta) f(y_1, \ldots, y_T | y_0, \theta)$. For AR(1), the marginal distribution of y_0 is obtained by considering that the process started in the infinite past so that $\mathrm{E}(y_0) = 0$ and $\mathrm{Var}(y_0) = \sigma^2 / (1 - \alpha^2)$. Consequently the complete likelihood function is

$$\begin{aligned} f(y_0, y | \theta) &= \sqrt{\tfrac{1-\alpha^2}{\sigma^2}} \exp\left(-\tfrac{1-\alpha^2}{2\sigma^2} y_0^2\right) \\ &\quad \times \sigma^{-T} \exp\left[-\tfrac{1}{2\sigma^2} \sum_{t=1}^{T} (y_t - \alpha y_{t-1})^2\right]. \end{aligned} \tag{5.33}$$

We must note of course that this complete likelihood function can be written only when the process is stationary. Zellner (1971: 189) shows that the influence of the initial condition on the posterior expectation of α decreases as the sample size grows.

Marginal approach: the question of the initial condition can be treated in a totally different way when y_0 is an unobserved random variable. It has to be provided with a density $f(y_0 | \theta)$. Then the likelihood function used to compute the posterior density of the parameters is obtained by integrating out y_0 from the joint density of the observables and unobservables:

$$f(y | \theta) = \int f(y | y_0, \theta) f(y_0 | \theta) dy_0. \tag{5.34}$$

In this approach, y_0 can be seen either as a missing observation or as a parameter. In the latter case, $f(y_0 | \theta)$ becomes a prior density. This makes no difference for inference. If $y_0 \sim N(0, \sigma^2 / (1 - \alpha^2))$, it is easy to verify that

$$f(y | \theta) \propto \sqrt{1 - \alpha^2} \, \sigma^{-T} \exp\left\{-\frac{1}{2\sigma^2} \left[\sum_{t=2}^{T} (y_t - \alpha y_{t-1})^2 + (1 - \alpha^2) y_1^2\right]\right\} \tag{5.35}$$

(by completing the square in y_0 and the properties of the normal density). This expression is exactly the same as that obtained for the exact approach, except that we have one observation less.

In the definitions of exogeneity and causality given in Subsection 5.2.1, we have used the conditional approach. Care should be taken in adapting these definitions to the marginal approach; see Florens and Mouchart (1985a) for details.

5.2.4 Non-stationarity

Bayesian inference with non-stationary data does not in principle raise specific difficulties like classical inference. Bayes' theorem obviously holds whether the data are stationary or not. The posterior density of a parameter or the predictive density of a future observation are conditional on the observed sample and contain all the information relevant for inference. But we have noted above that writing the complete likelihood function of an AR(1) model required the stationarity hypothesis because it not possible to define an invariant marginal distribution of y_0 in the AR(1) model in the case of a unit root ($\alpha = 1$). As a matter of fact, $y_0 \sim N(0, \sigma^2/(1-\alpha^2))$ is derived assuming that the process started in the infinite past. This assumption and the fact that y_0 is finite are not compatible with the possibility of a unit root or an explosive process.

Non-stationary data raise in fact conceptual difficulties which have led to the specific topics of unit roots and cointegration. These topics are treated in detail in Chapter 6 for unit roots and in Chapter 9 for cointegration. In this chapter, we suppose that the data are stationary.

5.3 Inference in ADL Models

5.3.1 Model Specification and Posterior Analysis

The ADL (Autoregressive Distributed Lag) model is defined by

$$\alpha(L)y_t = \beta(L)z_t + u_t, \tag{5.36}$$

where $u_t \sim IN(0, \sigma^2)$. The lag polynomials are defined by

$$\begin{aligned} \alpha(L) &= 1 - \alpha_1 L - \cdots - \alpha_p L^p, \\ \beta(L) &= \beta_0 + \beta_1 L + \cdots + \beta_p L^p. \end{aligned} \tag{5.37}$$

This is certainly one of the most widely used models in applied econometrics because it constitutes the general writing of 'error correction models', popularized by Davidson, Hendry, Srba, and Yeo (1978) for modelling the UK consumption function and later developed by Hendry and Richard (1982) and Hendry, Pagan, and Sargan (1984). For simplicity, we have restricted our attention to the case where there is only one exogenous variable z_t. The lag polynomials $\alpha(L)$ and $\beta(L)$ need not be of the same order p, but we can take p as the largest lag of all the polynomials by restricting coefficients to be equal to zero where needed. Using the conditional approach for the initial observations simplifies considerably both Bayesian and classical inference. Hence, we condition on the initial observations and we date them at $t = 0, -1, \ldots, -p+1$, i.e. we do not include the marginal density of the initial observations $f(y_0, \ldots, y_{1-p}|\theta, z_0, \ldots, z_{1-p})$ in the data density to compute the posterior density. For posterior analysis, if weak exogeneity of the z variables holds for β and σ^2, the results obtained for the static model (see Section 2.7) are directly applicable to the ADL case, provided we interpret the relevant densities and moments to be conditional on the initial observations.

5.3.2   *Truncation to the Stationarity Region*

The great question in dynamic regression models is of course that of stationarity. Let us consider for illustration the AR(1) model (5.31). The parameter α can in theory take any value, but we know that the behaviour of y_t is totally different if α is negative rather than positive while being less than one in absolute value, negative values introducing cycles. Values greater than one in absolute value induce non-stationarity and explosiveness. As we have chosen to be conditional on the initial values, stationarity does not matter for writing the likelihood function, but it is crucial for prediction. So there is interest in the possibility of introducing the information that the process is stationary. This kind of information is easy to introduce when $\alpha(L)$ is of degree 1, but becomes difficult for higher degrees. A convenient solution is just to truncate the region of integration to a subspace such as the stationarity region

$$A = \{\alpha : \text{ the roots of } \alpha(L) = 0 \text{ are out of the unit circle}\}. \qquad (5.38)$$

This amounts to incorporating in the prior density the indicator function of A as a multiplicative factor. The computation of posterior and predictive densities and moments has to be done by numerical integration in this case. Under a non-informative or a natural conjugate prior, the posterior density of the regression parameters α and β defined in (5.37) is Student. Draws of this density can be easily obtained. Truncated posterior moments and graphs of marginals are then obtained from these draws, rejecting the draws which do not lie in the region of stationarity. This is the rejection sampling method defined in Section 3.4.2. Note that truncation of the space of α modifies the posterior moments of all the parameters (not only of α). Computing the posterior probability of the set A (when truncation is not imposed a priori) corresponds to counting the percentage of sampled values of α that fall in A. The accepted sampled values of β serve to compute the truncated posterior moments. Obviously, if the posterior probability of A is close to one, the truncated and non-truncated results are not very different.

5.3.3   *Predictive Analysis*

For predictive analysis, we assume that strong exogeneity holds as defined in Section 5.2. The nice analytical results of the static regression model given in Section 2.7 are valid only for the case when h, the number of predictions, is equal to one. For more than one-step-ahead prediction, the predictive density is not known analytically, although its moments are. We illustrate the issue in a simple case, while the reader is referred to Koop, Osiewalski, and Steel (1995a) for more general results. We assume the model has one lag and one exogenous variable:

$$y_t = \alpha y_{t-1} + \beta_0 z_t + \beta_1 z_{t-1} + u_t, \tag{5.39}$$

and we want to compute the predictive density of y_{T+h} given the data on y and z for periods 0 to T (denoted X_0^T). Future observations for z are denoted $\tilde{Z}$. We know that

$$\begin{aligned}
y_{T+1}|X_0^T, \tilde{Z}, \beta, \sigma^2 &\sim N(\alpha y_T + \beta_0 z_{T+1} + \beta_1 z_T, \sigma^2), \\
y_{T+2}|y_{T+1}, X_0^T, \tilde{Z}, \beta, \sigma^2 &\sim N(\alpha y_{T+1} + \beta_0 z_{T+2} + \beta_1 z_{T+1}, \sigma^2), \\
&\cdots
\end{aligned} \tag{5.40}$$

while the posterior density of the parameters is

$$\beta, \sigma^2 | X_0^T \sim NIG(\beta_*, M_*, s_*, \nu_*), \tag{5.41}$$

where $\beta = (\alpha, \beta_0, \beta_1)'$. By the product of the two densities given by (5.40), we obtain the joint density of (y_{T+1}, y_{T+2}) conditional on the parameters and the sample, and we can integrate it with respect to y_{T+1}. Using Theorems A.14 and A.12 successively, the result is

$$\begin{aligned}
y_{T+2}|X_0^T, \tilde{Z}, \beta, \sigma^2 \sim N[&\alpha^2 y_T + \alpha\beta_0 z_{T+1} \\
&+ \alpha\beta_1 z_T + \beta_0 z_{T+2} + \beta_1 z_{T+1}, (1+\alpha^2)\sigma^2].
\end{aligned} \tag{5.42}$$

The next task is to integrate this density with respect to the parameters using the posterior density of β as defined in (5.41). However, there is no analytical solution because the conditional expectation $E(y_{T+2}|X_0^T, \tilde{Z}, \beta, \sigma^2)$ is not linear in the parameter β. Before explaining how one can compute numerically the predictive density of y_{T+2}, let us note that its moments can be computed analytically. For example,

$$\begin{aligned}
E(y_{T+2}|X_0^T, \tilde{Z}) &= E[E(y_{T+2}|X_0^T, \tilde{Z}, \beta)] \\
&= E(\alpha^2|X_0^T)\, y_T + E(\alpha\beta_0|X_0^T)\, z_{T+1} + E(\alpha\beta_1|X_0^T)\, z_T \\
&\quad + E(\beta_0|X_0^T)\, z_{T+2} + E(\beta_1|X_0^T)\, z_{T+1}
\end{aligned} \tag{5.43}$$

where the expectations in the last line are analytically known and easy to compute as they consist of first and second moments of the posterior Student density of β. More generally, for the h-step-ahead conditional expectation, moments of order h of the Student density are required, since the conditional expectation of y_{T+h} depends on α^h. For h larger than ν_* (the degrees of freedom of the Student density), these posterior moments do not exist; hence the predictive expectation of y_{T+h} does not exist. However, since $\nu_* \geq T$, the problem arises only for prediction at a long horizon. The rejection method devised above to restrict the domain of variation of the parameters to the stationarity region does not modify the analytical result obtained in (5.43) provided that the posterior expectations

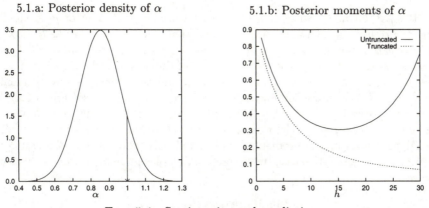

FIG. 5.1. Stationarity and prediction

of the parameters are obtained from the truncated Student posterior density of β. Finally, we explain how to compute numerically the predictive density of y_{T+2}. Obviously,

$$
\begin{aligned}
f(y_{T+2}|X_0^T, \tilde{Z}) &= \int \int \int \int f(y_{T+2}|X_0^T, \tilde{Z}, \alpha, \beta_0, \beta_1, \sigma^2) \\
&\quad \times \varphi(\alpha, \beta_0, \beta_1, \sigma^2|X_0^T)\, d\beta_0\, d\beta_1\, d\sigma^2\, d\alpha \\
&= \int f(y_{T+2}|X_0^T, \tilde{Z}, \alpha)\, \varphi(\alpha|X_0^T)\, d\alpha.
\end{aligned}
\tag{5.44}
$$

We notice from (5.42) that $f(y_{T+2}|X_0^T, \tilde{Z}, \alpha, \beta_0, \beta_1, \sigma^2)$ is a normal density, which, conditionally on α, has an expectation that is linear in β_0 and β_1, and a variance that is linear in σ^2. Given (5.41), by definition of the normal–inverted gamma-2 density and by Theorem A.11, we deduce that $\varphi(\beta_0, \beta_1, \sigma^2|X_0^T, \alpha)$ is a normal–inverted gamma-2 density. Hence the joint density

$$
f(y_{T+2}, \beta_0, \beta_1, \sigma^2|X_0^T, \tilde{Z}, \alpha)
$$

is also normal–inverted gamma-2 (by Theorem A.13). By Corollary A.15, it follows that $f(y_{T+2}|X_0^T, \tilde{Z}, \alpha)$ is a Student density with parameters

$$
\alpha^2 y_T + \mathrm{E}(\beta_0|X_0^T, \alpha)(z_{T+2} + \alpha z_{T+1}) + \mathrm{E}(\beta_1|X_0^T, \alpha)(z_{T+1} + \alpha z_T),
$$

s_*, $1 + \alpha^2$, and ν_*, while obviously $\varphi(\alpha|X_0^T)$ is also a Student density. The computation of the predictive density of y_{T+2} requires a unidimensional numerical integration in α, which can be done using a Simpson rule. More generally, for an ADL with p lags, Monte Carlo integration should be used with direct simulation of the posterior Student density of the parameters of the autoregressive polynomial $\alpha(L)$.

One should be careful about the interaction between prediction and stationarity. In a classical framework, prediction is done using a point estimate for α.

In the AR(1) model without a constant term, the prediction of y is equal to $\hat{y}_{T+h} = \hat{\alpha}^h y_T$. As soon as $\hat{\alpha} < 1$, the prediction converges to zero as $h \to \infty$. In a Bayesian framework, the predictive expectation of y_{T+h} is equal to $\mathrm{E}(\alpha^h|y)y_T$ and not to $\mathrm{E}(\alpha|y)^h y_T$. Consequently the tail of the posterior distribution of α can have a major influence on the prediction. To illustrate this, we have simulated an $N(0.85, 0.1)$ distribution for α, so that $\Pr(\alpha > 1) = 0.067$ (see Fig. 5.1.a). We have computed $\mathrm{E}(\alpha^h|y)$ for $h = 1, \ldots, 30$, once with the complete distribution of α and once with the distribution of α truncated to the stationarity region. The usual behaviour of the prediction is obtained only when α is restricted to the stationary region. Otherwise the prediction diverges after some value of h as can be seen in Fig. 5.1.b.

5.3.4   Inference on Long-run Multipliers

In ADL models, one is typically interested by inference on functions of the parameters β such as total multipliers measuring the transmission of shocks on the exogenous variables to the endogenous variable, and median or mean lags of these effects—see Harvey (1990: Section 7.2) for details. These quantities are often non-linear functions of β. For example, the total multiplier effect of z on y (or long-run elasticity if z and y are in logarithms) in (5.36) is

$$\eta = \beta(1)/\alpha(1), \tag{5.45}$$

provided of course that the model is stationary. In the ADL model, the total multipliers do not appear as regression coefficients. This may be a drawback if one wants to introduce prior information on total multipliers in a direct manner. For example, in a money demand equation, one could use a prior which says that the long-run elasticity of money with respect to income is close to one in probability, e.g. a (normal or Student) density with mean equal to one and standard deviation equal to 0.1. Within an ADL formulation, this must be done indirectly through the prior on the regression coefficients, may prove tedious and may be incompatible with some aspects of the prior information (note that with a natural conjugate prior or a Student–inverted gamma-2 prior on α and $\beta_0 + \beta_1$, the implied prior on η is skewed). An alternative approach uses the error correction mechanism (ECM) reparameterization of the ADL model. Starting from the ADL model (5.36), the ECM model can be written

$$a(L)\Delta y_t = a(y_{t-1} - \eta z_{t-1}) + b(L)\Delta z_t + u_t, \tag{5.46}$$

where $a = -\alpha(1)$ and η is as defined in (5.45). The lag polynomials $a(L)$ and $b(L)$ are of degree $p - 1$ and their coefficients are linear functions of the coefficients of the original corresponding polynomials $\alpha(L)$ and $\beta(L)$ (see Harvey 1990: 281). The introduction of this new parameterization raises specific issues which come from the non-linearity present in the definition of η. More precisely:

- A non-informative prior on the parameters of the linear ADL implies a different prior for the non-linear ECM because of the Jacobian of the transformation which is not equal to one.

- There is a local identification problem for η when a approaches zero because of the product $a \times \eta$ present in the ECM formulation. This problem is of course not present in the linear ADL.
- Bayesian inference is made slightly more tedious because of the non-linearity.

In order to detail all these issues, let us consider the simple case of one lag and one exogenous variable. The linear version of the model is

$$\Delta y_t = \beta_0 \Delta z_t + a y_{t-1} + \gamma z_{t-1} + u_t, \qquad (5.47)$$

where $a = \alpha - 1$. Its ECM reparameterization is

$$\Delta y_t = \beta_0 \Delta z_t + a(y_{t-1} - \eta z_{t-1}) + u_t, \qquad (5.48)$$

where $\eta = -\gamma/a$. Jeffreys' prior on the regression parameters of (5.47) and on σ^2 is

$$\varphi(a, \gamma, \beta_0, \sigma^2) \propto 1/\sigma^2, \qquad (5.49)$$

and the implied prior on the parameters of (5.48) is

$$\varphi(a, \eta, \beta_0, \sigma^2) \propto |a|/\sigma^2, \qquad (5.50)$$

because of the Jacobian of the non-linear transformation (in the case of k explanatory variables, the Jacobian $|a|$ is raised to the power k). The choice between the two parameterizations depends on the parameter of interest. If a is the sole parameter of interest, the ADL model formulation is the most convenient. If η is the parameter of interest, the ECM becomes more convenient and (5.50) indicates that the prior to consider may be more complex as it suggests a prior dependence between a and η.

Inference on non-linear functions of the parameters of the linear ADL model can be done easily by direct simulation as the posterior density of the regression parameters in (5.47) is a Student density under the usual type of prior. But it should be remarked that quantities like η, which have a denominator depending on $1 - \alpha$, do not have posterior moments, if the denominator has a positive probability density at zero. Requiring α to belong to the stationarity region implies the existence of posterior moments of η, and is coherent with the definition of η.

Let us now turn to the ECM. Instead of considering a ratio, we have the product $a \times \eta$ which introduces a local identification problem: at $a = 0$, the likelihood is flat in the direction of η (see Subsection 2.2.4 and in particular Example 2.5 for an illustration). The Bayesian solution to identification problems is to bring in prior information, not necessarily holding with probability 1 (exact restrictions). One solution is to exclude values of a which are too close to zero, and sometimes (like the empirical example of Section 5.6) this prior truncation does not contradict the evidence from the data. Another solution is just to use an informative prior for η, independent of a. A third solution, which is not very intuitive at first sight, is to introduce a prior dependence between a and η. We have seen that the non-informative prior (5.50) introduces a prior dependence, and we shall see below that this type of prior dependence solves the identification problem. A more general prior presenting such a dependence has been proposed by Schotman (1994). It is a normal density with a variance which is inversely related to $|a|$, such that the prior tends to a non-informative (flat) limit when $|a|$ tends to zero:

$$\varphi(\eta|a,\sigma^2) \propto \sqrt{\frac{|a|^r}{\sigma^2}} \exp\left[-\frac{m_0|a|^r}{2\sigma^2}\eta^2\right] \tag{5.51}$$

(the zero prior mean has been chosen just for convenience of exposition). The prior variance, equal to $\sigma^2/(m_0|a|^r)$, is a function of a, which ensures the prior dependence between η and a. The constant r is an adjustment hyperparameter that plays a major role in defining the prior dependence.

This prior can immediately be translated into a conditional normal prior for γ, applying the transformation $\eta = -\gamma/a$ of Jacobian $1/|a|$:

$$\varphi(\gamma|a,\sigma^2) \propto \sqrt{\frac{|a|^r}{a^2\sigma^2}} \exp\left[-\frac{m_0|a|^r}{2\sigma^2a^2}\gamma^2\right]. \tag{5.52}$$

When $r = 0$, we have a prior independence between η and a, but a prior dependence between γ and a. When $r = 2$, we have just the reverse situation. The case $r = 1$ represents an intermediate situation. When $m_0 = 0$ and $r = 2$, (5.51) becomes (5.50), and (5.52) becomes (5.49): the informative normal priors tend to the non-informative priors.

Let us now detail inference in the ECM (5.48) using the conditional prior (5.51) on $\eta|a$ and a flat prior on the other parameters. We take $m_0 = 0$ for simplicity; see Schotman (1994) for a complete treatment. The ECM model is non-linear in the parameters because of the product $a \times \eta$, but conditionally on a, it is linear in the remaining parameters. Let us introduce the following notation:

$$\begin{aligned} y_t(a) &= [\Delta y_t - a\,y_{t-1}], & y(a) &= [y_t(a)], \\ z_t'(a) &= [-a\,z_{t-1}, \Delta z_t], & Z(a) &= [z_t'(a)]. \end{aligned} \tag{5.53}$$

Then the ECM is

$$y_t(a) = z_t'(a)\beta + u_t, \tag{5.54}$$

where $\beta' = (\eta, \beta_0)$. The prior respects the property of conditional linearity. The posterior density of β given a is Student:

$$\varphi(\beta|y) \propto [s(a) + (\beta - \hat{\beta}(a))'Z'(a)Z(a)(\beta - \hat{\beta}(a))]^{-(T+k)/2}, \tag{5.55}$$

where the scalar $s(a)$ is equal to $y(a)'y(a) - y(a)'Z(a)[Z(a)'Z(a)]^{-1}Z(a)'y(a)$ and $\hat{\beta}(a) = [Z(a)'Z(a)]^{-1}Z(a)'y(a)$. The posterior density of a is the reciprocal of the integrating constant of this Student density times the factor $|a|^{r/2}$ which comes from the prior on a:

$$\varphi(a|y) \propto |a|^{r/2} |Z(a)'Z(a)|^{-1/2} s(a)^{-T/2}. \tag{5.56}$$

Let us partition the matrix $Z(a)$ as $(-aZ_1\ Z_2)$. Since

$$|Z(a)'Z(a)| = a^2 |Z_1'Z_1 - Z_1'Z_2(Z_2'Z_2)^{-1}Z_2'Z_1| |Z_2'Z_2|,$$

it follows that the posterior (5.56) can be simplified to

$$\varphi(a|y) \propto |a|^{r/2} a^{-1} s(a)^{-T/2}. \tag{5.57}$$

When r is smaller than two, this function tends to zero as a tends to zero, which creates numerical problems. Choosing $r = 2$ cancels this singularity and this choice is thus highly advisable. The posterior density of a has to be analysed numerically, using for instance a Simpson rule. The marginal posterior density of β is obtained using the techniques described in Section 3.2 for partially linear models.

Remark: Another feasible approach can be proposed for making inference in the ECM. Non-linearity comes from the product $a\eta$. So conditionally on a, we have seen that with (5.55) the posterior density of the remaining parameters is Student. Conversely, conditionally on η, the model is still linear. If we define

$$y = [\Delta y_t], \qquad Z'(\eta) = [y_{t-1} - \eta z_{t-1}, \Delta z_t], \qquad \delta' = [a, \beta_0], \tag{5.58}$$

the model can be written as

$$y = Z(\eta)\delta + u. \tag{5.59}$$

The posterior density of δ is Student, conditionally on η. This immediately suggests a Gibbs sampler. This nice symmetry is preserved only if the prior is natural conjugate. A prior like (5.51) or (5.50) destroys the initial symmetry. The identification problem can be solved with an informative prior on η of the normal–inverted gamma-2 type.

5.4 Models with AR Errors

The presence of autocorrelation in the error term of a regression model was first seen as a deficiency (Durbin and Watson 1950) since it violates one of the 'classical' hypotheses of the static regression model. But it soon appeared that the regression model with autocorrelated errors was an interesting dynamic model *per se* (see e.g. Sargan 1961 or 1964). Bayesian inference for this model started with Zellner and Tiao (1964). Richard (1977) considers the general case and Chib (1993) shows how the Gibbs sampler can be a nice solution to evaluate the posterior density.

5.4.1 *Common Factor Restrictions in ADL Models*

Models with autocorrelated errors can be interpreted as ADL models subject to common factor restrictions as explained for instance by Hendry and Mizon (1978). The simple ADL model (5.39) can also be written as

$$(1 - \alpha L)y_t = \beta_0 \left(1 + \frac{\beta_1}{\beta_0}L\right) z_t + u_t. \tag{5.60}$$

The restriction $\alpha = -\beta_1/\beta_0$ imposes a common root to the two lag polynomials. With this restriction, it is possible to divide both sides of (5.60) by $(1 - \alpha L)$ so that the model simplifies to

$$y_t = \beta_0 z_t + u_t, \quad \text{with } u_t = \alpha u_{t-1} + \epsilon_t, \tag{5.61}$$

where ϵ_t is a white noise. In the more general case of two exogenous variables, the unrestricted ADL model with p lags

$$\alpha(L)y_t = \beta(L)z_{1t} + \delta(L)z_{2t} + u_t \tag{5.62}$$

can have a maximum of p common factors. These commom factors are found by factorizing $\rho(L)$ out of $\alpha(L)$, $\beta(L)$, and $\delta(L)$ so that

$$\rho(L)\tilde{\alpha}(L)y_t = \rho(L)\tilde{\beta}(L)z_{1t} + \rho(L)\tilde{\delta}(L)z_{2t} + u_t, \tag{5.63}$$

which can be put immediately in the form of a regression model with autoregressive errors by dividing both members of (5.63) by $\rho(L)$. The dynamics of the impact on y_t of a shock on z_{1t} can still be rather different from that of a shock on z_{2t} if the number of common factors l is not too large compared with p. But it becomes strictly the same for $l = p$ as in this case we have a static model with autoregressive errors. So the model with autoregressive errors is a convenient simplification of the ADL model as it is more parsimonious. However, it is not recommended that common factor restrictions be imposed when they are rejected by the data. The empirical literature is full of examples of misspecified models due to abusive common factor restrictions: see e.g. Hendry and Mizon (1978) or Hoover (1988). See also Mizon (1995) for a theoretical discussion in the classical context. So it is important to test for the adequacy of common factor restrictions before imposing them.

5.4.2 *Bayesian Inference*

Let us consider the static regression model with autoregressive errors

$$\begin{aligned} y_t &= \beta' z_t + u_t, \\ \rho(L)u_t &= \epsilon_t, \end{aligned} \tag{5.64}$$

where z_t is a k-dimensional vector of exogenous variables, $\epsilon_t \sim IN(0, \sigma^2)$, and $\rho(L)$ is a lag polynomial of degree p. We call ρ the vector containing the p coefficient of $\rho(L)$. A considerable simplification occurs if we treat the initial conditions as given, i.e. we adopt the conditional approach. The integrating constant and the moments of the posterior density of β and ρ cannot be derived analytically, since the model is non-linear in the parameters as is clearly apparent when the two equations in (5.64) are combined. However, the model is bilinear in the sense that for given ρ it is linear in β, and for given β it is linear in ρ. This feature is clear if we write the model in the two equivalent ways:

$$
\begin{aligned}
y_t(\rho) &= \beta' z_t(\rho) + \epsilon_t, \\
y_t(\beta) &= \rho' z_t(\beta) + \epsilon_t,
\end{aligned}
\tag{5.65}
$$

where

$$
\begin{aligned}
y_t(\rho) &= \rho(L)y_t, \quad z_t(\rho) = \rho(L)z_t, \\
y_t(\beta) &= y_t - \beta' z_t, \quad z_t(\beta) = y_{t-1}(\beta), \ldots, y_{t-p}(\beta).
\end{aligned}
\tag{5.66}
$$

In the first line of (5.65), the model appears to be linear in β conditionally on ρ, and in the second line, it is linear in ρ conditionally on β. So we can treat these two conditional models as usual linear regression models.

This dichotomy can be exploited to set up a Gibbs sampler, provided it is preserved by the prior density. The prior density must belong to the natural conjugate family and verify the conditional independence property:

$$
\varphi(\beta, \rho, \sigma^2) = \varphi(\beta|\sigma^2)\, \varphi(\rho|\sigma^2)\, \varphi(\sigma^2).
\tag{5.67}
$$

A non-informative prior, obtained as the limit of the above natural conjugate densities, is also possible. The conditional posterior densities are easily obtained and have the following form:

$$
\begin{aligned}
\beta|\rho, \sigma^2, X_p^T &\sim NIG, \\
\rho|\beta, \sigma^2, X_p^T &\sim NIG, \\
\sigma^2|\beta, \rho, X_p^T &\sim IG_2.
\end{aligned}
\tag{5.68}
$$

The hyperparameters of the densities above are obtained by application of the standard formulae of natural conjugate analysis given in Section 2.7 once the model (5.64) is written in one of the canonical forms given in (5.65). This feature was exploited by Chib (1993) to design a Gibbs sampler algorithm to generate a Markov chain of random drawings of the posterior density of β, ρ, and σ^2. The prior can be multiplied by an indicator function of the stationarity region of ρ and the Gibbs algorithm keeps a drawing if it lies in the stationarity region. The paper of Chib (1993) provides examples.

Remarks:

1) The size of the integration problem can be reduced if we integrate out σ^2 analytically so that the conditional posterior densities of $\beta|\rho$ and $\rho|\beta$ become conditional Student densities. The Gibbs sampler, in this case, has only two blocks instead of three.

2) The Gibbs sampler algorithm can also be implemented with a joint Student prior density on β and ρ (or two independent Student densities, one on ρ, one on β): in this case $\beta|\rho, X_p^T$ and $\rho|\beta, X_p^T$ are 2-0 poly-t densities, which can be directly simulated using the algorithm presented in Appendix B.

This Gibbs algorithm hides a problem which is best understood if we write the joint posterior density of the model completely. Considering a uniform prior for simplicity of exposition, the conditional posterior density of β is Student:

$$\varphi(\beta|\rho) = f_t(\beta|\beta_*(\rho), s_*(\rho), M_*(\rho), T - k), \qquad (5.69)$$

where
$$\begin{aligned}
M_*(\rho) &= X(\rho)'X(\rho), \\
\beta_*(\rho) &= M_*^{-1}(\rho)X'y(\rho), \\
s_*(\rho) &= y'[I_T - X(\rho)(X(\rho)'X(\rho))^{-1}X(\rho)']y.
\end{aligned} \qquad (5.70)$$

From the integrating constant of this density, we get the marginal posterior density of ρ:

$$\varphi(\rho|y) \propto |M_*(\rho)|^{-1/2} s_*(\rho)^{-(T-k)/2}. \qquad (5.71)$$

When the first column of X is a constant term, the first diagonal element of $M_*(\rho)$ is equal to $T(1 - \sum_{i=1}^p \rho_i)^2$, which becomes null at the boundary of the stationarity region. The matrix $M_*(\rho)$ tends to a singular matrix. As a consequence, the Gibbs sampler may fail to converge when approaching the non-stationarity region. There are essentially two ways to cope with this problem. Chib (1993) uses an informative prior for β in all his Monte Carlo experiments. The precision matrix of a normal prior combines nicely with $M_*(\rho)$ and results in a regular matrix provided one is informative at least on the constant term. An alternative to this solution consists in centring the data and eliminating the constant term from $X(\rho)$. Truncation is not a good solution as the results may be sensitive to the truncation point. This type of problem is discussed in more detail in Chapter 6 in the context of unit root inference, in conjunction with the role of the initial conditions when the full likelihood approach is followed.

5.4.3 *Testing for Common Factors and Autocorrelation*

The greatest merit of models with autocorrelated errors is probably in providing a framework to check the specification of a maintained model against the omission of unknown lagged variables or of exogenous variables (e.g. seasonal dummy variables). The idea is quite simple: if one finds autocorrelation of order q in the residuals of an equation like (5.62) estimated under the assumption of uncorrelated errors, one should not conclude hastily that the correct specification is the same equation with autocorrelated errors. Such a finding may be simply indicating that an ADL model of order $p + q$ might be a better specification. Indeed, Monte Carlo studies in a classical framework have shown that Lagrange multiplier (LM) test statistics of autocorrelation have high power against omission of lagged variables.

Common factors and autoregressive errors are very much linked as already mentioned above. Consider the dynamic ADL model

$$y_t = ay_{t-1} + b_1 z_{1t} + b_2 z_{1t-1} + c_1 z_{2t} + c_2 z_{2t-1} + u_t. \qquad (5.72)$$

This is an unrestricted model and the posterior density of the parameters is a Student density provided the prior belongs to the natural conjugate family. A common factor corresponds to the non-linear restrictions

$$\delta_1 = a\,b_1 + b_2 = 0,$$
$$\delta_2 = a\,c_1 + c_2 = 0. \qquad (5.73)$$

These restrictions are non-linear, so the Bayesian F-test of linear restrictions developed in Section 2.7 is not applicable. However, the posterior density of δ can be simulated using a transformation of the draws of the Student posterior density. Bauwens and Rasquero (1993) build an approximate HPD region for this transformation and look if zero belongs to this region. The procedure works as follows. Suppose we have obtained N draws of the bivariate random variable δ. We can compute the sample mean $\bar{\delta}$ and sample variance V_δ of δ. Then we can use the same draws of δ to simulate the random variable ζ defined by

$$\zeta = (\delta - \bar{\delta})'V_\delta^{-1}(\delta - \bar{\delta}) \qquad (5.74)$$

and see if zero belongs to an HPD region of the simulated density.

If the common factor restriction is accepted, the model (5.72) can be simplified into a static model with no lags, but with autoregressive errors, a being the coefficient of autocorrelation. So starting from (5.72), a joint test of common factors ($\delta_1 = 0$, $\delta_2 = 0$) and autocorrelation ($a = 0$) can be constructed.

We can propose two competing procedures directly to detect autocorrelation. The Gibbs sampler algorithm detailed above produces draws of β and ρ (assuming convergence of the chain). The draws of ρ can be used to construct an approximate HPD region for ρ in order to check if it contains the point $\rho = 0$. The marginal posterior density of ρ defined by (5.71) can also be used as explained in Chapter 6 to construct such a region. This method is based on the exact posterior density of ρ in the model (5.64).

Another computationally much quicker method is based on inference in a linearized version of the model (5.64). When the two equations of (5.64) are combined, we get a non-linear regression model. When $p = 1$, the non-linearity is represented by the product $\rho\beta$ which can be linearized around preliminary estimates $\hat{\beta}$ and $\hat{\rho}$ so that $\beta\rho \simeq \hat{\beta}\hat{\rho} + (\rho - \hat{\rho})\hat{\beta} + (\beta - \hat{\beta})\hat{\rho}$. It is natural to take $\hat{\beta}$ equal to the posterior mean of β when $\rho = 0$ (or the OLS estimator under a diffuse prior), and $\hat{\rho} = 0$. This provides

$$y_t = \beta' z_t + \rho(y_{t-1} - \hat{\beta}' z_{t-1}) + \epsilon_t. \qquad (5.75)$$

We immediately recognize a static regression with the lagged OLS (or more generally Bayesian) residual of the same static regression. Pagan (1978) and Aprahamian, Lubrano, and Marimoutou (1994) recommended use of this regression

as a test regression for autocorrelation. Bauwens and Rasquero (1993) verified by
Monte Carlo experiments that this provides a good diagnostic. A test for higher
order autocorrelation is obtained by adding more lags of $\hat{u}_t = y_t - \hat{\beta}'z_t$. In this
case, the Bayesian F-test described in Subsection 2.7.5 can be used to compute
an HPD region to test for $\rho = 0$.

5.5   Models with ARMA Errors

Moving average (MA) or autoregressive moving average (ARMA) errors in a
regression model are not used very often in the econometric practice. The main
reason for this is probably that (classical) estimation of such models is more
difficult computationally than in the case of autoregressive errors, since least
squares methods cannot be used in the presence of an MA component. The
regression model with ARMA(1,1) errors is

$$
\begin{aligned}
y_t &= x_t'\beta + u_t, \\
(1 - \alpha L)u_t &= (1 - \phi L)\epsilon_t,
\end{aligned}
\tag{5.76}
$$

with $|\alpha| < 1$ to ensure the stationarity of u_t and $|\phi| < 1$ to guarantee the
invertibility of the MA polynomial. Combining these two equations gives

$$
y_t = \alpha y_{t-1} + \beta(x_t - \alpha x_{t-1}) + \epsilon_t - \phi\epsilon_{t-1},
\tag{5.77}
$$

which is a dynamic regression model with MA(1) errors and a common factor
restriction on the dynamics of y_t and x_t. This type of model can be justified in
different ways. One case is the Koyck or geometric distributed lag model

$$
y_t = \beta \sum_{j=0}^{\infty} \phi^j x_{t-j} + \epsilon_t,
\tag{5.78}
$$

which can be transformed into the autoregressive regression model with MA(1)
errors:

$$
y_t = \phi y_{t-1} + \beta x_t + \epsilon_t - \phi\epsilon_{t-1}.
\tag{5.79}
$$

The model of adaptive expectations also leads to the same type of structure, see
Harvey (1990: 229–230). So there are several motivations to consider inference
in this type of model.

5.5.1   Identification Problems

An MA(1) component introduces two types of difficulties in a dynamic model:
root cancellation and 'pile-up'. We take the model (5.76) with $\beta = 0$, so that we
have the ARMA(1,1) model commonly used in time series analysis. Rearranging
the terms, using the lag polynomial notation ($Ly_t = y_{t-1}$), and replacing α by
$\phi + \delta$, we get

$$
[1 - (\phi + \delta)L]y_t = (1 - \phi L)\epsilon_t.
\tag{5.80}
$$

If δ is equal to zero, the two lag polynomials in (5.80) are identical and can be
cancelled, so that y_t becomes a white noise. In the space of possible values of α

and ϕ, the likelihood function is flat over the directions $\alpha = \phi$, i.e. over all lines parallel to the main diagonal; see Fig. 2.1 for an illustration of a comparable case. Consequently the model is not globally identified.

The 'pile-up' problem was studied by DeJong and Whiteman (1993). It is best understood by considering the autocorrelation function of an MA(1) process. An MA process can be entirely summarized by its autocorrelation function. In the MA(1) process $y_t = \epsilon_t - \phi\epsilon_{t-1}$, the first-order autocorrelation is

$$\rho(1) = \frac{-\phi}{1 + \phi^2}, \tag{5.81}$$

and all higher order autocorrelations are zero. It is well known that one gets exactly the same result if ϕ is replaced by its inverse, or for the model $y_t = \epsilon_t - \epsilon_{t-1}/\phi$. As noted by DeJong and Whiteman (1993), this entails that $L(\phi, \sigma^2; y) = L(1/\phi, \sigma^2; y)$. This implies that in an inference exercise, when the 'true' parameter is close to one, there tends to be an accumulation of estimates of ϕ at one or very close to it (the so-called 'pile-up'). Consequently it is natural to constrain ϕ to be smaller than one, in order to eliminate this local identification problem, i.e. to consider only invertible MA processes.

We can now discuss the assessment of prior information for the model (5.77). The presence of exogenous regressors does not cause special problems so the usual types of prior can be used, e.g. the uninformative version for β and σ^2:

$$\varphi(\beta, \sigma^2) \propto 1/\sigma^2. \tag{5.82}$$

We thus suppose that the ARMA parameter $\theta' = (\alpha, \phi)$ is independent of the regression parameters. Adequate prior information could solve the problem of root cancellation. Kleibergen and Hoek (1995) have proposed use of Jeffreys' prior for α and ϕ in the ARMA(1,1) model. Jeffreys' prior is based on the information matrix. When a parameter value is not identified, the determinant of the information matrix is zero at the unidentified value, so that Jeffreys' prior puts a zero weight on such values. However, a non-informative prior for the ARMA(1,1) model can be constructed using a simpler argument. Let us express the ARMA(1,1) model as an infinite AR process by inverting $(1 - \phi L)$, assuming $|\phi| < 1$, and rearranging the terms to get

$$\epsilon_t = y_t - (\alpha - \phi) \sum_{j=1}^{\infty} \phi^{j-1} y_{t-j}. \tag{5.83}$$

Using the reparameterization

$$\begin{aligned} c_1 &= \alpha - \phi, \\ c_2 &= \phi(\alpha - \phi), \end{aligned} \tag{5.84}$$

of Jacobian $|\alpha - \phi|$, the model can be written as

$$\epsilon_t = y_t - c_1 y_{t-1} - c_2 y_{t-2} - c_2 \sum_{j=3}^{\infty} \left(\frac{c_2}{c_1}\right)^{i-2} y_{t-i}. \tag{5.85}$$

Kleibergen and Hoek (1995) claim that in this parameterization, the problem of root cancellation disappears. This suggests defining a flat prior on c_1 and c_2. Translated into the original parameter space, this prior is

$$\varphi(\alpha, \phi) \propto |\alpha - \phi|, \tag{5.86}$$

thus giving a zero weight to the lines $\alpha = \phi$ where the local identification problem exists. Note that (5.86) is not the Jeffreys' prior used by Kleibergen and Hoek (1995), but that it plays an equivalent role.

5.5.2   The Likelihood Function

The likelihood function of a regression model with ARMA(1,1) errors is in principle not difficult to construct. The density of the complete sample of T observations stacked in the vector y is a normal density with mean $X\beta$ (provided X contains no lag of y), and a variance–covariance matrix equal to $\sigma^2 V$ where σ^2 is the variance of ϵ_t and V a $T \times T$ matrix:

$$L(\beta, \sigma^2, \theta; y) \propto \sigma^{-T} |V|^{-1/2} \exp\left[-\frac{1}{2\sigma^2}(y - X\beta)'V^{-1}(y - X\beta)\right]. \tag{5.87}$$

The definition of V depends on the type of process considered. For instance, if u_t in (5.76) follows an MA(1) process, the matrix V is defined by

$$V = \begin{pmatrix} 1+\phi^2 & \phi & 0 & 0 & \cdot \\ \phi & 1+\phi^2 & \phi & 0 & \cdot \\ 0 & \phi & 1+\phi^2 & \phi & \cdot \\ 0 & 0 & \phi & 1+\phi^2 & \cdot \\ \cdot & & \cdot & & \cdot \end{pmatrix}. \tag{5.88}$$

For an MA(q) process, this expression is still tractable but becomes rather cumbersome to write for an ARMA(1,1) process. As it is very inefficient and even numerically dangerous to invert this matrix without taking its particular structure into account, two routes are possible to evaluate the likelihood function:

1. As usual, the complete likelihood function can be factorized into

$$L(\beta, \sigma^2, \theta; y) \propto \prod_{t=2}^{T} L(y_t | y_{t-1}, \ldots, y_1) \times L(y_1). \tag{5.89}$$

Thus the likelihood function is evaluated recursively as a product of conditional normal densities. One has of course to compute the conditional expectations and variances. If we define

$$\begin{aligned} v_t &= y_t - E(y_t | y_{t-1}, \ldots, y_1), \\ \sigma^2 f_t &= \text{Var}(v_t), \end{aligned} \tag{5.90}$$

the likelihood function can be rewritten

$$L(\beta, \sigma^2, \theta; y) \propto \prod_{t=1}^{T} (\sigma^2 f_t)^{-1/2} \exp\left[-\frac{1}{2\sigma^2} \sum_{t=1}^{T} v_t^2 / f_t\right]. \tag{5.91}$$

This is the prediction error method used to construct likelihood functions whenever there are dynamic unobserved components: see Harvey (1990: 104–108). The term prediction comes from the fact that best predictions are based on conditional expectations. The most efficient way to compute v_t and f_t numerically is to use the state space representation of the model and to apply the Kalman filter.

2. It is possible to get an analytical expression for the inverse of V in simple cases. Then this inverse is factorized by finding a matrix P such that $PP' = V^{-1}$. For instance, Balestra (1980) proposes a decomposition valid for the MA(1) process, so that the likelihood function (5.87) simplifies to

$$L(\beta, \sigma^2, \theta; y) \propto \sigma^{-T} |PP'|^{1/2}$$
$$\times \exp\left[-\frac{1}{2\sigma^2}(Py - PX\beta)'(Py - PX\beta)\right]. \tag{5.92}$$

Since the products Py and PX can also be best evaluated by recursions (once the structure of P is given), there is a direct link between the two methods; see Harvey (1990: 108).

A considerable simplification can be achieved if one supposes that the initial conditions of the process are given. In this case, $|V| = 1$ and the likelihood function reduces to a sum of squared residuals which can be constructed by a straightforward recursion. For the regression model with MA(1) errors, the matrix V simplifies to

$$V = \begin{pmatrix} 1 & \phi & 0 & 0 & \cdot \\ \phi & 1+\phi^2 & \phi & 0 & \cdot \\ 0 & \phi & 1+\phi^2 & \phi & \cdot \\ 0 & 0 & \phi & 1+\phi^2 & \cdot \\ \cdot & \cdot & \cdot & \cdot & \cdot \end{pmatrix}. \tag{5.93}$$

and we can verify that we indeed have $|V| = 1$. The factorization proposed by Balestra (1980) becomes much simpler as P is reduced to the lower triangular matrix

$$P = \begin{pmatrix} 1 & 0 & 0 & 0 & \cdot \\ -\phi & 1 & 0 & 0 & \cdot \\ \phi^2 & -\phi & 1 & 0 & \cdot \\ -\phi^3 & \phi^2 & -\phi & 1 & \cdot \\ \cdot & \cdot & \cdot & \cdot & \cdot \end{pmatrix}. \tag{5.94}$$

For evaluating the likelihood function (5.92), it suffices to define

$$y(\phi) = Py,$$
$$X(\phi) = PX.$$
(5.95)

These matrices can be constructed recursively according to

$$y_t(\phi) = y_t - \phi y_{t-1}(\phi),$$
$$x_t(\phi) = x_t - \phi x_{t-1}(\phi),$$
(5.96)

starting with $y_0(\phi) = 0$ and $x_0(\phi) = 0$.

In the case of the model (5.76) with exogenous variables, the recursions can be defined as follows. The model can be transformed into an infinite distributed lag regression model if we invert the MA lag polynomial $1 - \phi L$ to get

$$\frac{y_t(\alpha)}{1 - \phi L} = \frac{x'_t(\alpha)}{1 - \phi L}\beta + \epsilon_t,$$
(5.97)

where

$$y_t(\alpha) = y_t - \alpha y_{t-1} \ \text{ and } \ x_t(\alpha) = x_t - \alpha x_{t-1}.$$
(5.98)

By use of the decomposition

$$z_t/(1 - \phi L) = \sum_{j=0}^{t-1} \phi^j z_{t-j} + \phi^t \sum_{j=0}^{\infty} \phi^j z_{-j},$$
(5.99)

we can write

$$\epsilon_t = \sum_{j=0}^{t-1} \phi^j [y_{t-j}(\alpha) - x'_{t-j}(\alpha)\beta] + \phi^t \epsilon_0,$$
(5.100)

which is the recursion used in conditional maximum likelihood analysis to define the sum of squared residuals. It appears clearly that whenever $|\phi| < 1$, the influence of the initial value of ϵ_0 vanishes as t grows. So it is convenient to take $\epsilon_0 = 0$. But the error committed by imposing $\epsilon_0 = 0$ becomes serious when $|\phi| \geq 1$. Consequently maximum likelihood or Bayesian inference cannot be undertaken seriously for non-invertible processes with the conditional likelihood approach. By subtracting the expression of $\phi \epsilon_{t-1}$ from (5.100), one gets

$$\epsilon_t = y_t(\alpha) - x'_t(\alpha) + \phi \epsilon_{t-1},$$
(5.101)

which is the first recursion we are looking for. Applying the same type of reasoning to $y_t(\alpha)/(1 - \phi L)$ and $x_t(\alpha)/(1 - \phi L)$ in (5.97), we get the desired generalization of (5.96):

$$y_t(\theta) = y_t - \alpha y_{t-1} - \phi y_{t-1}(\theta),$$
$$x_t(\theta) = x_t - \alpha x_{t-1} - \phi x_{t-1}(\theta).$$
(5.102)

Note that these recursions have to start from $t = 2$, assuming $y_1(\theta) = x_1(\theta) = 0$ for the ARMA(1,1) model, while they start from $t = 1$ for the MA(1) model.

5.5.3   *Bayesian Inference*

Considering the likelihood function (5.87) and the prior (5.82), inference can be done conditionally on θ in the natural conjugate framework (see Section 2.7). The conditional posterior density of β is

$$\varphi(\beta|\theta, y) = f_t(\beta|\beta_*(\theta), s_*(\theta), M_*(\theta), T - k), \tag{5.103}$$

with

$$
\begin{aligned}
M_*(\theta) &= X'V^{-1}(\theta)X, \\
\beta_*(\theta) &= M_*^{-1}(\theta)X'V^{-1}(\theta)y, \\
s_*(\theta) &= y'[V^{-1}(\theta) - V^{-1}(\theta)X(X'V^{-1}(\theta)X)^{-1}X'V^{-1}(\theta)]y.
\end{aligned}
\tag{5.104}
$$

The posterior density of θ obtains as the integrating constant of the Student density times the determinant of V from the likelihood function

$$\varphi(\theta|y) \propto |V(\theta)|^{-1/2}|M_*(\theta)|^{-1/2}s_*(\theta)^{-(T-k)/2}\varphi(\theta). \tag{5.105}$$

If these formulae seem simple, they hide the fact that the structure of the $T \times T$ matrix V is quite complicated for the ARMA process and that finding a matrix P such that $PVP' = I_T$ is not trivial, as mentioned above. Judge, Griffiths, Carter Hill, Lütkepohl, and Lee (1985: 304–305) treat the regression model with MA(1) errors using a factorization of V proposed by Balestra (1980). Monahan (1983) factorizes the covariance matrix V extending the algorithm of Ansley (1979), but he restricts his attention to AR(2), MA(2), and ARMA(1,1) models with x_t being a constant term. He integrates the posterior density (5.105) by deterministic integration rules on the restricted region of stationarity and invertibility. Chib and Greenberg (1994) adopt a different route and consider the likelihood function (5.91) evaluated with the Kalman filter. Taking advantage of some new results concerning the state space representation of ARMA processes, they propose a Gibbs sampler algorithm for β, σ^2, and the starting values of the Kalman filter together with a Metropolis–Hastings step for the AR and MA parameters. Kleibergen and Hoek (1995) prefer to consider the simplification $\epsilon_0 = 0$ and use a special recursion to define $y(\theta)$ and $X(\theta)$. They use Jeffreys' prior and integrate the posterior density of θ by importance sampling.

Whatever the solution chosen to evaluate the likelihood function, we can propose the following type of algorithm to evaluate the posterior density. In the MA(1) case, it is easy to integrate ϕ using a Simpson rule. In the same loop of integration the posterior moments of β and σ^2 can be computed according to the rule of expectations of conditional expectations explained in Section 3.2. In the more general case of MA(q) or ARMA(p,q) errors, a griddy-Gibbs or a Metropolis–Hastings algorithm can be used to draw from the posterior of θ. Then conditionally on each draw of θ obtained from the sampler, the posterior moments of β are obtained by averaging conditional moments in the proper way.

5.6 Money Demand in Belgium

A widespread specification of a long-run money demand equation relates the real money stock (M) to a measure of real income (Y), an interest rate (R), and possibly a measure of the price level (P). We use data for Belgium over the period 1953–1982 with the following measured variables:

- Y: disposable income of households, in 1953 constant 10^8 BF;
- R: yearly average of interest rate on three-month treasury certificates, in percent per year;
- P: consumer price index (base 1953);
- M = M1/P, with M1 the yearly average M1 monetary stock, in current 10^8 BF.

The long-run functional form is

$$m = \eta_y y + \eta_r r + \eta_p p + \eta_0, \tag{5.106}$$

where m, y, and p denote the (natural) logarithms of the corresponding variables, and $r = \log(1 + R/100)$. Plots of levels and first differences of the data (see Fig. 5.2) suggest that levels may be non-stationary while first differences are stationary (except perhaps Δp).

Using the non-informative prior (5.50) and an ECM parameterization with one lag of all the variables, we get the following estimated equation at the posterior means (with posterior standard deviations between parentheses):

$$
\begin{aligned}
\Delta m_t = {} & \underset{[0.27]}{0.53}\,\Delta y_t - \underset{[0.30]}{0.78}\,\Delta r_t - \underset{[0.24]}{0.42}\,\Delta p_t \\
& - \underset{[0.19]}{0.65}\,(\,m_{t-1} - \underset{[0.20]}{1.14}\,y_{t-1} - \underset{[1.38]}{1.90}\,r_{t-1} - \underset{[0.14]}{0.38}\,p_{t-1} - \underset{[0.77]}{0.36}\,) + e_t.
\end{aligned}
$$

The results were computed by numerical integration on a, the coefficient of m_{t-1}—see (5.46)—using a Simpson rule over the interval $(-1.25, -0.01)$. Since the stationarity region in terms of a is the interval $(-2, 0)$, our choice implies a slight truncation of the integration range (at the right boundary), which hardly changes the results as the probability of a exceeding zero is very small (see the posterior density of a on Fig. 5.3.a).

The posterior densities of the long-run elasticities η_y, η_r, and η_p are contained in Figs 5.3.b–5.3.d. Results in accordance with the theory of money demand are that η_y is of the order of unity, and η_r is negative. The theory strongly suggests that η_p should be equal to zero (by homogeneity of degree 0 of demand with respect to the price level), but this restriction is rejected by the data since the posterior probability that this coefficient is negative is equal to one. A possible explanation is the discrepancy between the theoretical variables and the measured ones (in particular we have used the index of consumer prices as the general price level). Further investigations on this issue are beyond our illustrative purpose, which we pursue by showing the results when we introduce an informative prior stating that η_p has a mean equal to zero and a standard deviation equal

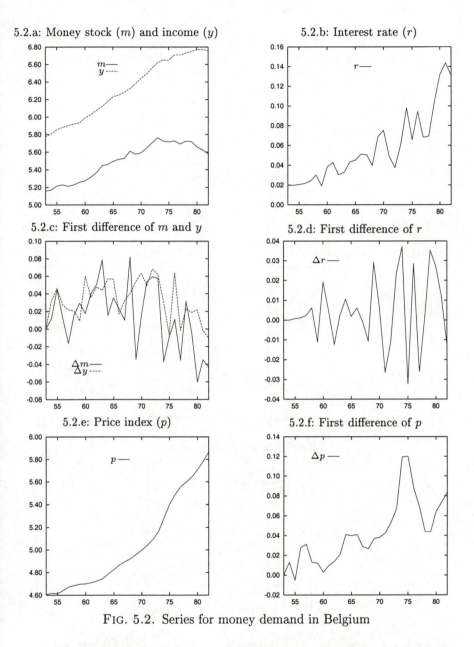

FIG. 5.2. Series for money demand in Belgium

to 0.1. The prior information was embedded in a natural conjugate density with parameters $\nu_0 = 5$, $s_0 = 0.9515 \times 10^{-3}$ (the latter being deduced from a prior R^2 equal to 0.98 which is of the order of the sample R^2), M_0 a null matrix except that its third diagonal element is equal to 0.0317 (implying the required prior

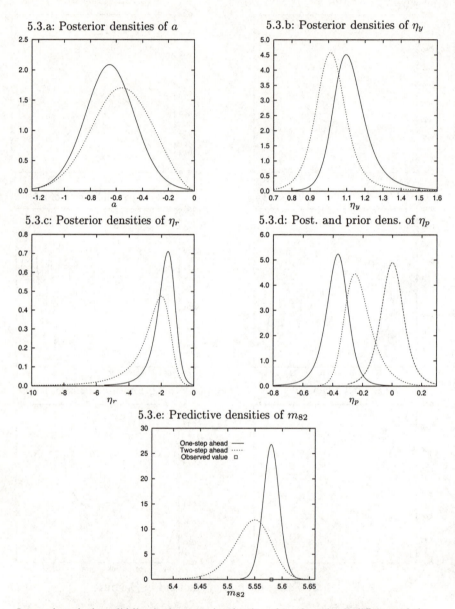

In panels a–d, the solid line is the posterior density when the prior is diffuse, and the dotted line is the posterior when the informative prior on η_p is used. The informative prior on η_p is also shown on panel d.

FIG. 5.3. Posterior and predictive densities for money demand

variance), and $\beta_0 = 0$. The estimated equation becomes

$$\Delta m_t = \underset{[0.28]}{0.77} \Delta y_t - \underset{[0.32]}{1.06} \Delta r_t - \underset{[0.25]}{0.25} \Delta p_t$$
$$- \underset{[0.22]}{0.57} \left(m_{t-1} - \underset{[0.16]}{1.03} y_{t-1} - \underset{[1.92]}{2.79} r_{t-1} - \underset{[0.10]}{0.22} p_{t-1} - \underset{[0.90]}{0.27} \right) + e_t.$$

The range of integration over a was again $(-1.25, -0.01)$, involving almost no truncation. The posterior densities are drawn on the same figures as above (together with the prior in the case of η_p). The influence of the prior on η_p is to move its posterior density towards zero, and it also modifies the densities of other parameters (see in particular a, η_r, and the coefficient of Δp_t). The one-step- and two-step-ahead predictive densities of m_{82} are shown in Fig. 5.3.e. The one-step-ahead one is a Student density and was obtained using data until 1981 and the observed values of y, r, and p in 1982. The two-step-ahead predictive density was computed as (5.44), using data until 1980, and the observed values of y, r, and p in 1981 and 1982. The observed value of m in 1982 (5.581) is quite close to the one-step-ahead predictive mean (5.580) but is about 1.1 standard deviations larger than the two-step-ahead predictive mean (5.540).

6

UNIT ROOT INFERENCE

6.1 Introduction

Let us consider the AR(1) model

$$y_t = \rho y_{t-1} + \epsilon_t, \tag{6.1}$$

where $\epsilon_t \sim N(0, \sigma^2)$. If $|\rho| < 1$, the mean of y_t is zero and its variance is $\sigma^2/(1 - \rho^2)$. The AR(1) process presents a unit root if $\rho = 1$; testing for a unit root is to test the point null hypothesis $H_0 : \rho = 1$. In this case, y_t is non-stationary. Its mean and its variance do not exist. It is not difficult to check by simulation that when $|\rho| < 1$, y_t has a strong tendency to return to its mean value (here zero) after it has experienced a shock. We shall see in the sequel that this is not true when $\rho = 1$ and that a shock in this case has an everlasting effect. When $\rho = 1$, y_t can be expressed as the cumulated sum of past errors, each receiving the same weight (see Section 6.3). We have a random walk in this case.

This unit root hypothesis has received much attention in the economic and econometric literature since the seminal paper of Nelson and Plosser (1982). Whether or not a series is mean reverting can make a lot of differences in macroeconomic theory. The main topics concern business cycle theory, permanent income theory, insiders–outsiders on the labour market, and the hysteresis of unemployment. The interested reader can consult King, Plosser, and Rebelo (1988), Hall (1978), and Blanchard and Summers (1986). The statistical problem of estimation and testing in autoregressive time series models when there is a unit or an explosive root is very old in the literature. The Cowles Commission already investigated this question for explosive roots with Rubin (1950) and Hurwicz (1950), followed by White (1958). The first modern reference for unit roots is Dickey and Fuller (1978). In the simple AR(1) model (6.1), the asymptotic distribution of the ordinary least squares estimator defined by $\hat{\rho} = \sum y_t y_{t-1}/\sum y_{t-1}^2$ presents a discontinuity at $\rho = 1$. Kadane, Chan, and Wolfson (1996) summarize this result as follows:

$$(\hat{\rho} - \rho)\sqrt{\sum y_{t-1}^2} \Rightarrow \begin{cases} N(0,1) & \text{if } \rho < 1 \\ \dfrac{0.5\,W(1)^2 - 1}{(\int_0^1 W(r)^2 dr)^{1/2}} & \text{if } \rho = 1 \\ t(0,1,1,1) & \text{if } \rho > 1, \end{cases} \tag{6.2}$$

where $W(.)$ is the standard Wiener process—see e.g. Hamilton (1994: Chap. 17) for details—$t(0,1,1,1)$ is the standard Student density with one degree of freedom (or Cauchy distribution)—see (A.31)—and '$\Rightarrow$' designates convergence in distribution as the sample size T tends to infinity. The asymptotic distribution is symmetric around zero in the stationary and the explosive cases, but asymmetric in the case of a unit root. In the stationary case, the speed of convergence of the OLS estimator towards its true value is of the order of $\sqrt{T}$. In the unit root case, the speed of convergence is much faster as it is of the order of T, but in this case, the estimator converges to a random quantity and no longer to its point true value. Moreover, adding a constant term or a trend complicates the asymptotic distribution in a non-trivial way. The practical consequence is that when one wants to test the null hypothesis of a unit root in a classical framework, one has to use special tables and to use different tables when a constant or a trend is added. With these new critical values, it is much more difficult to reject the null of a unit root. For instance, the 5 per cent asymptotic critical value for the one-sided test of $H_0 : \rho = 1$ against $H_1 : \rho < 1$ is -1.94 (-2.86 and -3.41 respectively when a constant and a trend are added) with the Dickey–Fuller tables, while it is only -1.65 with the usual normal table (independently of the presence of a constant or a trend). Nelson and Plosser (1982) built on these results to analyse the main US macroeconomic series. They concluded that most of them presented a unit root.

Testing for a unit root in a Bayesian framework is one of the most controversial topics in the econometric literature. There are several reasons for this:

- First of all, testing is one of the hot topics among classical and Bayesian statisticians, mainly because classical testing seems very often *ad hoc* to pure Bayesians. A classical test uses information that is not contained in the likelihood function and this violates the likelihood principle to which Bayesians stick. See Section 2.2 for more details on the likelihood principle.

- Secondly, the unit root hypothesis is a point hypothesis and Bayesians do not like testing a point hypothesis because it is not natural to compare an interval which receives a positive probability (the composite alternative $H_1 : \rho < 1$) with a point null hypothesis of zero mass (the null hypothesis $H_0 : \rho = 1$). See Section 1.10 for more details on testing.

- Finally, classical and Bayesian unit root tests do not give the same answer. This is a striking example where it is not possible to recover the classical results using a non-informative prior.

6.2 Controversies in the Literature

In this section, we try to analyse the main points of the controversy. The first and major controversy is between classical and Bayesian econometricians. This is best explained by the Sims and Uhlig (1991) 'helicopter tour' which by a Monte Carlo experiment manages to compare the classical and Bayesian approaches. But the Bayesian approach itself is not unified. We discuss in Subsection 6.2.2 the main variants and we try to determine in Subsection 6.2.3 what really matters for further discussions in this chapter.

6.2.1 *The Helicopter Tour*

For a Bayesian statistician, once the sample is observed, it is fixed and non-random and the sole source of uncertainty is the parameter. In the simple AR(1) model (6.1), if the ϵ_t are $IN(0,1)$ and if y_0 is given, $\hat{\rho}$ is a sufficient statistic and the likelihood function $l(\rho; \hat{\rho})$ has the form of a normal density in ρ, with mean $\hat{\rho}$, and variance $1/\sum y_{t-1}^2$. If $\varphi(\rho)$ denotes the prior density of ρ, then the product

$$\pi(\hat{\rho}, \rho) \propto l(\rho; \hat{\rho})\, \varphi(\rho) \tag{6.3}$$

is the joint density of the OLS estimator $\hat{\rho}$ and of the parameter ρ. The prior density can be chosen to be flat, i.e.

$$\varphi(\rho) \propto 1. \tag{6.4}$$

The function $\pi(\hat{\rho}, \rho)$ is a very convenient tool for comparing the Bayesian and the classical approaches of unit roots with a Monte Carlo experiment. For a fixed value of ρ, we can simulate the small-sample distribution of $\hat{\rho}$. For a chosen $\hat{\rho}$ we obtain the posterior density of ρ. Sims and Uhlig (1991) have designed such an experiment to compare Bayesian and classical results. They define a grid of 33 points for ρ, chosen in the interval [0.85, 1.10]. For each point of this interval, a vector of $T = 50$ values of y_t is generated according to $y_t = \rho y_{t-1} + \epsilon_t$ and the corresponding $\hat{\rho}$ computed. This is replicated 50,000 times. A good approximation of the graph of the bivariate density $\pi(\hat{\rho}, \rho)$ is obtained by constructing the histogram of the density of $\hat{\rho}$ for each value of ρ. This bivariate graph is shown from different angles in Figs 6.1.a–6.1.c.

- Figure 6.1.a represents the bivariate density $\pi(\hat{\rho}, \rho)$ when both axes are restrained to the range [0.85, 1.00] as the complete graph is dominated by explosive values.
- Figure 6.1.b shows the same bivariate density sliced at $\hat{\rho} = 1$, and Fig. 6.1.c shows the operation of the cut at $\rho = 1$.
- Figure 6.1.d gives two conditional densities extracted from the previous graphs: the solid line is $\varphi(\hat{\rho}|\rho = 1)$, the classical small-sample distribution of the OLS estimator under the null, and the dotted line is $\varphi(\rho|\hat{\rho} = 1, y)$, the Bayesian posterior density of ρ for a sample containing a unit root.

The remarkable fact is that the Bayesian posterior density of ρ is symmetric around $\hat{\rho}$ while the classical small-sample distribution of $\hat{\rho}$ is skewed to the left. When the uncertainty comes from the sample for fixed ρ, the distribution is non-standard. In Bayesian analysis the uncertainty comes from the parameter for a fixed sample and the posterior density of ρ is the same as in the regression model. Sims (1988) expressed great scepticism of the classical results and in particular for the discontinuity in asymptotic theory at $\rho = 1$ which leads to disconnected confidence intervals.[1] As a conclusion of their work, Sims and Uhlig

---

[1] A 95 per cent confidence interval is given by $\rho \in [\hat{\rho} \pm t\, \sigma_{\hat{\rho}}]$, with t the appropriate quantile. There are several ways of computing this interval depending on the distribution which is chosen

6.1.a: Surface   sliced   at   one   6.1.b: View of ρ along $\hat{\rho}$ = 1

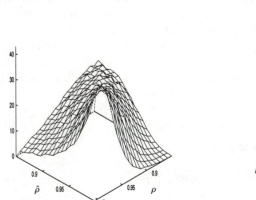

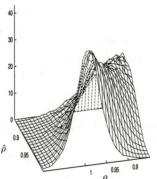

6.1.c: View of $\hat{\rho}$ along ρ = 1   6.1.d: Classical vs Bayesian ρ

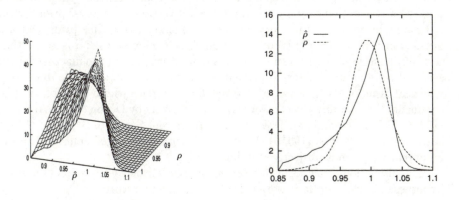

FIG. 6.1. The helicopter tour

(1991) recommend that in testing for a unit root, one should not consider special tables, but the usual Student tables. This is certainly a provocative conclusion. The problem is stated, but the paradox is not explained. Is the likelihood the culprit, or is the prior on ρ the culprit? We must try to uncover the mystery.

among those reported in (6.2) to calculate t. These different intervals do not necessarily overlap. In particular when a unit root is rejected using the normal distribution and accepted using the non-standard distribution, the intervals are disconnected. See Sims (1988) for more details.

6.2.2 Bayesian Routes to Unit Root Testing

The basic model for testing the unit root hypothesis is the AR(1) model (6.1). This model can be refined firstly so as to contain deterministic terms such as a constant and a trend, and secondly to incorporate lags of Δy_t in order to whiten the residuals. A parameterization in level and differences is convenient. In the AR(p) model, it separates the parameters α into $\rho = 1 - A(1)$ that concerns the long-run dynamics, and the short-term parameters called a^*; see formulae (6.82)–(6.84). Supposing that σ^2 is fixed, the prior density of α can be factorized as

$$\varphi(\alpha) = \varphi(\rho)\,\varphi(a^*|\rho). \qquad (6.5)$$

The marginal likelihood function of ρ is

$$l(\rho; y) \propto \int l(\rho, a^*; y)\,\varphi(a^*|\rho)\,da^*. \qquad (6.6)$$

This marginal likelihood function, combined with a prior on ρ, is the essential ingredient for testing the unit root hypothesis. A great deal of the controversy turns on the definition of an 'objective' non-informative prior $\varphi(\rho)$.

Phillips (1991a) claims that the difference in results between the classical and the Bayesian approaches comes from the flat prior (6.4) that puts too much weight on the stationarity region. He derived a version of Jeffreys' prior for the AR model in both the stationary and non-stationary cases. This prior, which is detailed in Section 6.5, tends to infinity quickly as ρ increases and is larger than one. With the resulting posterior, Phillips found that most of the macroeconomic series of Nelson and Plosser do present a unit root. His paper was published in a special issue of the *Journal of Applied Econometrics* where it is followed by comments that amplify the controversy, among others by DeJong and Whiteman (1991c), Schotman and van Dijk (1991b), Koop and Steel (1991), Sims (1991), and a reply by Phillips (1991b). Most of the comments judged Jeffreys' prior to be unrealistic from a subjectivist point of view.

The discussion concerns also, to a certain extent, the specification of the null hypothesis. Various options were considered in the literature:

- Many authors, including for instance Schotman and van Dijk (1991a), consider

$$H_0 : \rho = 1 \qquad \text{against} \qquad H_1 : \rho < 1. \qquad (6.7)$$

  This is a test of a simple hypothesis against a composite alternative. This option is adopted in most of the classical literature, see e.g. Dickey and Fuller (1978). The principal particularity is that no explosive value for ρ has to be considered. This test is treated by the posterior odds method with the Bayes factor

$$K_{01} = \frac{l(\rho = 1; y)}{\displaystyle\int_0^1 l(\rho; y)\,\varphi(\rho)\,d\rho}. \qquad (6.8)$$

The above formula of the Bayes factor follows by applying formula (1.94), with α, β, H_1, and B corresponding to ρ, $(a_*\ \sigma^2)$, $(0,1)$, and the parameter space of $(a_*\ \sigma^2)$, respectively. An advantage of the posterior odds principle is that the null and the alternative hypotheses are treated in a symmetric way. But (6.8) is not defined if $\varphi(\rho)$ is not a proper density (integrating to one) because the denominator of the Bayes factor is equal to the predictive density that is defined only if $\varphi(\rho)$ is a proper density. It is also meaningless if $l(\rho=1;y)$ is either zero or infinite (in fact, if it presents a singularity as defined in Section 6.4).

- Some authors like Phillips (1991a) and Lubrano (1995a) consider the problem as being instead

$$H_0 : \rho \geq 1 \qquad \text{against} \qquad H_1 : \rho < 1. \tag{6.9}$$

This is a test with two composite alternatives. The possibility of explosive values for ρ is explicitly considered. This type of test can be treated by posterior odds. But its main advantage is that it can be treated by considering a posterior confidence interval for ρ, or the posterior probability that $\rho > 1$:

$$\Pr(\rho > 1|y) = \int_1^\infty \varphi(\rho|y)\,d\rho, \tag{6.10}$$

which is defined whatever the type of the prior $\varphi(\rho)$, informative or diffuse, because we integrate the posterior density of ρ and we do not need the predictive density of the sample.

- Finally, some authors like DeJong and Whiteman (1991a, 1991b, 1991c) do not choose ρ as the parameter of interest. In an unrestricted AR(p) model like

$$y_t = a_1 y_{t-1} + \cdots + a_p y_{t-p} + \epsilon_t, \tag{6.11}$$

$\rho = \sum a_i = 1$ is considered to be the null hypothesis by most econometricians. DeJong and Whiteman prefer to consider the largest modulus of the roots of the characteristic equation

$$1 - \sum_{i=1}^{p} \alpha_i z^i = 0, \tag{6.12}$$

and to check if it is smaller or larger than one. It seems that this value is in general slightly smaller than ρ (ρ is usually positive). DeJong and Whiteman claim that this difference may be important and that when this approach is used, a unit root is really found less often. Using an unrestricted AR(3) model on the levels with a constant and a trend, DeJong and Whiteman (1991a) derived the posterior density of the dominant root for the 14 macroeconomic series of Nelson and Plosser (1982). They concluded that for 11 cases, the dominant root was smaller than one, which meant that the corresponding series were trend stationary. Their results

were obtained with a flat prior on the AR parameters and on the trend coefficient. DeJong and Whiteman (1991b) obtained the same type of results
for dividends and stock prices. See also DeJong and Whiteman (1989).

6.2.3 *What Is Important?*

The debate between considering the sum of the coefficients or the largest modulus
of the roots of the characteristic equation does not seem to be essential. Firstly,
Phillips (1991b) shows mathematically that $\rho = 1$ characterizes better the long-
term behaviour of a series than (6.12). Secondly, a Monte Carlo experiment shows
that the difference between the two approaches is negligible. We generated 1000
samples of 100 observations each distributed as a random walk. We estimated
then by OLS an AR(3) model and computed the largest root and the sum of the
AR parameters. Averaging the results over the 1000 samples, we obtained 0.982
for the largest root and 0.984 for the sum of the estimated AR coefficients, with
respective standard deviations of 0.038 and 0.032.

The question of the prior is a serious one as we would not like to use a
prior containing hidden messages. Besides, the choice of an informative or non-
informative prior on ρ conditions the type of test that can be computed. A point
null hypothesis requires a proper prior for ρ, or at least an integrable prior,
as a Bayes factor has to be computed. With a composite null hypothesis, this
requirement is no longer mandatory.

The previous discussion shows that it is still hard to understand what is really
going on. To be more precise we have to investigate the dynamic properties of the
AR(1) model in the presence of a unit root and understand why the presence or
the absence of deterministic components can make such a difference. Moreover,
if the initial condition does not matter in large samples of a stationary process,
this is not true for a non-stationary process. Once the model is understood,
we must be aware that Jeffreys' prior does not constitute a universal answer.
Firstly, there is not a single way to compute it. Secondly, Jeffreys' prior has
the general property of exactly compensating the singularities present in the
likelihood function.

6.3 Dynamic Properties of the AR(1) Model

It is important to realize that an observed time series corresponds in general to
the observation of a portion of a dynamic process that may have started either
in the infinite past or in a distant past. The initial observation y_0, or the initial
condition, is all we know about that past. It is important to achieve a correct
modelling of y_0 and to measure its impact when ρ approaches one.

6.3.1 *Initial Condition*

The dynamic properties of the AR(1) model and the role of the initial observation
are best understood when the model is written as an infinite MA process by
inversion of the lag polynomial $1 - \rho L$. In particular the role of y_0 appears
clearly when the inverse of the lag polynomial $1 - \rho L$ is split as follows:

$$(1 - \rho L)^{-1} = \sum_{i=0}^{\infty} \rho^i L^i = \sum_{i=0}^{t-1} \rho^i L^i + \rho^t L^t \sum_{i=0}^{\infty} \rho^i L^i. \tag{6.13}$$

When this decomposition is applied to $y_t = (1 - \rho L)^{-1} \epsilon_t$, $\rho^t L^t \sum_{i=0}^{\infty} \rho^i \epsilon_{t-i}$ is equal to $\rho^t y_0$ and the model becomes

$$y_t = \sum_{i=0}^{t-1} \rho^i \epsilon_{t-i} + \rho^t y_0. \tag{6.14}$$

The infinite MA representation implies that the initial condition is defined as

$$y_0 = \sum_{i=0}^{\infty} \rho^i \epsilon_{-i}$$
$$\sim N(0, \sigma^2/(1 - \rho^2)), \tag{6.15}$$

which is equivalent to $y_0 \sqrt{1 - \rho^2} = \epsilon_0$.

- When the process is stationary, i.e. when $|\rho| < 1$, $\lim_{i \to \infty} \rho^i = 0$. The process has a limited memory and is independent of its starting point. It reverts to its (zero) mean (it is said to be mean reverting).
- When $\rho = 1$, the process

$$y_t = \sum_{i=0}^{t-1} \epsilon_{t-i} + y_0 \tag{6.16}$$

is the accumulation of past shocks plus the initial observation. Its memory is infinite as there is no dampening of the role of y_0 and of each shock. The process is not mean reverting.

- When $\rho > 1$, the process diverges. The initial observation cannot have a finite value as this would contradict the fact that the process started in the infinite past.

When the process does not start at $-\infty$, but at some point of the past $t = -s$, with initial condition y_{-s-1}, instead of having the MA form $y_t = \sum_{i=0}^{\infty} \rho^i \epsilon_{t-i}$, we have

$$y_t = \sum_{i=0}^{t+s} \rho^i \epsilon_{t-i} + \rho^{t+s+1} y_{-s-1}$$
$$= \sum_{i=0}^{t-1} \rho^i \epsilon_{t-i} + \rho^t \sum_{i=0}^{s} \rho^i \epsilon_{-i} + \rho^{t+s+1} y_{-s-1}, \tag{6.17}$$

implying that

$$y_0 = \sum_{i=0}^{s} \rho^i \epsilon_{-i} + \rho^{s+1} y_{-s-1}. \tag{6.18}$$

This does not change the behaviour of the observed process. But a finite value of y_0 is compatible with $\rho > 1$ if we suppose that the process may be running for a small number of observations before being observable.

6.3.2   *Introducing a Constant and a Trend*

Deterministic terms play a key role in the dynamics of y_t and this dynamic pattern can be very different according to the parameterization of the model. We can distinguish two different parameterizations: a non-linear one and a linear one.

In time series analysis (see e.g. Granger and Newbold 1986: 17), it is common to parameterize the AR(1) model with a constant and a trend as

$$(1 - \rho L)\,(y_t - \mu - \delta t) = \epsilon_t. \tag{6.19}$$

In this model, the parameters have a direct interpretation: $\mu + \delta t$ represents the mean of y_t and δ is its rate of growth provided y_t is in logarithms. Writing (6.19) as

$$y_t = \rho y_{t-1} + \rho\delta + (1 - \rho)(\mu + \delta t) + \epsilon_t \tag{6.20}$$

shows that for $\rho = 1$, the intercept μ vanishes, the trend disappears, and δ becomes the drift of the process. This is in accordance with the fact that a random walk has no mean.

The AR(1) model with a constant and a trend appears to be a non-linear model. These non-linearities play a key role in the Bayesian approach as the parameter μ is not dentified under the null hypothesis of a unit root. This creates a singularity in the likelihood function and motivates a separate analysis for the cases with and without deterministic terms.

The non-linear AR(1) model is the reduced form of the unobserved component model adopted for instance in Zivot (1994), or of the regression model with autocorrelated errors when the regressors are the constant and the trend, see Lubrano (1995a). The non-linear AR(1) model was promoted by Schotman and van Dijk (1991a) and used by Lubrano (1995a), Uhlig (1994b), and Zivot (1994). Using (6.13), the non-linear AR(1) model with a constant and a trend can be written as

$$y_t - \mu - \delta t = \sum_{i=0}^{t-1} \rho^i \epsilon_{t-i} + \rho^t (y_0 - \mu). \tag{6.21}$$

The infinite MA representation gives the expression of the initial observation

$$y_0 = \mu + \sum_{i=0}^{\infty} \rho^i \epsilon_{-i} \tag{6.22}$$
$$\sim N(\mu, \sigma^2/(1 - \rho^2)),$$

which is equivalent to

$$y_0 \sqrt{1 - \rho^2} = \mu \sqrt{1 - \rho^2} + \epsilon_0. \tag{6.23}$$

When $\rho = 1$, the model simplifies to

$$y_t - \delta t = \sum_{i=0}^{t-1} \epsilon_{t-i} + y_0, \tag{6.24}$$

as μ cancels out from both sides of (6.21) and becomes unidentified as in the AR representation.

As the model (6.19) is non-linear in ρ, some authors like Phillips (1991a), following the classical tradition on unit roots, have preferred to consider the linear AR model

$$y_t = \rho y_{t-1} + \beta_0 + \beta_1 t + \epsilon_t. \tag{6.25}$$

Inverting $1 - \rho L$ in (6.25) and taking $t = 0$ gives the initial condition

$$y_0 \sim N(\beta_0/(1-\rho), \sigma^2/(1-\rho^2)), \tag{6.26}$$

so that

$$y_0 \sqrt{1 - \rho^2} = \beta_0 \sqrt{\frac{1+\rho}{1-\rho}} + \epsilon_0. \tag{6.27}$$

In theory, (6.25) is just a one-to-one reparameterization of the non-linear AR(1) model (6.19), with

$$\begin{cases} \rho = \rho \\ \beta_0 = (1-\rho)\mu + \rho\delta \\ \beta_1 = (1-\rho)\delta. \end{cases} \tag{6.28}$$

The Jacobian of the transformation from (ρ, μ, δ) to (ρ, β_0, β_1) is $(1 - \rho)^{-2}$. However, (6.25) presents some unappealing properties. Using the decomposition (6.13), the infinite MA representation of (6.25) is

$$\begin{aligned} y_t &= \rho^t y_0 + \beta_0 \sum_{i=0}^{t-1} \rho^i + \beta_1 \sum_{i=0}^{t-1} \rho^i(t-i) + \sum_{i=0}^{t-1} \rho^i \epsilon_{t-i} \\ &= \rho^t y_0 + \beta_0 \frac{1-\rho^t}{1-\rho} + \beta_1 \frac{t(1-\rho) + \rho^{t+1} - \rho}{(1-\rho)^2} + \sum_{i=0}^{t-1} \rho^i \epsilon_{t-i}. \end{aligned} \tag{6.29}$$

The dynamic behaviour of (6.25) is very different from that of (6.19):

- When $\rho < 1$, it is easy to see from (6.29) that the deterministic part of y_t is $O(t)$ if $\beta_1 \neq 0$ and $O(1)$ otherwise. We have the same property for the non-linear model (6.19) according to the value of δ.
- These similitudes of behaviour collapse when $\rho = 1$. The limit of (6.29) for $\rho \to 1$ is

$$y_t = y_0 + \beta_0 t + 0.5\beta_1 t(t+1) + \sum_{i=0}^{t-1} \epsilon_{t-i}. \tag{6.30}$$

Now the deterministic part of y_t is $O(t^2)$ when $\beta_1 \neq 0$ and $O(t)$ otherwise, because there is no link between ρ and the β coefficients. With (6.19), when $\rho = 1$, y_t is $O(t)$ if $\delta \neq 0$, and is $O(1)$ if $\delta = 0$.

When there is no deterministic term, y_t is of the same order under the null and under the alternative. When there is a constant or a trend, the non-linearity of (6.19) requires that y_t is of the same order under the null and the alternative. This property disappears with (6.25). This is the reason why the non-linear AR may be viewed as more suitable for a Bayesian analysis of the unit root as pointed out for instance in Schotman and van Dijk (1991a, 1991b) and Lubrano (1995a), and recognized in Phillips (1991b).

6.3.3 *Trend and Cycle Decomposition*

We examine here some side properties of AR models which are related to trend and cycle decomposition. This decomposition is often the prime goal of time series analysis. Suppose that we have an $AR(p)$ representation of a time series y_t and that this series incorporate exactly one unit root. According to the now usual terminology, this is an I(1) series (integrated of order 1) which becomes stationary or I(0) (integrated of order 0) by first differentiation. Consequently, we can write the Wold representation of that series

$$\Delta y_t = \delta + C(L)\epsilon_t \qquad (6.31)$$

where $C(L)$ is an infinite lag polynomial $C(L) = 1 + c_1 L + c_2 L^2 + \dots$. As Δy_t is stationary, $C(L)$ has all its roots outside the unit circle and we can define the following factorization

$$C(L) = C(1) - (1 - L)C^*(L) \qquad (6.32)$$

obtained by the Euclidean division of $C(L)$ by $(1 - L)$ where $c_j^* = \sum_{i=j}^{\infty} c_{i+1} + C(1) - 1$. We now combine (6.31) and (6.32) and integrate it to get the MA representation of the series in level. This gives

$$y_t = y_0 + \delta t + C(1)\sum_{j=0}^{t-1} \epsilon_{t-j} + C^*(L)\epsilon_t. \qquad (6.33)$$

This equation can be split into a system with

$$\begin{aligned} y_t &= Z_t + c_t \\ Z_t &= Z_{t-1} + \delta + C(1)\epsilon_t \\ c_t &= C^*(L)\epsilon_t. \end{aligned} \qquad (6.34)$$

The variable y_t is expressed as the sum of two components which are identified as being a stochastic trend Z_t and a cycle c_t. Z_t is a trend with growth rate δ. The coefficient $C(1)$ measures the importance of the stochastic part in the trend and more precisely the size of the permanent impact of a shock on the trend. It is commonly used as a measure of persistence. c_t is a cycle modelled as an invertible MA. Its AR representation exists and is stationary because $C^*(L)$ is invertible by assumption.

6.4   Pathologies in the Likelihood Functions

As explained in Subsection 5.2.3, depending on the treatment of the initial condition, we can consider the approximate (or conditional) likelihood function built from the conditional density $f(y_1 \ldots y_T | y_0, \theta)$, or the exact likelihood function obtained from the joint density of the sample and of the initial condition. As explained in Section 5.3, the conditional approach lends itself to powerful analytical results through the natural conjugate approach. On the contrary, the exact likelihood function introduces a non-linearity in the autoregressive coefficient and anyway relies on the stationarity of the process. As noted in Uhlig (1994b) the initial observation y_0 can tell a lot about the nature of the trend and the size of the root. As $y_0 \sim N(0, \sigma^2/(1 - \rho^2))$,

'the distance of the initial observation from the time trend can be compared with its standard deviation, based on the roots and the innovation variance of the series: for small roots, that distance should not be too big. Ignoring that information may lead to overstating the evidence in favour of trend stationarity'.

If the initial conditions bring in a lot of information in the likelihood function, they may also introduce pathologies when approaching the unit root. The same holds for the constant term. In this section, we analyse the pathologies of the likelihood function due to the initial condition in the case of the simple AR(1) model (6.1). The pathologies due to the constant term are analysed with the non-linear model (6.19) and the linear model (6.25).

6.4.1   Definitions

The marginal likelihood function (6.6) summarizes what the sample can say about the unit root. We would like the marginal likelihood function to be finite and positive at $\rho = 1$, and to be integrable over the interval [0,1] when combined with the prior density on ρ.

Definition 6.1 *A function $f(\theta)$ has an infinite singularity at $\theta = \theta_0$ if it tends to infinity as $\theta \to \theta_0$. The singularity is integrable if*

$$\int_{\bar{\Theta}} f(\theta)\, d\theta < \infty, \tag{6.35}$$

where $\bar{\Theta}$ is some open neighbourhood of θ_0.

Definition 6.2 *A function $f(\theta)$ has a zero singularity at $\theta = \theta_0$ if it tends to zero as $\theta \to \theta_0$.*

6.4.2   The Simple AR(1) Model

It is convenient for further reference to define

$$y_t(\rho) = y_t - \rho y_{t-1}. \tag{6.36}$$

As $\epsilon_t \sim N(0, \sigma^2)$, the *approximate* likelihood function of the model (6.1) is

$$l(\rho, \sigma^2; y|y_0) \propto \sigma^{-T} \exp\left[-\frac{1}{2\sigma^2} \sum_{t=1}^{T} y_t(\rho)^2 \right]. \tag{6.37}$$

The prior density is decomposed as follows:

$$\varphi(\rho, \sigma^2) = \varphi(\rho)\, \varphi(\sigma^2). \tag{6.38}$$

We leave unspecified for the moment the prior density of ρ for which an extensive discussion is provided in Section 6.5. We choose to be non-informative on σ^2 with

$$\varphi(\sigma^2) \propto 1/\sigma^2. \tag{6.39}$$

After integrating σ^2, the marginal approximate likelihood function of ρ is

$$l(\rho; y|y_0) \propto \left[\sum y_t(\rho)^2\right]^{-(T-1)/2}. \tag{6.40}$$

Theorem 6.3 *The marginal approximate likelihood function (6.40) of the simple AR(1) model (6.1) is non-zero and integrable at $\rho = 1$.*

Proof The result follows from the fact that the sum in (6.40) is strictly positive and finite (it is a sum of squared residuals).   □

The *exact* likelihood function is obtained by multiplying the density of y_0 given in (6.15) by the approximate likelihood function (6.37):

$$l(\rho, \sigma^2; y, y_0) \propto (1 - \rho^2)^{1/2}\sigma^{-(T+1)} \exp\left\{-\frac{1}{2\sigma^2}[(1 - \rho^2)y_0^2 + \sum y_t(\rho)^2]\right\}. \tag{6.41}$$

The resulting marginal exact likelihood function of ρ is

$$l(\rho; y, y_0) \propto (1 - \rho^2)^{1/2}\,[(1 - \rho^2)y_0^2 + \sum y_t(\rho)^2]^{-T/2}. \tag{6.42}$$

It is also bounded at $\rho = 1$, but equal to zero because of the term $(1 - \rho^2)^{1/2}$ coming from the distribution of the initial observation.

Theorem 6.4 *The marginal exact likelihood function (6.42) of the simple AR model (6.1) has a zero singularity at $\rho = 1$. No meaningful Bayes factor for the unit root hypothesis can be computed in this case.*

Proof Formula (6.42) is the product of a bounded and positive term times a term which is zero at $\rho = 1$.   □

The data density of y_0, when the process started at $t = -\infty$, exists only if the process is stationary. For explosive values of ρ, other hypotheses have to be made, as explained in Subsection 6.5.5.

6.4.3 *The Non-linear AR(1) Model with Constant*

To simplify the algebra, we consider the case where $\delta = 0$. When $\delta \neq 0$, the results of this subsection and the next one remain valid: see Lubrano (1995a) for the proofs. The model (6.19) with $\delta = 0$ is a linear regression model, conditionally on ρ:

$$y_t(\rho) = (1 - \rho)\mu + \epsilon_t. \tag{6.43}$$

The *approximate* likelihood function is

$$l(\mu, \sigma^2, \rho; y|y_0) \propto \sigma^{-T} \exp\left\{-\frac{1}{2\sigma^2} \sum_{t=1}^{T} [y_t(\rho) - (1 - \rho)\mu]^2\right\}. \tag{6.44}$$

The prior density (6.38) has to be completed for μ:

$$\varphi(\rho, \mu, \sigma^2) = \varphi(\rho)\,\varphi(\mu|\rho)\,\varphi(\sigma^2). \tag{6.45}$$

For the moment, the prior on μ is chosen to be flat:

$$\varphi(\mu|\rho) \propto 1. \tag{6.46}$$

The conditional posterior density of $\mu|\rho$ is Student as in the regression model:

$$\varphi(\mu|\rho, y, y_0) = f_t(\mu|\tilde{\mu}_*(\rho), \tilde{m}_*(\rho), \tilde{s}_*(\rho), T - 1), \tag{6.47}$$

where

$$\begin{aligned}
\tilde{m}_*(\rho) &= T(1 - \rho)^2, \\
\tilde{\mu}_*(\rho) &= \sum y_t(\rho)/[T(1 - \rho)], \\
\tilde{s}_*(\rho) &= \sum y_t^2(\rho) - [\sum y_t(\rho)]^2/T.
\end{aligned} \tag{6.48}$$

By integration of μ, we get a kernel of the marginal approximate likelihood function of ρ:

$$l(\rho; y|y_0) \propto [\tilde{s}_*(\rho)]^{-(T-1)/2} |\tilde{m}_*(\rho)|^{-1/2}. \tag{6.49}$$

A similar expression is found in Zellner and Tiao (1964), O'Brien (1970), and Richard (1977).

Theorem 6.5 *The marginal approximate likelihood (6.49) of the non-linear model (6.43) presents a non-integrable singularity at $\rho = 1$.*

Proof Formula (6.49) is composed of two terms. The first one is bounded as $\tilde{s}_*(\rho)$ is a sum of squared residuals. The second term $\tilde{m}_*(\rho)^{-1/2}$ is proportional to $(1 - \rho)^{-1}$ which is not integrable in any neighbourhood of one. □

The constant term introduces an infinite singularity at $\rho = 1$ in the likelihood function. This problem was first pointed out in O'Brien (1970) for the regression model with autocorrelated errors. It is coherent with the property that a random walk has no mean. With a flat prior on μ, the approximate likelihood function cannot be used for testing the unit root.

Let us now consider the *exact* likelihood function. From (6.22), we get the data density of y_0 which has to be combined with the approximate likelihood function (6.44):

$$l(\mu, \sigma^2, \rho; y, y_0) \propto (1 - \rho^2)^{1/2} \sigma^{-1} \exp\left[-\frac{1 - \rho^2}{2\sigma^2}(y_0 - \mu)^2 \right] \qquad (6.50)$$

$$\times\, l(\mu, \sigma^2, \rho; y|y_0).$$

Conditionally on ρ, $\sqrt{1 - \rho^2}(y_0 - \mu)$ and $y(\rho)$ have the same generic $N(0, \sigma^2)$ distribution. We are in the natural conjugate framework and we can apply the usual formulae to get the marginal exact likelihood function in ρ:

$$l(\rho; y, y_0) \propto [s_*(\rho)]^{-T/2}\, |m_*(\rho)|^{-1/2}\, (1 - \rho^2)^{1/2}, \qquad (6.51)$$

with

$$
\begin{aligned}
m_*(\rho) &= T(1 - \rho)^2 + (1 - \rho^2), \\
\mu_*(\rho) &= m_*^{-1}(\rho)\,[(1 - \rho)\textstyle\sum y_t(\rho) + (1 - \rho^2)\,y_0], \\
s_*(\rho) &= \textstyle\sum y^2(\rho) + y_0^2(1 - \rho^2) - \mu_*^2(\rho)\,m_*(\rho).
\end{aligned} \qquad (6.52)
$$

This function now behaves properly:

Theorem 6.6 *The marginal exact likelihood function (6.51) of the non-linear model (6.43) is non-zero and integrable at $\rho = 1$. It behaves as $s_*(\rho)$ around the unit root. It is well suited for computing a Bayes factor.*

Proof $s_*(\rho)$ is bounded for the same reason as before. We have to analyse the term

$$|m_*(\rho)|^{-1/2}\,(1 - \rho^2)^{1/2},$$

which has the same behaviour as

$$\frac{1 - \rho^2}{T(1 - \rho)^2 + (1 - \rho^2)} = \frac{1 + \rho}{T + 1 - \rho(T - 1)}.$$

At $\rho = 1$, this term is equal to one and $[s_*(\rho)]^{-T/2}$ becomes the leading term.
□

This theorem was proved in the general case of the regression model with autocorrelated errors in Lubrano (1995a); see also Zivot (1994) for the unobserved component model. The zero singularity introduced by the density of the initial condition exactly compensates the non-integrable singularity that the constant term introduces in the likelihood function of the non-linear model.

6.4.4 The Linear AR(1) Model with Constant

Phillips (1991a) uses the *approximate* likelihood function of the reduced form AR(1) model (6.25) (with $\beta_1 = 0$). This model is linear in ρ. But for ease of comparison, it is still interesting to write it as

$$y_t(\rho) = \beta + \epsilon_t \tag{6.53}$$

(using β instead of β_0). The approximate likelihood function is

$$l(\beta, \sigma^2, \rho; y|y_0) \propto \sigma^{-T} \exp\left\{ -\frac{1}{2\sigma^2} \sum_{t=1}^{T} [y_t(\rho) - \beta]^2 \right\}. \tag{6.54}$$

Let us use the prior density

$$\varphi(\beta|\rho) \propto 1 \tag{6.55}$$

for the moment. By the same type of reasoning as before, the marginal approximate likelihood function of ρ is

$$l(\rho; y|y_0) \propto [\tilde{s}_*(\rho)]^{-(T-1)/2}, \tag{6.56}$$

with $\tilde{s}_*(\rho)$ having the same definition as in (6.48).

Theorem 6.7 *The marginal approximate likelihood function (6.56) of the linear model (6.53) is bounded and integrable at $\rho = 1$.*

Proof This function is bounded and integrable as $\tilde{s}_*(\rho)$ is a sum of squared residuals. □

The *exact* likelihood function is obtained by multiplying the approximate likelihood function (6.54) with the distribution of the initial observation given by (6.26):

$$l(\beta, \sigma^2, \rho; y, y_0) \propto (1 - \rho^2)^{1/2} \sigma^{-1} \exp\left\{ -\frac{1 - \rho^2}{2\sigma^2} [y_0 - \beta/(1 - \rho)]^2 \right\} \tag{6.57}$$
$$\times \, l(\beta, \sigma^2, \rho; y|y_0).$$

The corresponding marginal exact likelihood function is

$$l(\rho; y, y_0) \propto [s_*(\rho)]^{-T/2} \, |m_*(\rho)|^{-1/2} \, (1 - \rho^2)^{1/2}, \tag{6.58}$$

where

$$m_*(\rho) = T + (1 + \rho)/(1 - \rho),$$
$$\beta_*(\rho) = m_*^{-1}(\rho) \left[\sum y_t(\rho) + (1 + \rho) y_0 \right], \tag{6.59}$$
$$s_*(\rho) = \sum y^2(\rho) + y_0^2(1 - \rho^2) - \beta_*^2(\rho) \, m_*(\rho).$$

As expected, the initial condition introduces a zero singularity.

Table 6.1 *Singularities at $\rho = 1$ in likelihood functions*

Likelihood	No constant	Non-linear	Linear
Approximate	(6.40)	(6.49)	(6.56)
	none	∞ non-integrable	none
Exact	(6.42)	(6.51)	(6.58)
	zero	none	zero

Theorem 6.8 *The marginal exact likelihood function (6.58) of the linear model (6.53) is bounded and integrable, but presents a zero singularity at $\rho = 1$. It cannot be used to compute a meaningful Bayes factor.*

Proof Formula (6.58) behaves like $(1 - \rho^2)(1 - \rho)/[T(1 - \rho) + 1 - \rho]$ which is zero for $\rho = 1$. □

In the linear model, the constant term does not introduce an infinite singularity in the likelihood function. But the density of the initial condition introduces a zero singularity. Consequently, the exact likelihood function is always zero at the unit root. With the linear model, it is not advisable to model the first observation when one wants to test for a unit root.

6.4.5 *Summary*

We summarize the main results of this section in Table 6.1 to conclude that there is a game of hide and seek between model specification and singularities in the likelihood function. For the moment it is not possible to draw definite conclusions as the marginal likelihood functions were derived under a flat prior. In the next section, we show how Jeffreys' prior interacts with these singularities.

6.5   The Exact Role of Jeffreys' Prior

As underlined by Zellner (1971: 217),

'Jeffreys has suggested that the square root of the determinant of the information matrix be taken as a diffuse prior pdf, *although not without great care and thought.*'

Thornber (1967) was the first to derive Jeffreys' prior for the stationary AR(1) model; see also Zellner (1971: Chap. 7). This prior underwent many variants in the literature:

- Phillips (1991a) explicitly considers the non-stationary case for Jeffreys' prior.
- Berger and Yang (1994) develop a reference prior for the stationary AR(1) model, which appears to be equivalent to Jeffreys' prior derived by Thornber (1967). Its symmetric counterpart is taken for the explosive case.
- Lubrano (1995a) considers a beta prior which can be made identical to Jeffreys' prior in the stationary case. He extends its range to consider explosive values.

These variants have of course different properties. Jeffreys' prior was advocated by Phillips (1991a) as being *the* solution to the Bayesian controversy about unit root inference. In fact the sole diversity of priors shows that this is not so straightforward even in the simple AR(1) model.

In this section, we derive the different variants of Jeffreys' prior for the AR(1) model. All the calculations related to the information matrix are based on the approximate likelihood function. We relegate to an appendix in this chapter the derivation of Jeffreys' prior using the exact likelihood function, and we show in this appendix that the two calculations lead to asymptotically equivalent results.

6.5.1 *Jeffreys' Prior Without Deterministic Terms*

For the approximate likelihood function (6.37), the information matrix is diagonal. Assuming that $y_0 = 0$, its diagonal elements are

$$
\begin{cases}
-\mathrm{E}\left(\dfrac{\partial^2 \log l}{\partial \sigma^2}\right) = \dfrac{T}{2\sigma^4}, \\[3mm]
-\mathrm{E}\left(\dfrac{\partial^2 \log l}{\partial \rho^2}\right) = \dfrac{1}{\sigma^2}\mathrm{E}(\textstyle\sum_{t=1}^{T} y_{t-1}^2) = \dfrac{1}{\sigma^2}\mathrm{E}(\textstyle\sum_{t=0}^{T-1} y_t^2).
\end{cases}
\tag{6.60}
$$

When the process is stationary, the expectation can be calculated using the infinite MA representation of y_t (see Section 6.3) which implies that $\mathrm{E}(y_t^2) = \sigma^2/(1 - \rho^2)$. Consequently,

$$
\varphi_J(\rho) \propto \frac{1}{\sqrt{1 - \rho^2}}.
\tag{6.61}
$$

This is the prior derived by Thornber (1967). It presents an integrable singularity at $\rho = 1$ since

$$
\int \varphi_J(\rho)\, d\rho = \arcsin(\rho) \quad \text{so that} \quad \int_0^1 \varphi_J(\rho)\, d\rho = \pi/2.
\tag{6.62}
$$

Despite the fact that this is a non-informative prior, it can be used to compute a Bayes factor. This prior is also a particular beta density defined over $[-1,1]$ since it is of the type

$$
\varphi(\rho) \propto (1 + \rho)^{\alpha-1}(1 - \rho)^{\beta-1},
\tag{6.63}
$$

with $\alpha = \beta = 0.5$.

An important issue is how to deal with explosive values of ρ, if we want to test $\rho < 1$ against $\rho \geq 1$. Phillips (1991a) uses the decomposition (6.13) which serves to express the infinite MA representation conditionally on the first observation y_0. With this representation,

$$E(y_t^2|y_0) = E(\rho^t y_0 + \sum_{i=0}^{t-1} \rho^i \epsilon_{t-i})^2$$
$$= \rho^{2t} y_0^2 + E(\epsilon_t^2) \sum_{i=0}^{t-1} \rho^{2i} \tag{6.64}$$
$$= \rho^{2t} y_0^2 + \frac{1 - \rho^{2t}}{1 - \rho^2} \sigma^2.$$

Combining (6.60) and (6.64), and assuming $y_0 = 0$ as the analysis is conditional on y_0, Jeffreys' prior for the non-stationary case is obtained after taking the square root:

$$\varphi_P(\rho) \propto \frac{1}{\sqrt{1 - \rho^2}} \sqrt{1 - \frac{1 - \rho^{2T}}{T(1 - \rho^2)}}. \tag{6.65}$$

This is the prior advocated by Phillips (1991a). Its limit as ρ tends to one is equal to $\sqrt{0.5(T - 1)}$ (by use of L'Hospital's rule). When $\rho < 1$, (6.65) is asymptotically (in T) equivalent to Thornber's prior (6.61). When $\rho \geq 1$, the second square root becomes asymptotically dominant.

Noticing the similarity between Jeffreys' prior in the stationary case and the beta prior, Lubrano (1995a) suggests considering a beta prior defined not simply on $[-1,1]$, but on a slightly extended range so as to allow for slightly explosive values:

$$\varphi_L(\rho) \propto (1 + \upsilon - \rho^2)^{-1/2}, \tag{6.66}$$

where υ is a small positive number which translates the integrable singularity of (6.61) from 1 to $\sqrt{1 + \upsilon}$.

Berger and Yang (1994) choose another route and develop a reference prior[2] for the AR(1) model. It turns out that the reference prior, which is defined only for the stationary case, is identical to (6.61). To extend their prior to the non-stationarity region, Berger and Yang suggest symmetrizing their prior by considering the transformation $\tilde{\rho} = 1/\rho$ of Jacobian $1/\rho^2$, which gives

$$\varphi_B(\rho) = \begin{cases} 1/[2\pi\sqrt{1 - \rho^2}] & \text{if } |\rho| < 1 \\ 1/[2\pi|\rho|\sqrt{\rho^2 - 1}] & \text{if } |\rho| \geq 1. \end{cases} \tag{6.67}$$

Let us compare the advantages and the drawbacks of these different priors when they try to cope with explosive values. For the stationarity region, they all constitute acceptable approximations of the flat prior.

- Phillips' prior (6.65) explodes over the non-stationarity region. This prior could be rationalized by the following argument. Explosive values of ρ are less and less likely as the sample size grows. This prior, being of the order of ρ^{2T}, compensates for the stationarity message of the sample and favours the unit root. But it is still dominated by the likelihood function as the latter decreases at the rate $\exp(-k\rho^2)$ (with $k > 0$). However, one of the most

---

[2] Reference priors are defined in Chapter 4. See Berger and Yang (1994) for more details on the computation of the reference prior for the AR(1) model.

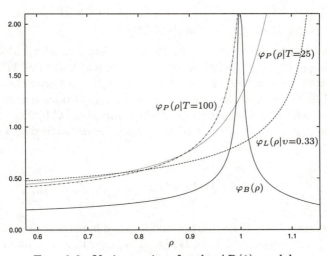

FIG. 6.2. Various priors for the AR(1) model

criticized aspects of Phillips' prior (see the comments and references in the special issue of the *Journal of Applied Econometrics* mentioned above) is that it is of order ρ^{2T}. This prior will be dominated by the sample only for large values of ρ. As shown in Fig. 6.2 (where all the priors were normalized to one between -1 and 1), (6.65) goes to infinity quicker and quicker as the sample size grows. This is a rather undesirable feature.

- Lubrano's prior (6.66) goes to infinity when $\rho > 1$, but at a speed which is governed only by v. It has an integrable singularity at $\rho = \sqrt{1+v}$. This prior has a subjective aspect since the statistician can select the v he or she believes in. In particular, one can choose v so as to give an equal weight to the stationarity and to the non-stationarity regions. These regions can be defined symmetrically as $[\sqrt{v}, 1]$ and $[1, \sqrt{1+v}]$. The respective integrals of $\varphi_L(\rho)$ are $\pi/2 - 2\arctan(\sqrt{v})$ and $\arctan(\sqrt{v})$. These integrals are equal for $v = 0.333$.

- The symmetrized reference prior of Berger and Yang is particularly attractive as it recognizes that there is something special at $\rho = 1$, where it presents an integrable singularity. But it gives decreasing weights to explosive values. As it gives an equal weight to stationary and non-stationary values of ρ and as it is a proper density, it is readily usable to compute posterior odds. Its shape is roughly in accordance with the prior advocated by Kadane, Chan, and Wolfson (1996), which is a mixture of two normal densities and of a discrete density at $\rho = 1$. Kadane, Chan, and Wolfson (1996) have elicited this mixture prior with the predictive method for an AR(1) model of the US GNP. They assign a weight of 0.85 for the stationarity region, 0.05 for the explosive region, and 0.10 for the unit root.

6.5.2 *Choosing a Prior for the Simple AR(1) Model*

How can we compare these four priors (including the flat prior)? Does Jeffreys' prior of Phillips solve the statistical puzzle of Sims and Uhlig (1991)? To answer these questions, we compute the risk functions of the posterior mean of ρ (see Definition 1.2) for each of the four priors in the AR(1) inference problem. If a risk function uniformly dominates the others in the sense of having the smallest risk for all values of ρ, the associated prior could be declared the 'best' one. So we compute

$$\int [\mathrm{E}(\rho|y) - \rho_0]^2 f(y|\rho_0) \, dy \simeq \frac{1}{N} \sum_{i=1}^{N} [\mathrm{E}(\rho|y_i) - \rho_0]^2, \qquad (6.68)$$

where y_i is a draw from $f(y|\rho_0)$. This computation is realized by a Monte Carlo experiment, as in Berger and Yang (1994). The algorithm is as follows:

1) Define a grid of values of ρ between 0.80 and 1.10.
2) Run a loop from 1 to 1000:
   2-a) For each value of ρ, generate a sample of size 50 using $y_t = \rho y_{t-1} + \epsilon_t$ with $y_0 = 0$.
   2-b) Compute the posterior expectation[3] of ρ with the flat prior, Berger and Yang's prior, Lubrano's prior, and Phillips' prior using the marginal likelihood function (6.40).
3) After the loop, compute the sample averages (6.68).

A graph of the four risk functions is given in Fig. 6.3 and it reveals interesting features:

- The flat prior $\varphi_U(\rho)$ is uniformly dominated by all the other priors. We find the usual result here that the OLS estimator $\hat{\rho}$ is downward biased.
- For values of ρ below 0.85, Lubrano's prior $\varphi_L(\rho)$ dominates. For values of $\rho \in [0.85, 0.975]$, Berger and Yang's prior $\varphi_B(\rho)$ dominates. For values of ρ above 0.975, Phillips' prior $\varphi_P(\rho)$ dominates. If we exclude the flat prior, no prior is uniformly dominated.
- The priors of Berger and Yang and of Lubrano behave very similarly and are close substitutes.
- Phillips' prior, despite its counterintuitive shape, performs best around the unit root and for explosive values, but poorly for the stationarity region.
- All priors, including the flat prior, have a small risk for explosive values of ρ.

We can provisionally conclude that the statistical paradox is solved if we exclude the flat prior and use one of the three versions of Jeffreys' prior together

---

[3] The one-dimensional integral is evaluated with Simpson's rule on 33 points. For Lubrano's prior, $v = 0.333$. The integration bounds are chosen with $\rho_{inf} = \sqrt{v + 0.001}$ and $\rho_{sup} = \sqrt{1 + v - 0.001}$.

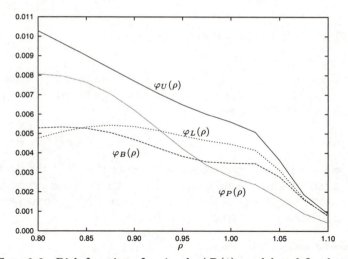

FIG. 6.3. Risk functions for simple AR(1) model and fixed y_0

with the conditional likelihood function in the AR(1) model without a constant term. With an adequate prior, the Bayesian results should not be so different from the classical ones in this case. The marginal exact likelihood function (6.42) cannot be used as it presents a zero singularity at $\rho = 1$.

6.5.3 Jeffreys' prior with Deterministic Terms

As explained in Subsection 4.3.4, Jeffreys' prior is invariant to the parameterization. This means that we need only compute Jeffreys' prior for the non-linear model. By using the adequate Jacobian, we immediately have the corresponding Jeffreys' prior for the linear model. Assuming that $y_0 = \mu$, instead of $y_0 = 0$ (since we proceed conditionally on y_0 and μ is the mean of y_0), the information matrix block related to σ^2 and ρ of the approximate likelihood function (6.44) is the same as in the case without deterministic terms. Moreover, the diagonal element related to μ of the information matrix is

$$-\mathrm{E}\left(\frac{\partial^2 l}{\partial \mu^2}\right) = \frac{T(1-\rho)^2}{\sigma^2}, \tag{6.69}$$

and the off-diagonal elements related to μ are equal to zero. The resulting Jeffreys' prior can be decomposed into a marginal prior on σ^2, which is proportional to $1/\sigma^2$, a conditional prior on ρ, which is independent of μ and σ^2 and is identical to (6.61) or (6.65) (depending on the hypothesis made for the calculation of the variance of y_t), and a conditional prior on μ:

$$\varphi(\mu|\rho,\sigma^2) \propto (1-\rho)/\sigma. \tag{6.70}$$

If we decide to apply Jeffreys' principle separately to σ^2 and then to the other parameters, we arrive at a similar prior, except for μ:

$$\varphi(\mu|\rho) \propto (1 - \rho), \tag{6.71}$$

i.e. a prior independent of σ^2.

In the linear model $y_t = \beta + \rho y_{t-1} + \epsilon$, the parameter β is related to μ by the transformation $\beta = (1 - \rho)\mu$ of Jacobian $1/(1 - \rho)$. Consequently, by transformation of (6.71), we get

$$\varphi(\beta|\rho) \propto 1. \tag{6.72}$$

Jeffreys' prior for the constant term is a flat prior (for β) in the linear model, and a prior (on μ) which tends to zero when ρ tends to one in the non-linear model. This zero singularity of the prior of μ at $\rho = 1$ is a consequence of the lack of identification of μ when ρ is equal to one.

6.5.4 *Playing with Singularities*

In the non-linear model, the constant term creates an infinite singularity which is removed when the density of y_0 is accounted for (see Table 6.1). Jeffreys' prior (6.71) on μ is an alternative solution to remove this singularity as it presents a zero singularity. However, we shall see below that this solution is not very efficient.

Let us first consider the marginal approximate likelihood functions (6.49) and (6.56). We have the following theorem:

Theorem 6.9 *Jeffreys' prior (6.71) on μ removes the non-integrable singularity of the marginal likelihood function (6.49). The resulting posterior,*

$$\varphi(\rho|y) \propto \tilde{s}_*(\rho)^{-(T-1)/2}\, \varphi(\rho), \tag{6.73}$$

with $\tilde{s}_*(\rho)$ as defined in (6.48), is bounded and integrable at $\rho = 1$. This posterior is identical to that obtained with the linear model when combining Jeffreys' prior (6.71) on β with (6.56).

Proof By multiplying (6.71) and (6.49), we get

$$l(\rho; y|y_0) \propto [\tilde{s}_*(\rho)]^{-(T-1)/2}\, |\tilde{m}_*(\rho)|^{-1/2}\, (1 - \rho).$$

The definition of $\tilde{m}_*(\rho)$ given in (6.48) implies that

$$|\tilde{m}_*(\rho)|^{-1/2}\, (1 - \rho) = 1/\sqrt{T},$$

so that (6.73) follows. The second result of the theorem follows by the invariance property of Jeffreys' prior.   □

With Jeffreys' prior, the marginal posterior density of ρ behaves exactly in the same way as in the model with no constant term. It is proportional to a sum of squared residuals. The benefit of having a non-linear model with a constant term is lost.

Remarks:

1) We used a flat prior for both μ and β in Section 6.4. These priors cannot hold at the same time as a flat prior on β implies a prior on μ equal to $1 - \rho$ because of the Jacobian of the transformation of β to ρ.

2) Schotman and van Dijk (1991a) remove the singularity introduced by the constant term with an adequate prior on μ which is based on the distribution (6.22) of y_0.

3) Schotman (1994) has proposed the following prior density for constant terms in non-linear AR(1) models (see also Uhlig 1994a):

$$\varphi(\mu|\rho, \sigma^2) \propto (1 - \rho)^{p/2} \sigma^{-1} \exp\left[-\frac{K}{2\sigma^2}|1 - \rho|^{-p}\right]. \tag{6.74}$$

Jeffreys' prior (6.70) on μ corresponds to $K = 0$ and $p = 2$.

4) O'Brien (1970) introduces a prior on ρ which is proportional to $1 - \rho$. It kills the infinite singularity of (6.49) at $\rho = 1$. His prior on μ is flat.

Let us now consider the marginal exact likelihood functions (6.51) and (6.58). This time, the zero singularity is transmitted to the posterior so that the result is not very interesting for analysing a unit root problem.

Theorem 6.10 *When combined with the marginal exact likelihood function (6.51), Jeffreys' prior (6.71) introduces a zero singularity in the posterior density of ρ, which is given by*

$$\varphi(\rho|y, y_0) \propto s_*(\rho)^{-T/2} \sqrt{\frac{(1 - \rho^2)(1 - \rho)}{T + 1 - \rho(T - 1)}} \, \varphi(\rho), \tag{6.75}$$

where $s_*(\rho)$ is defined in (6.52). The posterior density of ρ is the same in the non-linear and linear models.

Proof The marginal likelihood function (6.58) obtained with a flat prior on β, which happens also to be Jeffreys' prior, has a zero singularity. By changing the parameterization, the corresponding marginal likelihood function is (6.51) times the Jacobian of the transformation, which is $1 - \rho$, that is to say Jeffreys' prior on μ. □

The main results are summarized in Table 6.2. The conclusion is that Jeffreys' prior applied to all the parameters does not give very satisfactory results. When we consider the exact likelihood function, in every case we have a zero singularity at the unit root. No sensible unit root inference result can be obtained in this case. When considering the approximate likelihood function, the posterior density is well behaved but there is no difference between the linear and the non-linear models. So all the efforts made to introduce in the model the essential dynamic characteristics of a process following a random walk are ruined by Jeffreys' prior. We have here another example of the danger of applying Jeffreys' principle in an automatic way.

Table 6.2 *Singularities at $\rho = 1$ in Jeffreys' prior and posterior*

Model	No constant	Non-linear	Linear
Jeffreys' prior	Integrable	Zero	Integrable
Approximate likelihood	none (6.40)	∞ non-integrable (6.49)	none (6.56)
Posterior	none	none (6.73)	none (6.73)
Exact likelihood	zero (6.40)	none (6.49)	zero (6.56)
Posterior	zero	zero (6.75)	zero (6.75)

The singularities of Thornber's prior on ρ are the same as those of Jeffreys' prior.

6.5.5 Bayesian Unit Root Testing

Jeffreys' prior should not be thrown away, but the recommendation is not to use Jeffreys' prior completely, and in particular the implied Jeffreys' prior for μ. The model that manages to incorporate all the dynamic characteristics of a random walk is the non-linear model with a constant term. The non-integrable singularity is removed by modelling the initial condition. Using a flat prior on μ, the marginal exact likelihood function (6.51) behaves nicely when approaching the unit root (see Theorem 6.6). The choice of the prior on ρ is free.

To determine which prior gives the 'best' results in this case, we compute the risk functions of the posterior mean of ρ for the different priors. A technical problem arises for computing the risk for values of ρ greater than one. Explosive values of ρ were discarded when modelling y_0, because an explosive process cannot have been running for ever. To cope with this question, Uhlig (1994b) supposes that the process starts at $t = -s$. This implies that

$$y_0 | \rho, \sigma^2 \sim N(\mu, \sigma^2 q(\rho, s)) \tag{6.76}$$

with

$$q(\rho, s) = \sum_{i=0}^{s} \rho^{2i} = \frac{1 - \rho^{2(s+1)}}{1 - \rho^2}. \tag{6.77}$$

For $s \to \infty$, this function is equal to $1/(1 - \rho^2)$ (provided $\rho < 1$) and we go back to the usual modelling of y_0. For $s = 0$, this function is equal to one (fixed initial condition). For $s \to \infty$, (6.76) becomes (6.22). We can find other functions that behave like (6.77) at polar cases, in particular

$$q(\rho, v) = \frac{1 + v}{1 + v - \rho^2}, \tag{6.78}$$

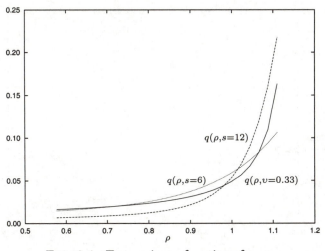

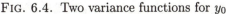

FIG. 6.4. Two variance functions for y_0

which is related to the prior (6.66). For $v = 0$, we go back to the usual modelling of y_0. For $v \to \infty$, this function is equal to one. In between, it is possible to find s and v so that they have a similar behaviour in ρ (see Fig. 6.4).

The advantage of $q(\rho, v)$ over $q(\rho, s)$ is that it leads to simpler calculations (see in particular the appendix for deriving the information matrix). The exact likelihood function of the non-linear model with a constant term becomes

$$l(\rho, \mu, \sigma^2, v; y, y_0) \propto q(\rho, s)^{-1/2} \sigma^{-(T+1)/2}$$
$$\times \exp\left\{ -\frac{1}{2\sigma^2} \left[(y_0 - \mu)^2/q(\rho, s) + \sum(y_t - \rho y_{t-1} - (1 - \rho)\mu)^2 \right] \right\}.$$
$$(6.79)$$

The marginal exact likelihood function is

$$l(\rho; y, y_0) \propto s_*(\rho)^{-T/2} m_*(\rho)^{-1/2} q(\rho, s)^{-1/2}, \qquad (6.80)$$

with

$$m_*(\rho) = T(1 - \rho)^2 + 1/q(\rho, s),$$
$$\mu_*(\rho) = m_*^{-1}(\rho) \left[(1 - \rho) \sum y_t(\rho) + y_0/q(\rho, s) \right], \qquad (6.81)$$
$$s_*(\rho) = \sum y_t^2(\rho) + y_0^2/q(\rho, s) - mu_*^2(\rho) m_*(\rho).$$

At $\rho = 1$, this function is bounded and integrable. It behaves in the same way as (6.51). The algorithm of Subsection 6.5.2 used to compute the risk functions is modified as follows:

1) Define a grid of values of ρ between 0.80 and 1.10.
2) Run a loop from 1 to 1000:

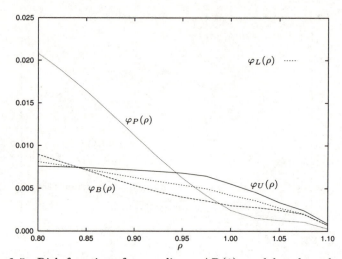

FIG. 6.5. Risk functions for non-linear AR(1) model and random y_0

2-a) For each value of ρ, generate a sample of size 50 using $y_t = \rho y_{t-1} + \epsilon_t$ with $y_0 = 1$.

2-b) Compute the posterior expectation of ρ with the flat prior, Berger and Yang's prior, Lubrano's prior, and Phillips' prior using the marginal likelihood function (6.80).

3) After the loop, compute the sample averages (6.68).

In step 2-b, the posterior expectation of ρ can be computed with either (6.77) and $s = 9$, or (6.78) and $v = 0.33$. As the results were the same, only the last case is reported in Fig. 6.5.

When the initial condition is modelled, no prior is uniformly the best. However, Phillips' prior really does not behave satisfactorily for stationary values of ρ below 0.92. If we exclude this prior, the prior advocated by Berger and Yang very slightly dominates the other two.

6.5.6 *Can We Test for a Unit Root Using a Linear Model?*

The alternative solution to testing for a unit root is of course to use the linear model without modelling the initial condition, together with the complete Jeffreys' prior. This is the solution advocated by Phillips (1991a). In Fig. 6.6, we compare the risk function of this procedure to the risk function of the criticized flat prior for ρ combined with the marginal exact likelihood function (6.80). The latter is already available from the previous subsection.

The comparison is striking: Jeffreys' prior advocated by Phillips is uniformly dominated. We can conclude this investigation by saying that the flat prior is by no means responsible for the statistical paradox. It is a matter of model, of constant term, and of likelihood function (through the initial condition).

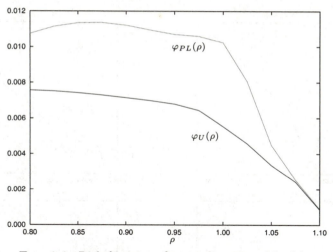

FIG. 6.6. Risk functions for non-linear model with
flat prior and linear model with Phillips' prior

6.6   Analysing the Extended Nelson–Plosser Data

The exact likelihood function together with either a flat prior or the symmetrized reference prior was found to be the preferred model for testing the unit root hypothesis. In order to apply this method to the Nelson–Plosser data set extended by Schotman and van Dijk (1991b), we must generalize it to include a deterministic linear trend term, and to consider an autoregressive model of order larger than one.

6.6.1   The AR(p) Model with a Deterministic Trend

For empirical applications, the AR(1) model is usually too restrictive and is extended to

$$A(L)(y_t - \mu - \delta t) = \epsilon_t, \tag{6.82}$$

where $A(L) = 1 - a_1 L - \ldots - a_p L^p$. This lag polynomial has a unit root if $A(1) = 0$. Instead of considering the sum of the coefficients, it is convenient to isolate the presence of a possible unit root by the reparameterization

$$A(L) = (1 - \rho L) + (1 - L)A^*(L), \tag{6.83}$$

where

$$\begin{aligned}
\rho &= 1 - A(1), \\
A^*(L) &= a_1^* L + \cdots + a_{p-1}^* L^{p-1}, \\
a_j^* &= \sum_{i=j}^{p-1} a_{i+1}, \quad j = 1, \ldots, p-1.
\end{aligned} \tag{6.84}$$

If we replace $A(L)$ by its reparameterization in (6.83), we get

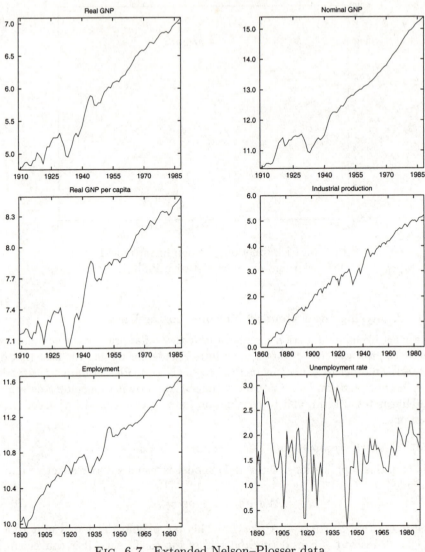

FIG. 6.7. Extended Nelson–Plosser data

$$y_t(\rho) = [(1 - \rho)\mu + \rho\delta] + (1 - \rho)\delta t + A^*(L)(\Delta y_t - \delta) + \epsilon_t. \qquad (6.85)$$

The addition of $p - 1$ lags of Δy_t together with a trend introduces an extra non-linearity in the model. Following Lubrano (1995a), we can replace the last δ in (6.85) by $\hat{\delta}$, the empirical mean of Δy_t. This simplifies matters since the marginal likelihood function of ρ keeps the same structure as in the case $p = 1$. Let us define $x'_t = [1, t]$ and

$$x'_t(\rho) = [x'_t - \rho x'_{t-1}, \Delta y^*_{t-1}, \ldots, \Delta y^*_{t-p+1}], \qquad (6.86)$$

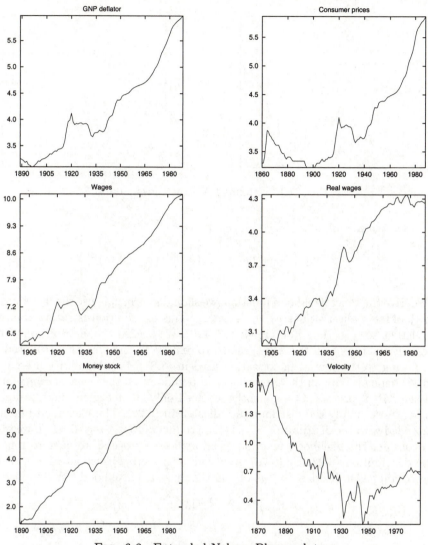

FIG. 6.8. Extended Nelson–Plosser data

where $\Delta y_t^* = \Delta y_t - \hat{\delta}$. Using a matrix notation for stacking the T observations together, the model can be put in the regression format

$$y(\rho) = X(\rho)\beta + \epsilon, \qquad (6.87)$$

where $\beta = (\mu, \delta, a_1^*, \ldots, a_{p-1}^*)'$. In an AR($p$) model, the approximate likelihood function is conditional on the first p observations:

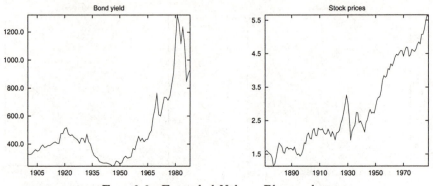

FIG. 6.9. Extended Nelson–Plosser data

$$l(\rho, \mu, \delta, a^*, \sigma^2; y|y_0, y_1, \ldots, y_{p-1},) \propto \sigma^{-(T-p+1)/2}$$
$$\times \exp\left\{-\frac{1}{2\sigma^2}[y(\rho) - X(\rho)\beta]'[y(\rho) - X(\rho)\beta]\right\}. \tag{6.88}$$

To derive the exact likelihood function, we should in principle use the distribution of the first p observations $y_0, y_1, \ldots, y_{p-1}$. This distribution is rather complex to derive, see e.g. Hamilton (1994: 123–125). We needed the distribution of the first observation y_0 in the AR(1) model to remove the singularity introduced by μ. Owing to the special factorization used in (6.85), the singularity present in (6.88) depends only on the product $(1 - \rho)\mu$ and not on the other parameters a^* of the AR(p) process. Consequently, we need only the marginal distribution of y_0, or more simply the distribution indicated in (6.22). The likelihood function extended with the distribution of y_0 is the product of (6.22) and (6.88). If we want to consider the likelihood function of an explosive process, we have to replace the distribution (6.22) by (6.76) eventually using $q(\rho, v)$ instead of $q(\rho, s)$. By proceeding as in Section 6.5, we obtain the marginal likelihood function in ρ:

$$l(\rho; y, y_0) \propto s_*(\rho)^{-(T-p+1)/2} |M_*(\rho)|^{-1/2} q(\rho, s)^{-1/2}, \tag{6.89}$$

where

$$M_*(\rho) = X'(\rho)X(\rho) + \begin{pmatrix} 1/q(\rho, s) & 0 \\ 0 & 0 \end{pmatrix},$$
$$\beta_*(\rho) = M_*^{-1}(\rho)\left[X'(\rho)y(\rho) + \begin{pmatrix} y_0/q(\rho, s) \\ 0 \end{pmatrix}\right], \tag{6.90}$$
$$s_*(\rho) = y'(\rho)y(\rho) + y_0^2/q(\rho, s) - \beta_*'(\rho)M_*(\rho)\beta_*(\rho).$$

6.6.2 *The Empirical Results*

The Nelson–Plosser data set has been used by several authors for comparing unit root tests, see e.g. Perron (1989), Phillips (1991a), and others. These annual data cover the main macroeconomic indicators of the United States. They start between 1860 and 1900 and end in 1970. Schotman and van Dijk (1993) have

Table 6.3 *Unit root tests on the extended Nelson–Plosser data set*

Series	Start	p	Trend	ADF	Non-lin. K_{01}	Non-lin. $\Pr(\rho \geq 1\|y)$	Linear $\Pr(\rho \geq 1\|y)$
Real GNP	1909	2	yes	−3.52*	0.76*	0.033*	0.002*
Nominal GNP	1909	2	yes	−2.06	5.75	0.146	0.066
Real GNP per cap.	1909	2	yes	−3.59*	0.67*	0.031*	0.002*
Industrial prod.	1860	2	yes	−3.62*	0.42*	0.014*	0.040*
Employment	1890	2	yes	−3.47*	0.37*	0.011*	0.003*
Unemployment rate	1890	4	no	−4.04*	0.02*	0.001*	0.001*
GNP deflator	1889	2	yes	−1.62	18.6	0.259	0.132
Consumer prices	1860	4	yes	−1.22	33.7	0.211	0.185
Nominal wages	1900	2	yes	−2.40	4.78	0.104	0.029*
Real wages	1900	2	yes	−1.71	7.07	0.220	0.292
Money stock	1889	2	yes	−2.91	0.97*	0.014*	0.007*
Velocity	1869	2	yes	−1.62	19.1	0.492	0.211
Bond yield	1900	4	no	−1.35	7.88	0.225	0.240
Stock prices	1871	2	yes	−2.44	7.02	0.228	0.063

* Indicates when the unit root hypothesis is rejected at the 5 per cent probability level.

extended the series until 1988. All the series are plotted in Figs 6.7 to 6.9. The end of the sample proved to be highly informative in the sense that the conclusion of Nelson and Plosser (1982) that all the series except the unemployment rate were I(1) was invalidated for three series according to Schotman and van Dijk (1991b). We have analysed these series with three methods:

1) The Bayes factor (6.8) can be computed using the exact likelihood function (6.88) of the non-linear model provided that a proper prior is used for ρ. Thornber's prior is a good candidate as it is integrable over [0,1]. However, the complete Jeffreys' prior cannot be used as shown above. The prior on μ has to be chosen flat. Any other integrable prior on ρ can be used. We used Lubrano's prior (6.66) with $v = 0.333$.

2) When (6.88) is extended so as to cover explosive values of ρ, it is possible to compute a 95 per cent posterior confidence interval of ρ and to see if it contains the unit root, or to compute the tail area after $\rho = 1$. Any type of prior for ρ is eligible. As for the Bayes factor, we took Lubrano's prior.

3) The marginal likelihood function (6.56) of the linear model, conditional on y_0, can be used together with Phillips' prior to compute the same tail area.

To analyse the data set, we selected the number of additional lags with the Schwarz criterion computed with the first model and we added a trend whenever the graph of the data suggested to do so.

The results are grouped in Table 6.3, and the posterior densities are contained in Figs 6.10 to 6.12. We quickly see that the classical and the Bayesian results are in a fair agreement if we adopt a 5 per cent probability level. The classical

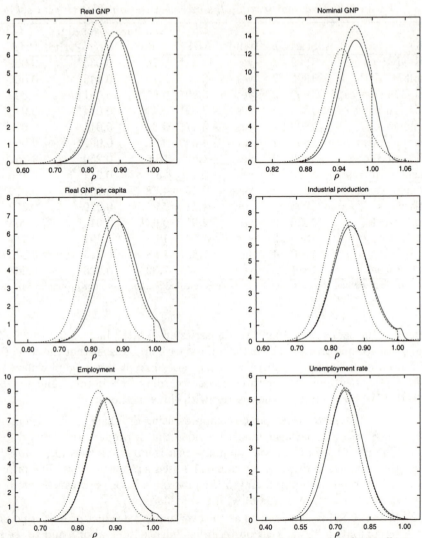

The solid line is the posterior density of ρ computed with Lubrano's prior, the non-linear model, and the exact likelihood. The dashed line corresponds to the same posterior, but truncated to the range [0,1]. The dotted line is the posterior of ρ corresponding to the linear model with Phillips' prior.

FIG. 6.10. Posterior densities for the Nelson–Plosser data

ADF test rejects the unit root in five cases out of 14. Posterior odds or posterior probabilities computed with the non-linear model reject the unit root in six identical series, while the Phillips approach rejects it in one more case. The classical test finds a unit root in the money stock while none of the Bayesian tests does. The Phillips test is the only one to reject the unit root for the nominal

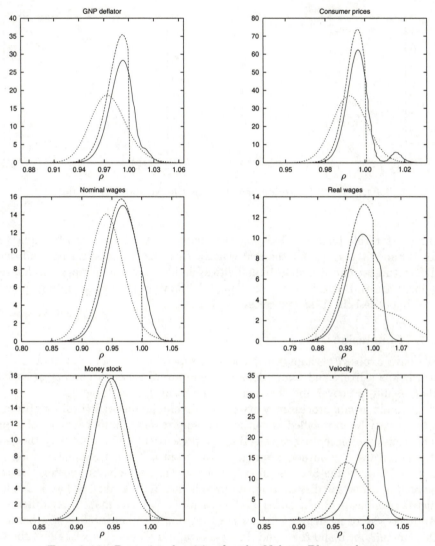

FIG. 6.11. Posterior densities for the Nelson–Plosser data

wages.

From a decisional point of view, it makes no difference to use a posterior odds or a posterior confidence interval, provided the same prior and likelihood function are used. Note that the range of integration is not the same. It is truncated to [0,1] for the posterior odds and not truncated for the posterior confidence interval. Consequently, the region above one does not contain spurious information.

It is clearly apparent from the graphs of the posterior densities of ρ that the linear model is 'biased' against the unit root. Jeffreys' prior manages to correct

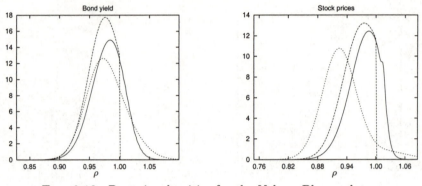

FIG. 6.12. Posterior densities for the Nelson–Plosser data

slightly for this bias by distorting the shape of the density to the right (see for instance the graph for the real wages). But this correction is not sufficient. Truncating at one can hide bimodalities, as in the consumer price index and velocity cases. But this does not change the final decision of accepting the unit root hypothesis in these two series.

6.7 Conclusion

We have exposed perhaps a heterodox viewpoint about the unit root debate, which was a lively and funny debate. There are of course a number of aspects that we did not cover and that may be important for the topic.

A random walk process may experience several jumps. In an ordinary process, a temporary jump is called an outlier and a permanent jump a structural break. The decision of accepting or rejecting the presence of a unit root may thus well depend on the way outliers are taken into account. The normal distribution has thin tails, while the Student distribution has thicker tails. Supposing that the error has a normal distribution, as in this chapter, or that it has a Student distribution, as in Hoek, Lucas, and van Dijk (1995), can make a big difference. Another way of modelling outliers is to introduce the possibility of a break in the constant term and the trend. In a classical framework, Perron (1989) showed that when the breaks are taken into account, most of the unit roots found in the Nelson–Plosser data set disappear. Franses, Hoek, and Paap (1997), in the context of seasonality, show also that a structural mean shift can substantially alter the conclusion concerning the presence or the absence of a unit root.

The unit root hypothesis was defined inside a finite order AR process. If the true process contains an MA component, a sufficiently high order for the AR part can compensate for the absence of the MA part (which is not so easy to infer on, as seen in Chapter 5). However, a highly parameterized model is not usually a good solution, so that it may be preferable to introduce an MA part. Moreover, too parsimonious an AR process can present a unit root that could be cancelled just by the presence of an MA part. Consequently MA errors may be important.

Chib and Greenberg (1994) propose a regression model with stationary ARMA errors, but possibly including an unrestricted autoregressive part. They adjust an AR(1) with a constant and a trend on the quarterly US real GNP covering the period 1951.2 to 1988.4. Their model includes an MA(2) error process which is highly significant. They conclude in favour of the presence of a unit root.

A unit root is important as it implies the persistence of shocks. When a unit root is imposed, the AR process becomes $\alpha(L)(\Delta y_t - \delta) = \epsilon_t$. The stochastic trend present in the series is defined by $S_t = S_{t-1} + \delta + \epsilon_t/\alpha(1)$. The size of $\phi(1) = 1/\alpha(1)$ measures the importance of a shock on the stochastic trend. For a deterministic trend, we have of course $\phi(1) = 0$. Schotman and van Dijk (1993) compute this quantity for the GNP of 16 countries. Here again, taking into account a possible MA part would give more flexibility to the measure. Uhlig (1994a) on the contrary recommends not to pretest for the unit root so as to take into account the uncertainty about the unit root when computing impulse response functions. Finally, there are more recent models, called ARFIMA (for autoregressive fractionally integrated moving average), that take into account persistence in a more refined way than ARIMA models. Koop, Ley, Osiewalski, and Steel (1997) conduct a Bayesian analysis of such models.

6.8   Appendix: Jeffreys' Prior with the Exact Likelihood

Jeffreys' prior was built using the approximate likelihood function in Section 6.5, i.e. discarding the information provided by the distribution of y_0. In this appendix, we show how taking into account the distribution of the initial condition modifies Jeffreys' prior. For the stationary case, these priors are asymptotically equivalent. The non-stationary case is more complex as y_0 must be modelled in a special way. This is because a non-stationary process with $\rho > 1$ cannot have been running for ever.

In a multiparameter framework, the direct application of Jeffreys' principle leads to taking the determinant of the information matrix. However, in practice it is usual to consider only the diagonal elements of the matrix, otherwise the calculations are too tricky and the prior is difficult to interpret. In the case of the exact likelihood, the information matrix is not fully diagonal, as it is with the approximate likelihood.

The Stationary Case

This prior was first derived by Zellner (1971: appendix to Chap. 7). The log likelihood function of the non-linear model, obtained from (6.50), is

$$\log l(\rho, \mu, \sigma^2; y, y_0) = \frac{1}{2}\log(1 - \rho^2) - \frac{T+1}{2}\log\sigma^2$$

$$- \frac{1}{2\sigma^2}[(1 - \rho^2)(y_0 - \mu)^2 + \sum(y_t - \rho y_{t-1} - (1 - \rho)\mu)^2].$$

(6.91)

The second-order direct derivatives are

$$\frac{\partial^2 \log l}{\partial(\sigma^2)^2} = \frac{T+1}{2\sigma^4} - \frac{1}{\sigma^6}[(1-\rho^2)(y_0 - \mu)^2 + \sum(y_t - \rho y_{t-1} - (1-\rho)\mu)^2],$$

$$\frac{\partial^2 \log l}{\partial\mu^2} = -\frac{1}{\sigma^2}[1 - \rho^2 + T(1-\rho)^2], \tag{6.92}$$

$$\frac{\partial^2 \log l}{\partial\rho^2} = -\frac{1+\rho^2}{(1-\rho^2)^2} + \frac{1}{\sigma^2}[(y_0 - \mu)^2 - \sum_{t=1}^{T}(y_{t-1} - \mu)^2].$$

Taking minus the expectation with respect to the distribution of y_t gives

$$-\mathrm{E}\frac{\partial^2 \log l}{\partial(\sigma^2)^2} = \frac{(T+1)\sigma^2}{2\sigma^6} - \frac{T+1}{2\sigma^4} = \frac{T+1}{2\sigma^4},$$

$$-\mathrm{E}\frac{\partial^2 \log l}{\partial\mu^2} = \frac{1}{\sigma^2}[1 - \rho^2 + T(1-\rho)^2], \tag{6.93}$$

$$-\mathrm{E}\frac{\partial^2 \log l}{\partial\rho^2} = \frac{1+\rho^2}{(1-\rho^2)^2} + \frac{T-1}{1-\rho^2}.$$

The infinite MA representation of $y_t - \mu$ and the distribution of y_0 provide the necessary expectations. Jeffreys' prior is obtained by taking the square root of the diagonal elements of the information matrix. If we apply Jeffreys' principle separately to σ^2 and to the other parameters, the prior of μ becomes independent of σ^2. We obtain

$$\varphi(\sigma^2) \propto 1/\sigma^2,$$

$$\varphi(\mu|\rho) \propto \sqrt{T(1-\rho)^2 + 1 - \rho^2},$$

$$\varphi(\rho) \propto \sqrt{\frac{T}{1-\rho^2}} \sqrt{\left[1 + \frac{2\rho^2}{T(1-\rho^2)}\right]}. \tag{6.94}$$

We have separated the terms coming from the likelihood of the sample $(y_1, \ldots, y_T)$ and from the initial condition y_0. When $T \to \infty$, the terms coming from the initial condition become negligible and Jeffreys' prior is then identical to that derived using the approximate likelihood function.

The Non-stationary Case

Uhlig (1994b) gives the expression of Jeffreys' prior using $q(\rho, s)$ given in (6.77) together with the likelihood function (6.79). But the second-order derivatives are very tedious. In this appendix, we use $q(\rho, v)$ given in (6.78), instead of $q(\rho, s)$, because this simplifies a lot of the results. The initial observation is supposed to be distributed as

$$y_0 \sim N\left(\mu, \sigma^2 \frac{1+v}{1+v-\rho^2}\right). \tag{6.95}$$

The log likelihood function of the non-linear model, supposing $\sigma^2 = 1$ (since we apply Jeffreys' principle separately to the other parameters), is

$$\log l(\rho, \mu, v; y, y_0) = \tfrac{1}{2}\log(1+v-\rho^2)$$
$$- \tfrac{1}{2}\left[(y_0 - \mu)^2 \frac{1+v-\rho^2}{1+v} + \sum(y_t - \rho y_{t-1} - (1-\rho)\mu)^2\right]. \tag{6.96}$$

The second-order direct derivatives are

$$\frac{\partial^2 \log l}{\partial \mu^2} = -\frac{1+v-\rho^2}{1+v} - T(1-\rho)^2,$$
$$\frac{\partial^2 \log l}{\partial \rho^2} = -\frac{1+v+\rho^2}{(1+v-\rho^2)^2} + \frac{(y_0-\mu)^2}{1+v} - \sum_{t=1}^{T}(y_{t-1}-\mu)^2. \tag{6.97}$$

Taking the square root of minus the expectation of the expression in the first line directly gives the prior of $\mu|\rho$:

$$\varphi(\mu|\rho) \propto \sqrt{T(1-\rho)^2 + \frac{1+v-\rho^2}{1+v}}. \tag{6.98}$$

For $v = 0$, we go back to the stationary case derived in the previous subsection. For large values of T, the prior becomes very close to Jeffreys' prior (6.71) computed with the approximate likelihood function.

The prior $\varphi(\rho)$ requires more calculations. Taking minus the expectation of the second derivative leads to

$$-\mathrm{E}\frac{\partial^2 \log l}{\partial \rho^2} = \frac{1+v+\rho^2}{(1+v-\rho^2)^2} - \frac{1}{1+v-\rho^2} + \sum_{t=0}^{T-1}\mathrm{E}(y_t-\mu)^2. \tag{6.99}$$

Using $y_t - \mu = \sum_{i=0}^{t-1}\rho^i \epsilon_{t-i} + \rho^t(y_0 - \mu)$ we get

$$\mathrm{E}(y_t-\mu)^2 = \mathrm{E}(\sum_{i=0}^{t-1}\rho^i \epsilon_{t-i})^2 + \rho^{2t}\mathrm{E}(y_0-\mu)^2 + 2\rho^t \mathrm{E}(y_0-\mu)\mathrm{E}(\sum_{i=0}^{t-1}\rho^i \epsilon_{t-i})$$
$$= \frac{1-\rho^{2t}}{1-\rho^2} + \rho^{2t}\frac{1+v}{1+v-\rho^2},$$

$$\tag{6.100}$$

as the third term is zero and $\sigma^2 = 1$. Let us compute the required sums:

$$\sum_{t=0}^{T-1} \frac{1-\rho^{2t}}{1-\rho^2} = \frac{1}{1-\rho^2}\left[T - \frac{1-\rho^{2T}}{1-\rho^2}\right],$$

$$\sum_{t=0}^{T-1} \rho^{2t} \frac{1+v}{1+v-\rho^2} = \frac{1+v}{1+v-\rho^2}\left[\frac{1-\rho^{2T}}{1-\rho^2}\right]. \tag{6.101}$$

Finally,

$$\varphi(\rho) \propto \sqrt{\frac{1+v+\rho^2}{1+v-\rho^2}\left[(1+v)\frac{1-\rho^{2T}}{1-\rho^2} - 1\right] + \frac{1}{1-\rho^2}\left[T - \frac{1-\rho^{2T}}{1-\rho^2}\right]}. \tag{6.102}$$

The last term is exactly Phillips's prior (6.65) (where the proportionality comes from neglecting the factor $T^{1/2}$). The first terms come from the initial condition. For very small v, the joint Jeffreys' prior has the same behaviour as in the stationary case. There is a zero singularity around the unit root. When v increases, this singularity is progressively removed.

Remarks:

1) Jeffreys' prior represents the exact counterpart of the properties of the likelihood function: zero singularity versus infinite singularity and vice versa.

2) Uhlig (1994b) reports the following result for the information matrix:

$$-\mathrm{E}\frac{\partial^2 l}{\partial \rho^2} = \frac{1}{2}\frac{q'(\rho,s)^2}{q(\rho,s)^2} + \frac{1}{1-\rho^2}\left(T - \rho^{2s}\frac{1-\rho^{2T}}{1-\rho^2}\right), \tag{6.103}$$

using $q(\rho,s)$ instead of $q(\rho,v)$. The prior he considers is formed by Jeffreys' prior *stricto sensu* multiplied by the density of the first observation.

7

HETEROSCEDASTICITY AND ARCH

7.1 Introduction

In Chapter 5, we studied the linear regression model supposing that the conditional variance of the endogenous variable is constant over time. In this chapter, we are going to relax this assumption, i.e. to study heteroscedastic regression models. To motivate the study of particular formulations of heteroscedasticity, it is quite instructive to introduce a regression model with random coefficients:

$$y_t = x_t'\beta_t + \epsilon_t, \qquad \epsilon_t \sim IN(0, \sigma^2), \tag{7.1}$$

where β_t is supposed to be drawn independently from a normal density of mean β and variance Σ:

$$\beta_t \sim IN(\beta, \Sigma). \tag{7.2}$$

The Bayesian analysis of a particular case of this model has been proposed by Griffiths, Drynan, and Prakash (1979). In the absence of repeated observations on the 'individuals' indexed by t, it is necessary to integrate out all the β_t, in order to make inference on the remaining parameters β, Σ, and σ^2. From (7.1) and (7.2), it is easy to conclude (by successively using Theorems A.14 and A.12) that

$$y_t|\beta, \sigma^2, \Sigma \sim N(x_t'\beta, \sigma^2 + x_t'\Sigma x_t). \tag{7.3}$$

This result shows that a regression model with random coefficients and constant variance can be transformed into a regression with constant coefficients and heteroscedastic error term.

In this chapter, we focus our attention on the linear regression model with heteroscedasticity, i.e. quite generally

$$y_t = x_t'\beta + \epsilon_t, \qquad \epsilon_t \sim IN(0, \sigma_t^2). \tag{7.4}$$

There are many ways to specify how the conditional variance σ_t^2 varies with the index t. Maybe the most widespread formulation, at least with cross-section data, assumes that σ_t^2 is a known function of observable variables z_t and unknown parameters α:

$$\sigma_t^2 = \sigma^2 h(z_t, \alpha). \tag{7.5}$$

The variables z_t are assumed to be exogenous, in the sense that their distribution does not depend on y_{t+i} ($\forall i \geq 0$) and on the parameters of the model. In some cases, there may be parametric restrictions between β and α, as in the case where $h(z_t, \alpha) = h(x'_t \beta)$. Typically, the latter situation prevents (even partly) analytical posterior results from being obtained, so that the posterior density of the parameters has to be treated fully by numerical integration. This is why we do not cover this case. When β and α are completely variation free, (7.4)–(7.5) are the model studied by Breusch and Pagan (1979) from a classical viewpoint and by Bauwens and Lubrano (1991) from a Bayesian viewpoint.

Another very widespread model for σ_t^2, in the case of time series data, is to assume that it depends on past innovations, i.e.

$$\sigma_t^2 = \sigma^2 \, h(\epsilon_{t-1}, \ldots, \epsilon_{t-p}, \alpha). \tag{7.6}$$

This particular class of heteroscedasticity was first introduced by Engle (1982) and is named autoregressive conditional heteroscedasticity (ARCH). The simplest case is when $h(.) = 1 + \alpha \, \epsilon_{t-1}^2$, the ARCH(1) model. A Bayesian treatment of the ARCH model was first given by Geweke (1988b, 1989b). ARCH models were further developed by Bollerslev (1986) with the generalized autoregressive conditional heteroscedasticity model (GARCH). Kleibergen and van Dijk (1993) and Bauwens and Lubrano (1996) gave a Bayesian treatment of this model and of some of its extensions.

A common feature of (7.5) and (7.6) is that the function $h(.)$ is *deterministic*: for a given parameter value, once the conditioning information set is specified, the variance is uniquely determined by the function $h(.)$. Another possibility is to specify the variance as a *stochastic* function. This has been proposed as an alternative to ARCH models, namely with the class of 'stochastic volatility' (hereafter SV) models. In the simplest SV regression model, the logarithm of the variance of ϵ_t is specified as

$$\log \sigma_t^2 = \log \sigma^2 + \alpha \log \sigma_{t-1}^2 + u_t, \tag{7.7}$$

where u_t is a random variable, e.g. $\sim IN(0, 1)$ and independent of ϵ_t. SV models are much more difficult to estimate than ARCH models, because the computation of the likelihood function requires integration of the joint distribution of y_t and σ_t^2 (for $t = 1, \ldots, T$) with respect to the T stochastic variances (since they are not observable). Even with a simple model like (7.7), the integral is not known analytically. It may even be argued that Bayesian estimation of SV models is easier than ML estimation, see e.g. Jacquier, Polson, and Rossi (1994).

What is the reason for taking care of heteroscedasticity? In a classical framework, heteroscedasticity induces an inconsistency in the estimator of the variance of the ordinary least square estimator. Although the estimator itself is unbiased, the usual t-statistics are no longer correct. In a Bayesian framework, sampling properties are not of interest. But even if the parameters of the variance σ_t^2 are nuisance parameters, neglecting the heteroscedasticity may result in a posterior distribution for the regression coefficients which is different from what it is when the heteroscedasticity is taken into account. Not considering the 'right' model may have a cost which can be measured by a loss of utility which depends on the statistical or decisional problem considered.

Modelling the variance can also be interesting in itself, whether in the classical or Bayesian framework. Understanding and forecasting the behaviour of the variance of a series is of prime importance for financial markets as σ_t^2 is usually taken as a proxy for risk. By assuming some parametric form of heteroscedasticity, it is possible to draw inference not only on the parameters β of the regression function but also on the parameters α inducing the variability of the variance across the sample. It is then possible to compute a predictive distribution of a future variance, i.e. to predict the risk.

This chapter is organized as follows. Section 7.2 deals with the case of functional heteroscedasticity, corresponding to (7.5). The next three sections deal successively with ARCH models, GARCH models, and some special topics linked to these models. Section 7.6 proposes a general method to detect heteroscedasticity. The last section concludes.

7.2 Functional Heteroscedasticity

The regression model we consider is (7.4)–(7.5) where z_t is a set of ℓ variables. The elements of z_t may be functions of x_t, including the limit case $z_t = x_t$. We exclude that z_t has a constant because its role is taken by σ^2: we assume that $h(.)$ is defined so that $h(z_t, 0) = 1$. For $\alpha = 0$, we are back to the homoscedastic model. The formulation (7.5) covers two cases:

1) Multiplicative heteroscedasticity, with

$$\sigma^2 h(z_t'\alpha) = \sigma^2 \exp(z_t'\alpha), \quad \forall \alpha \in \mathbb{R}^\ell. \tag{7.8}$$

2) Additive heteroscedasticity, with

$$\sigma^2 h(z_t'\alpha) = \sigma^2 + z_t\tilde{\alpha} \quad \text{with } \tilde{\alpha} = \alpha/\sigma^2, \tag{7.9}$$

to which we must impose the positivity condition

$$h(z_t'\alpha) > 0, \quad \forall \alpha \in A \subset \mathbb{R}^\ell. \tag{7.10}$$

If $z_t > 0$, a sufficient condition is that α belongs to the positive orthant.

For example, the regression model (2.38) with a change of variance from σ_1^2 to σ_2^2 at date $T_1 + 1$ is an additive heteroscedasticity model with z_t the indicator variable of $t > T_1$, i.e. $\sigma_t^2 = \sigma^2 + \alpha z_t$, with $\sigma^2 = \sigma_1^2$, and $\alpha = \sigma_2^2 - \sigma_1^2$, with the restriction $\alpha > -\sigma^2$.

7.2.1 *Prior Density and Likelihood Function*

The parameters of the model are β, σ^2, and α. It is obvious that if α is known, the model defined by (7.4)–(7.5) can be transformed into a homoscedastic regression model by dividing y_t and x_t by the square root of $h(z_t, \alpha)$. Conditionally on α, all the results of the Bayesian analysis of the linear model given in Section 2.7 can be used. It is therefore convenient to factorize the prior density as

$$\varphi(\beta, \sigma^2, \alpha) = \varphi(\beta|\sigma^2)\,\varphi(\sigma^2)\,\varphi(\alpha), \qquad (7.11)$$

and to specify a normal–inverted gamma-2 density for σ^2 and β:

$$\sigma^2 \sim IG_2(s_0, \nu_0), \quad \beta|\sigma^2 \sim N(\beta_0, \sigma^2.M_0^{-1}). \qquad (7.12)$$

Another possible choice is a Student density for β, independent of σ^2 (see Subsection 4.5.2). The prior on α can be chosen freely as the analysis must be completed by numerical integration on this parameter, along the principles defined in Section 3.2.

Concerning the definition of a non-informative prior, using the square root of the determinant of the information matrix, following Jeffreys' invariance principle, gives a complicated prior because the information matrix is not block diagonal between the parameters σ^2 and α. For β and σ^2, it is convenient to take $1/\sigma^2$ as a diffuse prior, as in the homoscedastic model. A non-informative prior on α can be defined to be flat on the domain of admissible values, which is called A hereafter:

$$\varphi(\alpha) \propto 1 \quad \text{if } \alpha \in A. \qquad (7.13)$$

In order to write the likelihood function, we define y as the vector of the T observations on the endogenous variable, X as the $T \times k$ matrix of observations on the exogenous variables, and the $T \times T$ diagonal matrix

$$H(\alpha) = \text{diag}(1/h(z_1'\alpha),\, 1/h(z_2'\alpha),\, \ldots,\, 1/h(z_T'\alpha)). \qquad (7.14)$$

The likelihood function can be written as

$$l(\beta, \sigma^2, \alpha; y)$$

$$\propto \sigma^{-T} |H(\alpha)|^{1/2} \exp\left[-\frac{1}{2\sigma^2}(y - X\beta)'H(\alpha)(y - X\beta) \right]$$

$$\propto \sigma^{-T} |H(\alpha)|^{1/2} \exp\left(-\frac{1}{2\sigma^2}\{[\beta - b(\alpha)]'X'H(\alpha)X[\beta - b(\alpha)] + s(\alpha)\} \right),$$

$$\qquad (7.15)$$

where

$$b(\alpha) = [X'H(\alpha)X]^{-1}X'H(\alpha)y,$$
$$s(\alpha) = y'[H(\alpha) - H(\alpha)X(X'H(\alpha)X)^{-1}X'H(\alpha)]y. \qquad (7.16)$$

The last expression shows that, conditionally on α, this likelihood function has the same form as that of a homoscedastic regression model. Note that $b(\alpha)$ is the weighted least squares estimator of β.

7.2.2 Posterior Analysis

Using the prior (7.12), it is obvious that the conditional posterior density of $\beta|\alpha$ is Student:

$$\beta|\alpha, y \sim t_k(\beta_*(\alpha), s_*(\alpha), M_*(\alpha), \nu_*), \qquad (7.17)$$

where

$$
\begin{aligned}
M_*(\alpha) &= M_0 + X'H(\alpha)X, \\
\beta_*(\alpha) &= M_*^{-1}(\alpha)[M_0\beta_0 + X'H(\alpha)y], \\
s_*(\alpha) &= s_0 + s(\alpha) + b'(\alpha)X'H(\alpha)Xb(\alpha) - \beta_*(\alpha)'M_*(\alpha)\beta_*(\alpha), \\
\nu_* &= \nu_0 + T.
\end{aligned}
\qquad (7.18)
$$

The marginal posterior density of α is obtained as the inverse of the integrating constant of (7.17) times $H(\alpha)^{1/2}$ (from the likelihood function) times the prior density of α:

$$\varphi(\alpha|y) \propto |H(\alpha)|^{1/2}\,|M_*(\alpha)|^{-1/2}\,s_*(\alpha)^{-(\nu_*-k)/2}\,\varphi(\alpha). \qquad (7.19)$$

Modelling heteroscedasticity with exogenous variables may not be parsimonious. There is a tendency for the modeller to use several variables in z_t, such as the squares of the exogenous variables of the regression. As explained in Section 7.6, an auxiliary regression based on the squared 'Bayesian residuals' can be used to select the variables of z_t. If the dimension of α is one or two, one can use deterministic rules of integration to get marginal posterior results on the parameters. Otherwise, one has to resort to Monte Carlo integration methods.

Whatever Monte Carlo technique is used, it should take advantage of the knowledge that the conditional posterior density of β is Student. This can be exploited to marginalize the conditional posterior moments of β by the technique of Rao–Blackwellization: see formulae (3.41)–(3.43). As numerical integration has to be performed on α, the difficulty comes of course from the fact that the posterior density of α does not belong to a known class of densities. To simulate random draws from it, several possibilities are open:

1) The griddy-Gibbs sampler (see Subsection 3.4.3).
2) The Metropolis–Hastings algorithm (see Subsection 3.4.3).
3) Importance sampling (see Subsection 3.4.2).

For the last two methods, an importance function has to be defined for α. Its choice is not too complex in the case of multiplicative heteroscedasticity. Positive and negative values of α are admissible. A normal or Student approximation to the log posterior, centred on the posterior mode of α, is a good starting point. The case of additive heteroscedasticity is more delicate as the domain of definition of α is restricted. A normal or Student importance function is still possible, but the use of the prior (7.13) means that all the sampled values of α not in A must be rejected. Thus the method may be very inefficient. In that case, the griddy-Gibbs sampler turns out to be convenient, since it directly uses the relevant domain of integration.

7.2.3   A Test of Homoscedasticity

As $h(z_t, 0) = 1$, a test for homoscedasticity is a test of $\alpha = 0$. Since this is a sharp hypothesis, the principle of posterior odds is not very convenient (it would require giving a positive probability to the point 0 and use of a mixed discrete and continuous prior). Homoscedasticity can be 'accepted' if the point 0 belongs to a 95 per cent HPD region of α. If α is of dimension 1, this region is an interval that can be easily found. In the multi-dimensional case, finding an HPD region is more difficult, since there is no guarantee that the posterior density of α is symmetric. An approximate HPD region can be built by considering the transformation of α defined by

$$\xi = [\alpha - E(\alpha|y)]' \text{Var}(\alpha|y)^{-1} [\alpha - E(\alpha|y)]. \tag{7.20}$$

We accept homoscedasticity if

$$\xi_* = E(\alpha|y)' \text{Var}(\alpha|y)^{-1} E(\alpha|y) \tag{7.21}$$

belongs to the (95 per cent) HPD interval of ξ. The posterior density of ξ can be obtained by Monte Carlo simulation, using the same draws as for computing the marginal posterior results. If one has stored the sample of α values generated to get the posterior moments $E(\alpha|y)$ and $\text{Var}(\alpha|y)$, one can again use the same draws of α to compute ξ for each α, and then trace a smoothed histogram of the posterior density of ξ.

7.2.4   Application to Electricity Consumption

Bauwens, Fiebig, and Steel (1994) consider the electricity consumption of a sample of 174 Australian households and explain this consumption by the ownership of 11 categories of electric appliances, four socio-economic variables, and three composite variables mixing appliance ownership and the size of the household or the size of the house. For 108 households, there was direct metering of electricity consumption for some of the appliances. The purpose of the study was to make inferences on the end-use electricity consumption concerning the 11 appliances (conditional demand analysis). The variability of the number of appliances owned by the households should cause a heteroscedastic effect. Let us call y_t the total electricity consumption, x_t the vector of 19 exogenous variables (including the constant term), and z_t the total number of appliances owned by household t. The model is

$$y_t = x_t'\beta + u_t, \qquad u_t \sim N(0, \sigma^2 z_t^\alpha). \tag{7.22}$$

The hypothesis of homoscedasticity corresponds to $\alpha = 0$. One problem with this model of electricity consumption is that it may very easily produce negative appliance consumptions due to imprecision in the data. Positivity constraints have to be introduced on several elements of β. As Bauwens, Fiebig, and Steel (1994) fixed α equal to one, their posterior density of β is a Student density from which it is easy to generate random draws and retain only those which

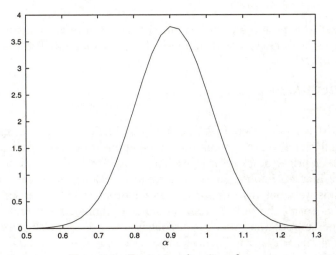

FIG. 7.1. Posterior density of α
for the end-use electricity consumption model

pass the positivity constraints. Truncated moments of β are thus computed by a simulation technique.

As an extension to this analysis, we consider α to be unknown. Rejection sampling (for the positivity restrictions on β) is used in this case within the loop of integration over α, from the conditional posterior density of β given α, which is still Student, see (7.17). Conditional truncated moments are then cumulated to be marginalized with respect to α. Under a diffuse prior, the posterior expectation of α is equal to 0.91, and the standard deviation to 0.11. The posterior density of α was evaluated by Simpson's rule using 33 points. For each point of α, 1000 draws of β were generated, out of which only an average of 54 draws were accepted. The graph of the posterior density of α, given in Fig. 7.1, shows firstly that the value 1 chosen by Bauwens, Fiebig, and Steel (1994) was very reasonable, and secondly that the heteroscedastic effect cannot be avoided. Inference results obtained for β are not very different from those reported in the first column of Table 3 in Bauwens, Fiebig and Steel (1994) and are not reproduced here.

As an alternative to Simpson integration, a direct simulation method was tried as follows. The marginal density of α was first numerically evaluated by the trapezoidal rule with 66 points. Random draws of α were generated by inversion of the distribution function, and were used to compute the conditional posterior density of $\beta|\alpha$, from which random draws of β were simulated. The method was less efficient in terms of computational time than the method of the previous paragraph, but it can be easily generalized for a higher dimension of α. It corresponds to a griddy-Gibbs sampling on α and then to a direct simulation of the conditional posterior of β. The simulation of β was necessary only because of the need to impose the positivity restrictions on several elements of β. Without such restrictions, it would be more efficient to marginalize the conditional moments of β.

7.3 ARCH Models

7.3.1 *Introduction*

Even if ARCH models were first introduced by Engle (1982) in an application to the UK inflation rate, their main domain of application concerns financial series such as stock prices, stock returns, exchange rates, and interest rates. The theory of efficient markets implies that the changes in stock prices are independent over time; if this were not true, opportunities for profit would arise. As information is available to all the agents, they would react immediately and compete for these opportunities that would consequently vanish. This suggests a random walk model $\Delta y_t = e_t$ with $\text{Cov}(e_t, e_{t-j}) = 0$, for any $j > 0$. In finance, e_t is often interpreted as the 'news' arriving on the market. The observation of financial series often reveals that important price fluctuations are followed by periods of relative quiet (see Fig. 7.2 for an example). This effect is called volatility clustering. It suggests a form of temporal dependence between the squares of e_t, such that $\text{Cov}(e_t^2, e_{t-j}^2) \neq 0$, for some $j > 0$. These non-zero covariances are not compatible with the (unconditional) normality of e_t. Suppose that $e_1 \sim N(0,1)$ and $e_2|e_1 \sim N(0, \sigma^2(e_1^2))$, meaning that the conditional variance of e_2 is a function of e_1. Then $\text{Cov}(e_1^2, e_2^2) = \text{Cov}[e_1^2, \text{E}(e_2^2|e_1^2)] = \text{Cov}[e_1^2, \sigma^2(e_1^2)] \neq 0$. Moreover, the unconditional distribution of e_2 cannot be normal because the conditional variance of e_2 depends on e_1 (see Theorem A.14).

The idea behind the building of ARCH processes is that the square of Δy_t follows an autoregressive process. The question of course is to determine if this type of model is able to mimic correctly the behaviour of financial series. In addition to volatility clustering, financial series display two stylized facts (see for instance Pagan 1996, or Teräsvirta 1996): fat tails or leptokurtosis, i.e. a large excess kurtosis (compared with the normal distribution), and an autocorrelation function of the squares which starts at a low value and decays rather slowly.

As an example, let us consider the monthly series of the exchange rate of the US dollar against the German mark (DM), taken in first difference, covering the period 1960.1–1991.6. It is plotted in Fig. 7.2. Its empirical kurtosis is equal to 19.45. The first autocorrelation of the squares is 0.25, varies somewhat till the sixth autocorrelation with a peak at 0.33, and then declines gradually to zero.

ARCH models gave rise to an enormous literature which is reviewed in Bera and Higgins (1993) and Bollerslev, Engle, and Nelson (1994), for statistical properties and procedures, and Bollerslev, Chou, and Kroner (1992) for empirical applications in finance. Bayesian inference was developed by Geweke (1988b, 1989b) for ARCH models, and by Kleibergen and van Dijk (1993) and Bauwens and Lubrano (1998) for GARCH models.

The rest of this section is organized as follows. After a review of the statistical properties of ARCH processes with zero mean, we present the Bayesian analysis

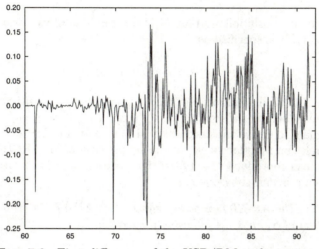

FIG. 7.2. First difference of the USD/DM exchange rate

of these models and illustrate it with the USD/DM series. Next, we consider the case of regression models with ARCH errors. The next section treats the more general GARCH case.

7.3.2 *Properties of ARCH Processes*

Engle (1982) introduces a quite simple but powerful model which is based on the distinction between the *marginal* variances and the *conditional* variances of a series. If y_t represents a return (typically the log-price differential of an asset), market efficiency means that y_t is an uncorrelated stochastic process with zero mean (or more generally a martingale difference sequence). Thus the price (in logarithms) is supposed to behave like a random walk (more generally a martingale). Conditionally on its past denoted $\mathcal{I}_{t-1}$, the variable y_t is modelled as

$$y_t = \epsilon_t \sqrt{h_t}. \tag{7.23}$$

The ϵ_t process is assumed to be a martingale difference sequence with the following moments:

$$\begin{aligned}
\mathrm{E}_{t-1}(\epsilon_t) &= 0, \\
\mathrm{E}_{t-1}(\epsilon_t^2) &= 1, \\
\mathrm{E}_{t-1}(\epsilon_t^3) &= 0, \\
\mathrm{E}_{t-1}(\epsilon_t^4) &= \lambda,
\end{aligned} \tag{7.24}$$

where $\mathrm{E}_{t-1}(.)$ denotes the conditional expectation $\mathrm{E}(.|\mathcal{I}_{t-1})$. Alternatively, the ϵ_t sequence can be assumed IID, but the independence assumption cannot be replaced by uncorrelatedness. The unit variance hypothesis in (7.24) is an identification restriction (if the variance was left free, there would be a redundant parameter). It obviously follows that h_t is the *conditional* variance of y_t (with respect to $\mathcal{I}_{t-1}$). It is specified as

$$h_t = \omega + \alpha_1 y_{t-1}^2 + \cdots + \alpha_p y_{t-p}^2, \qquad (7.25)$$

which is the ARCH(p) equation. In order to guarantee the positivity of h_t, the parameters must satisfy the conditions $\omega > 0$ and $\alpha_i \geq 0$, $\forall i \leq p$.

We are going to derive the unconditional moments of order 1 to 4 of y_t, and the autocorrelation function of y_t^2, in the simple case of an ARCH(1) process, and see if it can reproduce the stylized facts about financial series that were recalled in the previous subsection.

Theorem 7.1 *The ARCH(1) process defined by (7.23)–(7.25) (with $p = 1$, and using α instead of α_1) has the following properties:*

(i) $E(y_t) = E(y_t^3) = 0$.
(ii) $E(y_t^2) = E(h_t) = \omega/(1 - \alpha)$ *if* $0 \leq \alpha < 1$.
(iii) *The kurtosis coefficient of y_t is given by*

$$KC = \lambda \frac{1 - \alpha^2}{1 - \lambda\alpha^2} \quad \text{if } \alpha < \sqrt{\lambda^{-1}}. \qquad (7.26)$$

(iv) *The autocorrelation function of y_t^2 is given by $\rho_j = \alpha^j$ ($j = 0, 1, \ldots$).*

Proof By the law of the iterated expectation, for all $j > 0$,

$$E(y_t^j) = E(h_t^{j/2} \epsilon_t^j) = E[h_t^{j/2} E_{t-1}(\epsilon_t^j)], \qquad (7.27)$$

whence (i) follows by using (7.24).

For $j = 2$, (7.27) gives $E(y_t^2) = E(h_t)$, assumed to be finite. By writing the ARCH(1) equation $h_t = \omega + \alpha y_{t-1}^2$ as $h_t = \omega + \alpha h_{t-1}\epsilon_{t-1}^2$, and taking the expectation on both sides (with respect to the random variables ϵ_{t-1}, ϵ_{t-2}, $\ldots$), we get

$$E(h_t) = \omega + \alpha E(h_{t-1}),$$

which gives (ii) if the process is stationary, since then $E(h_t) = E(h_{t-1})$. This can hold only if $\alpha < 1$, which is a covariance stationarity condition.

For $j = 4$, (7.27) gives $E(y_t^4) = \lambda E(h_t^2)$, assumed to be finite. By squaring the ARCH(1) equation, and taking the expectation, we get

$$E(h_t^2) = \omega^2 + \alpha^2 \lambda E(h_{t-1}^2) + 2\omega\alpha E(h_{t-1}).$$

If the process is stationary, this equation can be solved for $E(h_t^2)$. Dividing $E(y_t^4)$ by the square of $E(y_t^2)$ gives the kurtosis coefficient as in (7.26).

To obtain the autocorrelation function of y_t^2, a convenient way is to add y_t^2 to both sides of the ARCH(1) equation which can be written as

$$y_t^2 = \omega + \alpha y_{t-1}^2 + v_t, \tag{7.28}$$

where $v_t = y_t^2 - h_t = (\epsilon_t^2 - 1) h_t$ is an innovation for y_t^2 since

$$E(v_t) = E[(\epsilon_t^2 - 1) h_t] = E[h_t \, E_{t-1}(\epsilon_t^2 - 1)] = 0,$$
$$E(v_t \, v_{t-i}) = 0 \qquad \forall i \geq 1,$$
$$E(v_t \, y_{t-i}^2) = 0 \qquad \forall i \geq 1.$$

The ARCH(1) process is equivalent to an AR(1) process on y_t^2. The autocorrelation function of y_t^2 follows directly from the standard formulae for the AR(1) process. $\square$

Volatility clustering is induced directly by the parameter α: if h_{t-1} is large (or small), it is likely that y_{t-1} is large (or small), so that the next conditional variance tends to be large (or small), the more so as α is large. The formula (7.26) shows that whatever the distribution of ϵ_t, the kurtosis of the unconditional distribution of y_t is larger than that of the conditional distribution (λ), as soon as $\alpha > 0$ and $\lambda > 1$. For example, for a normal distribution, $\lambda = 3$, and $KC = 3.062, 3.273, 4.84, 9$ if $\alpha = 0.10, 0.20, 0.30, 0.40$, respectively. The ARCH process induces excess kurtosis, but α must be large enough for this effect to be strong. But if α is large, the first autocorrelation of the squared returns is also large, which is in contradiction with the stylized fact that the autocorrelation function starts at a rather low value and declines rather slowly. The ARCH(1) process, with the single parameter α, is not flexible enough to accommodate all the stylized facts. This conclusion is also true even with an ARCH process of higher order ($p > 1$). One solution is to assume a Student distribution with unit variance and ν degrees of freedom for ϵ_t (see the remark at the end of Subsection 7.4.1). For instance, with five degrees of freedom, $\lambda = 3 (\nu - 2)/(\nu - 4) = 15$, and $KC = 9.18, 9.79, 13.50, \infty$, corresponding to the same values of α as above. Another solution is to use a GARCH process (see Subsection 7.4.1). Both solutions were proposed by Bollerslev (1987, 1986).

Let us remark that even if the moments of the unconditional distribution of y_t can be derived, the form of the distribution is not known. All we can say is that it is symmetrical around zero if the conditional distribution of ϵ_t is also symmetrical, and that it is more leptokurtic than the conditional distribution (if $\lambda > 1$).

The covariance stationarity condition for the ARCH(1) process of y_t is $\alpha < 1$. For the ARCH(p) process, it is the same, defining $\sum_{i=1}^{p} \alpha_i = \alpha$. This condition ensures that the second moments exist. For the ARCH(1) case, Nelson (1990) has shown that the process can be strictly stationary even if $\alpha > 1$. The condition for strict stationarity is $E[\ln(\alpha \epsilon_t^2)] < 0$, provided that $\omega > 0$ (see Subsection 7.5.1). If $\epsilon_t \sim N(0,1)$, strict stationarity holds if $\alpha < 3.4$. This is an example of a process that can be strictly stationary without being covariance stationary, because its second moments do not exist.

Finally, let us point out that the ARCH model is useless when ω is equal to zero. It is easy to check that $\mathrm{Var}(y_t) = \mathrm{E}(h_t) = 0$, implying that y_t is equal to its expectation with probability equal to 1 (provided $\alpha < 1$).

7.3.3   *Likelihood Function and Posterior Density*

To write the likelihood function of the ARCH model (7.23)–(7.25), we add the hypothesis

$$\epsilon_t \sim N(0,1). \tag{7.29}$$

The model is dynamic through the conditional variance equation. Because the unconditional distribution of y_t is not known analytically, we cannot complete the likelihood function with the density of the initial conditions. Therefore, we use the conditional likelihood function

$$l(\theta; y, \mathcal{I}_0) = \prod_{t=1}^{T} f(y_t | \mathcal{I}_{t-1}, \theta), \tag{7.30}$$

with $\theta' = (\omega \; \alpha_1 \ldots \alpha_p)$, $y = (y_1 \ldots y_T)$, and $\mathcal{I}_0$ the vector of initial conditions $(y_0, y_{-1}, \ldots, y_{1-p})$. Each conditional density $f(y_t | \mathcal{I}_{t-1}, \theta)$ is $N(0, h_t)$. The initial conditions can be treated either as parameters for inference, or as observed quantities, in which case it is natural to use the first observations as initial conditions. The last option gives the likelihood function

$$l(\theta; y, \mathcal{I}_0) \propto \prod_{t=1}^{T} h_t^{-1/2} \exp \left(-\frac{1}{2} \sum_{t=1}^{T} y_t^2 / h_t \right). \tag{7.31}$$

Imposing the positivity and the stationarity conditions $0 \leq \alpha < 1$ in estimation is a problem for ML estimation, as often also with inequality restrictions. In Bayesian inference, this is not a problem if one simulates the posterior and rejects the draws that do not verify the inequality. This corresponds to imposing the inequality condition through the prior. This approach has been advocated by Geweke (1988b, 1989b). Obviously, there may be a computational efficiency problem if there are many rejections (e.g. because the process is close to being non-stationary).

Engle (1982) proposed a linear declining structure on the coefficients α_i of the ARCH(p) model to reduce drastically the number of parameters (from $p+1$ to 2). The equation (7.25) is replaced by

$$h_t = \omega + 2\alpha \sum_{j=1}^{p} \frac{p+1-j}{p(p+1)} y_{t-j}^2. \tag{7.32}$$

As $\sum_{j=1}^{p}(p+1-j)/(p(p+1)) = 0.5$ and $(p+1-j)/(p(p+1)) > 0$, $\forall j \leq p$, the stationarity condition is again that α must be smaller than one.

It should be obvious that the the likelihood function (7.31) does not belong to the exponential family. There is no alternative for treating the posterior density other than to evaluate it by numerical integration. For the ARCH(1), or the parsimonious ARCH(p) defined by (7.32), a deterministic rule of integration (such as a compound Simpson rule) can be used to compute the posterior results. In the general ARCH(p) case, with p larger than 1, a Monte Carlo technique, such as importance sampling, can be used. Rejections are needed to impose the positivity restrictions, and optionally the stationarity condition.

Since numerical integration is used, any type of prior density can be chosen. A convenient diffuse prior for the parameters ω and α of an ARCH(1) or parsimonious ARCH(p) is

$$\varphi(\omega, \alpha) \propto 1 \text{ if } \omega > 0 \text{ and } \alpha \in [0, 1[. \tag{7.33}$$

When numerically computing the posterior results on the parameters, it is straightforward to compute the posterior results for any conditional variance since h_t is a function of the parameters and the data. For instance, with an ARCH(1), we get

$$\begin{aligned}
\mathrm{E}(h_t|y) &= \mathrm{E}(\omega|y) + \mathrm{E}(\alpha|y)\, y_{t-1}^2, \\
\mathrm{Var}(h_t|y) &= \mathrm{Var}(\omega|y) + \mathrm{Var}(\alpha|y)\, y_{t-1}^4 + 2\, \mathrm{Cov}(\omega, \alpha|y)\, y_{t-1}^2.
\end{aligned} \tag{7.34}$$

7.3.4 Predictive Densities

Predictive densities of ARCH models have been analysed by Geweke (1989b) using a simulation technique. Geweke considers the prediction of y_{T+1}^{T+s} (i.e. the s postsample values) and of h_{T+1}^{T+s}. However, it is useful, as in other dynamic models, to distinguish between the prediction of y_{T+1} for which the predictive density belongs to the same family as the generating process (conditionally on the error variance parameters) and that of y_{T+j}, $j \geq 2$, for which this result no longer holds. For ease of exposition, in this subsection we consider only the ARCH(1) case.

The predictive density of y_{T+1} is given by

$$f(y_{T+1}|y) = \int_\Theta f(y_{T+1}|y, \theta)\, \varphi(\theta|y)\, d\theta, \tag{7.35}$$

where $f(y_{T+1}|y, \theta)$ is a normal density with zero mean and variance $h_{T+1} = \omega + \alpha y_T^2$. Conditionally on θ, h_{T+1} is known as y_T^2 is observed. The predictive moments of y_{T+1} are

$$\begin{aligned}
\mathrm{E}(y_{T+1}|y) &= \mathrm{E}_{\theta|y}[\mathrm{E}(y_{T+1}|y, \theta)] = 0, \\
\mathrm{Var}(y_{T+1}|y) &= \mathrm{E}_{\theta|y}[\mathrm{Var}(y_{T+1}|y, \theta)] + \mathrm{Var}_{\theta|y}[\mathrm{E}(y_{T+1}|y, \theta)] \\
&= \mathrm{E}_{\theta|y}(h_{T+1}|y, \theta) \\
&= \mathrm{E}(\omega|y) + \mathrm{E}(\alpha|y)\, y_T^2.
\end{aligned} \tag{7.36}$$

Thus we have partly analytical results as in Chapter 5 for dynamic regression models.

For predicting y_{T+2} we have the same type of results conditionally on y_{T+1}, but as we want to predict y_{T+2} given y_T, we have to integrate out y_{T+1} by numerical integration:

$$f(y_{T+2}|y) = \int_{\Theta} \left[\int_{\mathbf{R}} f(y_{T+2}|y_{T+1}, y, \theta) f(y_{T+1}|y, \theta) \, dy_{T+1} \right] \varphi(\theta|y) \, d\theta. \quad (7.37)$$

Both $f(y_{T+2}|y_{T+1}, y, \theta)$ and $f(y_{T+1}|y, \theta)$ are normal densities of zero mean and variances h_{T+2} and h_{T+1}, respectively, but the resulting density in the inner integral, $f(y_{T+2}|y, \theta)$, is not of a known form. Geweke (1989b) evaluates the predictive density and moments of y_{T+2} by simulation. However, the conditional predictive moments can still be evaluated analytically:

$$\begin{aligned}
\mathrm{E}(y_{T+2}|y, \theta) &= \mathrm{E}(\sqrt{h_{T+2}}\,\epsilon_{T+2}|y, \theta) \\
&= \mathrm{E}(\sqrt{h_{T+2}}|y, \theta) \, \mathrm{E}(\epsilon_{T+2}|y, \theta) = 0, \\
\mathrm{E}(y_{T+2}^2|y, \theta) &= \mathrm{E}(h_{T+2}\,\epsilon_{T+2}^2|y, \theta) \\
&= \mathrm{E}(h_{T+2}|y, \theta) \, \mathrm{E}(\epsilon_{T+2}^2|y, \theta) = \mathrm{E}(h_{T+2}|y, \theta).
\end{aligned} \quad (7.38)$$

We are left with the computation of the conditional predictive expectation of h_{T+2}:

$$\begin{aligned}
\mathrm{E}(h_{T+2}|y, \theta) &= \omega + \alpha\, \mathrm{E}(h_{T+1}\epsilon_{T+1}^2|y, \theta) \\
&= \omega + \alpha\, \mathrm{E}(h_{T+1}|y, \theta) \\
&= \omega + \alpha\,(\omega + \alpha\, y_T^2).
\end{aligned} \quad (7.39)$$

For horizon s, this expectation becomes

$$\mathrm{E}(h_{T+s}|y, \theta) = \omega \sum_{j=0}^{s-1} \alpha^j + \alpha^s y_T^2, \quad (7.40)$$

and for $s \to \infty$, it converges to $\omega/(1 - \alpha)$.

All these results are conditional on θ. Predictive moments are obtained by numerical integration over θ in the procedure used to compute posterior moments of θ. For instance,

$$\mathrm{E}(h_{T+s}|y) = \int_{\Theta} \left[\omega \sum_{j=0}^{s-1} \alpha^j + \alpha^s y_T^2 \right] \varphi(\theta|y) \, d\theta. \quad (7.41)$$

To draw the graph of the predictive density of y_{T+s}, with $s \geq 2$, Geweke (1989b) proposed a simulation method which is based on the following scheme, conditionally on θ:

$$\begin{aligned}
\epsilon_{T+s} &\sim N(0, 1), \\
h_{T+s} &= \omega + \alpha\, y_{T+s-1}^2, \\
y_{T+s} &= \sqrt{h_{T+s}}\,\epsilon_{T+s}.
\end{aligned} \quad (7.42)$$

One draws a standard normal variable, then computes h_{T+s} and y_{T+s}, starting at $s = 1$ with the starting value y_T^2. Draws are used to build a histogram of the predictive density of y_{T+s} according to a predetermined grid. Once a draw of $y_{T+s}|y,\theta_j$ is obtained, we have to determine in which cell of the histogram it falls, increment the value of this cell by one, multiply by the value of $\varphi(\theta_j|y)$, and multiply by the weight of the Simpson or trapezoidal rule at point j. For one point θ_j, N draws of $y_{T+s}|y,\theta_j$ have to be generated.

7.3.5 Application to the USD/DM Exchange Rate

An ARCH(3) model was fitted to the differenced series of the US dollar versus German mark exchange rate for the period 1960.1–1991.6. A graph of the series is given in Fig. 7.2. To avoid possible underflows in computations, we divided the series by its standard deviation $s_y = 0.0558$. Consequently the scale of ω is changed. The posterior expectations and standard deviations of the parameters, computed under the diffuse prior (7.33), are shown (in an obvious way) in the estimated ARCH equation

$$h_t = \underset{[0.054]}{0.38} + \underset{[0.079]}{0.42} \times 2 \times \sum_{j=1}^{3} \frac{p+1-j}{p(p+1)} y_{t-j}^2. \tag{7.43}$$

They were computed using a bivariate Simpson rule with 33 points on each axis. To find the unscaled posterior moments of ω, we must multiply the posterior expectation by s_y^2 and the posterior variance by s_y^4, which gives $E(\omega|y) = 0.00115$ and $\sigma_{\omega|y} = 0.000162$.

We see that the posterior expectation of α is lower than $1/\sqrt{3}$, but its range of integration goes beyond this value. To compute an implied kurtosis, we decided to compute the expected kurtosis by truncating the posterior of α at $1/\sqrt{3}$. The result is 6.30, which is much lower than the sample value of 19.45. The expected autocorrelation at order 1 is of course the posterior expectation of α and is 0.42, which is much higher than the empirical value of 0.25.

The posterior correlation between α and ω is equal to -0.57, which is neither very strong nor very small. This negative relation can be seen on the graph of the bivariate posterior density given in Fig. 7.3. The number of lags was chosen so as to minimize the posterior expectation of ω. A too low value for p produces a high value of $E(\omega|y)$. This value decreases rapidly when adding extra lags. It increases slightly when the number of lags becomes too important.

The graph of the marginal posterior density of α, given in Fig. 7.4, shows that there is definitely an ARCH effect in the data, as the value 0 is far in the left tail of the posterior density.

The graph of the posterior expectations of h_t for the sample, given in Fig. 7.5, shows (by comparison with Fig. 7.2) that the model manages to track the volatility of the data fairly well, even if it cannot 'fit' the empirical kurtosis.

7.3.6 Regression Models with ARCH Errors

In the ARCH model (7.23)–(7.25), the mean of y_t is equal to zero. This is unduly restrictive in many cases. The introduction of a conditional mean equation with regressors is necessary in many applications. Let us give some examples:

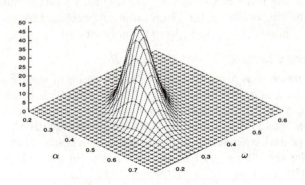

FIG. 7.3. Bivariate posterior density of α and ω

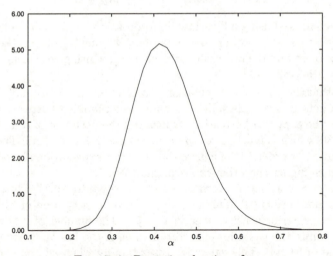

FIG. 7.4. Posterior density of α

- If y_t is a financial return, and the asset is risky, there should be a risk premium relative to a risk-free asset, inducing a positive mean, which could be time varying. Moreover, the model assumes some form of market efficiency. The endogenous variable y_t is the first difference of the asset price p_t (usually in logarithms): $y_t = \Delta \ln p_t$. If we want to test this hypothesis, we have to change the model from $y_t = e_t = \epsilon_t \sqrt{h_t}$ where e_t is the ARCH error term to

$$\Delta \ln p_t = \mu + (\rho - 1) \ln p_{t-1} + e_t. \tag{7.44}$$

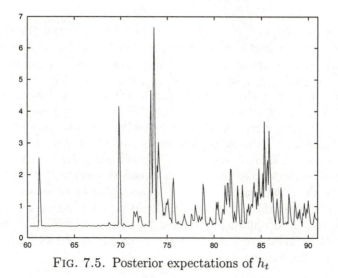

FIG. 7.5. Posterior expectations of h_t

The null hypothesis of market efficiency corresponds to $\mu = 0$ and $\rho = 1$. This is a unit root test in the presence of conditional heteroscedasticity. Moreover, as documented by Campbell, Lo, and MacKinley (1997: Chap. 2), positive autocorrelation of order 1 is quite usual for a stock market index and could be induced by non-synchronous trading of the index components (1997: Chap. 3).

• Engle (1982) used an ARCH model to estimate a price inflation equation for the UK. He was thus interested in both the parameters of an ARCH process on the error terms and in the regression coefficients of the price equation.

The presence of k extra regressors x_t does not change the fundamental properties of the ARCH model, but it complicates the computations. The model is

$$
\begin{aligned}
y_t &= x_t'\beta + e_t, \\
e_t &= \sqrt{h_t}\,\epsilon_t, \qquad \epsilon_t \sim N(0, 1), \\
h_t &= \omega + \alpha_1 e_{t-1}^2 + \cdots + \alpha_p e_{t-p}^2.
\end{aligned}
\tag{7.45}
$$

The increased computational burden in (7.45) comes from the fact that it is not possible to separate the parameters of the regression function from those of the conditional variance. This is directly obvious if e_{t-j}^2 is replaced by its value $(y_{t-j} - x_{t-j}'\beta)^2$. So it is not possible to make inference on β conditionally on the variance parameters in a partially natural conjugate framework, so as to integrate out β analytically as in the heteroscedastic model presented in Section 7.2. A Gibbs sampler is also not directly implementable. The solution of Geweke (1988b, 1989b) and Kleibergen and van Dijk (1993) is to proceed by Monte Carlo integration using importance sampling for all the parameters. They use a Student importance function (plus antithetic drawings in the case of Geweke).

An alternative solution proposed by Bauwens and Lubrano (1996) consists in implementing a griddy-Gibbs sampler (as described in Subsection 3.4.3). With a relatively small number of draws, this method can give accurate posterior moments and precise graphs of the univariate marginal densities.

In order to reduce the computational burden, we can use an approximate solution for inference in the above model. The idea is to force the separability between the regression parameters and the variance parameters called α hereafter (so α includes ω and the α_i parameters of the ARCH equation). We start by making inference on β ignoring the ARCH part, using the results of Section 2.7. This gives a posterior mean for β, which we call b hereafter (it is the least squares estimator if the prior is diffuse). We compute 'Bayesian residuals' $\hat{e}_t = y_t - x_t'b$, lag them, and inject them into the conditional variance equation to get $\hat{h}_t$. These 'estimates' of the conditional variances no longer depend on β, but are still functions of α. Then, we conduct inference on the model as a heteroscedastic regression model, written as

$$
\begin{aligned}
y_t &= x_t'\beta + e_t, \\
e_t &= \sqrt{\hat{h}_t}\, \epsilon_t \qquad \epsilon_t \sim N(0,1), \\
\hat{h}_t &= \omega + \alpha_1 \hat{e}_{t-1}^2 + \cdots + \alpha_p \hat{e}_{t-p}^2.
\end{aligned}
\tag{7.46}
$$

This model uses the fact that β has to be estimated by a technique similar to weighted least squares, but treats β as fixed for inference on $\alpha = (\omega\ \alpha_1\ \ldots\ \alpha_p)$. Inference on this model can be done using the formulae (7.11)–(7.16), where $\sigma^2 = 1$ and $h(z_t, \alpha) = \hat{h}_t$. Using the prior (7.13) for instance, the conditional posterior density of β is normal with mean $b(\alpha)$ and covariance matrix equal to the inverse of $X'H(\alpha)X$. It is normal rather than Student as in (7.17), because σ^2 is equal to one as this parameter is subsumed implicitly in α.

The marginal posterior density of α is

$$
\varphi(\alpha|y) \propto \varphi(\alpha)\, |H(\alpha)|^{1/2}\, |X'H(\alpha)X|^{-1/2} \exp\left[-\tfrac{1}{2}s(\alpha)\right].
\tag{7.47}
$$

Clearly, the model (7.46) is an approximation of the exact model (7.45). Thus it yields approximate posterior results for β and α. But the approximation can be expected to be good, because the information matrix is block diagonal between β and α as shown in Engle (1982). The computing time may be considerably shortened compared with the exact method. Another use of this approximation would be to calibrate the moments of an importance function for the exact model, using the results of the approximate model.

Let us illustrate these techniques using the exchange rate series already used in Subsection 7.3.5. We added extra lagged variables as regressors and we ended up with the same ARCH(3) structure as before. It was necessary to introduce one lag of the level and one lag of the differences, but not a constant term. With a diffuse prior, the posterior results are

$$\Delta y_t = \underset{[0.00067]}{-0.0013} y_{t-1} + \underset{[0.058]}{0.30} \, \Delta y_{t-1},$$

$$h_t = \underset{[0.054]}{0.41} + \underset{[0.14]}{0.70} \times 2 \times \sum_{j=1}^{3} \frac{p+1-j}{p(p+1)} e_{t-j}^2. \tag{7.48}$$

We see that the posterior mean of α has almost doubled compared with (7.43) (for clarity, the variable y_t in (7.43) is exactly Δy_t above). The implied kurtosis has to be evaluated on a very restricted range of α and is 4.72. This value is even smaller than before (because of the truncation), and the first-order autocorrelation of the squares of Δy_t is greater (0.70). The presence of a unit root is questionable. The coefficient of y_{t-1} is very small, but the probability that $\rho > 1$ is only 0.022. Thus this exchange rate series has no unit root and can be predicted with a nearly integrated AR(2) on the levels, at least on the period considered.

These results were obtained using a griddy-Gibbs sampler initialized at the the maximum likelihood estimates. The first 50 draws were discarded. Moments and marginals were obtained with 500 draws and 33 points for evaluating the conditionals. Convergence was checked with CUMSUM plots and achieved very quickly. The computational time was 2 minutes on a Pentium Pro 150MHz.

Let us now present the empirical results obtained with the approximate model:

$$\Delta y_t = \underset{[0.00070]}{-0.0016} y_{t-1} + \underset{[0.069]}{0.34} \, \Delta y_{t-1},$$

$$h_t = \underset{[0.052]}{0.41} + \underset{[0.13]}{0.69} \times 2 \times \sum_{j=1}^{3} \frac{p+1-j}{p(p+1)} e_{t-j}^2. \tag{7.49}$$

The implied kurtosis is 4.51. It is remarkable that these inference results do not differ much from the exact ones. The posterior expectations are roughly the same. The posterior standard deviations of the regression coefficients are slightly larger, while the posterior standard deviations of the ARCH coefficients are slightly lower. On this particular example, we can conclude that this type of approximation is very good. And the computational time for the bivariate Simpson integration was 3.79 seconds (for 33×33 points), which means a computing efficiency ratio of the order of 40.

7.4   GARCH Models

With ARCH models, the conditional variance of y_t changes over time according to a distributed lag process of the squared errors. A more flexible but parsimonious lag structure may be required. Bollerslev (1986) introduced the GARCH model as a generalization of the ARCH one. The generalization amounts to adding a distributed lag of the conditional variance to the ARCH terms. The GARCH(p,q) model generalizes eqn (7.25) to

$$h_t = \omega + \alpha_1 y_{t-1}^2 + \cdots + \alpha_p y_{t-p}^2 + \gamma_1 h_{t-1} + \cdots + \gamma_q h_{t-q}, \tag{7.50}$$

adding q positive parameters. In many empirical applications, it is found that a GARCH(1,1) model is sufficient. With $p = q = 1$, the scedastic function (7.50) is written as

$$h_t = \omega + \alpha y_{t-1}^2 + \gamma h_{t-1}. \tag{7.51}$$

In this section, we concentrate on the GARCH(1,1) process.

7.4.1 Properties of GARCH Processes

Moments of GARCH models were first computed by Bollerslev (1986). The next theorem generalizes the results of Theorem 7.1 to the GARCH(1,1) model:

Theorem 7.2 *The GARCH(1,1) process defined by (7.23), (7.24), and (7.51) has the following properties:*

(i) $E(y_t) = E(y_t^3) = 0$.

(ii) $E(y_t^2) = E(h_t) = \omega/(1 - \alpha - \gamma)$ *if* $0 \leq \alpha + \gamma < 1$.

(iii) *The kurtosis coefficient of* y_t *is given by*

$$\mathrm{KC} = \lambda \frac{(1 + \alpha + \gamma)(1 - \alpha - \gamma)}{1 - \lambda \alpha^2 - \gamma^2 - 2\alpha\gamma} \quad \text{if } \lambda \alpha^2 + \gamma^2 + 2\alpha\gamma < 1. \tag{7.52}$$

(iv) *The autocorrelation function of* y_t^2 *is given by* $\rho_1 = \dfrac{\alpha(1 - \gamma^2 - \alpha\gamma)}{1 - \gamma^2 - 2\alpha\gamma}$, *and*

$$\rho_j = (\alpha + \gamma)\rho_{j-1} \ (j \geq 2).$$

Proof The proof of the first three results is done in the same way as for the ARCH(1) case, noting in particular that, using (7.23), the GARCH(1,1) equation (7.51) can be written as

$$h_t = \omega + h_{t-1}(\alpha \epsilon_{t-1}^2 + \gamma). \tag{7.53}$$

To obtain the ACF, one adds y_t^2 to both sides of (7.51), moves h_t to the right hand side, and gets

$$y_t^2 = \omega + (\alpha + \gamma)y_{t-1}^2 + v_t - \gamma v_{t-1}, \tag{7.54}$$

where $v_t = y_t^2 - h_t$ is a martingale difference that is an innovation for y_t^2, see the proof of Theorem 7.1. This equation shows that a GARCH(1,1) process is equivalent to an ARMA(1,1) process for y_t^2, with autoregressive coefficient $\alpha + \gamma$, and MA coefficient $-\gamma$. The ACF follows by the standard formulae for the ARMA(1,1) model.   □

The covariance stationarity condition is $\alpha + \gamma < 1$. There are also positivity restrictions, to preclude non-positive variances. As γ can be null, we also have $0 < \alpha < 1$. Note that α cannot be equal to zero while γ is different from zero: as a matter of fact, $\alpha = 0$ implies

$$(1 - \gamma L)y_t^2 = \omega + (1 - \gamma L)v_t, \tag{7.55}$$

so that there is a common factor in the AR and MA polynomials: h_t becomes constant. Finally, it is usual to impose that $0 \leq \gamma < 1$.

The GARCH(1,1) model is a very parsimonious extension of the ARCH(1) model, since the ARMA(1,1) corresponds to an AR(∞) (invertibility follows from the restriction $\gamma < 1$). With $\gamma = 0$ we are back to the ARCH(1) case.

The condition of existence of the kurtosis coefficient (KC), given in (7.52), can be expressed as $\alpha < (\sqrt{\lambda + \gamma^2 (1 - \lambda)} - \gamma)/\lambda$. When $\gamma = 0$, this condition is the same as in the ARCH(1) model. But when $\gamma > 0$, α has to be lower than $\sqrt{1/\lambda}$. Notice KC depends not only on α as in the ARCH(1) model, but also on γ, which gives more flexibility to accommodate the leptokurtosis of financial series. For instance, if γ tends to one, α has to tend to zero for the existence of KC. Consequently, the fourth moment can still exist when the sum $\alpha + \gamma$ approaches one, provided that α is sufficiently low.

The GARCH specification introduces flexibility in the autocorrelation structure of y_t^2 as well as in the kurtosis. The ACF depends on both α and γ. It declines geometrically at the rate $\alpha + \gamma$. One can have $\alpha + \gamma$ close to one, implying a slowly decreasing autocorrelation function, with α small enough so that KC exists. But with normal errors, it is rather difficult to have at the same time a low value of ρ_1 and a high value of KC. For example, if $\alpha = 0.1$, $\gamma = 0.8$, and $\lambda = 3$, which corresponds to the normal distribution, $\rho_1 = 0.14$, and KC $= 3.35$, which is not much higher than 3; if $\alpha = 0.165$ and $\beta = 0.8$, $\rho_1 = 0.39$ and KC $= 15$. More flexibility is obtained by using a Student distribution: if $\alpha = 0.1$, $\gamma = 0.8$, and $\lambda = 9$, which corresponds to a Student distribution with five degrees of freedom (and unit variance), KC $= 15.5$. To conclude, we can say that the GARCH(1,1) model can reproduce the stylized facts of financial series much better than the ARCH(1) model, especially if the distribution of the innovation is itself fat tailed. It should be noted, however, that the value of KC and of the first autocorrelation are very sensitive with respect to the parameter values. For instance, with a normal distribution, $\alpha = 0.15$ and $\gamma = 0.82$ give $\rho_1 = 0.38$ and KC $= 12.6$, while $\alpha = 0.17$ and $\gamma = 0.80$ give $\rho_1 = 0.43$ and KC $= 136.38$.

Remark on the Student distribution: When considering the use of a Student distribution instead of a normal one for ϵ_t, we have alluded to the fact that the variance of ϵ_t has to be equal to one, since this is an assumption—see (7.24). To impose this condition, the Student distribution should be defined as in (A.31) with parameters $\mu = 0$, $s = 1$, $m = 1/(\nu - 2)$, and ν degrees of freedom (or $s = \nu - 2$ and $m = 1$). It should be noted that KC of a $t(0, s, m, \nu)$ distribution exists only if $\nu > 4$, but that it does not depend on the ratio s/m; see (A.33). If one uses a $t(0, 1, 1/\nu, \nu)$ distribution, the variance of ϵ_t is equal to $\nu/(\nu - 2)$ (if $\nu > 2$), and some results of Theorem (7.2) have to be modified (only the result (i) remains valid as such). Teräsvirta (1996) provides general formulae that encompass this case.

7.4.2 *Extensions of GARCH Processes*

In all the ARCH models we have reviewed up to now, the conditional variance of y_t is a symmetric function of past shocks: the 'news impact curve', which is the graph of h_t against ϵ_{t-1}, is symmetric (around zero). But as underlined for

instance by Nelson (1991) (see also the references cited therein), the volatility
in stock markets tends to rise more in response to bad news than to good news.
To cope with this empirical fact, Nelson (1991) has introduced the EGARCH
(Exponential GARCH) model

$$\log h_t = \omega + \theta \epsilon_{t-1} + \alpha(|\epsilon_{t-1}| - \mathrm{E}|\epsilon_{t-1}|) + \gamma \log h_{t-1}. \qquad (7.56)$$

On a logarithmic scale, the news impact curve is a piecewise linear function with
slope $\theta + \alpha$ when $\epsilon_t > 0$ and $\theta - \alpha$ when $\epsilon_t < 0$. If α is positive and θ is negative,
the volatility increases more after a negative shock than after a positive one of
the same amplitude. As the logarithm of h_t is modelled, there is no positivity
constraint to introduce on the parameters to avoid negative values of h_t. The
conditional variance is an exponential function (hence the name EGARCH). The
moments of the EGARCH process are not known and the statistical properties
of this model are not very clear when approaching non-stationarity as underlined
in Pagan (1996).

Zakoian (1994) proposed another formulation of the asymmetric effect which
is inspired by the non-linear time series literature (see Chapter 8). The conditional standard deviation follows an ARMA process with a different AR coefficient when y_t is smaller or greater than a given threshold which is chosen to be
fixed and equal to zero:

$$\sqrt{h_t} = \omega + \alpha^+ y_{t-1}^+ + \alpha^- y_{t-1}^- + \gamma \sqrt{h_{t-1}}, \qquad (7.57)$$

where $y_{t-1}^+ = y_{t-1}$ times the indicator function of $y_{t-1} > 0$, while $y_{t-1}^- = y_{t-1}$
times the indicator function of $y_{t-1} \leq 0$. There is no need for positivity constraints on the parameters as the square of $\sqrt{h_t}$ is taken. This is convenient for
optimizing the likelihood function. But Zakoian (1994) introduces the positivity
constraints to compute moments. Glosten, Jagannathan, and Runkle (1993) have
proposed a related specification which has been used by Bauwens and Lubrano
(1998). It is formulated directly on the conditional variance, with

$$h_t = \omega + \alpha^+ (y_{t-1}^+)^2 + \alpha^- (y_{t-1}^-)^2 + \gamma h_{t-1}. \qquad (7.58)$$

Its advantage is that the symmetric GARCH is nested within (7.58). All the parameters have to be positive in order to guarantee a positive h_t. The expectation
of y_t is zero and its variance is equal to

$$\mathrm{E}(h_t) = \frac{\omega}{1 - 0.5(\alpha^+ + \alpha^-) + \gamma}. \qquad (7.59)$$

Compared with the symmetric GARCH, α is replaced by the average of α^+ and
α^-. The same property is true for the kurtosis. The autocorrelation function is
not known.

7.4.3 *Inference in GARCH Processes*

The likelihood function of a GARCH(1,1) process can be written as (7.31), with the new formulation of h_t, under the hypothesis of conditional normality. One needs an initial value h_0 in addition to y_0 (unless they are considered as parameters). A convenient solution is to take h_0 equal to the empirical variance of the sample.

If $\epsilon_t \sim t(0, 1, 1/(\nu - 2), \nu)$ is assumed (with $\nu > 2$), the likelihood function is

$$l(\theta; y, \mathcal{I}_0) \propto \prod_{t=1}^{T} \left[\Gamma\left(\frac{\nu+1}{2}\right) / \Gamma\left(\frac{\nu}{2}\right) \right] [(\nu - 2) h_t]^{-1/2} \left[1 + \frac{y_t^2}{(\nu - 2) h_t} \right]^{-(\nu+1)/2},$$

(7.60)

while if $\epsilon_t \sim t(0, 1, 1/\nu, \nu)$ is assumed, the likelihood function becomes

$$l(\theta; y, \mathcal{I}_0) \propto \prod_{t=1}^{T} \left[\Gamma\left(\frac{\nu+1}{2}\right) / \Gamma\left(\frac{\nu}{2}\right) \right] (\nu h_t)^{-1/2} \left[1 + \frac{y_t^2}{\nu h_t} \right]^{-(\nu+1)/2}. \quad (7.61)$$

An advantage of the latter formulation is that ν can be smaller than two, in which case the conditional variance does not exist. Note that with (7.60), the conditional variance is h_t, and that with (7.61), it is $h_t \nu / (\nu - 2)$ (if it exists).

A 'non-informative' prior that imposes the positivity restrictions can be taken to be the improper flat prior

$$\varphi(\omega, \alpha, \gamma) \propto 1 \quad \text{if } \omega > 0, \quad \alpha > 0, \quad \gamma > 0. \quad (7.62)$$

One can also impose the stationarity condition. In the case of a Student distribution, one must also provide a prior for ν. Bauwens and Lubrano (1998: Theorem 1) have shown that a flat prior $\varphi(\nu) \propto 1$ if $\nu > 0$ implies an improper posterior in a finite sample which is thus not integrable. This happens because the likelihood function (7.61) tends to a positive value when ν tends to infinity. Intuitively, it is not possible to discriminate between large values of ν with a finite sample. The prior on ν must therefore compensate this deficiency of the likelihood function by tending to zero quickly enough. Bauwens and Lubrano (1998) propose as possible priors for ν: a uniform prior on a finite interval, a half Cauchy prior (i.e. a Cauchy density centred at zero but truncated to the positive values), and an exponential distribution. A flat prior on $\log \nu$ (i.e. proportional to $1/\nu$) is not sufficient.

The extension to a regression model with GARCH errors is straightforward: in the likelihood function, one has to replace y_t by e_t as defined by (7.45), and the prior must be enlarged to the regression parameters.

The posterior density has to be evaluated numerically. Kleibergen and van Dijk (1993) have used importance sampling with a Student importance function. Geweke (1994) has used a Metropolis–Hastings algorithm. Bauwens and Lubrano (1998) have used the griddy-Gibbs sampler and made some comparison of this algorithm with the previous ones. They concluded that the griddy-Gibbs sampler seems easier to design in GARCH models, even if it may be more demanding in computing time.

7.4.4 *Application to the USD/DM Exchange Rate*

Let us again consider the USD/DM exchange rate series, with a regression equation as in (7.48), and a GARCH(1,1) specification instead of a parsimonious ARCH(3). With normal errors and a flat prior composed of (7.62) and a prior proportional to one for the regression coefficients, the posterior results are

$$\Delta y_t = \underset{[0.00066]}{-0.0014} y_{t-1} + \underset{[0.059]}{0.31} \Delta y_{t-1},$$
$$h_t = \underset{[0.030]}{0.069} + \underset{[0.050]}{0.14} e_{t-1}^2 + \underset{[0.069]}{0.79} h_{t-1}. \tag{7.63}$$

Computations were made using the griddy-Gibbs sampler, with 1000 draws (after discarding 50 draws to warm up the sampler). The posterior correlation matrix shows that the correlation coefficients are small or virtually equal to zero, except between the GARCH parameters (especially ω and γ, which slows down the convergence of the Gibbs sampler). Its lower triangular part is equal to

$$\begin{bmatrix} 1 \\ 0.72 & 1 \\ -0.93 & -0.86 & 1 \\ 0 & 0 & 0 & 1 \\ 0 & 0 & 0 & 0.12 & 1 \end{bmatrix},$$

where the order of the parameters is ω, α, γ, the regression coefficients of y_{t-1}, and those of Δy_{t-1}.

From (7.63), we conclude that there is definitely a GARCH effect, with a rather low α and a relatively high γ. Their sum, equal to 0.93 in mean, implies a slowly decreasing ACF, while the posterior mean of ρ_1 (computed on the truncated range $\alpha + \gamma < 1$) is equal to 0.27, which fits the sample value of 0.25 well. The posterior kurtosis, computed on a truncated range corresponding to 91 per cent of the draws, is 5.91, still much lower than the empirical value. With the ARCH specification, the truncated posterior kurtosis is 4.72 and the posterior mean of ρ_1 is 0.70. The posterior density of $\rho - 1$ (the regression coefficient of y_{t-1}) is rather concentrated and the posterior probability that ρ is greater than one is very low (0.011). The unit root hypothesis is not at all favoured by this model of the exchange rate series. This last conclusion is, however, not robust to the distributional assumption on the error term. If we consider Student errors with the likelihood function (7.61), the inference results are

$$\Delta y_t = \underset{[0.000086]}{-0.000035} y_{t-1} + \underset{[0.051]}{0.31} \Delta y_{t-1},$$
$$h_t = \underset{[0.00031]}{0.00044} + \underset{[0.066]}{0.28} e_{t-1}^2 + \underset{[0.070]}{0.49} h_{t-1}, \tag{7.64}$$

and $E(\nu|y) = 1.83$, with a posterior standard deviation of 0.24. The griddy-Gibbs sampler converged faster in this case as the strongest posterior correlation is -0.85 (between α and γ). The results were obtained using 1000 draws plus 50 for warming up and the same flat prior as above, times a Cauchy prior on ν.

The posterior mean and standard deviation of ν suggest that even the conditional variances do not exist (the h_t can still be interpreted as spread parameters). As $\Pr(\rho > 1|y) = 0.24$, the Student GARCH model favours the unit root hypothesis for the exchange rate series much more than the normal GARCH model. This example shows that inference on the unit root hypothesis can be very sensitive to the distribution of the error term in financial series. This was also noted by Kleibergen and van Dijk (1993), contrary to the results of Geweke (1993) who investigated macroeconomic annual time series which are, however, characterized by much less heteroscedasticity.

7.5   Stationarity and Persistence

As mentioned in Subsection 7.3.1, the squared returns of a financial asset are often characterized by a slowly decreasing autocorrelation function, or equivalently by a certain degree of persistence of a past shock on the future conditional variances. As shown in (7.54), the square of a GARCH(1,1) process is an ARMA(1,1) process with autoregressive coefficient equal to $\alpha + \gamma$, which should be close to one to fit the relatively slow decrease of the ACF. By analogy with stochastic processes having a unit root in the mean, a persistence in the conditional variance should correspond to the unit root $\alpha + \gamma = 1$. Engle and Bollerslev (1986) introduced integrated GARCH models (IGARCH) noting that in some series the data favour such a configuration. For the the exchange rate series of the dollar against the mark analysed in the previous section assuming normal errors, the posterior expectation of $\alpha + \gamma$ is equal to 0.93, and the standard deviation is 0.035, so that only 1.3 per cent of the probability is above one—see the results in (7.63). We can conclude that in this case the integration for the variance process is not supported by the data. Moreover, as underlined by Geweke (1986b), the h_t process, even when it has a unit root, does not behave like a random walk because all the h_t are positive by construction. With this brief introduction, we can feel that stationarity and persistence in GARCH(1,1) processes are special topics that have to be discussed carefully.

7.5.1   *Stationarity*

A stochastic process is weakly or covariance stationary if its first two moments are bounded and independent of the time index. The same process is strictly stationary if the data density is invariant by translation of the time index. These two notions coincide when the joint density of the observations is normal because the normal distribution is defined by its first two moments. But it is possible to find non-normal processes where one definition of stationarity is verified while the other is not. GARCH processes are one of these examples as shown by Nelson (1990). One of the reasons is that even if the conditional distribution of the observations is assumed to be normal, the marginal distribution is not normal and is not of any known form as emphasized in Subsection 7.4.1.

Let us consider the GARCH(1,1) process

$$y_t = \epsilon_t \sqrt{h_t},$$
$$h_t = \omega + h_{t-1}(\alpha \epsilon_{t-1}^2 + \gamma), \tag{7.65}$$

where the ϵ_t process is IID, with zero mean and unspecified variance (to cover the Student case when the variance is not equal to one).

Weak stationarity conditions have in fact been obtained in Subsection 7.4.1 and correspond to a condition of existence of the second moments of y_t. The marginal expectation of y_t is zero and the marginal variance is

$$E(y_t^2) = \frac{\omega}{1 - \alpha E(\epsilon_t^2) - \gamma}. \tag{7.66}$$

This is the result given in Theorem 7.2 when $E(\epsilon_t^2) = 1$. It follows that $\alpha E(\epsilon_t^2) + \gamma < 1$ is the condition for weak stationarity.

As $y_t = \epsilon_t \sqrt{h_t}$ and ϵ_t is strictly stationary by assumption, Nelson (1990) has shown that strict stationarity is equivalent to the measurability of h_t as a function of the ϵ_t process. This means that this function, or the stochastic process it generates, should not converge either to zero or to infinity. By successive substitutions of h_{t-i} in (7.65), Nelson (1990) expresses h_t as a function of past values of ϵ_t and of the initial condition h_0:

$$h_t = h_0 \prod_{i=1}^{t}(\alpha\epsilon_{t-i}^2 + \gamma) + \omega \left[1 + \sum_{j=1}^{t-1}\prod_{i=1}^{j}(\alpha\epsilon_{t-i}^2 + \gamma) \right], \tag{7.67}$$

which can also be written as

$$h_t = h_0 \, G_t + \omega \sum_{j=0}^{t-1} G_j, \tag{7.68}$$

with $G_0 = 1$ and $G_j = \prod_{i=1}^{j}(\alpha\epsilon_{t-i}^2 + \gamma)$. We have first the following theorem in Nelson (1990) which shows that $\omega = 0$ is a pathological case:

Theorem 7.3 When $\omega = 0$, the conditional variance h_t converges to zero if $E\left[\log\left(\alpha \epsilon_t^2 + \gamma\right)\right] < 0$ and to plus infinity otherwise.

Proof From (7.65), for $\omega = 0$,

$$\log h_t = \log h_{t-1} + \log\left(\alpha\epsilon_{t-1}^2 + \gamma\right)$$
$$= \log h_{t-1} + \mu + \eta_t$$

where $\mu = E\left[\log\left(\alpha\epsilon_{t-1}^2 + \gamma\right)\right]$ and $\eta_t = \log\left(\alpha\epsilon_{t-1}^2 + \gamma\right) - \mu$. Clearly, η_t has zero mean and is stationary. Thus $\log h_t$ behaves like a random walk with drift $E\left[\log\left(\alpha\epsilon_{t-1}^2 + \gamma\right)\right]$. A random walk converges to $+\infty$ or $-\infty$ according to the sign of its drift. By taking the exponential, we get the desired result. $\square$

This result can also be interpreted in the following way. When $\mathrm{E}\left[\log\left(\alpha\,\epsilon_t^2 + \gamma\right)\right] < 0$, the initial conditions of the recurrence equation (7.67) in h_t have no long-term influence. In other words, $G_t = \prod_{i=1}^{t}(\alpha\epsilon_{t-i}^2 + \gamma)$ converges to zero.

When $\omega > 0$, h_t includes the factor $\omega\sum_{j=0}^{t-1} G_j$. For the process to be strictly stationary, we have to prove that G_j converges sufficiently quickly to zero (at an exponential rate in j) so that when $t \to \infty$, its sum is strictly positive and bounded. This result is shown in Nelson (1990: appendix of theorem 2). Consequently, we can state the following theorem which is inspired by Nelson (1990):

Theorem 7.4 *When $\omega > 0$, the GARCH(1,1) process is strictly stationary and ergodic if and only if $\mathrm{E}\left[\log(\alpha\,\epsilon_t^2 + \gamma)\right] < 0$.*

A variant of this theorem was proved in Kleibergen and van Dijk (1993). See also Bollerslev, Engle, and Nelson (1994) for some additional comments. Weak stationarity guarantees that the marginal variance of the process exists while strict stationarity simply guarantees that the process itself exists. By a simple application of Jensen's inequality, we can show that strict stationarity is a much weaker requirement than weak stationarity in GARCH(1,1) processes.

7.5.2 Measures of Persistence

In an AR(1) model like $y_t = \alpha y_{t-1} + \epsilon_t$, the question of persistence is whether a shock (ϵ_t) at date t has a lasting effect on the future values of y_t. If there is a unit root ($\alpha = 1$), $y_t = y_0 + \sum_{i=1}^{t}\epsilon_i$, and a shock at date t has an everlasting effect on future values. If $\alpha < 1$, ultimately the effect of a shock disappears, although if α is close to one, it vanishes slowly (the effect after i periods being α^i, which is the derivative of y_{t+i} with respect to ϵ_t). With GARCH models, we are interested in whether the effect of a shock on future conditional variances is persistent or eventually vanishes.

We can define the impact of an initial shock ϵ_0 on the conditional variance h_t as

$$\lim_{t\to\infty} \mathrm{E}\frac{\partial h_t}{\partial \epsilon_0^2}. \tag{7.69}$$

This corresponds to what Nelson (1990) calls persistence in L^1, a particular case of formula (36) of his paper. The reason for taking the expectation in (7.69) is that the derivative depends on all ϵ_i between dates 0 and t. Assuming that h_0 is independent of the ϵ_t sequence (which is itself an independent sequence), from (7.67), the expected derivative is equal to

$$
\begin{aligned}
\mathrm{E}\frac{\partial h_t}{\partial \epsilon_0^2} &= \mathrm{E}(h_0)\,\mathrm{E}\left[\frac{\partial\prod_{i=1}^{t}(\alpha\epsilon_{t-i}^2 + \gamma)}{\partial \epsilon_0^2}\right] \\
&= \mathrm{E}(h_0)\,\mathrm{E}\left[\prod_{i=1}^{t-1}(\alpha\epsilon_{t-i}^2 + \gamma)\right]\mathrm{E}\left[\frac{\partial(\alpha\epsilon_0^2 + \gamma)}{\partial \epsilon_0^2}\right] \\
&= \mathrm{E}(h_0)\left[\alpha\mathrm{E}(\epsilon^2) + \gamma\right]^{t-1}\alpha.
\end{aligned}
\tag{7.70}
$$

We have persistence (in the sense of the everlasting effect of a shock) if (7.70) converges to a finite and non-zero quantity when $t \to \infty$. This condition is verified if $\alpha E(\epsilon^2) + \gamma = 1$. The everlasting impact of a shock is then given by α.

If the variance of ϵ is equal to one, persistence occurs if there is a unit root in the GARCH(1,1) process ($\alpha + \gamma = 1$). This corresponds to the IGARCH model of Engle and Bollerslev (1986). Engle and Mustafa (1992) use $\alpha [\alpha + \gamma]^{s-1}$ as a measure of persistence of a shock at time t on h_{t+s} in near IGARCH models.

The condition for persistence is slightly different when $\epsilon \sim t(0, 1, 1, \nu)$, as then ϵ_t does not have variance equal to one. It becomes

$$\alpha \frac{\nu}{\nu - 2} + \gamma = 1 \qquad (\text{if } \nu > 2). \tag{7.71}$$

The measure of persistence of Engle and Mustafa (1992) could be generalized to $\alpha[\gamma + \alpha\nu/(\nu - 2)]^{s-1}$.

Persistence occurs in the absence of weak stationarity. While not being weakly stationary, the process generating the y_t can still be strictly stationary since the condition for strict stationarity, which is $E \log (\alpha\epsilon_t^2 + \gamma) < 0$, is less stringent than the condition for weak stationarity. The condition for strict stationarity implies that the posterior expectation of h_t does not explode as t tends to infinity and thus can be predicted. We can now remark that the analytical formulae of the predictive moments given in Subsection 7.3.4 exist only under the weak stationarity condition. On the contrary, the simulation method described at the end of the next subsection requires only the strict stationarity condition.

7.5.3 *Application to the USD/DM Exchange Rate*

Stationarity requires that

$$\text{WSC} = 1 - \alpha - \gamma > 0 \tag{7.72}$$

for weak stationarity, and

$$\text{SSC} = E \left[\log \left(\alpha \epsilon_t^2 + \gamma\right)\right] < 0 \tag{7.73}$$

for strict stationarity, when the error term is normal. The stationarity conditions are functions of the parameters, so that from the Bayesian viewpoint, one can compute the posterior probability of WSC and SSC. Once a simulated sample of the joint posterior density of the parameters is available, it is easy to compute the posterior density of these functions. Once a draw of θ is obtained, it is straightforward to calculate $1 - \alpha - \gamma$:

$$\text{WSC}_i = 1 - \alpha_i - \gamma_i. \tag{7.74}$$

After N draws, we can plot the posterior density of these values. The probability that WSC > 0 is approximated by the proportion of positive values. Computing

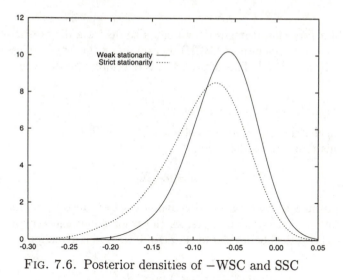

FIG. 7.6. Posterior densities of $-$WSC and SSC

the posterior density of SSC is slightly more demanding. For each draw of θ, we have to simulate M draws of ϵ according to an $N(0, 1)$ distribution, and evaluate

$$\text{SSC}_i = \frac{1}{M} \sum_{j=1}^{M} \log{(\alpha_i \, \epsilon_j^2 + \gamma_i)}, \qquad (7.75)$$

where ϵ_j is a draw of ϵ.

In Fig. 7.6, one finds the posterior densities of $-$WSC and SSC for the model (7.63) with normal errors (for ease of presentation, the graph of WSC times -1 is given instead of that of WSC). The probability of weak stationarity is 0.987 and the probability of strict stationarity is 0.996. Consequently, the h_t are predictable, but there may be some problems in using the predictive formulae of Subsection 7.3.4, since there is a small probability of getting explosive values $(\alpha + \gamma > 1)$. The solution to this problem is to reject the explosive values. With Student errors, the conclusion is quite different. The posterior probability that ν is larger than two is not negligible (0.22). But weak stationarity cannot hold if the conditional variances h_t do not exist, which requires $\nu > 2$. Thus it does not make sense to compute a posterior probability of weak stationarity as WSC should be defined as $1 - \gamma - \alpha \nu / (\nu - 2)$: one would reject too high a proportion of draws to get meaningful results. But one can compute the probability of strict stationarity, since it does not rely on ν being larger than two, but simply that $\nu > 0$. The result is 0.71 which means that the strict stationarity condition is not very well verified, which casts some doubts on the model.

7.6   Bayesian Heteroscedasticity Diagnostic

Most classical heteroscedasticity tests are based on the examination of the residuals of the linear regression model; see for instance the references in Pagan

(1984). In a Bayesian framework, we can also devise a diagnostic for detecting heteroscedasticity (including ARCH) by examining the Bayesian residuals of the linear regression model. This approach was developed by Bauwens and Lubrano (1991).

7.6.1 *Properties of Bayesian Residuals*

Let us consider the regression model $y = X\beta + u$ with $u \sim N(0, \sigma^2 I_T)$. The error term of this model is by definition

$$u = y - X\beta. \tag{7.76}$$

The error term is a theoretical notion, defined before any observation takes place. The predictive density of u expresses the prior belief the econometrician has about the theoretical behaviour of the error term and is given for a single element of u by

$$
\begin{aligned}
p(u_t) &= \int p(u_t|\sigma^2)\,\varphi(\sigma^2)\,d\sigma^2 \\
&= \int f_N(u_t|0,\sigma^2)\,f_{Ig}(\sigma^2|\nu_0, s_0)\,d\sigma^2 \\
&= f_t(u_t|0, s_0, 1, \nu_0),
\end{aligned} \tag{7.77}
$$

where $\varphi(\sigma^2) = f_{Ig}(\sigma^2|\nu_0, s_0)$ is the prior density of σ^2. The predictive moments are

$$
\begin{aligned}
\mathrm{E}(u_t) &= 0, \\
\mathrm{Var}(u_t) &= s_0/(\nu_0 - 2) = \mathrm{E}(\sigma^2).
\end{aligned} \tag{7.78}
$$

It is convenient to express (7.77) as

$$u_t \sim t(0, 1, 1, \nu_0)\,\sqrt{s_0/\nu_0}. \tag{7.79}$$

The predictive distribution of the square of the error term is the same as that of a Fisher random variable times a constant:

$$u_t^2 \sim F(1, \nu_0)\, s_0/\nu_0. \tag{7.80}$$

Its expectation is

$$\mathrm{E}(u_t^2) = \frac{s_0}{\nu_0 - 2} = \mathrm{E}(\sigma^2). \tag{7.81}$$

The Bayesian residual is also defined as $u = y - X\beta$, but it exists only after the sample has been observed and inference made on the regression parameters. Consequently, the posterior density of the Bayesian residual is a transformation of the posterior density of β. Under a natural conjugate prior, we know that the posterior density of β is Student with parameters β_*, s_*, M_*, and ν_*, see (2.89)–(2.93). Consequently,

$$\varphi(u|y) = f_t(u|y - X\beta_*, (X\,M_*^{-1}X')^+, s_*, \nu_*), \tag{7.82}$$

where $^+$ stands for the Moore–Penrose inverse. This is a singular Student density with expectation

$$\begin{aligned}
E(u|y) &= y - X E(\beta|y) \\
&= y - X \beta_* \\
&= u^*,
\end{aligned} \tag{7.83}$$

and variance

$$\begin{aligned}
\text{Var}(u|y) &= X \text{Var}(\beta|y) X' \\
&= X M_*^{-1} X' s_* / (\nu_* - 2) \\
&= P_{X*} s_* / (\nu_* - 2).
\end{aligned} \tag{7.84}$$

By marginalization, we get the posterior distribution of a single Bayesian residual:

$$\varphi(u_t|y) = f_t(u_t|u_t^*, s_*, (P_t^*)^{-1}, \nu_*), \tag{7.85}$$

where

$$\begin{aligned}
u_t^* &= y_t - x_t' \beta_*, \\
P_t^* &= x_t' M_*^{-1} x_t.
\end{aligned} \tag{7.86}$$

We can express the distribution of a Bayesian residual as

$$u_t - u_t^* \sim t(0, 1, 1, \nu_*) \sqrt{P_t^* s_*/\nu_*}, \tag{7.87}$$

so that the square of a centred Bayesian residual is a Fisher random variable times a constant:

$$(u_t - u_t^*)^2 \sim F(1, \nu_*) P_t^* s_*/\nu_*. \tag{7.88}$$

Its posterior expectation is

$$E[(u_t - u_t^*)^2|y] = E(u_t^2|y) - u_t^{*2} = \frac{\nu_*}{\nu_* - 2} P_t^* \frac{s_*}{\nu_*} = E(\sigma^2|y) P_t^*. \tag{7.89}$$

There is a great difference between the classical and Bayesian residuals. The classical residual has a zero mean. Under a diffuse prior, the Bayesian residual has a mean equal to the classical residual. The classical residual has a variance which is proportional to the tth diagonal element of $M_X = I_T - X(X'X)^{-1}X'$. Under a diffuse prior the posterior variance of the Bayesian residual is proportional to the tth diagonal element of $P_X = I_T - M_X$.

7.6.2 A Diagnostic Procedure

A Bayesian test can be based on the comparison between what the error term should be (its predictive density) and what the Bayesian residual actually is (its posterior density). We have understood that what we are interested in is the distribution of the squares. It is quite difficult to compare two multivariate densities. We can proceed with an approximation which consists in comparing their expectation by means of an auxiliary regression. Namely, we want to compare the predictive expectation (7.81) and the posterior expectation (7.89). If they are roughly equal, we have

$$u_t^{*\,2} = \frac{s_0}{\nu_0 - 2} - \frac{s_*}{\nu_* - 2} P_t^* + \epsilon_t, \tag{7.90}$$

with ϵ_t being an innovation. But this regression does not constitute a test regression as no direction of test as been specified. Let us now suppose that the distribution of the error term is

$$u_t \sim N(0, \sigma_t^2), \tag{7.91}$$

and let us define an inverted gamma-2 prior density for σ_t^2:

$$\varphi(\sigma_t^2) = f_{Ig}(\sigma_t^2 | \nu_0, \sigma^2 + z_t'\alpha). \tag{7.92}$$

This prior density represents a direction of test which is precise as soon as the set of variables z_t is chosen. The new predictive density of the error term is

$$\begin{aligned} p(u_t | z_t, \sigma^2, \alpha) &= \int p(u_t | \sigma_t^2)\, \varphi(\sigma_t^2)\, d\sigma_t^2 \\ &= f_t(u_t | 0, \sigma^2 + z_t'\alpha, 1, \nu_0). \end{aligned} \tag{7.93}$$

Considering the square of the error term, we get

$$u_t^2 | z_t, \sigma^2, \alpha \sim F(1, \nu_0)\, (\sigma^2 + z_t'\alpha)/\nu_0, \tag{7.94}$$

with expectation

$$\mathrm{E}(u_t^2 | z_t, \sigma^2, \alpha) = (\sigma^2 + z_t'\alpha)/(\nu_0 - 2). \tag{7.95}$$

Let us now compare the posterior expectation of the squared Bayesian residuals with the predictive expectation of the squared error term. We get the following test regression:

$$u_t^{*\,2} = \alpha_0 + \alpha_1 P_t^* + z_t'\alpha + \epsilon_t. \tag{7.96}$$

This regression says if the posterior expectation of the squared residuals can be explained only by a constant term and a correction term given by P_t^*, or if extra regressors representing a direction of test for heteroscedasticity are necessary. Homoscedasticity corresponds of course to $\alpha = 0$. The variables z_t can represent various directions of heteroscedasticity. Several choices of z_t are possible:

- A general heteroscedasticity test corresponds to including in z_t the squares and the cross-products of the exogenous variables x_t.
- If the variance is constant, but changes after a certain date, or if it is constant within groups of observations, but varies between groups, appropriate dummy variables form z_t.
- Finally, an ARCH test is obtained if z_t is defined as lagged values of $u_t^{*\,2}$.

The regression (7.96) looks very much like the classical test regressions surveyed by Pagan (1984) but is nevertheless different due to the term P_t^* and to the use of Bayesian residuals (which incorporate the effect of the prior information). For an increasing number of observations, the term P_t^* approaches zero and the classical and Bayesian test regressions coincide under a diffuse prior. From a classical point of view, the extra regressor P_t^* can be viewed as a small-sample correction term.

7.6.3 Applications to Electricity and Exchange Rate Data Sets

Let us now apply the test procedure given by the regression (7.96) to the electricity consumption data set already described in Subsection 7.2.4. We have 282 observations, corresponding to the 172 households, plus 108 of them for which direct metering was also made. The 't-statistic' of the regression coefficient of the heteroscedasticity variable (number of appliances owned by a household) is 2.11. This means that zero is out of the 95 per cent HPD interval, confirming the heteroscedastic effect already found in Subsection 7.2.4. We should also note that in this case the variable P_t^* has a great impact with a 't-statistic' of 6.14.

For the exchange rate data set which has 377 observations, we have tried a regression with three lags of the squared Bayesian residuals. The 'F-statistic' corresponding to these regression coefficients is 8.40. With this value, we have a very small tail probability in an $F(3, 369)$ distribution. In this regression the correcting factor P_t^* has very little impact. However, this impact is important when the number of lags is equal to one, but decreases quickly as the number of lags increases. Once again, the presence of heteroscedasticity (ARCH) is detected by the Bayesian test.

7.7 Conclusion

Testing for heteroscedasticity can be done in two different ways. We can test for the null of homoscedasticity in a particular heteroscedastic model as this corresponds to the parametric restriction $\alpha = 0$ in functional heteroscedastic models, or to $\alpha = \gamma = 0$ in a GARCH(1,1) model. The alternative approach is to conduct a misspecification search in a homoscedastic regression model by examining its squared Bayesian residuals. This approach is easy to implement and allows for different test directions. But as in the classical framework, it is not possible to find a direction representing GARCH. It is only possible to test for the ARCH direction.

We used the exchange series between the US dollar and the German mark to illustrate the different refinements of ARCH models and see the type of information we could extract from the series. The final model we got is not quite satisfactory as the condition for strict stationarity is not fully satisfied. This could be interpreted as an indication of misspecification. A quick look at the graph of the series shows that it behaves quite differently before and after 1973. Before 1973, the volatility is small except for two very short periods. After that date, the variance is greater. This suggests a structural change in the variance process, and maybe outliers in the first subperiod. This topic should be investigated further.

Financial analysts are particularly interested in the modelling of the volatility of a stock price or a stock index, as volatility is taken as a proxy for risk which is a major ingredient of theoretical pricing functions such as the Black and Scholes formula. However, these theoretical pricing formulae assume a risk which is constant. Attempts to plug directly the estimated or predicted volatility into for instance the Black and Scholes formula for option pricing, such as in Noh, Engle, and Kane (1994), violate this assumption of constancy. In a rational world the theoretical price for a European option on an asset with stochastic volatility is the expected value of the payoffs discounted by the risk-free interest rate (see Ghysels, Harvey, and Renault 1995). Engle and Mustafa (1992) propose a direct simulation of this expected value in a classical context. Bauwens and Lubrano (1998) propose a similar method based on the predictive density of future conditional volatilities (using an asymmetric GARCH model).

GARCH models are particularly attractive as they offer a parsimonious parameterization for modelling the dynamics of the volatility of a series, and are easy to estimate. However, we have seen that they do not always manage fully to reproduce the charactersitics of financial series. GARCH models suffer from the fact that with a single error term they have to cope with the error of observation for the mean and with the dynamics of the volatility. Stochastic volatility models may be seen as an extension of GARCH models. They introduce a second error term to describe the volatility, which gives a greater flexibility to the model. However, there is a high price to pay as the evaluation of the likelihood function requires the evaluation of an integral the dimension of which is the size of the sample. Jacquier, Polson, and Rossi (1994) have proposed a Bayesian treatment of this type of model, using in particular the Gibbs sampler to compute the likelihood function. Shephard and Pitt (1997) have refined and extended this approach; see also Shephard (1996) for other references. Uhlig (1997) uses a different approach which generates analytical results. Other solutions could be considered. We could try to simplify the problem using alternative formulations of the economic model such as the ones contained in Heston (1993) or Stein and Stein (1991). We could also tackle the numerical integration problem using the accelerated importance sampling method devised by Danielson and Richard (1993) and developed by Richard and Zhang (1997).

8

NON-LINEAR TIME SERIES MODELS

8.1 Introduction

In a dynamic linear regression model, the conditional expectation of the endogenous variable is a *linear* combination of the predetermined variables. The type of models we analyse in this chapter corresponds to a data generating process which is both dynamic and non-linear. This means that the conditional expectation of the endogenous variable is a *non-linear* function of the exogenous variables and of lags of the endogenous variable. The interest in this type of model started quite a long time ago with threshold and switching regression models. See Quandt (1958) for the classical side and Bacon and Watts (1971) for the Bayesian side. But it gained a revival in recent econometric literature with for instance the book by Granger and Teräsvirta (1993), and papers dealing with the asymmetry of the business cycle between recession and expansion phases, such as Hamilton (1989), Potter (1995), or Tiao and Tsay (1994).

In the linear regression model, the regression coefficients β are fixed over time. One particularly interesting way of introducing a non-linearity is to suppose that the conditional expectation of the endogenous variable follows two or more regimes. In the two-regime case, we have

$$
\begin{aligned}
\mathrm{E}(y_t|x_t) &= x_t'\beta_1 \quad \text{(first regime)}, \\
\mathrm{E}(y_t|x_t) &= x_t'\beta_2 \quad \text{(second regime)}.
\end{aligned}
\tag{8.1}
$$

The choice between the two regimes is driven by a transition function $F(\tilde{z}_t'\theta)$ which takes values between zero and one. Usually $F(.)$ is chosen either in the class of cumulative distribution functions (cdfs) or in the class of Dirac functions. We can write

$$
y_t = [1 - F(\tilde{z}_t'\theta)]\, x_t'\beta_1 + F(\tilde{z}_t'\theta)\, x_t'\beta_2 + \epsilon_t.
\tag{8.2}
$$

This class of models covers a wide range of non-linearities, but does not exhaust all the possible cases of non-linearities in time series. In particular one can think of the mixture model introduced by Lindgren (1978) and later developed by Hamilton (1989).

To specify (8.2), we have to choose a transition function $F(.)$ and the switching variables contained in $\tilde{z}_t$. We can distinguish two types of models which are quite different for the treatment of inference:

- The first class of model corresponds to models with a threshold. There is no common element between β and θ. The vector $\tilde{z}_t$ is of dimension 2. It is composed of a variable the nature of which is left unspecified for the moment and of a constant term. Conditionally on θ, the model is linear and θ must be treated by numerical integration.

- The second class of model has been advocated by Ginsburgh, Tishler, and Zang (1980), Richard (1980), or Sneessens (1985) as a reasonable approximation to the disequilibrium models of Maddala and Nelson (1974). The switching rule is based on the difference $x'_t\beta_2 - x'_t\beta_1$. Consequently all the elements of β are contained in θ. There is no conditional linearity in a part of the parameters. The posterior density of the parameters does not belong to any class of tractable densities. It has to be analysed by Monte Carlo integration, e.g. using importance sampling.

According to this distinction, we separate our presentation into two main parts. In the first part (Sections 8.2 to 8.5), we deal with some of the threshold models that have been proposed in the literature. They all present identification or integrability problems, sometimes rather tricky ones. These models are amenable to a common statistical treatment. This part draws heavily on Lubrano (1999). In the second part (Section 8.6), we discuss the analysis of the one-market disequilibrium model.

8.2   Inference in Threshold Regression Models

One of the main characteristics of threshold regression models is that the parameter vector can be divided into 'linear' parameters (β and σ^2) and 'non-linear' parameters (θ); that is to say, these models are linear in β conditionally on θ. Conditional inference on β and σ^2 can be conducted analytically (in the natural conjugate framework). The posterior density of θ has of course to be computed numerically, as well as the marginal moments of β and σ^2, following the principles outlined in Section 3.2. An alternative approach that consists in treating the complete density of all the parameters by Monte Carlo integration appears less efficient from a computational viewpoint; see e.g. Pfann, Schotman, and Tschernig (1996). In particular, the posterior density of θ can be difficult to integrate. This pleads in favour of the use of deterministic integration rules such as the iterative Simpson rule to integrate out θ, when this parameter is of small dimension (as is usually the case).

8.2.1   *A Typology of Threshold Models*

A typology of threshold regression models is provided firstly by the nature of the switching function $F(.)$, which can be step or smooth, and secondly by the nature of the switching variable $\tilde{z}_t$, which can be the time index or a continuous variable.

- A step transition function is built around a Dirac function which is zero when a linear combination of $\tilde{z}_t$ is negative and one otherwise. A smooth transition function replaces the Dirac function usually by a cumulative distribution function which is mostly the logistic function, as advocated by

Teräsvirta (1994). These functions, taking values in [0,1], have the particularity that their value changes not only according to the sign of the linear combination of $\tilde{z}_t$, but also according to its value.

- One possible candidate for $\tilde{z}_t$ is the time index and a constant term. These models introduce the possibility of a structural break at an unknown date. There is a huge literature on the subject, mainly classical, starting with Quandt (1958) in a maximum likelihood framework and Ferreira (1975) in a Bayesian framework. For instance, Perron and Vogelsang (1992) test for a unit root in the presence of a structural change at an unknown date while Gregory and Hansen (1996) test for cointegration in the same context. On the Bayesian side, we found, for example, DeJong (1996) who tests for unit roots with a structural break in the US GNP and Lubrano (1995b) who looks for a possible break in a cointegrated wage equation adjusted on French data.

- Regression models where the change of regime depends on a continuous variable, not necessarily growing over time, allow for an unknown number of changes of regime during the sample period. They are mainly represented by SETAR models (self-exciting threshold autoregressive models) which can be viewed as an alternative to linear ARMA models. The switching variable is a lag of y_t. As the change of regime is self-exciting, these models are particularly interesting for prediction. Bacon and Watts (1971) started a long Bayesian literature on threshold regression models which continued with Geweke and Terui (1993), Peguin-Feisolle (1994), Chen and Lee (1995), and found applications in finance with, for example, Pfann, Schotman, and Tschernig (1996) or Forbes, Kalb, and Kofman (1997).

The argument of the switching function is $\tilde{z}_t'\theta$. In the simplest case, to which we limit our attention in the first sections of this chapter, $\tilde{z}_t$ is composed of a variable and of a constant term, say $\tilde{z}_t = (z_t, 1)$. In this case, θ has to be partitioned in (θ_1, θ_2) such that

$$
\begin{aligned}
\tilde{z}_t'\theta = z_t\theta_1 + \theta_2 &= \theta_1\left(z_t + \frac{\theta_2}{\theta_1}\right) \\
&= \gamma(z_t - c).
\end{aligned}
\tag{8.3}
$$

With this reparameterization, γ measures the smoothness of the transition in a smooth transition function. It is restricted to be non-negative, so that large positive values of $z_t - c$ are associated with the second regime (since $F[\gamma(z_t - c)]$ is then close to one), and large negative values of $z_t - c$ are associated with the first regime. The switching is determined by the value of $z_t - c$ and c is called the threshold parameter. A step transition is the limit of a smooth transition when γ tends to infinity. In a step transition model, the dimension of θ is reduced to one.

The interpretation of the threshold c depends of course on the nature of the switching variable z_t. The useful range of c is determined by the empirical range of z_t as the switching operates by comparing c with z_t. When z_t is the time index, it is common practice to change the name of the threshold c and to call it τ to stress the fact that the threshold is a date and thus a discrete parameter. When z_t is a continuous variable another parameter may appear as in SETAR models like that considered in Geweke and Terui (1993). In these models, z_t is the lagged endogenous variable, i.e. $z_t = y_{t-d}$, and d is called a delay parameter. It is a statistical question to determine the value of d. In the Bayesian literature (see e.g. Geweke and Terui 1993 or Koop and Potter 1995), d is treated as a parameter for which a posterior density is derived. In this case, d is an element of θ. We could also decide that it is part of the specification of the model as for instance the lag length in AR models. Then, d should be determined with an information criterion as for instance Tong and Lim (1980) do in a classical framework. In this chapter, we consider the determination of d as a model choice problem and not as an inference problem; hence we do not derive a posterior density for d.

8.2.2 Notation

For practical computations it is useful to reparameterize the model (8.2) as

$$y_t = x_t'\beta_1 + F(\tilde{z}_t'\theta)\, x_t'(\beta_2 - \beta_1) + \epsilon_t, \tag{8.4}$$

which suggests defining

$$
\begin{aligned}
x_t'(\theta) &= [x_t', F(\tilde{z}_t'\theta)\, x_t'], \\
\beta' &= [\beta_1^k, \beta_2' - \beta_1'],
\end{aligned}
\tag{8.5}
$$

so that the model can be written in the more compact form

$$y_t = x_t'(\theta)\beta + \epsilon_t. \tag{8.6}$$

In the homoscedastic case, the variance of ϵ_t is σ^2. If we allow for different variances in each regime, we have a heteroscedastic model where

$$\mathrm{Var}(\epsilon_t) = \sigma_1^2[1 - F(\tilde{z}_t'\theta)] + \sigma_2^2 F(\tilde{z}_t'\theta). \tag{8.7}$$

The same transition function is supposed to drive the transition of the mean and of the variance. For the moment, we have left the general notation θ, which means that we propose a general analysis of the model, irrespective of the nature of the transition function and irrespective of the nature of the switching variable. We also suppose that the value of the delay parameter d is given.

Finally let us note that the model is not fundamentally changed if we allow for a different set of regressors x_{it} in each regime. Supposing that k_1 and k_2 are the dimensions of these sets of regressors, we define $k = k_1 + k_2$ as the total number of regressors in the model. So k represents the total number of regressors in the model and k_1, k_2 the number of regressors in each regime, even if $k_1 = k_2$.

8.2.3 *Posterior Analysis in the Homoscedastic Case*

Under a normality assumption, the likelihood function of model (8.6) is

$$L(\beta, \theta, \sigma^2; y) \propto \sigma^{-T} \exp\left\{ -\frac{1}{2\sigma^2} \sum_{t=1}^{T} [y_t - x_t'(\theta)\beta]^2 \right\}. \qquad (8.8)$$

Following the distinction between linear and non-linear parameters, it is useful to decompose the prior density into

$$\varphi(\beta, \sigma^2, \theta) = \varphi(\beta, \sigma^2)\, \varphi(\theta). \qquad (8.9)$$

We can make any choice for $\varphi(\theta)$, as this parameter has to be integrated out numerically anyway. Moreover, we want to be free to choose the prior on θ according to the particular non-linear model which is analysed. On the contrary, it is interesting to remain in the natural conjugate framework for the prior on β and σ^2 as we can integrate out these parameters analytically. Therefore, we have the following prior densities:

$$\begin{aligned} \varphi(\beta|\sigma^2) &= f_N(\beta|\beta_0, \sigma^2 M_0^{-1}), \\ \varphi(\sigma^2) &= f_{Ig}(\sigma^2|\nu_0, s_0). \end{aligned} \qquad (8.10)$$

The conditional posterior densities of β and σ^2 result from the application of standard formulae of natural conjugate analysis (see Section 2.7):

$$\begin{aligned} \varphi(\beta|\theta, y) &= f_t(\beta|\beta_*(\theta), s_*(\theta), M_*(\theta), \nu_*), \\ \varphi(\sigma^2|\theta, y) &= f_{Ig}(\sigma^2|\nu_*, s_*(\theta)), \end{aligned} \qquad (8.11)$$

where

$$\begin{aligned} M_*(\theta) &= M_0 + \sum_{t=1}^{T} x_t(\theta)\, x_t'(\theta), \\ \beta_*(\theta) &= M_*^{-1}(\theta)\, [\sum_{t=1}^{T} x_t(\theta)\, y_t + M_0\beta_0], \\ s_*(\theta) &= s_0 + \beta_0' M_0 \beta_0 + \sum_{t=1}^{T} y_t^2 - \beta_*'(\theta)\, M_*(\theta)\, \beta_*(\theta), \\ \nu_* &= \nu_0 + T. \end{aligned} \qquad (8.12)$$

The posterior density of θ is proportional to the inverse of the integrating constant of the above Student density times the prior density of θ:

$$\varphi(\theta|y) \propto |s_*(\theta)|^{-(T-k)/2}\, |M_*(\theta)|^{-1/2}\, \varphi(\theta). \qquad (8.13)$$

This density has to be analysed numerically to compute its integrating constant and its moments. It typically presents some important pathologies that are explained in detail in Section 8.3. The marginal posterior densities of β and σ^2 follow by

$$\varphi(\beta|y) = \int \varphi(\beta|\theta, y)\, \varphi(\theta|y)\, d\theta, \qquad (8.14)$$

$$\varphi(\sigma^2|y) = \int f_{Ig}(\sigma^2|\nu_*, s_*(\theta))\,\varphi(\theta|y)\,d\theta. \tag{8.15}$$

Marginal moments are obtained by application of formulae explained in Section 3.2. A marginal expectation is the expectation of a conditional expectation and a marginal variance is the sum of the expectation of a conditional variance plus the variance of the conditional expectation.

8.2.4 *Posterior Analysis for the Heteroscedastic Case*

Let us now consider the model (8.6) with a changing variance of the error term given by (8.7). We can reparameterize (8.7) as

$$\text{Var}(\epsilon_t) = \sigma^2[(1 - F(\tilde{z}_t'\theta)) + \phi\,F(\tilde{z}_t'\theta)] = \sigma^2 h_t(\theta, \phi), \tag{8.16}$$

where $\sigma^2 = \sigma_1^2$, $\phi = \sigma_2^2/\sigma_1^2 \in [0, +\infty[$. The same analysis as in Subsection 8.2.3 can be reproduced, provided we rescale the data. Let us define

$$\begin{aligned} y_t(\theta, \phi) &= y_t/\sqrt{h_t(\theta, \phi)}, \\ x_t(\theta, \phi) &= x_t(\theta)/\sqrt{h_t(\theta, \phi)}. \end{aligned} \tag{8.17}$$

The likelihood function of the model is

$$L(\beta, \theta, \sigma^2, \phi; y) \propto \sigma^{-T} \left[\prod_{t=1}^{T} h_t(\theta, \phi)\right]^{-1/2} \exp\left\{-\frac{1}{2\,\sigma^2}\sum_{t=1}^{T}[y_t(\theta, \phi) - x_t'(\theta, \phi)\beta]^2\right\}. \tag{8.18}$$

We have the additional parameter ϕ for which the prior density could be an inverted gamma-2 so as to take its positivity into account, or more simply a non-informative one like

$$\varphi(\phi) \propto 1/\phi. \tag{8.19}$$

We can use the same prior information on β and on σ^2 as before, noting simply that in this case the prior density of β is conditional on σ^2 which is the error variance in the first regime. The conditional posterior density of β is a Student density

$$\varphi(\beta|\theta, \phi, y) = f_t(\beta|\beta_*(\theta, \phi), s_*(\theta, \phi), M_*(\theta, \phi), \nu_*), \tag{8.20}$$

and that of σ^2 is an inverted gamma-2

$$\varphi(\sigma^2|\theta, \phi, y) \propto f_{Ig}(\sigma^2|\nu_*, s_*(\theta, \phi)), \tag{8.21}$$

where

$$\begin{aligned} M_*(\theta, \phi) &= M_0 + \sum_{t=1}^{T} x_t(\theta, \phi)\,x_t'(\theta, \phi), \\ \beta_*(\theta, \phi) &= M_*^{-1}(\theta, \phi)\,[\sum_{t=1}^{T} x_t(\theta, \phi)\,y_t(\theta, \phi) + M_0\beta_0], \\ s_*(\theta, \phi) &= s_0 + \beta_0'M_0\beta_0 + \sum_{t=1}^{T} y_t(\theta, \phi)^2 - \beta_*'(\theta, \phi)\,M_*(\theta, \phi)\,\beta_*(\theta, \phi), \\ \nu_* &= \nu_0 + T. \end{aligned} \tag{8.22}$$

The joint posterior density of θ and ϕ is obtained from the inverse of the integrating constant of the above Student density, the first factor of the likelihood, and the prior densities of θ and ϕ:

$$\varphi(\theta, \phi | y) \propto [\prod h_t(\theta, \phi)]^{-1/2} |s_*(\theta, \phi)|^{-(T-k)/2} |M_*(\theta, \phi)|^{-1/2} \varphi(\theta) \varphi(\phi). \quad (8.23)$$

Compared with (8.13), the dimension of the numerical integration is increased by one. The marginal posterior densities of β and σ^2 follow by marginalization:

$$\varphi(\beta | y) = \int \int f_t(\beta | \beta_*(\theta, \phi), s_*(\theta, \phi), M_*(\theta, \phi), \nu_*) \, \varphi(\theta, \phi | y) \, d\theta \, d\phi, \quad (8.24)$$

$$\varphi(\sigma^2 | y) \propto \int \int f_{Ig}(\sigma^2 | \nu_*, s_*(\theta, \phi)) \, \varphi(\theta, \phi | y) \, d\theta \, d\phi. \quad (8.25)$$

The latter corresponds to the posterior density of the variance of the error term in the first regime. In order to find the posterior density of $\sigma_2^2 = \sigma^2 \phi$, we use the one-to-one transformation from (σ^2, ϕ, θ) to $(\sigma_2^2, \phi, \theta)$ of Jacobian ϕ. Then

$$\varphi(\sigma_2^2, \phi, \theta | y) \propto \phi \times f_{Ig} \left(\frac{\sigma_2^2}{\phi} | \nu_*, s_*(\theta, \phi) \right) \varphi(\theta, \phi | y). \quad (8.26)$$

The marginal density and moments of σ_2^2 can be computed by numerical integration on ϕ and θ.

To check if the unequal variance model is favoured by the data, we can look at the posterior density of ϕ. If 1 belongs to a 95 per cent HPD interval of ϕ, the two variances σ_1^2 and σ_2^2 can be considered to be equal at this level of confidence.

Remark: Another type of treatment of the unequal variance case was given by Geweke and Terui (1993) (see also Pole and Smith 1985) when the transition between the two regimes is abrupt. Their formulation takes advantage of the fact that β_1 and β_2 are independent conditionally on θ. Consequently the conditional posterior densities of β_1 and β_2 are independent Student densities and there is no extra non-linear parameter ϕ; see Lubrano (1999) for more details. However, their formulation is not compatible with our reparameterization and does not allow recovery of the posterior correlations between β_1 and β_2. This correlation matrix is interesting for a specification search and for a test of linearity, as of course these parameters are not marginally independent.

8.2.5 Predictive Density for the SETAR Model

If the considered model is self-exciting, i.e. $z_t = y_{t-d}$, the change of regime is endogenous, which is not the case if $z_t = t$. Prediction becomes as interesting as in linear AR models, except that now, turning points may have a better chance of being correctly predicted owing to the endogeneity of the switching mechanism. Let us consider a simple version of the SETAR model with

$$y_t = \beta_1 y_{t-1} + F[\gamma(y_{t-1} - c)]\delta y_{t-1} + \epsilon_t. \tag{8.27}$$

Let y^* be a set of s future observations of y_t, i.e. $y_{T+1}, \ldots, y_{T+s}$, and $g(y^*)$ a function of the future observations. We want to compute the expected value of this function. For adequate choices of $g(.)$, we can get the expectation, variance, and density function of the future observations. The posterior expectation of this function is

$$
\begin{aligned}
E[g(y^*)|y] &= E_\zeta[E_{y^*}(g(y^*)|y,\zeta)] \\
&= \int_\zeta \left[\int_{\mathbf{R}^s} g(y^*)\, p(y^*|y,\zeta)\, dy^* \right] \varphi(\zeta|y)\, d\zeta,
\end{aligned}
\tag{8.28}
$$

where $p(y^*|y,\zeta)$ is the density of future observations and ζ represents all the parameters of the model (θ, β, and σ^2). To evaluate these integrals, we can use a simulation method. For given values of σ^2, β, and θ, it is easy to simulate n_2 sets of future observations y^*, starting from the observed y_T, by the recursion

$$y_{T+f} = \beta_1\, y_{T+f-1} + F[\gamma(y_{T+f-1} - c)]\,\delta\, y_{T+f-1} + \epsilon_{T+f} \tag{8.29}$$

inherent to the model. This only requires generation of each ϵ_{T+f} from the $N(0,\sigma^2)$ distribution. Conditionally on θ we know analytically the posterior densities of β and σ^2 which are respectively Student and inverted gamma-2, see (8.11). Consequently, n_1 random drawings β_i and σ_i^2 can be obtained conditionally on θ. The predictive moments of y can be computed in the same loops of the numerical integration procedure that is used to compute the posterior moments. The expectation $E[g(y^*)|y]$ is approximated by

$$\int \frac{1}{n_1 n_2} \sum_{i=1}^{n_1} \sum_{j=1}^{n_2} g(y_j^*|\beta_i, \sigma_i^2, \theta)\, d\theta, \tag{8.30}$$

where y_j^* is a simulated value of y^*. This is a mix of a deterministic integration rule (for γ and c) and a direct Monte Carlo simulation (for the future observations and the other parameters).

8.3 Pathological Aspects of Threshold Models

We examine the peculiarities of the posterior density (8.13) of the non-linear parameter θ. They depend on the type of the transition variable $\tilde{z}_t$ and on the form of the transition function $F(.)$. We then discuss the identification problems that are present for certain values of θ.

8.3.1 *The Nature of the Threshold*

The previous developments give the impression that whatever $F(.)$ and $\tilde{z}_t$ are, the posterior densities of the parameters are always the same. This is not true as the choice of the switching function $F(.)$ and of the transition variable z_t can have an enormous influence on the shape of the posterior density of the threshold c (or τ in a time index regression).

As the change of regime depends on the value of $z_t - c$, the useful domain of definition of c is determined by the minimum and the maximum of the sample values of z_t. If z_t is a time index, the threshold τ represents a date and is by nature a discrete parameter. Its posterior density is discrete on equally spaced points and integration over τ is done by summation. Each point of the density represents a probability. On the contrary, if z_t is a continuous variable, c is a continuous parameter with a posterior density that is generally continuous. However, if the transition function is abrupt, the posterior density of c presents discontinuities at a finite number of points. Let us assume that we have sorted the observations of the switching variable z_t in ascending order. The continuous parameter c has to be compared with these sorted observations. Between two consecutive observations, c can vary without modifying the sample classification and consequently the likelihood function. Thus the marginal likelihood function $l(c; y)$ is a step function which looks like a histogram with $T - 1$ cells. For T tending to infinity, the length of the steps (or the cells of the histogram) tend to zero provided the distribution of z_t is absolutely continuous with respect to the Lebesgue measure over the real line. In this case, the posterior density $\varphi(c|y)$ tends to a continuous density. Integration over c can be done by deterministic integration rules, independently of the spacing between two consecutive values of the ordered z_t.

The functions $l(c; y)$ or $\varphi(c|y)$ typically do not have a bell shape (the shape of the usual densities). A consequence is that maximum likelihood estimation is difficult: the likelihood function is not differentiable and may be multimodal. Any classical measure of uncertainty for c seems unfeasible. The Bayesian approach, on the contrary, causes no problem as we simply have to average on the domain of definition of c.

8.3.2 *Identification in Abrupt Transition Models*

The change between the two regimes is done via a step transition function $ID(z_t - c)$ defined by

$$ID(z_t - c) = \begin{cases} 0 & \text{if } z_t \geq c \\ 1 & \text{if } z_t < c. \end{cases} \tag{8.31}$$

$ID(.)$ is an indicator function (or Dirac function, also called Heaviside function). Replacing $F(\tilde{z}_t'\theta)$ by (8.31) in (8.4), the model is written

$$y_t = x_t'\beta_1 + ID(z_t - c)\, x_t'(\beta_2 - \beta_1) + \epsilon_t, \tag{8.32}$$

and

$$x_t'(\theta) = x_t'(c) = [x_t', \, ID(z_t - c) \, x_t'].$$ (8.33)

Various models correspond to this framework depending on the choice made for z_t. In Quandt (1958), Ferreira (1975), Lubrano (1993, 1995b), and many other papers, z_t is the time index ($z_t = t$). The purpose of this choice is to analyse the presence of a structural break at an unknown point of time. In Geweke and Terui (1993) or Chen and Lee (1995), z_t is a continuous variable and more precisely the lagged endogenous variable y_{t-d}.

This model presents a serious identification problem whether z_t is the time index or a continuous variable. In regime i, the number of observations T_i must be greater than the number of regressors k_i. Let us assume that we have sorted z_t in ascending order and the other variables accordingly (this is done naturally if $z_t = t$). The model is not changed even if it is dynamic. The threshold c has to be compared with the ordered values of z_t, called oz_t hereafter. This first regime is active as long as c is lower than oz_t for some value T_1 of t, which is the number of observations in the first regime. The second regime becomes active when c becomes larger than oz_t for some t. There is then T_2 observations in the second regime. The model is identified if $T_1 > k_1$ and $T_2 > k_2$. There are two different ways of solving this identification problem. In the linear regression model, a rank deficiency ($T < k$) is solved by introducing prior information on the regression coefficients β. This would solve only a part of the problem as there is an additional parameter (c or τ). On the contrary, adequate prior information on the threshold parameter that guarantees a sufficient number of observations per regime would definitively solve the problem.

When z_t is the time index, the prior on τ has to be discrete, since τ is a discrete parameter. A 'non-informative' prior assigns an equal mass to each integer $1, 2, \ldots, T$. The prior on τ has to take into account the above-mentioned identification problem. It should give a zero weight to unfeasible regime classifications:

$$\varphi(\tau) = \begin{cases} 0 & \text{if } \tau < k_1 \text{ or } \tau > T - k_2 \\ \dfrac{1}{T - k_1 - k_2} & \text{for each other point of the sample.} \end{cases}$$ (8.34)

Ferreira (1975) used the following variant to this prior:

$$\varphi(\tau) \propto [\tau \, (T - \tau)]^{1/2}.$$ (8.35)

The weights in (8.35) are taken from of a beta density on the interval $[0, T]$. Ferreira extended the prior (8.35) to

$$\varphi(\tau) \propto [\tau \, (T - \tau) \, |M_*(\tau)|]^{1/2},$$ (8.36)

in order to cancel a term coming from the posterior density of τ which is

$$\varphi(\tau | y) \propto |s_*(\tau)|^{-(T-k)/2} \, |M_*(\tau)|^{-1/2} \, \varphi(\tau).$$ (8.37)

This is a discrete density as τ is a discrete parameter and it has to be integrated out by discrete summations, in particular for computing the marginal posterior density of β:

$$\varphi(\beta|y) \propto \sum_{\tau=1}^{T} \varphi(\beta|\tau, y)\, \varphi(\tau|y). \qquad (8.38)$$

Posterior results, as reported in Ferreira (1975) for an artificial sample, do not seem to be importantly affected by variants of the prior density on τ.

When z_t is a continuous variable, the threshold c is a continuous parameter, which acts like a location parameter. A non-informative prior for c can be taken to be constant. But it has to give a zero weight to unfeasible regime classifications, so it is defined by

$$\varphi(c) \propto \begin{cases} 0 & \text{if } c < oz_{k_1} \text{ or } c > oz_{T-k_2} \\ 1 & \text{otherwise.} \end{cases} \qquad (8.39)$$

This prior simply expresses the information that the break has the same probability of occurring anywhere within the observed sample, and not outside or at its boundaries. The posterior density of c, given by

$$\varphi(c|y) \propto |s_*(c)|^{-(T-k)/2}\, |M_*(c)|^{-1/2}\, \varphi(c), \qquad (8.40)$$

is discontinuous at a finite number of points given by the sample values of z_t, but it is continuous (and constant) between two consecutive values of z_t. This parameter can be integrated out by a deterministic rule so that

$$\varphi(\beta|y) \propto \int \varphi(\beta|c, y)\, \varphi(c|y)\, dc. \qquad (8.41)$$

8.3.3 Identification in Smooth Transition Models

A smooth transition between the two regimes is obtained by replacing the step indicator function (8.31) by a smooth monotonically increasing function $F(.)$ with $F(-\infty) = 0$ and $F(\infty) = 1$. $F(.)$ is usually chosen to be a cdf (cumulative distribution function). Teräsvirta (1994) advocates the use of the logistic function

$$F[\gamma(z_t - c)] = \frac{1}{1 + \exp[-\gamma(z_t - c)]}. \qquad (8.42)$$

The parameter γ determines the degree of smoothness of the transition and is chosen to be positive in order to define the transition function uniquely. Other transition functions than the logistic one can be proposed, but the result is insensitive to this choice as shown in Bacon and Watts (1971). With a smooth transition function, the model (8.32) is changed into

$$y_t = x_t'\beta_1 + F[\gamma(z_t - c)]x_t'(\beta_2 - \beta_1) + \epsilon_t, \qquad (8.43)$$

and

$$x'_t(\theta) = x'_t(\gamma, c) = [x'_t, F[\gamma(z_t - c)] x'_t]. \qquad (8.44)$$

We have seen that an identification problem arises in the step transition model whenever there are fewer observations than variables in a given regime. When the transition is smooth, it is no longer possible to classify unambiguously an observation as belonging to a single regime and consequently the previous identification problem does not occur. However, the smooth transition function introduces new problems: a local identification problem at $\gamma = 0$ and an integrability problem due to its behaviour when $\gamma \to \infty$.

8.3.3.1 *Identification at $\gamma = 0$* When $\gamma = 0$, the transition function (8.42) is constant (and equal to $1/2$) whatever the value of c, which means that c is no longer identified. For $\gamma = 0$, the model is in fact linear as it is reduced to

$$y_t = x'_t\beta_1 + 0.5\, x'_t(\beta_2 - \beta_1) + \epsilon_t. \qquad (8.45)$$

The parameter $\delta = \beta_2 - \beta_1$ is also no longer identified, and the matrix $M_*(\gamma = 0, c)$ defined in (8.13) is singular due to perfect collinearity, except of course when x_{1t} and x_{2t} have no common elements. Consequently the posterior density of γ and c as given in (8.13) tends to infinity when γ tends to zero (assuming of course that the prior is flat), since the factor depending on $s_*(\theta)$ is bounded ($s_*(\theta)$ being a sum of squared residuals). Numerical problems for evaluating the posterior density may occur for small positive values of γ, depending on the sample configuration. This problem is general to models presenting non-linearities in the parameters (see the discussion in Subsection 2.2.4). In order to solve this local identification problem, one can introduce prior information on δ. When M_0 is zero, $M_*(\gamma = 0, c)$ given by the convolution formulae in (8.12) is singular. But with sufficient prior information, $M_*(\gamma = 0, c)$ becomes regular. What is the minimum prior information required? When $\gamma \simeq 0$, the model becomes linear and thus δ can take any value and in particular zero (in the case where the two regimes have the same regressors). So $\mathrm{E}(\delta) = 0$ is a good and simple choice. When γ is far from zero, there is no need for this special prior information, so the prior precision has to be a function of γ. A normal prior could be

$$\varphi(\beta|\sigma^2, \gamma, c) = f_N(\beta|0, \sigma^2 M_0^{-1}(\gamma)), \qquad (8.46)$$

where

$$M_0(\gamma) = \begin{pmatrix} 0 & 0 \\ 0 & N_0/\exp(\gamma) \end{pmatrix}. \qquad (8.47)$$

with N_0 being the identity matrix times a constant. A more complex choice is $N_0(\gamma, c)$ which normalizes the determinant of $M_*(\gamma = 0, c)$ to one, at least when the regressors are the same in the two regimes. This is obtained with

$$N_0(\gamma, \tau) = 0.25 \left[\sum x_t x'_t F(\gamma(z_t - c)) \right]^{-1}.$$

This prior information has the same effect as the prior (8.36) used by Ferreira (1975), but only for small values of γ.

8.3.3.2 *Integrability* The density of γ and c has another pathology, which has to do with its behaviour when γ tends to infinity: it does not tend to zero, so it is not integrable if a flat prior is used for γ. The reason for this behaviour is that when γ tends to infinity, the smooth transition model (8.43) tends to the step transition model (8.32) since the smooth transition function (8.42) tends to a Dirac function. It follows that the likelihood function of the smooth transition model tends to the likelihood function of the step transition model, which has a strictly positive value by definition. Therefore the marginal likelihood function of γ is $O(1)$ as $\gamma \to \infty$, so that under a flat prior for γ, the posterior density is not integrable. To ensure the integrability of the posterior density, one solution is to restrict the range of integration of γ to a bounded interval like $(0, M)$. This raises the issue of the choice of M, and of the sensitivity of the posterior results to this choice. Another solution is to use a prior on $(0, \infty)$, which tends to zero quickly enough at its right tail. The prior should be at least $O(\gamma^{1+v})$ with $v > 0$. A possible choice of prior is the truncated Cauchy density

$$\varphi(\gamma) \propto (1 + \gamma^2)^{-1} \quad \text{if } \gamma > 0 \tag{8.48}$$

(the scale parameter of the Cauchy density has been set equal to one, but this restriction is not necessary). Another possible choice is a gamma (in particular an exponential) density.

In order to define a prior density for γ, the scale of measurement of this parameter must be fixed. A convenient way to do this is to divide the series $z_t - c$ by the standard deviation of the series z_t; see Granger and Teräsvirta (1993: 123). This has at least the advantage of making γ independent of the unit of measurement of z_t. When z_t is a time index, γ is linked to the periodicity of the observations. The scaling can be done by dividing t by $N \times S = T$ where N is the number of years and S the number of observations per year. In this case the standard deviation of the resulting time index (t/T) is $\sqrt{0.083333 - 0.083333/T^2}$. Consequently it is preferable to divide the time index t by $T \times \sqrt{0.083333}$ instead of simply T (when T is large).

Once suitable prior information is defined, the joint posterior density of γ and c is well defined over the parameter space including the point $\gamma = 0$. Its expression is

$$\varphi(\gamma, c|y) \propto |s_*(\gamma, c)|^{-(T-k)/2} |M_*(\gamma, c)|^{-1/2} \varphi(\gamma) \varphi(c). \tag{8.49}$$

In the case where z_t is a time index, this density is peculiar as it is discrete in c and continuous in γ. By numerical integration of γ, we can compute the discrete probabilities attached to each of the $T - k$ possible values of the threshold. By discrete summation over the threshold, we get the posterior density and moments of γ.

The interpretation of the regression coefficients β is not as obvious with a smooth transition as with a step one. When the change of regime is abrupt, the value of the transition function is either zero or one. So the regimes are clearly defined, and the regression coefficients are the partial derivatives of y_t with respect to x_t in each regime. When the transition is smooth, the change of regime is gradual, and the partial derivatives are weighted averages of β_1 and β_2, with weights that vary from one observation to another. Thus it is rather difficult to compare the inference results on β in the two models.

Remark: When z_t is the time index, there is presumably only one change at a particular point of time. When z_t is continuous and stationary, many changes of regime can occur for a given sample. But all these changes have to obey the same transition function which has constant parameters: the threshold c and the speed of change γ are always the same irrespective of the size of the jump given by z_t. This restriction may be part of the explanation.

8.4 Testing for Linearity and Model Selection

The numerous possibilities among the different cases of non-linearity induce some very natural questions which can be rather hard to answer. The first question is of course to know if a non-linear model is necessary to give a correct account of the behaviour of the data. Some tests presented in the classical literature do not specify a precise model for the alternative (such as the RESET test, the bispectrum test, or tests based on Voltera expansions). But for most of the tests, such as the ones presented for instance in Tsay (1989) or in Lin and Teräsvirta (1994), the data are supposed to follow a particular non-linear model under the alternative. These classical tests should be more powerful as they are based on a precise direction, even if they may be powerful against other directions. There does not seem to be a Bayesian equivalent literature on this topic. We present some Bayesian directions in this section. Besides the Lagrange multiplier tests of Luukkonen, Saikkonen, and Teräsvirta (1988) and Teräsvirta (1994), there is a vast literature on likelihood ratio tests in non-linear models based on the paper of Andrews and Ploberger (1994). Koop and Potter (1999) present the Bayesian counterpart of this literature. The second question of interest concerns the determination of the switching variable z_t. There is no universal answer to this question. The economic problem under consideration of course gives some natural choices which are very helpful. In the breaking point literature for instance, z_t is a time trend. In the switching regime literature, z_t is a continuous variable which is usually suggested by economic theory. But z_t governs the switching with some delay, so that it appears as z_{t-d} where d is called the delay parameter. This parameter has to be determined and we propose a model selection procedure below.

8.4.1 *Model Selection*

In the linear regression model

$$y_t = x_t'\beta + u_t, \tag{8.50}$$

the conditional expectation of y_t is supposed to be equal to $x_t'\beta$. In the spirit of the augmented regressions of Pagan (1984), reinterpreted in a Bayesian framework by Aprahamian, Lubrano, and Marimoutou (1994), we can see if a better fitting conditional expectation can be found for y_t. The search is conducted in regression directions by means of a set of additional variables. Once these additional variables are found, we have to compare two regression models using, for instance, a Bayesian information criterion. Model choice is best made when it is possible to embed the initial and the alternative models inside a general model. The problem here is that the alternative model is non-linear. Thus we have to find a general linear model that approximates the non-linear model and admits the particular linear model as a restriction. The linear model (8.50) becomes non-linear by adding the term $x_t'\delta F[\gamma(z_{t-d} - c)]$. Linearity is recovered when $\gamma = 0$. A general linear model, approximating the non-linear model, can be found by linearization of $F(.)$ around $\gamma = 0$ in the non-linear model. In the classical literature, Luukkonen, Saikkonen, and Teräsvirta (1988) showed that a third-order Taylor expansion of $F(.)$ in general preserves many of the characteristics of the transition function. It gives

$$F[\gamma(z_{t-d} - c)] \simeq \alpha_0 + \alpha_1 z_{t-d} + \alpha_2 z_{t-d}^2 + \alpha_3 z_{t-d}^3. \qquad (8.51)$$

The augmented regression for detecting a non-linear direction becomes

$$y_t = x_t'\beta + x_t'\delta_1 z_{t-d} + x_t'\delta_2 z_{t-d}^2 + x_t'\delta_3 z_{t-d}^3 + \epsilon_t. \qquad (8.52)$$

The choice between the linear model (8.50) and the non-linear approximation (8.52) can be made on the basis of the Schwarz (1978) Bayesian information criterion (BIC).

Looking for non-linearity by means of a linear augmented regression has many advantages. Firstly, there is no need to make inference in a non-linear model. Secondly, in order to estimate the augmented regression, we have to fix a value for d. Choosing a d that minimizes the Schwarz criterion maximizes the chances of detecting non-linearity and gives the most plausible value for d. So in the same procedure, we test for non-linearity and select the best value for d. The Schwarz criterion includes a penalty for large models and is thus a protection for over-parameterization. The way is thus prepared to estimate a particular non-linear model.

8.4.2 *A Lnearity Test Based on the Posterior Density*

Let us now consider the reverse situation. A particular non-linear model has been specified and estimated. We ask ourselves if the incorporated non-linearity is necessary to give a good account of the behaviour of the data. As indicated above, the problem can be tackled by posterior odds as in Koop and Potter (1999). But as linearity occurs when $\delta = 0$ (or also for $\gamma = 0$ in the smooth transition model), linearity can be tested by constructing a posterior confidence interval for δ (or γ). Cook and Broemeling (1996) propose the evaluation of such an interval for δ using a simulation method.

There is a fundamental difficulty in testing for linearity which is known as Davies' problem (Davies 1977). Linearity occurs for $\gamma = 0$, but under this restriction δ is not identified. Testing for $\delta = 0$ leads exactly to the same situation for γ. This means that we cannot test for linearity in the absence of prior information. In fact Davies' problem has already been discussed (without naming it) in Section 8.3. In the step transition model, there is linearity when $\delta = 0$. In this case, c or τ is not identified. But if the prior on c or τ has enough points in each regime, the posterior of both δ and c or τ is perfectly defined. In the smooth transition model, γ complicates the situation. When we integrate over γ, starting at $\gamma = 0$, δ is not identified. The proposed informative prior (8.46) on δ solves the problem.

The marginal posterior density of δ can be easily derived and is given in the following theorem for the smooth transition model.

Theorem 8.1 *The marginal posterior distribution*

$$\varphi(\delta|y) = \int f_t\left(\delta|\delta_*(\gamma, c), M_{22.1}^*(\gamma, c), s_*(\gamma, c), T - k\right) \varphi(\gamma, c|y)\, d\gamma\, dc \qquad (8.53)$$

is a proper density whatever the value of γ when the prior for γ is the truncated Cauchy (8.48) and that of δ is the conditional normal (8.46).

Proof Formula (8.53) results from the properties of the Student density, see Appendix A. The hyperparameters are conformable partitions of (8.12) with

$$\beta_*(\gamma, c) = \begin{pmatrix} \beta_1^*(\gamma, c) \\ \delta_*(\gamma, c) \end{pmatrix}$$

$$M_*(\gamma, c) = \begin{pmatrix} M_{11}^*(\gamma, c) & M_{12}^*(\gamma, c) \\ M_{21}^*(\gamma, c) & M_{22}^*(\gamma, c) \end{pmatrix} \qquad (8.54)$$

$$M_{22.1}^*(\gamma, c) = M_{22}^*(\gamma, c) - M_{21}^*(\gamma, c) M_{11}^{*-1}(\gamma, c) M_{12}^*(\gamma, c).$$

$M_*(\gamma = 0, c)$ is a regular matrix under the prior (8.46). The posterior density $\varphi(\gamma, c|y)$ is fully integrable under the Cauchy prior (8.48) and the normal prior (8.46). □

In order to build a multivariate posterior confidence interval for δ, one can consider a quadratic transformation $\xi(\gamma, c)$ of δ, defined by

$$\xi(\gamma, c) = [\delta - \delta^*(\gamma, c)]' M_{22.1}^*(\gamma, c) [\delta - \delta^*(\gamma, c)] \frac{T - k}{k_2 s_*(\gamma, c)}. \qquad (8.55)$$

Conditionally on γ and c, $\xi(\gamma, c)$ is distributed as a Fisher random variable with k_2 and $T - k$ degrees of freedom. Let us define

$$\xi_0(\gamma, c) = \delta_*'(\gamma, c)\, M_{22.1}^*(\gamma, c)\, \delta_*(\gamma, c) \frac{T - k}{k_2 s_*(\gamma, c)}, \qquad (8.56)$$

which is the value of $\xi(\gamma, c)$ when $\delta = 0$. The probability that $\xi(\gamma, c)$ exceeds $\xi_0(\gamma, c)$ can be obtained from the $F(k_2, T - k)$ distribution and is denoted $p_{\xi_0(\gamma, c)}$.

It is the posterior 'p-value' associated to $\xi_0(\gamma, c)$, and it is conditional on γ and c. The marginal posterior p-value,

$$p = \int p_{\xi_0(\gamma,c)}\, \varphi(\gamma, c|y)\, d\gamma\, dc, \tag{8.57}$$

can be computed during the numerical integration procedure used to obtain the marginal posterior results on β. Linearity can be accepted if p is larger than 5 or 10 per cent.

Remark: Another way to do the test is to compute the average value of $\xi_0(\gamma, c)$

$$\xi_0 = \int \xi_0(\gamma, c)\, \varphi(\gamma, c|y)\, d\gamma\, dc, \tag{8.58}$$

and to compute the marginal probability

$$p_2 = \Pr[\xi > \xi_0]. \tag{8.59}$$

This must be done by simulation of the marginal posterior distribution of ξ. The simulation is done by drawing γ and c according to their joint posterior distribution, then by drawing δ conditionally on the drawn values of γ and c, and finally by transforming the drawn value of δ in ξ by (8.55). Once a large sample of drawn values of ξ has been simulated, it is easy to estimate the probability that ξ exceeds ξ_0. An approximation of this probability can be obtained easily by taking ξ to be an $F(k_2, T - k)$ random variable, but it is likely to underestimate the tail probability.

8.4.3 A Numerical Example

Let us consider a random sample of size 100 generated from

$$y_t = \beta_0 + \beta_1 x_t + \epsilon_t, \tag{8.60}$$

where $\epsilon_t \sim N(0, 0.25)$, x_t is generated from a uniform distribution over $[0,1]$, and $\beta_0 = \beta_1 = 1$. We have fitted two structural break models on the sample, a step transition one and a smooth transition one, and with these two models we test the presence of non-linearity by testing $\delta = 0$. For this particular sample the results are displayed in Table 8.1.

For both models, the expected value of the break date is close to the middle of the sample, with a very large standard deviation. In each case the upper tail probability of the test indicates that linearity cannot be rejected.

8.5 Empirical Applications

This section contains two empirical applications. In the first one, we deal with a French consumption function, and we look for a structural break in the marginal propensity to consume and its return to equilibrium. The second application looks for asymmetries in the US business cycle.

Table 8.1 *Linearity tests for an artificial sample*

	β_{01}	β_{11}	β_{02}	β_{12}	τ	γ	BIC	Tail-p
Linear	1.10	0.78					3.58	
	[0.11]	[0.19]						
Step	0.99	0.86	0.15	0.016	50.7		3.56	0.45
	[0.23]	[0.38]	[0.29]	[0.56]	[25.2]			
Smooth	1.02	0.82	0.13	0.017	49.8	5.66	3.57	0.60
	[0.20]	[0.32]	[0.24]	[0.42]	[24.5]	[5.55]		

Figures in square brackets are posterior standard deviations. Figures above them are posterior expectations. The last column gives the tail probabilities p for the linearity restriction, as defined in (8.57).

8.5.1 *A Consumption Function for France*

A very simple consumption function relates the logarithm of real consumption to the logarithm of real disposable income. This formulation implies that in the long run the saving ratio is constant provided the long-run elasticity equals unity. Carruth and Henley (1990) pointed out that this ratio has declined a lot in the late 1980s in the UK leading to the predictive failure of many existing consumption functions. The French economy seems also to have experienced a fall in its saving ratio; see Fig. 8.1, which displays the ratio between C, real consumption, and Y, real disposable income. This is the mean propensity to consume displayed for quarterly data covering the period 1963.1–1991.4 from the Laroque (INSEE) database. It remained fairly stationary till 1977, despite the first oil shock of 1974. As noted by Villa (1996), profits were the first to be affected by the oil shock of 1974 which was transmitted only lately to wages. The share of wages in real GNP increased till 1977 and eventually till 1982. Income distribution and consumption played a countercyclical role. Adjustments operated later with the conjugate effects of wage and fiscal policies.

This change in the structure of earnings is difficult to incorporate for modelling consumption and attempts to introduce personal wealth as an explanatory variable (see e.g. Hendry and von Ungern-Sternberg 1981 for the UK or Villa 1996 for France) may be seen as proxies for modelling this change. We prefer to investigate if allowing for a temporal change in the mean propensity to consume restores the stability of the traditional consumption function, and where the break happens. With a log linear model, a temporary break on the constant term is all we need.

The basic formulation of the consumption function we use is

$$\Delta \log C_t = \delta + \delta_0 \, d69.2 + \gamma \Delta \log C_{t-4} + \beta_0 \Delta \log Y_t \\ + (\alpha - 1)[\log C_{t-1} - \nu \log Y_{t-1}] + \epsilon_t, \tag{8.61}$$

where $d69.2$ is a dummy variable which takes into account the effect of the important wage increase that followed the Matignon-negotiations in the second

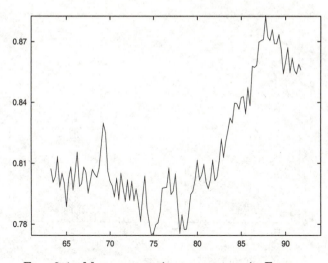

FIG. 8.1. Mean propensity to consume in France

quarter of 1969. The steady state is $\log C = \log K + \nu \log Y$, K being the mean propensity to consume if $\nu = 1$. In a dynamic equilibrium where $\Delta \log Y = g_y$ and $\Delta \log C = g_c = \nu g_y$, the log of the mean propensity to consume is given by

$$\log K = \frac{\delta}{1-\alpha} + g_y \frac{\beta_0 - (1-\gamma)\nu}{1-\alpha}. \tag{8.62}$$

A first estimation of this equation with a non-informative prior produces a result where no long-term solution comes in. The Schwarz criterion attached to this linear regression is -4.926. In order to detect a possible misspecification, we built an augmented regression by adding a trend, a squared trend, and a cubic trend. These extra variables represent the direction of a possible non-linearity in the constant term. This augmented regression is preferred to the initial model as it has a Schwarz criterion of -4.931. In a first attempt, we made inference in a model with a single break in the constant term. This model is preferred to the linear one on the basis of the Schwarz criterion (-5.030). A break clearly appears in 1984.1. However, the long-term elasticity ν of consumption to income is lower than one and the values of the implied mean propensity to consume were mainly unrealistic.

An everlasting increase in the mean propensity to consume implied by a single break model is improbable and the normal situation is a return to stable equilibrium after a certain delay. The following step function models this situation with a first break at time $t = \tau_1$ and a return to the previous equilibrium at time $t = \tau_2$:

$$ID(\tau_1, \tau_2) = ID(t - \tau_2) - ID(t - \tau_1) \qquad \text{with } \tau_1 < \tau_2. \tag{8.63}$$

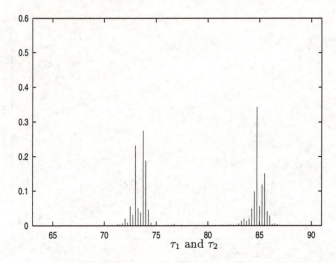

FIG. 8.2. Double threshold of step transition model
for the French consumption function

This function is equal to zero when t is outside the interval $[\tau_1, \tau_2]$, and one in between. When this type of transition function is plugged into the linear model, the unit elasticity hypothesis is accepted. The final results are:

$$\Delta \log C_t = \underset{[0.0041]}{-0.0088} - \underset{[0.0017]}{0.0071} ID(\tau_1, \tau_2) + \underset{[0.0067]}{0.019} \, d69.2$$
$$- \underset{[0.078]}{0.26} \, \Delta \log C_{t-4} + \underset{[0.069]}{0.23} \, \Delta \log Y_t - \underset{[0.022]}{0.11} \, \log(C/Y)_{t-1}$$

$$E(\sigma^2|y) = 0.000432$$
$$\text{Schwarz} = -5.051$$

Figure 8.2 represents on the same graph the posterior densities of the two parameters τ_1 and τ_2. Both densities integrate separately to one. For identification reasons, the ranges of numerical integration cannot overlap. They were chosen by trial and error. Finally, τ_1 was integrated over 1970.1–1978.1 and τ_2 over 1978.2– 1987.2.

This model has many remarkable features:

- The unit long-run elasticity is accepted when it was rejected with the single break model.

- The expectation of τ_2 is 1984.1 with a standard deviation of three quarters. There is thus a well-marked break at the same date as in the single break model. The expectation of τ_1 is 1973.3 with a standard deviation of three quarters. Consequently another well-marked break appears before this.

- The mean propensity to consume is $0.92 \exp(-9.36g_y)$ in the long-term equilibrium, but seems lower at $0.87 \exp(-9.36g_y)$ during the period of

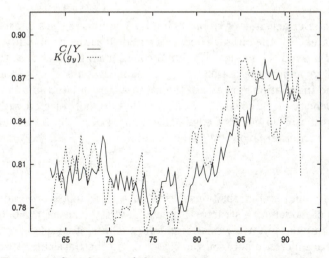

FIG. 8.3. Simulation of the mean propensity to consume
with the double threshold model

adjustment. With $g_y \in [0, 0.02]$, these figures are within an order of magnitude of the data. Figure 8.3 reproduces these data (C/Y) and $K(g_y)$ with g_y smoothed by a moving average of order 5. The two series follow a similar path. Even if the constant term is lower during the intermediate regime between 1973 and 1984, the resulting dynamic mean propensity to consume, $K(g_y)$, is slightly decreasing till 1975, but increases between 1978 and 1986, following the path shown by the ratio C/Y. The model thus manages to cope with the change in the structure of earning.

The final question is to evaluate what would bring in a smooth transition function. The generalization of the double step transition function is

$$F(\gamma, \tau_1, \tau_2) = \frac{1}{1 + \exp[\gamma(t - \tau_1)(t - \tau_2)]}. \tag{8.64}$$

This transition function was first suggested as a generalization of an exponential smooth transition function by Jansen and Teräsvirta (1996). With the conditional normal prior on δ and the truncated Cauchy prior on γ, inference results are as follows:

$$\Delta \log C_t = \underset{[0.0047]}{-0.0092} - \underset{[0.0043]}{0.012} \, F(\gamma, \tau_1, \tau_2) + \underset{[0.0069]}{0.019} \, d69.2$$
$$- \underset{[0.079]}{0.24} \, \Delta \log C_{t-4} + \underset{[0.070]}{0.26} \, \Delta \log Y_t - \underset{[0.025]}{0.10} \, \log(C/Y)_{t-1}$$

$$\mathrm{E}(\sigma^2|y) = 0.000453$$
$$\mathrm{Schwarz} = -5.003.$$

The posterior densities of τ_1 and τ_2 in Fig. 8.4 indicate the same modes for the breaking dates. But the message becomes muddled as the probability is smoothly distributed around the modes. The jump comes from the fact that the posterior densities of τ_1 and τ_2 are presented on the same graph and they both integrate to one. The integration ranges are the same as in the step function case. The posterior density of γ indicates that high values are not rejected with a mean of 10 and a posterior 95 per cent confidence interval of [0,23]. As a matter of fact, the Schwarz criterion favours the step function.

Remarks:

1) Smooth and step transitions based on a time index are two alternative ways of modelling a structural break. The step transition model is simpler to manipulate in a Bayesian framework and is often used first. There are marked difference between the classical and the Bayesian approaches. In a classical framework, τ is determined by a grid search, comparing a suite of conditional linear regressions. As a result inference on β gives a conditional estimator, with a fixed sample separation in the step transition case. In the Bayesian approach, on the contrary, τ is integrated out, so $E(\beta|y)$ is a marginal estimator which depends not on a single sample separation, but on the most likely and averaged sample separations. So even with a step transition function, the Bayesian model accounts for a rather smooth transition, depending on the sample configuration. This being said, it becomes harder to strictly separate the step and smooth transition models from a modelling point of view in a Bayesian framework.

2) The graph of the posterior density of τ in a step transition model gives direct intuitive results concerning the degree of abruptness of the switching. If most of the probability appears for one value of τ, this is confirmation of an abrupt change. If, on the contrary, most of the probability is scattered around one value of τ with a nice bell shape, this is evidence of a gradual transition.

3) In a smooth transition model, a high value of γ approximates the behaviour of the step transition model. When can $E(\gamma|y)$ be considered as high? Firstly, γ must be made scale free by an appropriate normalization of z_t. Usual practice consists in dividing it by its standard deviation. Secondly, the right tail of the posterior density of γ behaves like that of the truncated Cauchy prior. When the Cauchy prior is normalized to one on $[0, \infty]$, it has the property that the tail probability after 12.706 is equal to 5 per cent and after 63.66 to 1 per cent. One can then conclude that $E(\gamma|y)$ is large if it is greater than 12 or greater than 66. However, the Schwarz criterion is certainly more secure for choosing between the step and the smooth transition functions.

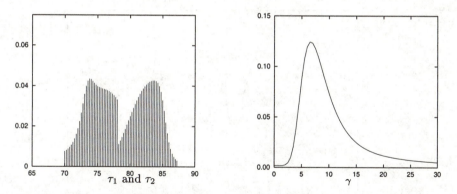

FIG. 8.4. Smooth transition parameters for French consumption function

8.5.2 *United States Business Cycle Asymmetries*

Business cycle asymmetries have been discussed for quite a long time in the literature, starting with the research conducted in the NBER during the 1920s. Possible asymmetries concern the fact that periods of recession present different dynamics from the periods of expansion. For instance, Keynes—quoted by Granger and Teräsvirta (1993: 141)—argued that periods of recession are more violent but shorter than periods of expansion. Graphical methods were first used to detect possible asymmetries. Non-linear time series models provide a more formal way to examine this issue.

Hamilton's (1989) model explains the changes in the log of real quarterly US GNP over the period 1951.2–1984.4 using a discrete shift between two regimes where the shift obeys a Markov process. His model reproduces the usual turning points of the US business cycle as determined by the NBER. Boldin (1996) showed that Hamilton found only a local maximum of the likelihood function and that his results were not robust to an extension of the sample period. Potter (1995), using the same data but for the period 1947.1–1990.4, adjusts a two-regime step transition TAR(5) model with unequal variances where $d = 2$ and $c = 0$. If his model seems to fit the data correctly, the linearity tests he reports, based on Hansen's (1996) theoretical results, reject linearity at 10 per cent, but not at 5 per cent. Hansen (1996) himself settles on a statistical artefact for non-linearity in the US GNP. However, tests presented in Tiao and Tsay (1994) do confirm the non-linearity of the US GNP. Teräsvirta and Anderson (1992) stress that an industrial production index (IPI) has a greater variance than the GNP series and thus is more amenable for displaying non-linearity.

We consider both the US real GNP and the IPI for the period 1960.1–1994.1. The data come from the OECD database. They are seasonally adjusted for the GNP. Monthly, non-seasonally-adjusted data are available for the IPI. We converted them to quarterly by averaging. We then take the fourth difference of these two series to make them stationary and to remove possible remaining sea-

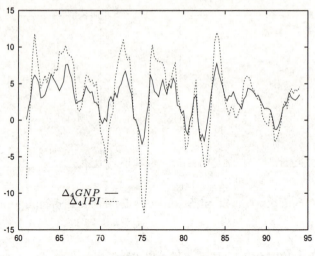

FIG. 8.5. US business indicators

sonality. The resulting series are displayed in Fig. 8.5. We try first to verify the presence of non-linearity by analysing a sequence of augmented regressions as described in Section 8.4. An AR(5) model fits best for both series, but leads to very messy augmented regressions as 15 supplementary regressors are needed. An AR(1) model is probably misspecified, but nevertheless picks up a lot of the variance of the series. Let us now compare the linear AR(1) model with a sequence of augmented regressions where d varies between 1 and 5. Results are presented in Table 8.2.

Table 8.2 *Auxiliary regressions for US GNP and IPI*

			Real GNP			
d	-	1	2	3	4	5
BIC	−3.91	−3.81	−3.87	−3.86	−3.90	−3.80
p-value F-test	-	0.74	0.036	0.069	0.006	0.87
		Industrial production index				
d	-	1	2	3	4	5
BIC	−2.63	−2.52	−2.62	−2.66	−2.55	−2.53
p-value F-test	-	0.89	0.004	0.001	0.25	0.68

The first line corresponds to the value of d, the second line to the Schwarz criterion (BIC) attached to the initial regression and then to the augmented regression. The last line corresponds to the classical F-test for the nullity of the coefficients of the auxiliary regressors. Small p-values reject linearity. According the the classical F-test, linearity is rejected at the 5 per cent and 1 per cent level, with an optimal d of 4. If, on the contrary, we follow the Schwarz criterion,

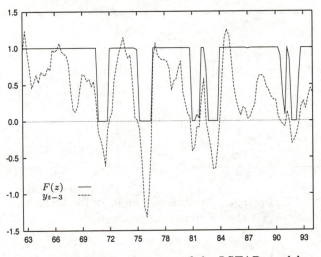

FIG. 8.6. Transition function of the LSTAR model
for the US industrial production index

linearity is not rejected. If we consider an AR(5) model, linearity is also not rejected by the classical p-value. This is in agreement with some of the empirical results mentioned above.For the US IPI, linearity is rejected at the classical level of 1 per cent. The BIC selects the non-linear model with $d = 3$. This is in agreement with the results of Teräsvirta and Anderson (1992) on a smaller sample size. These results are confirmed with an AR(5) model.

We only adjusted an LSTAR model on the IPI data. There is not enough evidence in favour of non-linearity in the GNP data. Let us call y_t the transformed variable $\Delta_4 IPI$. We used a restricted uniform prior on c (over the range $[-1.4, 0.4]$), a Cauchy prior on γ (over the range $[0, 120]$), and a conditional normal prior on δ. We started with a model including six lags of y_t and ended up with

$$
y_t = \underset{[0.54]}{-1.60} + \underset{[0.11]}{1.05}\, y_{t-1} - \underset{[0.91]}{0.36}\, y_{t-2} - \underset{[0.19]}{1.06}\, y_{t-4} + \underset{[0.20]}{0.58}\, y_{t-5}
$$
$$
+ \{1 + \exp[-\underset{[26]}{34}\, (y_{t-3} + \underset{[0.26]}{0.40}\,)]\}^{-1}
$$
$$
\times\, (\underset{[0.66]}{1.92} + \underset{[0.10]}{0.26}\, y_{t-1} + \underset{[0.21]}{0.96}\, y_{t-4} - \underset{[0.22]}{0.58}\, y_{t-5})
$$

$$E(\sigma^2|y) = 2.477$$
$$\text{Schwarz} = 6.056.$$

As the transition variable was normalized by its standard deviation, the posterior expectation of γ can be interpreted directly. With a value of 34, the transition between expansions and recessions is quite abrupt; see the corresponding graph of $F(z)$ in Fig. 8.6 which is shown together with the rescaled series $z = y_{t-3}$. Note that with a shorter sample (ending in 1986), $E(\gamma|y)$ was much lower. This

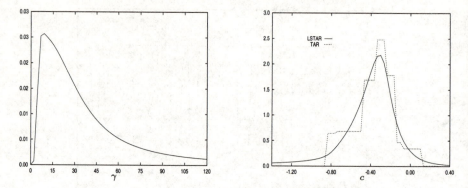

FIG. 8.7. Posterior densities of γ and c of the LSTAR model
for the US industrial production index

is in agreement with the remark made at the end of Subsection 8.3.3.

The step transition model has a Schwarz criterion of 6.045, which is slightly better than that of the smooth transition model. There is no major change in the regression coefficients. The posterior density of the threshold is displayed in Fig. 8.7 on the same graph as for the smooth case. It shows how the shape of this posterior density is modified by the nature of the threshold. It is less scattered, but of course presents a series of points where it is not continuous. Incidentally, it is still centred on zero, which again suggests that the threshold could be pinpointed by this value. In this case the model is reduced to a linear regression model with multiplicative dummy variables.

The model is characterized by very different dynamic behaviour between the two regimes. Teräsvirta and Anderson (1992) suggest computing the modulus of the dominant root of the lag polynomial for each regime. We have a dominant complex root of modulus 1.123 for the recession regime and 0.830 for the expansion regime. Consequently, the dynamics of the expansion is stationary, while the dynamics of the recession is explosive, suggesting that recessions are short lived and violent. Out of 127 observations, 25 are in the recession regime, while 102 are in the expansion regime.

8.6   Disequilibrium Models

In the previous sections, we supposed that in the product $\tilde{z}_t'\theta$, $\tilde{z}_t' = (z_t, 1)$ and $\theta' = (1, c)$. If z_t contains more than one variable, special problems appear which we examine in this section. We confine ourselves to step transitions. It is convenient to use slightly different notation and consider explicitly the case where the two regimes have no common exogenous variables. The basic model is

$$y_t = \delta_t x_{1t}'\beta_1 + (1 - \delta_t)x_{2t}'\beta_2 + \epsilon_t, \tag{8.65}$$

where δ_t is a dichotomous variable defined by

$$\delta_t = \begin{cases} 1 & \text{if } z_t'\alpha < 0 \\ 0 & \text{otherwise.} \end{cases} \tag{8.66}$$

Pole and Smith (1985) propose a Bayesian analysis of this model when the switching rule (8.66) and the regime equation (8.65) have no common element. Lubrano (1985) examines the same model but where $z_t' = (x_{1t}', x_{2t}')$ and $\alpha' = (\beta_1', -\beta_2')$. Both models have in common that the posterior density of β is a piecewise Student density over cones with vertex at the origin which are defined by the step switching rule. This model is linked to disequilibrium models as detailed below.

Econometric disequilibrium models were introduced by Fair and Jaffee (1972). They describe the functioning of a market when prices are sticky. Adjustments have to be done by quantities. The exchanged quantity Q_t is thus equal to the minimum of demand D_t and supply S_t:

$$
\begin{aligned}
Q_t &= \min(D_t, S_t), \\
D_t &= x_{1t}'\beta_1 + u_{1t}, \\
S_t &= x_{2t}'\beta_2 + u_{2t}.
\end{aligned}
\tag{8.67}
$$

Q_t is equal to the minimum of two random quantities. Ginsburgh, Tishler, and Zang (1980) propose instead to consider a model where the exchanged quantity is equal to the minimum of expected demand and expected supply, plus a random error. The error term is thus pushed out of the min condition:

$$y_t = \min(x_{1t}'\beta_1,\, x_{2t}'\beta_2) + \epsilon_t. \tag{8.68}$$

Richard (1980) and Sneessens (1985) argued that this formulation should be preferred to the more traditional one given above, because it displays nicer statistical and empirical properties. In our notations, the model we consider is (8.65) with

$$\delta_t = \begin{cases} 1 & \text{if } x_{1t}'\beta_1 - x_{2t}'\beta_2 < 0 \\ 0 & \text{otherwise.} \end{cases} \tag{8.69}$$

This is the pure or canonical disequilibrium model. If prices or other variables are taken as regime indicators, the switching rule is given by (8.66) where z_t represents the regime indicator variables. We start by treating the canonical form and continue with the second case.

8.6.1 Maximum Likelihood Estimation

The maximum likelihood procedure we now explain helps to understand the structure of the likelihood function. Let us define d_t as

$$d_t = x_{1t}'\beta_1 - x_{2t}'\beta_2. \tag{8.70}$$

The model can be written as

$$y_t = x'_{1t}\beta_1 - \max(0, d_t) + \epsilon_t. \tag{8.71}$$

The idea of Tishler and Zang (1981) consists in smoothing out the kink of the function $\max(0, d_t)$ located at $d_t = 0$ by a smooth differentiable transition function. Let us define a neighbourhood of the kink by $|d_t| < v$ where v is a small positive number. A smooth transition function approximating the max operator is

$$q_v(d_t) = \begin{cases} 0 & \text{if } d_t < -v \\ \dfrac{d_t^2}{4v} + \dfrac{d_t}{2} + \dfrac{v}{4} & \text{if } -v < d_t < v \\ d_t & \text{if } v < d_t. \end{cases} \tag{8.72}$$

Under a normality assumption, the likelihood function is

$$l(\beta, \sigma^2; y) \propto \sigma^{-T} \exp\left\{ -\frac{1}{2\sigma^2} \sum_{t=1}^{T} [y_t - x'_{1t}\beta_1 - q_v(d_t)]^2 \right\}. \tag{8.73}$$

This function is differentiable up to first order and can be maximized with a gradient method. It is recommended to start with a large value of v (compared with the mean of y_t). In a second step, the value of v is sharply decreased; the function is maximized again using the previous optimum as a starting point. The algorithm stops when $|d_t| > v$, $\forall t$. This means that the algorithm stops when all the observations are unambiguously classified. The method thus provides as a by-product a deterministic classification of the observations between the two regimes, indicating which belongs to the demand side, and which belongs to the supply side. The classification is zero–one and deterministic. The Bayesian approach, on the contrary, because β is random, is able to produce a probability assessment about the obtained classification.

8.6.2 *The Structure of the Posterior Density*

The T-dimensional auxiliary parameter $\delta = (\delta_t)$ implicitly defines a cone C^δ with vertex at the origin in the parameter space of β:

$$C^\delta = \{\beta \,|\, \delta_t \, d_t - (1 - \delta_t) \, d_t \leq 0, \, t = 1, \ldots, T\}. \tag{8.74}$$

Over a particular cone C^δ, the posterior density of β is Student provided the prior density on β and σ^2 belongs to the natural conjugate class. Let us consider the same prior as in (8.10). Then the conditional posterior of β is

$$\varphi(\beta|y, \delta) = f_t(\beta|\beta_*(\delta), s_*(\delta), M_*(\delta), \nu_*), \tag{8.75}$$

where the definitions of $M_*(\delta)$, $\beta_*(\delta)$, $s_*(\delta)$, and ν_* can be easily deduced from (8.12), just by replacing θ by δ. The posterior density of δ is a multivariate discrete density defined by

$$\varphi(\delta|y) \propto |M_*(\delta)|^{-1/2} s_*(\delta)^{-\nu_*}, \tag{8.76}$$

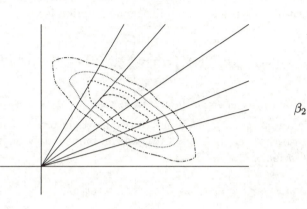

β_2

β_1

FIG. 8.8. Contours of the likelihood
function for min models

since δ_t can be either zero or one. The marginal posterior of β is obtained by a summation of the piecewise Student densities over the different cones:

$$\varphi(\beta|y) \propto \sum_{\delta \in D} \varphi(\beta|y,\delta)\, ID(C^\delta)\, \varphi(\delta|y). \qquad (8.77)$$

It is convenient to decompose the posterior density in this way to understand its structure. The parameter δ is an auxiliary parameter which is perfectly determined as soon as β is given. For this reason we did not introduce a specific prior for δ. In the next subsection, we shall see how prior information on β can be translated into prior regime probabilities.

For the moment, however, (8.77) is very convenient for showing that the model may have serious identification problems as discussed in Lubrano (1985). Among the T^{k-1} possible cones, very few fulfil the condition that there are more observations per regime than parameters in the corresponding regression. For these cones, the matrix $M_*(\delta)$ is singular when the prior density of β is non-informative and thus the posterior (8.77) is not defined. The problem is not desperate because from Fig. 8.8, it is easy to understand that a great number of cones are not going to be covered by the useful part of the likelihood function. Consequently, if the likelihood function is sufficiently concentrated, there will be no identification problem for a given sample. But if the likelihood function is slightly non-informative in just one direction, a bad cone may appear in this direction and the posterior becomes degenerate just for this cone. So it is wise to be informative on β in this type of model. In practical computations (to be discussed below), the following likelihood function is used:

$$l(\beta, \sigma^2; y) \propto \sigma^{-T} \exp\left\{-\frac{1}{2\sigma^2} \sum_{t=1}^{T} [y_t - \min(x'_{1t}\beta_1, x'_{2t}\beta_2)]^2\right\}. \tag{8.78}$$

8.6.3 Elicitation of Prior Information on β

Prior information on β has direct consequences in terms of regime probabilities. If the prior has the form of (8.10), we can immediately deduce the form of the implied prior of d_t:

$$\varphi(d_t|x_t) = f_t(d_t|x'_t\beta_0, s_0, (x'_t M_0^{-1} x_t)^{-1}, \nu_0), \tag{8.79}$$

where $x'_t = (x'_{1t}, x'_{2t})$. Regime probabilities result from

$$\Pr(\delta_t = 1|x_t) = \int_{-\infty}^{0} \varphi(d_t|x_t)\, d\, d_t. \tag{8.80}$$

The elicitation is done as follows:

1) Values of the hyperparameters of (8.10) are assigned on the basis of the procedures described in Chapter 4.

2) The consequences of these assignments are explored in terms of induced regime probabilities and possibly revised if the implied regime classification is counterintuitive.

A practical tool for the evaluation of (8.80) is given by the logistic approximation. Defining $a_t = -x_t/\sqrt{x'_t M_0^{-1} x_t\, s_0/\nu_0}$, we have

$$p_t = \Pr(\delta_t = 1|x_t) \simeq F(a'_t\beta_0) = \left[1 + \exp\left(-\frac{\pi}{\sqrt{3}}a'_t\beta_0\right)\right]^{-1}. \tag{8.81}$$

Let us now consider the reverse situation. We have information on the regime classification from business survey data or macroeconomic data such as the unemployment rate for the labour market. We can form probabilistic judgements on each p_t and represent these judgements by a beta prior density of parameters n_t and r_t denoted

$$\varphi(p_t) = f_\beta(p_t|r_t, n_t), \tag{8.82}$$

with $\mathrm{E}(p_t) = r_t/n_t$. This prior information cannot be used directly in the model. It has to be translated into probability judgements on β. We look for the β_0 which is the most likely to have produced these assignments on the regime classification. This is done by solving

$$\max_{\beta_0} \prod_{t=1}^{T} f_\beta(F(a_t'\beta_0)|n_t, r_t), \tag{8.83}$$

where $F(.)$ is given in (8.81). This is identical to the maximization of the likelihood function of a logit model. This method has certain implications which should be noted:

1) We have to know the value of M_0 as it appears in the definition of a_t. Extending Zellner's (1986b) argument on g priors, we have

$$M_0 = \sum_{t=1}^{T} \begin{bmatrix} x_{1t}x_{1t}' \, p_t^2 & 0 \\ 0 & x_{2t}x_{2t}' \, (1-p_t)^2 \end{bmatrix}. \tag{8.84}$$

2) It is conditional on x_t. As soon as $T > k$, the preassigned regime probabilities are no longer necessarily compatible with the existence of a unique prior on β. The usual misspecification tools available with the logit model then give an indication on the ability of the model to be coherent with our prior opinions.

3) Finally, the value found for β_0 is defined up to a multiplicative scalar. A calibration has to be done, using the implied d_t as a guide.

8.6.4 Numerical Evaluation of the Posterior Density

Conditionally on δ_t, β is a Student random vector; conditionally on β, δ is a vector of Bernoulli random variables. But the joint density of β and δ_t is degenerate because δ is known as soon as a value is given to β. It does not make sense to use the Gibbs sampler simply because of the perfect correlation between β and δ.

A numerical method for evaluating the posterior density of β should ignore δ, and consider inference on δ as a by-product of the inference on β. Various possibilities exist to integrate the posterior density of β. Lubrano (1985) uses an importance sampling method with a Student importance function calibrated on $M_*(\hat\delta)$, $\beta_*(\hat\delta)$, and $s_*(\hat\delta)$, where $\hat\delta$ is the sample separation found by maximum likelihood. This calibration proves not to be optimal, but gives initial estimates of the posterior expectation and variance of β, which are used in a second round to recalibrate the importance function. Lubrano (1985) applied this method to an artificial sample generated with the following model:

$$y_t = \min(x_{1t}\beta_1, x_{2t}'\beta_2) + u_t, \qquad u_t \sim N(0, 0.1^2), \tag{8.85}$$

with 15 observations, $k_1 = 1$, and $k_2 = 2$. The exogenous variables are drawn according to a uniform distribution on $[0,1]$ and $\beta_1 = 0.8$, $\beta_2' = (0.5, 0.2)$. With the obtained sample, there are seven observations in the first regime. With a diffuse prior on the parameters, posterior results are reasonable in this simple and well-conditioned example. With 15,000 drawings, we get a relative precision of the integral of 2.1 per cent (and a coefficient of variation of the ratio of posterior density to importance function equal to 0.65). The most striking fact is that 98 per cent of the probability is obtained with only seven cones when the theoretical number was $T^{k-1} = 225$. The total number of detected cones is 25.

Table 8.3 *Posterior results for the min model*

β_{11}	β_{21}	β_{22}
0.984	0.472	0.295
(0.14)	(0.088)	(0.088)
1%	0.78%	1.18%

These results, displayed in Table 8.3, are fairly convincing, but the problem is simple as there is no constant term in the model. As a matter of fact, constant terms may induce instability. This is rather easy to understand. If each equation contains a constant term, a change in the difference of the constant terms suffices to induce a change in d_t. This creates a difficulty in small samples which is removed by adequate prior information. If the dimension of the integration is not too important, the griddy-Gibbs sampler described in Chapter 3 could be efficient.

8.6.5 *Endogenous Prices and Other Regime Indicators*

The presence of a regime indicator can greatly simplify inference in disequilibrium models. The movement of prices, for instance, has been taken as a regime indicator, rising prices being the sign of an excess demand and declining prices a sign of excess supply. Real wages play the same role for the labour market, but as they have an autonomous tendency (due for instance to the rise of productivity), their action on market tensions is less easy to identify. This kind of information can be used to elicit a prior density on β, as was explained above. In this case, the model remains the same. Or we can decide to implement directly in the model the action of these variables as regime indicators. Consequently δ_t in (8.65) is no longer determined via the min condition, but by the sign of the linear combination $z_t'\alpha$ as in (8.66), where z_t contains the indicator variables. The parameters α and β are supposed to be a priori independent. We are back to the framework of Section 8.2. Various configurations are interesting to discuss for z_t.

1) z_t is univariate. This is the case for instance when z_t represents Δp_t, the variation of prices. Then, because of the normalization rule, there is no parameter to estimate in the switching function. The sample separation becomes deterministic and the model, given this sample separation, is linear.

2) An unknown threshold is introduced. A switching occurs for instance when the rate of growth of wages is greater than an unknown level c. This case was amply discussed in the previous sections.

3) z_t is composed of two or more continuous variables. This case was examined by Pole and Smith (1985) when the dimension of z_t is two. The inequality $z_t'\alpha < 0$ determines cones in the α space. Some data configurations may cause problems and lead in some cases to bimodal posterior densities in small samples. For more details, see that paper.

It is interesting to discuss inference in the third case. As the dimension of α may be larger than two or three, the use of product rules as suggested in Section 8.2 is not very efficient. But as β and α have no element in common, it is quite possible to implement a Gibbs sampler as done for instance in Pfann, Schotman, and Tschernig. The conditional posterior density of β is Student and easy to simulate. The posterior density of α does not belong to a known class of densities and may be extremely peculiar as emphasized in Section 8.3 for the univariate case. Consequently special generators must be built using either rejection techniques or techniques inspired by the griddy-Gibbs (numerical inversion of the conditional cumulative density). Note that an importance sampling method using a global importance function (like the Student or even a poly-t) may not be efficient because the marginal posterior of α is discontinuous. The same applies to the Metroplis–Hastings algorithm.

8.7 Conclusion

Bayesian methods are feasible for analysing non-linear time series models. In the case of a step switching (switching rules based on inequalities), Bayesian methods appear to be easier than classical ones as they are not in conflict with the non-differentiability of the likelihood function. Bayesian methods proceed by averaging over the parameter space. Osiewalski and Welfe (1998) for instance analyse a two-equation wage–price model where price indexation occurs only above an unknown threshold c. Their posterior density of c has no obvious maximum. It is a collection of pieces, the shape of which is determined by the presence of a Jacobian generated by the simultaneity of the model.

We have tried to show that many of the switching regime models presented in the literature can be analysed in the same framework and can be treated by deterministic integration rules in dimension 1 or 2. Deterministic integration is particularly interesting in those cases as the posterior densities of the parameter θ which we have to integrate are really badly behaved. If the dimension of θ grows, the Gibbs sampler becomes a useful method as was demonstrated in many papers. But for low dimensions, deterministic rules are quick and precise, which is of great interest to start a specification search.

Much more complicated models have been treated in the Bayesian literature. They all need to resort to Monte Carlo integration. Lubrano (1986) considers extensions of the disequilibrium model to the two-market case with Monte Carlo methods to elicit prior information on the parameters. Koop and Potter (1995) study an autoregressive threshold model where the variable governing the switching is built recursively during inference which is conducted using the Gibbs sampler. Ghysels, McCulloch, and Tsay (1998) propose a periodic switching regime model where the change of regime follows a seasonal Markov process. The model is also estimated using the Gibbs sampler. Related references are Albert and Chib (1993) and McCulloch and Tsay (1993).

9

SYSTEMS OF EQUATIONS

9.1 Introduction

Systems of equations can be defined in several forms: multivariate regression models, systems of seemingly unrelated regression equations (SURE), vector autoregressive (VAR) models, possibly with moving average components, simultaneous equation models (SEM). This chapter aims to review how Bayesian inference can be applied to some of these models. Section 9.2 covers VAR models which are formally equivalent to multivariate regression models which may be subject to parametric restrictions. When the variables modelled by the VAR are stationary after differencing them once, there arises the interesting possibility of cointegration between their levels. This type of model, also called VECM (vector error correction mechanism) model is studied in Section 9.3. VAR models can be open or closed, depending on whether exogenous variables are included or not. In the former case, the model can be considered as the reduced form of a system of simultaneous equations. The analysis of such 'structural' open VAR models is not undertaken in this book, but a brief guide to the literature on this topic is provided in the last section.

9.2 VAR Models

9.2.1 Unrestricted VAR Models and Multivariate Regression

In Section 5.2, we show how to reduce a VAR model having normal errors to a dynamic regression equation. Bayesian analysis of the normal VAR system is relatively straightforward, if we condition on the initial observations. It generalizes the analysis of a regression equation (Section 2.7). We write the VAR as

$$A(L)x_t = c + \epsilon_t \tag{9.1}$$

where

$$A(L) = I_n - A_1 L - A_2 L^2 - \cdots - A_p L^p \tag{9.2}$$

is a polynomial of degree p in the lag operator, and $\epsilon_t \sim N_n(0, \Sigma)$ and independent of ϵ_s for $s \neq t$. In (9.1), we have included a vector of intercepts (c), and we could include other terms like a trend term and dummy variables. At the present stage we assume that no restrictions are imposed on the parameters c and A_i, implying that all equations of the system have the same explanatory variables (p

lags of each variable in x_t). The VAR system is then in the form of a mutivariate regression model written as

$$y_t = B'z_t + \epsilon_t, \qquad \epsilon_t \sim IN_n(0, \Sigma) \tag{9.3}$$

where y_t, z_t, and B are of dimension $n \times 1$, $k \times 1$, and $k \times n$, respectively. The VAR model (9.1) corresponds to

$$
\begin{aligned}
y_t &= x_t \\
z_t &= (1 \; x'_{t-1} \; x'_{t-2} \; \ldots \; x'_{t-p})' \\
B' &= (c \; A_1 \; A_2 \; \ldots \; A_p) \\
k &= (n \times p) + 1.
\end{aligned}
\tag{9.4}
$$

The matrix version of (9.3) for T observations (plus p initial ones in the VAR case) is

$$Y = ZB + E, \qquad E \sim MN_{T \times n}(0, \Sigma \otimes I_T) \tag{9.5}$$

where Y, Z, and E are obtained by stacking the row vectors y'_t, z'_t, and ϵ'_t, respectively, and MN denotes a matricvariate normal distribution as defined by (A.60). The following theorem provides the main posterior results of the Bayesian analysis of (9.3) with a non-informative prior density. The non-informative prior density is proportional to the square root of the determinant of the information matrix block of Σ (Jeffreys' prior); its computation must take care of the symmetry restrictions on Σ (see Richard 1975). This prior can also be obtained as the kernel of an $IW_n(S, \nu)$ (Inverted Wishart) density—see (A.96)—when the parameters take the particular values $S = 0$ and $\nu = 0$, which are on the boundary of the parameter space.

Theorem 9.1 *Under the non-informative prior*

$$\varphi(B, \Sigma) \propto |\Sigma|^{-(n+1)/2} \tag{9.6}$$

the posterior densities of the parameters of (9.5) are given by

$$
\begin{aligned}
B &\sim Mt_{k \times n}(\hat{B}, Z'Z, S, T - k) \\
\Sigma &\sim IW_n(S, T)
\end{aligned}
\tag{9.7}
$$

where

$$
\begin{aligned}
\hat{B} &= (Z'Z)^{-1}Z'Y \\
S &= Y'M_Z Y = Y'Y - Y'Z(Z'Z)^{-1}Z'Y.
\end{aligned}
\tag{9.8}
$$

Proof Using (A.60), the posterior density is

$$
\begin{aligned}
\varphi(B, \Sigma | Y, Z) &\propto |\Sigma|^{-(T+n+1)/2} \exp\{-\tfrac{1}{2}\mathrm{tr}\ \Sigma^{-1}(Y - ZB)'(Y - ZB)\} \\
&= |\Sigma|^{-(T+n+1)/2} \exp\{-\tfrac{1}{2}\mathrm{tr}\ \Sigma^{-1}[S + (B - \hat{B})'Z'Z(B - \hat{B})]\} \\
&\propto f_{MN}^{n \times k}(B | \hat{B}, \Sigma \otimes (Z'Z)^{-1}) \; f_{IW}^n(\Sigma | S, T).
\end{aligned}
\tag{9.9}
$$

The first part of (9.7) follows by application of Theorem A.19. Posterior moments follow from the properties of the matricvariate Student distribution for B, see

Subsection A.2.7, and of the inverted Wishart distribution for Σ, see A.2.6.

□

We have not given Theorem 9.1 for the case of a natural conjugate prior, because the latter is too restrictive to be useful: the prior covariance matrix of every column of B has the same correlation structure, since it is proportional to the same matrix (the prior counterpart of $(Z'Z)^{-1}$). We refer to Drèze and Richard (1983: Section 4) for more details and additional results (in particular for the definition of an extended natural conjugate prior which overcomes the inherent restrictiveness of the natural conjugate prior). Typically, the practical definition of an informative prior density for this type of model is difficult since it involves the choice of a large number of parameters. A particular informative prior has been defined by Litterman for VAR models and is explained below.

9.2.2 *Restricted VAR Models and SURE Models*

It may happen that the parameters of a VAR are subject to restrictions such that the explanatory variables are not the same in all equations. For example, in the partition defined by (5.18), the Granger non-causality restriction (5.26) implies that the lags of some variables do not appear in some equations while they do in the other ones. Another example is the inclusion of a linear trend or seasonal dummy variables in some equations but not in others. In such a case, the matrix B in (9.3) is subject to zero restrictions. These restrictions may complicate the derivation of the posterior results under the prior (9.6) (when B is restricted, this prior is meant to bear on the unrestricted parameters). In the proof of Theorem 9.1, the last line of (9.9) may not be true, i.e. the posterior density of B_c (the restricted B) is not necessarily (and typically is not) a matricvariate normal distribution with the given expectation and covariance matrix. It is if the structure of the restrictions is such that we can apply (A.68) or one of its particular cases (A.64) and (A.66) (where X stands for B_c). Otherwise, the only thing we can state is that the posterior density of B_c is a conditional density of a matricvariate Student density, i.e. we know the form of its kernel, but not its properties. It can be expressed as

$$\varphi(B_c|Y, Z) \propto |S + (B_c - \hat{B})'Z'Z(B_c - \hat{B})|^{-T/2}. \tag{9.10}$$

Posterior results have to be computed by Monte Carlo integration. Bauwens (1984) and Richard and Steel (1988) used importance sampling.

The VAR model (9.1) can be cast in the form of a SURE model, which is a set of regression equations (possibly with different regressors) whose error terms are correlated. This way of considering the VAR is especially useful when its parameters are restricted as described above. The SURE model can be written as

$$Y_i = Z_i\beta_i + E_i, \qquad i = 1, \ldots, n \tag{9.11}$$

where Y_i, Z_i, and β_i are of dimension $T \times 1$, $T \times k_i$, and $k_i \times 1$ respectively. In compact matrix format, we write

$$y = \mathcal{Z}\beta + \epsilon \qquad (9.12)$$

where

$$y = \begin{pmatrix} Y_1 \\ Y_2 \\ \vdots \\ Y_n \end{pmatrix} \qquad \beta = \begin{pmatrix} \beta_1 \\ \beta_2 \\ \vdots \\ \beta_n \end{pmatrix} \qquad \epsilon = \begin{pmatrix} E_1 \\ E_2 \\ \vdots \\ E_n \end{pmatrix} \qquad (9.13)$$

and

$$\mathcal{Z} = \begin{pmatrix} Z_1 & 0 & \cdots & 0 \\ 0 & Z_2 & \cdots & 0 \\ \vdots & \vdots & & \vdots \\ 0 & 0 & \vdots & Z_n \end{pmatrix}. \qquad (9.14)$$

The distribution of the $Tn \times 1$ vector ϵ is assumed to be $N_{Tn}(0, \Sigma \otimes I_T)$; this is actually the same hypothesis as in (9.5) since $\epsilon = \text{vec } E$. Another useful expression of the system (9.12) is

$$Y = W B_c + E \qquad (9.15)$$

with Y and E as in (9.5) and

$$W = (Z_1\ Z_2\ \ldots\ Z_n)$$

$$B_c = \begin{pmatrix} \beta_1 & 0 & \cdots & 0 \\ 0 & \beta_2 & \cdots & 0 \\ \vdots & \vdots & & \vdots \\ 0 & 0 & \vdots & \beta_n \end{pmatrix}. \qquad (9.16)$$

The matrix W is not of full column rank if some equations share the same explanatory variables (e.g. a constant). An example of a bivariate VAR with one lag and non-causality of x_2 for x_1 that can be put easily in the form of (9.12) or (9.15) is:

$$x_{1,t} = \beta_{11} x_{1,t-1} + c_1 + \epsilon_{1,t}$$
$$x_{2,t} = \beta_{21} x_{1,t-1} + \beta_{22} x_{2,t-1} + c_2 + \epsilon_{2,t}.$$

Posterior marginal densities for the SURE model are not available analytically, but full conditional densities of β and Σ are available and can be used to define a Gibbs sampling algorithm with two blocks (see Subsection 3.4.3), as in Percy (1992).

Theorem 9.2 *Under the non-informative prior*

$$\varphi(\beta, \Sigma) \propto |\Sigma|^{-(n+1)/2}$$

the following conditional posterior densities of the parameters of (9.12) or (9.15) are available:

$$\beta|\Sigma \sim N_k(\hat{\beta}, \left[\mathcal{Z}'(\Sigma^{-1} \otimes I_T)\mathcal{Z}\right]^{-1})$$
$$\Sigma|\beta \sim IW_n(Q, T)$$

(9.17)

where $k = \sum_{i=1}^n k_i$ and

$$\hat{\beta} = \left[\mathcal{Z}'(\Sigma^{-1} \otimes I_T)\mathcal{Z}\right]^{-1} \mathcal{Z}'(\Sigma^{-1} \otimes I_T)y$$
$$Q = (Y - WB_c)'(Y - WB_c).$$

(9.18)

Proof Conditionally on Σ, (9.12) is a normal linear regression model, so that

$$\varphi(\beta, \Sigma|Y, \mathcal{Z}) \propto |\Sigma|^{-(T+n+1)/2} \exp\left[-\tfrac{1}{2}(y - \mathcal{Z}\beta)'(\Sigma^{-1} \otimes I_T)(y - \mathcal{Z}\beta)\right]$$
$$= |\Sigma|^{-(T+n+1)/2} \exp -\tfrac{1}{2}\left\{\left[s + (\beta - \hat{\beta})'\mathcal{Z}'(\Sigma^{-1} \otimes I_T)\mathcal{Z}(\beta - \hat{\beta})\right]\right\}$$

where $s = y'(\Sigma^{-1} \otimes I_T)y - \hat{\beta}'\mathcal{Z}'(\Sigma^{-1} \otimes I_T)\mathcal{Z}\hat{\beta}$. The posterior conditional density of $\beta|\Sigma$ follows directly. To obtain the complementary conditional density, we use (9.15), so that

$$\varphi(\beta, \Sigma|Y, \mathcal{Z}) \propto |\Sigma|^{-(T+n+1)/2} \exp\left[-\tfrac{1}{2}\text{tr } \Sigma^{-1}(Y - WB_c)'(Y - WB_c)\right]$$

whence the result follows immediately by definition of the inverted Wishart density given in (A.96). □

Remark: If $Z_1 = Z_2 = \cdots = Z_n = Z$ of (9.5) in the SURE formulation (9.11), $\hat{\beta}$ of (9.18) is equal to vec $\hat{B}$ of (9.8); see e.g. Hamilton (1994: 318).

In the case of two equations ($n = 2$), and if W is of full rank, Drèze and Morales (1976) have shown that the marginal posterior density of β_1 (or of β_2) belongs to the class of 1-1 poly-t densities, whose moments are available analytically and where marginal densities can be evaluated by one-dimensional numerical integration (see Richard and Tompa 1980, and Subsection A.2.8). For a larger system, marginal densities are not available analytically, but the conditional density of $\beta_1|\beta_2, \ldots, \beta_n$ is multivariate Student with known parameters (even if W is of reduced rank)—see Drèze and Richard (1983: Lemma 6.4 and Corollary 6.5). This result could be used in a Gibbs sampling algorithm whose blocks would be $\beta_1, \beta_2, \ldots, \beta_n$. These results hold more generally under the extended natural conjugate prior density of Drèze and Morales.

9.2.3 *The Minnesota Prior for VAR Models*

Litterman and Sims have defined a prior for the VAR model (9.1)–(9.2); see e.g. Doan, Litterman, and Sims (1984) and the references quoted in that paper. It is called the 'Minnesota' (or 'Litterman') prior in the literature since Litterman wrote his doctoral dissertation at the University of Minnesota. This prior is informative on all the coefficients of the A_i matrices, and non-informative on the other parameters. The prior expectation says that the VAR system consists of n random walks, i.e. the prior mean of A_i is zero for $i \geq 2$, and the prior mean of A_1 is equal to I_n (the identity matrix). Obviously, this prior mean does not make sense for all types of series: for example, if we have quarterly data with a seasonal pattern, it is the prior mean of A_4 that should be an identity matrix, or if x_t is already the first difference of a series, there should be no identity matrix in the prior. The prior covariance matrix of all the parameters in the A_i matrices is diagonal. For a given equation of the VAR, the standard deviation of the corresponding diagonal element of A_1 is a fixed value (say λ), meaning that one is of course not sure that this parameter is equal to one; the standard deviation of the coefficient of lag i of the same variable is equal to λ/i, reflecting the idea that the larger the lag, the more likely the coefficient is to be close to zero. The standard deviations of the coefficients of the lags of every other variable in the equation have the same decreasing pattern. For lag i of the variable x_j in equation k, the standard deviation is $\lambda\theta\sigma_k/i\sigma_j$, where θ is a scalar between 0 and 1 to incorporate the idea that the lags of x_j ($j \neq k$) are more likely to have zero coefficients than the lags of x_k in equation k. The ratio σ_k/σ_j of the standard deviations of the error terms is a way to take account of the difference in the variability of the different variables. Thus for a given equation, the elicitation of the prior moments requires two values, λ and θ, which can be the same for all the equations. For example, for the first equation of a bivariate VAR with two lags (the prior means and standard deviations are given in parentheses):

$$x_{1,t} = \underset{(1,\lambda)}{\alpha_{11}x_{1,t-1}} + \underset{(0,\lambda/2)}{\alpha_{12}x_{1,t-2}} + \underset{(0,\theta\lambda\sigma_1/\sigma_2)}{\beta_{11}x_{2,t-1}} + \underset{(0,\theta\lambda\sigma_1/2\sigma_2)}{\beta_{12}x_{2,t-2}} + \epsilon_{1,t}. \tag{9.19}$$

The Minnesota prior is a normal distribution with the described mean and diagonal covariance matrix

$$\beta|\sigma_1, \sigma_2, \ldots, \sigma_n \sim N_k(\beta_0, M_0^{-1}) \tag{9.20}$$

where σ_i ($i = 1$ to n) is the square root of the ith diagonal element of the covariance matrix Σ. Note that M_0^{-1} depends on these parameters. The non-zero diagonal elements of M_0 are the inverses of the variances of the coefficients on which one is informative (as described above). The zero diagonal elements of M_0 correspond to the parameters on which one is not informative (like the intercepts), and the corresponding elements of β_0 are set to zero. So β_0 consists of ones for the diagonal elements of A_1 and zeros everywhere else.

The marginal posterior density of the parameters β when the Minnesota prior is used is not known analytically. The conditional density of $\beta|\Sigma$ can be shown to be normal:

$$\beta|\Sigma, X_T \sim N_k(\beta_*, V_*) \tag{9.21}$$

where X_T denotes the sample observations used to compute the posterior results and

$$\begin{aligned} \beta_* &= V_*^{-1}\left[M_0\beta_0 + \mathcal{Z}'(\Sigma^{-1} \otimes I_T)y\right] \\ V_* &= M_0 + \mathcal{Z}'(\Sigma^{-1} \otimes I_T)\mathcal{Z}. \end{aligned} \tag{9.22}$$

The proof is a straightforward extension of the proof of the first result in (9.17). The second result of (9.17) does not apply, because the Minnesota prior is not in the natural conjugate (or extended natural conjugate) family. In empirical work, the posterior (9.21) has been conditioned on $\Sigma = S/T$, the ML estimate—see (9.8) for the definition of S. We conjecture that the unconditional posterior mean of β is not likely to differ much from β_* evaluated at $\Sigma = S/T$. The conditional covariance matrix surely underestimates the unconditional one.

Sometimes, the matrix Σ is assumed to be diagonal, with the advantage that V_* is block diagonal since M_0 is also block diagonal (each block corresponding to one equation), and thus easier to invert to compute β_*.

The influence of the Minnesota prior on the posterior results of the VAR coefficients is twofold. Firstly, the precision of the 'estimates' is improved because of the usual adding up of prior and sample precisions. Secondly, the posterior means of the coefficients on which the sample is weakly informative are shrunk towards the prior means (most of them being null), and away from the least squares estimates (which are the posterior means under a non-informative prior). In VAR models, it is rather customary to find least squares estimates which are very imprecisely determined, so the prior may help to shrink these coefficients to less 'extreme' values than the least squares values. This usually helps to improve the predictions of the model. For a set of macroeconomic series, the VAR model with the Minnesota prior has indeed been found to be often a better prediction tool than the VAR model without the prior (i.e. least squares predictions); see Litterman (1986) for an account of such comparisons. An interesting paper in that respect is that of Kadiyala and Karlsson (1997), who use the Minnesota prior and also other prior densities (in particular the extended natural conjugate prior) that incorporate the same prior moments on the parameters as the Minnesota prior.

The predictive expectation of x_{T+h} is computed by recursive substitution. Let us illustrate the method for a forecast horizon of two periods ($h = 2$) and a VAR model with two lags (neglecting the intercept vector). Since

$$
\begin{aligned}
x_{T+2} &= A_1 x_{T+1} + A_2 x_T + \epsilon_{T+2} \\
&= (A_1^2 + A_2) x_T + A_1 A_2 x_{T-1} + \epsilon_{T+2} + A_1 \epsilon_{T+1}
\end{aligned}
$$

it follows that

$$
\mathrm{E}(x_{T+2}|X_T, \Sigma) = \mathrm{E}(A_1^2 + A_2|X_T, \Sigma) x_T + \mathrm{E}(A_1 A_2|X_T, \Sigma) x_{T-1}
$$

The above predictive mean is easily computed using the posterior (9.21) conditioned on $\Sigma = S/T$, since it requires uncentred first and second moments of a normal distribution. For a longer forecast horizon, higher moments are needed. They can be computed by applying analytical results on moments of normal distributions or by direct simulation of the normal posterior; see Subsection 3.4.1 for an explanation of the method of direct simulation, and Kadiyala and Karlsson (1997) for an application of this approach on two VAR models. The same tool can be used to compute posterior results on impulse response functions. A complete Bayesian analysis requires computation of

$$E(x_{T+h}|X_T) = E_{\Sigma|X_T}\left[E(x_{T+h}|X_T, \Sigma)\right], \tag{9.23}$$

i.e. integration with respect to the posterior of Σ (just like it requires computation of the marginal posterior of β). For a forecast horizon of one period, conditioning on Σ should not make a big difference for the predictive mean, but for longer horizons this is more controversial. A possible strategy to complete the analysis of posterior and predictive results by marginalization of Σ is to use an importance function for Σ: a natural candidate is the inverted Wishart density in (9.7). An alternative route is to use a prior which has the same mean and covariance matrix as (9.20) when $\Sigma = S/T$ but is independent of Σ.

9.3 Cointegration and VAR Models

9.3.1 *Model Formulation*

In the previous section, we explained that the Minnesota prior pushes the VAR system (9.1) towards a system of random walks, $\Delta x_t = c + \epsilon_t$. The innovations of the random walks are correlated. Obviously this specification could be sensible for trending time series since a random walk with drift exhibits a long-run movement, since $x_t = x_0 + ct + \sum_{i=1}^{t} \epsilon_i$. The trend contains a deterministic part and a stochastic part. Cointegration between series arises when they have the same stochastic trend, although they do not have the same 'cycle' (stationary component). More formally, the n I(1) series x_t are cointegrated if there exists r linear combinations of the series which are I(0) (with $0 < r < n$). Let β be an $n \times r$ matrix of rank r such that $\beta'x_t$ is I(0). This matrix is obviously not uniquely defined, since $H\beta'x_t$ is also I(0) for any $r \times r$ full rank matrix H, but we shall tackle this issue in due course. If the VAR system (9.1)–(9.2) is the data generating process of x_t, and x_t is subject to r cointegrating relations, there exists an $n \times r$ matrix α of rank r such that

$$A(1) = I_n - \sum_{i=1}^{p} A_i = -\Pi = -\alpha\beta' \tag{9.24}$$

(see Engle and Granger 1987). It is usually of prime interest to make inference on the cointegrating matrix β, so that a formulation of the VAR system where β appears explicitly is quite useful. This is known as the VECM representation of the VAR system, where VECM stands for 'vector error (or equilibrium) correction mechanism (or model)', obtained by transforming (9.1) into (see e.g. Hamilton: Ch. 11)

$$\begin{aligned}
\Delta x_t &= c + \sum_{i=1}^{p-1} \Pi_i \Delta x_{t-i} + \Pi x_{t-1} + \epsilon_t \\
&= c + \sum_{i=1}^{p-1} \Pi_i \Delta x_{t-i} + \alpha\beta' x_{t-1} + \epsilon_t \\
&= c + \sum_{i=1}^{p-1} \Pi_i \Delta x_{t-i} + \alpha z_{t-1} + \epsilon_t
\end{aligned} \tag{9.25}$$

where

$$\begin{aligned}
\Pi_i &= \sum_{j=i+1}^{p} A_j \ (i = 1 \ldots p-1) \\
\Pi &= -A(1) = \alpha\beta' \\
z_t &= \beta' x_t.
\end{aligned} \tag{9.26}$$

The variables in z_t are interpretable as the error correcting (or disequilibrium) terms in so far as $\beta' x_t = 0$ is meaningful as an economic model linking the components of x_t. Note that for $p = 1$, the VECM reduces to $\Delta x_t = c + \alpha \beta' x_{t-1} + \epsilon_t$, which differs from a system of n random walks by the presence of the error correcting term (which is 'neglected' by the Minnesota prior). If this term is not present, cointegration is not possible ($r = 0 \Leftrightarrow \Pi = 0$) and we have a stationary VAR on the first difference of x_t. If Π is of rank n, we have a stationary VAR on the level of x_t (we can set $\Pi = \alpha$ and $\beta = I_n$). The coefficient α_{ij} gives the *ceteris paribus* influence of $z_{j,t-1}$, the jth disequilbrium term, on $\Delta x_{i,t}$. Inference on α is also of prime interest for the economic interpretation of the VAR system, since the larger the coefficient (in absolute value), the faster the adjustment of $x_{i,t}$ towards its long-run equilibrium value.

Remark: In (9.25) the constant term c can be replaced by a set of deterministic components ψD_t, where D_t (of dimension $m \times 1$) may include a linear trend and dummy variables besides a constant, and ψ is an $n \times m$ matrix of parameters. Moreover, the deterministic components are not included in the cointegrating space, which implies for example that the levels x_t have a linear trend if D_t includes a constant. If this is not in agreement with the data, it is possible to incorporate D_t in the cointegrating space, by restricting ψ as $\psi = \alpha \psi_0'$ where ψ_0' is the $r \times m$ matrix of coefficients of the deterministic components in the cointegrating relations which become $\beta' x_t + \psi_0' D_t$. This modification can be easily taken into account in all the subsequent results (by redefining β and x_t to include ψ_0 and D_t, respectively).

9.3.2 *Identification Issues*

The parametrization of the long-run impact reduced rank matrix Π as the product $\alpha \beta'$ raises an identification issue: Π is obviously identified since (9.25) is linear in Π, but α and β are not identified since one can factorize Π equivalently as $(\alpha H^{-1})(H \beta') = \alpha_* \beta_*'$ by choosing any $r \times r$ full rank matrix H. The parameterization in terms of α and β identifies the cointegrating space (the row space of Π) and the adjustment space (the column space of Π). Without restrictions, the individual elements of β and α are not identified. In the paper of Bauwens and Lubrano (1996), on which this section is based, it is shown that the matrices α and β must be subject to r^2 restrictions (see Theorem 2.1 of that paper). Since they have a total of $2nr$ elements, there are many ways to impose the required number of restrictions, but all the possible ways do not imply identification. A sufficient condition requires that given a structure (α, β) subject to r^2 restrictions, an equivalent structure $(\alpha_*, \beta_*) = (\alpha H^{-1}, \beta H')$ satisfying the same restrictions can be obtained only if H is a diagonal matrix, or an identity matrix if one element of each column of β is normalized to -1. In the sequel, we assume that these r normalization restrictions are imposed, since they amount to choosing one normalized variable in each cointegrating relation. The remaining $r(r - 1)$ restrictions can be imposed on the matrix of adjustment coefficients α, on the matrix of cointegrating vectors β, or on both.

The system of equations $\beta' x_t = 0$, which is the long-run solution of the cointegrated VAR, is a set of simultaneous equations. One is usually interested in trying to interpret it as a meaningful economic model for x_t (e.g. a supply and demand market model, a macroeconomic model, etc.). Such a 'structural' interpretation requires identification of the parameters individually (e.g. the price elasticity of demand, the elasticity of money demand with respect to an interest rate, etc.). A practical solution is to impose restrictions on β and to leave α unrestricted. This solution turns out to be also the easiest for the computation of the posterior density of β. Let us denote the r cointegrating vectors by β_i ($i = 1 \ldots r$). Linear restrictions on β_i (not including the normalization of one element to -1) may be formalized by the relations

$$R_i \beta_i = h_i \quad (i = 1 \ldots r) \tag{9.27}$$

where R_i is a full rank $s_i \times n$ matrix of known constants, and h_i is a vector of known constants. Johansen (1995) and Johansen and Juselius (1994) provide formal conditions for identification of β. Essentially, every vector β_i is identified if every s_i is greater than or equal to $r - 1$, and no linear combination of the other columns of β can satisfy the restrictions imposed on β_i, so that H can only be an identity matrix. These conditions are akin to the usual conditions for the identification of a linear simultaneous equation model.

9.3.3 Likelihood Function and Prior Density

The key to a Bayesian analysis of (9.25) (as well as to ML estimation) is to notice that the model is linear in the parameters conditionally on β. One can then use the results of Subsection 9.2.1 on the Bayesian analysis of multivariate regression models. To do this, we write the second line of (9.25) for the T observations in the matrix format

$$Y = X\Gamma + Z\beta\alpha' + E = X\Gamma + \tilde{Z}\alpha' + E = \tilde{W}B + E \tag{9.28}$$

where

$$Y = \begin{pmatrix} \Delta x_1' \\ \Delta x_2' \\ \vdots \\ \Delta x_T' \end{pmatrix} \quad Z = \begin{pmatrix} x_0' \\ x_1' \\ \vdots \\ x_{T-1}' \end{pmatrix} \quad E = \begin{pmatrix} \epsilon_1' \\ \epsilon_2' \\ \vdots \\ \epsilon_T' \end{pmatrix}$$

$$X = \begin{pmatrix} 1 & \Delta x_0' & \cdots & \Delta x_{2-p}' \\ 1 & \Delta x_1' & \cdots & \Delta x_{3-p}' \\ \vdots & \vdots & & \vdots \\ 1 & \Delta x_T' & \cdots & \Delta x_{T-p+1}' \end{pmatrix} \quad \Gamma = \begin{pmatrix} c' \\ \Pi_1' \\ \vdots \\ \Pi_{p-1}' \end{pmatrix} \tag{9.29}$$

$$\tilde{W} = (X \; \tilde{Z}) = (X \; Z\beta) \quad B = \begin{pmatrix} \Gamma \\ \alpha' \end{pmatrix}.$$

Let g be the number of columns of X and the number of rows of Γ, so that $g = 1 + n(p - 1)$. Then $k = g + r$ is the number of columns of $\tilde{W}$. Conditionally on β, $Y = \tilde{W}B + E$ is exactly in the form of (9.5). Therefore the likelihood function of the parameters is proportional to the first line of (9.9) (substituting $\tilde{W}$ for Z).

In principle, any prior density on the unrestricted elements of β can be used, since we shall see that the computation of the posterior density and moments of β has to be done numerically except in a special case. This is a merit of our approach since β contains parameters for which one may have prior information originating from other studies or from economic theory. An informative prior on the adjustment coefficient matrix α may also be useful. For example, if x_t is partitioned into $x_{1,t}$ ($n_1 \times 1$) and $x_{2,t}$ ($n_2 \times 1$), and α is partitioned into α_1 ($n_1 \times r$) and α_2 ($n_2 \times r$) (with $n_1 + n_2 = n$), setting $\alpha_2 = 0$ implies the weak exogeneity of x_2 with respect to x_1 for the parameter β—see Urbain (1992). So one may wish to specify an informative prior for α_2, with prior mean equal to zero. Or one may have prior information based on theoretical reasoning that some adjustment coefficients should be null, and one may wish to impose such restrictions through a prior rather than exactly. Prior information on α could be implemented through a natural conjugate prior density (but we have mentioned in Subsection 9.2.1 that this type of prior is rather restrictive). Any other prior than non-informative or natural conjugate requires numerical integration on α and β. For the other parameters (Γ and Σ), we do not bother about defining informative prior densities, since one does not have very often genuine prior information about them. In the sequel, we use the non-informative prior (9.6) for B and Σ of the multivariate regression model times a prior density on β:

$$\varphi(\beta, B, \Sigma) \propto |\Sigma|^{-(n+1)/2} \varphi(\beta). \tag{9.30}$$

The above prior is not Jeffreys' prior. The latter depends on all the parameters in a way that precludes analytical integration of any parameter; see Kleibergen and van Dijk (1994a) for the computation of Jeffreys' prior, and its use in VECM systems.

Remark: Note that we use β as an argument of density functions even if some elements of β are known with probability 1.

9.3.4 *Posterior Results*

Theorem 9.3 gives a useful factorization of the posterior density.

Theorem 9.3 *For the VECM model defined by (9.28) where α is unrestricted and β is subject to the identifying linear restrictions (9.27), and for the prior (9.30), the posterior density can be factorized as*

$$
\begin{aligned}
&\text{(1) } \Sigma|B, \beta, X_T \sim IW_n((Y - \tilde{W}B)'(Y - \tilde{W}B), T) \\
&\text{(2) } B|\beta, X_T \sim Mt_{k \times n}(\tilde{B}, \tilde{W}'\tilde{W}, \tilde{S}, T - k) \\
&\quad where
\end{aligned}
$$

$$
\tilde{B} = (\tilde{W}'\tilde{W})^{-1}\tilde{W}'Y
$$
$$
\tilde{S} = (Y - \tilde{W}\tilde{B})'(Y - \tilde{W}\tilde{B})
$$

$$
\text{(3) } \varphi(\beta|X_T) \propto \varphi(\beta)|\beta'W_0\beta|^{l_0}/|\beta'W_1\beta|^{l_1} \tag{9.31}
$$
$$
\quad where
$$

$$
l_0 = (T - k - n)/2 \qquad l_1 = (T - k)/2
$$
$$
W_0 = Z'M_X Z
$$
$$
W_1 = Z'M_Y \left[I_T - X(X'M_Y X)^{-1}X'\right] M_Y Z
$$
$$
= Z'M_X \left[I_T - Y(Y'M_X Y)^{-1}Y'\right] M_X Z,
$$
$$
with M_X = I_T - X(X'X)^{-1}X', \text{ and likewise for } M_Y.
$$

Proof As mentioned above, conditionally on β, (9.28) is a multivariate regression model, so that (2) follows directly from Theorem 9.1. The first line of (9.9) (with $\tilde{W}'\tilde{W}$ substituted for $Z'Z$) and (A.96) yield (1) directly. The posterior kernel of β is obtained as the prior multiplied by the integral of the second line of (9.9) with respect to Σ and B, i.e. the inverse of the integrating constant of the matricvariate Student density of result (2):

$$
\varphi(\beta|X_T) \propto \varphi(\beta) |\tilde{S}|^{-(T-k)/2} |\tilde{W}'\tilde{W}|^{-n/2}. \tag{9.32}
$$

By applying formulae for the determinants of partitioned matrices, we get

$$
|\tilde{S}| = |Y'Y - Y'\tilde{W}(\tilde{W}'\tilde{W})^{-1}\tilde{W}'Y| = |\tilde{W}'\tilde{W}|^{-1} |\tilde{W}'M_Y\tilde{W}| |Y'Y|
$$
$$
|\tilde{W}'\tilde{W}| = |X'X| |\tilde{Z}'M_Y\tilde{Z}|
$$
$$
|\tilde{W}'M_Y\tilde{W}| = |X'M_Y X| |\tilde{Z}'M_Y\tilde{Z} - \tilde{Z}'M_Y X(X'M_Y X)^{-1}X'M_Y\tilde{Z}|.
$$

The result (3) follows by substituting the latter equalities and the definition of $\tilde{Z}$ in (9.32), neglecting the factors that do not depend on β. More details can be found in Bauwens and Lubrano (1996), on which this section is based. $\square$

Remark: The algebraic derivation of $\varphi(\beta|X_T)$ does not require that β be subject to any restrictions, such as defined by (9.27) or by a normalization rule. However explicitly incorporating the restrictions on β is important for interpreting $\varphi(\beta|X_T)$ (as well as the prior) as the density of the unrestricted elements of β. Otherwise the density of unrestricted β, conditioned on exact restrictions on β, may not be defined uniquely, as explained in Subsection 4.6.1.

If $\varphi(\beta)$ is constant, the posterior density (9.31) is proportional to the ratio of the determinants of two matrices that are quadratic forms in β, raised to positive powers. W_0 is the matrix of sums of squares and cross-products of the residuals of a least squares regression of Z on X. W_1 is the same type of matrix of a regression of $M_Y Z$ on $M_Y X$, and can also be computed from a regression of $M_X Z$ on $M_X Y$.

In order to use the results of Theorem 9.3, we must be able to compute the marginal density of any element of β and to summarize it by its quantiles and its moments if they exist. If there is a single cointegrating vector, some analytical results are available; if there are several vectors, we have to resort to numerical integration.

9.3.4.1 *The Case of a Single Cointegrating Vector* If the rank of cointegration is equal to one, β is a vector. We assume that one element of β is normalized to -1, since this is sufficient for identification. We say that the order of overidentification of β is the number of linear restrictions imposed on β in addition to the normalization. We can then specialize Theorem 9.3 to the following corollary which states the relation between the order of overidentification and the order of existence of the posterior moments of β.

Corollary 9.4 *Let* $r = 1$, $\beta = (-1 \ \beta'_*)'$, *and* $P\beta_* = w$, *with* $P\,(s \times n - 1, 0 \le s < n - 1)$ *and* $w\,(s \times 1)$ *known:*
  (i) If $\varphi(\beta) \propto 1$, $\varphi(\beta|X_T)$ *is a 1-1 poly-t density. The density is integrable, and it has finite moments of order equal to* s, *the order of overidentification of* β.
  (ii) If $\varphi(\beta)$ *is a Student density with* ν *degrees of freedom,* $\varphi(\beta|X_T)$ *is a 2-1 poly-t density that has finite moments of order equal to* $n + \nu - 1$.

Proof If $P\beta_* = w$, there exists a matrix Q of dimension $n - 1 \times q$, with $q = n-s-1$, such that $\beta_* = Q\tilde{\beta}$, where $\tilde{\beta}$ is a vector of q unrestricted parameters. In (9.31), $\beta'W_\bullet\beta$ (where $W_\bullet$ is W_0 or W_1) is a scalar when $r = 1$, and can be written as

$$(-1 \ \ \tilde{\beta}'Q') \begin{pmatrix} f_\bullet & g'_\bullet \\ g_\bullet & A_\bullet \end{pmatrix} \begin{pmatrix} -1 \\ Q\tilde{\beta} \end{pmatrix} = s_\bullet + (\tilde{\beta} - b_\bullet)'H_\bullet(\tilde{\beta} - b_\bullet) \quad (9.33)$$

where $H_\bullet = Q'AQ$, $b_\bullet = H_\bullet^{-1}Q'g_\bullet$, and $s_\bullet = f_\bullet - b'_\bullet H_\bullet b_\bullet$. With a constant prior, (9.31) becomes

$$\varphi(\tilde{\beta}|X_T) \propto [s_0 + (\tilde{\beta} - b_0)'H_0(\tilde{\beta} - b_0)]^{l_0}/[s_1 + (\tilde{\beta} - b_1)'H_1(\tilde{\beta} - b_1)]^{l_1} \quad (9.34)$$

which is the kernel of a 1-1 poly-t density, see Subsection A.2.8. In a q-variate 1-1 poly-t density with exponents l_0 and l_1, the condition $2(l_1 - l_0) - q > m$ is sufficient for the existence of moments of order m (including $m = 0$ for integrability). In (9.34), $2(l_1 - l_0) - q = s + 1$; hence moments of order s of $\tilde{\beta}$ are finite. If $\varphi(\tilde{\beta})$ is Student, (9.34) is multiplied by the prior kernel,

$$\left[1 + (\tilde{\beta} - b_2)'H_2(\tilde{\beta} - b_2) \right]^{-l_2}, \quad (9.35)$$

where b_2 and H_2 are the prior parameters, and $l_2 = (\nu + q)/2$. The condition for existence of mth moments is $2(l_2 + l_1 - l_0) - (n - s - 1) = n + \nu > m$; hence moments of order $n + \nu - 1$ are finite. □

With a flat prior on β, the posterior is always integrable, but without overidentifying restrictions it does not possess finite moments, even in large samples.

This result can be viewed as the Bayesian counterpart of Phillips' (1994) result that the ML estimator of β has no integer moments in finite samples.

When the posterior density of β is poly-t, its moments and marginal densities can be computed by the algorithms of Richard and Tompa (1980) included in the Bayesian Regression Programme (BRP) of Bauwens, Bulteau, Gille, Longrée, Lubrano, and Tompa (1981); see below for an example.

9.3.4.2 *The Case of Several Cointegrating Vectors* In the case of more than one cointegrating vector, the class of distributions to which the posterior of β belongs is a matricvariate generalization of the class of poly-t densities ('poly-matrix-t'). Not much is known about the properties of poly-matrix-t densities. The properties of poly-t densities do not extend trivially to this class. Moreover, the identification restrictions (9.27) complicate the situation, in the same way as restrictions complicate (9.7) to (9.10). Since we cannot analytically obtain the posterior marginal density or moments of the cointegrating vectors, we have to resort to numerical integration techniques. Bauwens and Lubrano (1996) used importance sampling in an example with two cointegrating vectors. They show that the posterior *conditional* density of a column of β, given the remaining columns, is a 1-1 poly-t density. They incorporate the conditional density of β_1 given β_2 in the importance function, and build a Student approximation to the marginal density of β_2 (see the paragraphs 'Methods to choose an importance function' in Subsection 3.3.2). They also apply formulae (3.41)–(3.43) (where α and β are replaced by β_1 and β_2, respectively). Another possibility suggested in that paper is to use Gibbs sampling, since a choice of the 'full conditional densities' (defined in Subsection 3.4.3) of the posterior of β is precisely the conditional 1-1 poly-t densities defined previously. They can be simulated with an algorithm of Bauwens and Richard (1985). This Gibbs sampling algorithm has not been implemented in an example because the simulation of a 1-1 poly-t density has a relatively high fixed cost. The fixed cost would be incurred rN times, which is typically a large number (N being the Monte Carlo sample size, and r the cointegrating rank). Moreover, this algorithm cannot work if the prior is informative in such a way that the full conditional posterior densities are no longer poly-t. For these reasons, Bauwens and Giot (1998) have applied the griddy-Gibbs sampler to the example of Bauwens and Lubrano; results obtained with this method are provided in one of the examples that follow.

9.3.5 *Examples*

9.3.5.1 *A Money Demand Equation* For an illustration with a single cointegrating vector, we use three variables that can define a money demand equation for Belgium. They are regrouped in $x_t = (m_t\ y_t\ r_t)'$ following the notation of model (9.25). In x_t, m_t is the log of deflated money stock (M1), y_t is the log of deflated disposable income of households, and r_t is the log of $(1 + R_t)$, R_t being the interest rate on three-month treasury certificates. With annual data trending upwards over the sample period 1953–1982, we use two lags ($p = 2$) and leave the intercept unrestricted. The cointegrating vector is $(-1\ \beta_y\ \beta_r)$, normalized on

Table 9.1 *Money demand: ML and posterior results on β*

	β_y	β_r
ML estimate (s.e.)	0.94 (0.09)	−3.85 (1.03)
Flat prior:		
Mode and median	0.88 0.92	−3.32 −3.63
0.1 and 0.9 deciles	0.69 1.29	−7.95 −0.75
Truncated flat prior:		
Prior mean (s.d.)	1.00 (0.29)	−4.00 (4.62)
Posterior mean (s.d.)	0.94 (0.17)	−3.86 (2.16)
Prior intervals	0.50 1.50	−12.0 4.0
Student prior:		
Prior mean (s.d.)	1.00 (0.20)	−4.00 (1.00)
Posterior mean (s.d.)	0.94 (0.08)	−3.90 (0.77)

m. The same data are analysed in Subsection 5.3.3 in a single-equation model.

Using the prior (9.30) with $\varphi(\beta_y, \beta_r) \propto 1$ (a flat prior), the posterior density of $(\beta_y \beta_r)$ is a 1-1 poly-t density (see Corollary 9.1). We report the graphs of the marginal densities of β_y and β_r in Fig. 9.1. The densities display long and fat tails, reflecting that they are integrable but do not possess finite moments. In Table 9.1, we report their mode, median, first and last deciles, and for comparison the ML estimates with their standard errors.

The Bayesian estimates (mode or median) are not very different from the ML ones, which is not surprising given the flat prior. They are consistent with the interpretation of the cointegrating relation as a money demand equation, with a long-run income elasticity of the order of one, and a negative interest rate elasticity. We also define a Student prior density on β, with 12 degrees of freedom, prior mean equal to 1 for β_y and to −4 for β_r, corresponding prior standard deviations equal to 0.2 and 1, and no correlation. The parameters of the Student prior (9.35) are $l_2 = (10 + 1)/2 = 5.5$, $b_2 = (1 - 4)'$, and H_2 the diagonal matrix obtained by solving (A.83) for the precision matrix P (H_2 in our context). The marginal prior and posterior densities are shown in Fig. 9.1. The posterior density is now a 2-1 poly-t with finite moments of order 14 ($\nu + n - 1$ in Corollary 9.1). Posterior moments are given in Table 9.1.

The Bayesian results show that the estimation of β_y and especially β_r is far from being accurate, even if this is not surprising given the small size of the sample. The imprecision of the ML estimates can be measured only with the asymptotic standard errors, which give too optimistic a view of precision by comparison with the Bayesian results (under a flat prior). Note that with the informative prior we have chosen, the posterior means are very close to the ML results, since

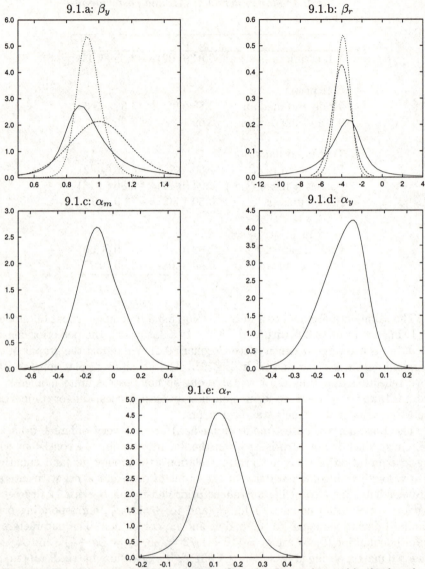

The solid line is the posterior density under a flat prior. In panels a and b, the dotted line is the posterior under a Student prior, and the Student prior is also shown.

FIG. 9.1. Money demand: prior and posterior densities

the prior means are also quite close to the ML estimates. The posterior standard deviations are slightly smaller than the asymptotic standard deviations. Our informative prior includes the amount of prior precision that is needed to reproduce roughly the classical asymptotic standard errors. Such classical stan-

Table 9.2 *Money demand: posterior results on* α

	α_m	α_y	α_r
Posterior mean	−0.10	−0.09	0.12
Posterior s.d.	(0.17)	(0.10)	(0.10)

dard errors are not usually reported in empirical studies: see e.g. Johansen and Juselius (1994), Urbain (1995), and several papers quoted by Johansen (1991). To assess the impact of the Student prior on the posterior standard deviations, we give in Table 9.1 the posterior moments obtained with a truncated flat prior, i.e. the prior of β_y and of of β_r are uniform on $(0.5, 1.5)$ and $(-12, 4)$, respectively. Graphs of the posterior are not reported since they are identical to those in the case of the flat prior, except that the curves are shifted vertically (as they have to be renormalized). The posterior standard deviations are at least twice as large with the truncated prior than with the Student prior.

The results with the flat and the Student prior were computed using the Bayesian Regression Programme, whereas the results with the truncated prior were computed using the griddy-Gibbs sampler (see Subsection 3.4.3), with 10,000 (plus 50 discarded) draws. The execution time was 80 seconds on a Pentium Pro 150 (with GAUSS). Using the Gibbs sample of β, we also computed the posterior results, given in Table 9.2 and in Fig. 9.1 (panels c–e), on $\alpha' = (\alpha_m \, \alpha_y \, \alpha_r)$ (where, for example, α_m is the coefficient of the error correction term $\beta' x_t$ in the money demand equation of the VAR model). Since α' is the last row of the matrix B—see (9.29)—which has a matricvariate Student distribution by Theorem 9.3, we can use (A.117) to deduce that α' also has a matricvariate Student distribution. Next, by applying (A.121) to the latter distribution, we see that each element of α' has a univariate Student distribution, conditionally on β. Then we can marginalize the conditional moments and densities of α' given β, using the relations between conditional and marginal moments and densities (see Section 3.2). Note that there is no truncation involved in the computation of the results on α, except indirectly through the truncation of β. The results indicate that perhaps the interest rate is 'error correcting' and that money and income are not, but this is rather tentative since we have too small a sample to draw strong conclusions.

9.3.5.2 Import Demand and Prices

This is an example with two cointegrating vectors on five variables, taken from Urbain (1995). The variables (in logarithms) are the import volume (m), the real GNP (y), the import price in foreign currency (pf), the effective exchange rate (ex), and the domestic price (pd). We have quarterly data for Belgium over the period 1970, second quarter, to 1990, second quarter. The model is (9.25) with $x_t = (m_t \; y_t \; pf_t \; ex_t \; pd_t)'$, p equal to four, and the constant replaced by ψD_t, where D_t includes the constant and three quarterly dummies (see the remark at the end of Subsection 9.3.1). The first cointegrating vector is normalized on ex and the second on m:

Table 9.3 *Import demand and prices: moments of β*

Parameter	Posterior	Prior	Density	Range
β_m	0.21 (0.11)	0.20 (0.12)	Uniform	−0.20 0.60
β_y	0.01 (0.10)	0.00 (0.10)	Normal	−0.35 0.35
β_f	0.58 (0.09)	0.60 (0.20)	Uniform	0.25 0.95
β_d	0.01 (0.08)	0.00 (0.10)	Normal	−0.30 0.30
γ_y	1.02 (0.07)	1.00 (0.10)	Normal	0.75 1.30
γ_f	0.00 (0.10)	0.00 (0.10)	Normal	−0.40 0.40
γ_x	−0.25 (0.28)	−0.23 (0.43)	Uniform	−1.30 0.85
γ_d	0.39 (0.16)	0.40 (0.35)	Uniform	−0.20 1.00

$$ex = \beta_m\, m + \beta_y\, y + b_f\, pf + b_d\, pd$$
$$m = \gamma_y\, y + \gamma_x\, ex + c_f\, pf + c_d\, pd.$$

Bauwens and Lubrano (1996) introduced two exact restrictions on each relation to identify the coefficients and to ensure the existence of the posterior variances. These restrictions are: $\beta_y = 0$, $bf + bd = 0$, $\gamma_y = 1$, and $\gamma_x = c_f$. Instead of imposing the restrictions exactly, we can impose them through a prior density. Firstly, we reparameterize the two cointegrating relations so as to have zero restrictions:

$$ex + pf - pd = \beta_m\, m + \beta_y\, y + \beta_f\, (pf - pd) + \beta_d\, pd$$
$$m = \gamma_y\, y + \gamma_x\, (ex + pf - pd) + \gamma_f\, (pf - pd) + \gamma_d\, pd$$

with $\beta_f = b_f + 1$, $\beta_d = b_f + b_d$, $\gamma_f = c_f - \gamma_x$, and $\gamma_d = c_d + c_f$. Secondly, we define a normal prior density on $(\beta_y\ \beta_f\ \gamma_y\ \gamma_f)$. The prior mean is centred on the value of the exact restrictions mentioned above: $(0\ 0\ 1\ 0)$. The covariance matrix is diagonal, and each standard deviation is equal to 0.1. The prior on the other parameters is flat on finite intervals described below. These intervals have been selected in order to avoid significant truncation of the posterior density.

In Table 9.3, we report the posterior means and standard deviations of the parameters of the cointegration matrix β, and in Table 9.4 we report the results on the elements of the matrix α (e.g. the entry at the intersection of the 'm' row and the 'First CI vector' column is the posterior mean of α_{11}, the coefficient of the first cointegrating vector in the equation of Δm_t in the VAR model). The results were computed with the griddy-Gibbs sampler applied to the eight parameters of the cointegrating vectors. The Monte Carlo sample size was 10,000 (after discarding 50 draws), but the results after 5,000 draws are almost identical. The range of integration of each parameter is given in Table 9.3. Note that since finite ranges are used, the normal prior is slightly truncated (so that the prior moments in Table 9.3 are approximate). The results on α were computed as for the previous example on money demand. Graphs of prior and posterior densities of the cointegrating vector parameters are shown in Figs 9.2 and 9.3.

The first cointegrating vector (evaluated at the posterior means) indicates that the deviation of the exchange rate from purchasing power parity ($ex +$

Table 9.4 *Import demand and prices: posterior moments of* α

Equation	First CI vector	Second CI vector
m	0.23 (0.24)	0.33 (0.23)
y	0.24 (0.23)	0.05 (0.20)
pf	0.03 (0.13)	0.04 (0.12)
ex	0.29 (0.14)	0.16 (0.12)
pd	0.05 (0.08)	-0.06 (0.07)

$pf - pd$) is stationary if it is corrected by $0.2m + 0.58(pf - pd)$. Given that imports are a very composite aggregate good, and that pf and pd are price indices for different goods (imported and domestic goods are not identical), we cannot expect a perfect purchasing power parity relation between ex, pd, and pf. The second relation indicates that imports are cointegrated with GNP (with unitary elasticity), import prices expressed in domestic currency (with elasticity -0.25), and domestic prices (with elasticity 0.69), but the long-run homogeneity of the price effect is clearly rejected by the data (γ_d would be equal to zero); this may also be attributed to the difference between the composition of domestic and imported goods. The same conclusions were drawn by Bauwens and Lubrano (1996), using exact restrictions.

The results on α indicate that the GNP and the two price variables of the VAR model are not 'error correcting', and could be treated as exogenous for β. This implies also that the innovations of these three I(1) variables determine the stochastic trend of the system. Moreover, the past disequilibrium in the purchasing power parity relation seems to correct only the exchange rate equation, while the past disequilibrium in the import demand relation corrects the import and perhaps the exchange rate equations.

9.3.6 *Selecting the Cointegration Rank*

For obtaining the previous theoretical results and in the examples, the cointegrating rank (r) was assumed known. We favour the viewpoint that an empirical cointegration analysis should be based on a theoretical economic model that defines equilibrium economic relations, so that a cointegration study is 'confirmatory' rather than 'exploratory'. Of course, it is not because a theoretical model defines equilibrium relations that they will be necessarily found in a particular data set. A discrepancy between the theoretical and empirical models can be due to several reasons, such as too small a sample or a lack of correspondence between measured and theoretical variables. Therefore, we believe that inference conditional on an assumed value of r is often a sensible approach, especially in small samples. But this does not preclude trying to make inference on the value of r. The most well-known and used classical test is the trace test of Johansen (1991). On the Bayesian side, the topic of selecting the cointegrating rank has not yet given very useful and convincing results. Using a posterior odds

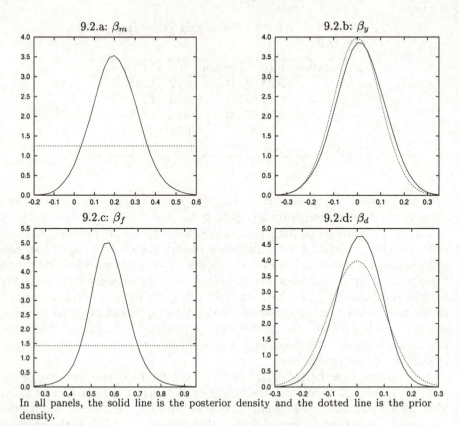

In all panels, the solid line is the posterior density and the dotted line is the prior density.

FIG. 9.2. Import demand and prices: prior and posterior densities

approach leads to rather heavy computations and requires definition of proper prior densities, see Kleibergen and Paap (1997). Bauwens and Lubrano (1996) use an informal approach. They compute the posterior distribution of the ordered eigenvalues of the matrix $\Pi'\Pi$ from the VECM formulation of the VAR model when cointegration is not imposed; see the first line of (9.25). Since if Π has a reduced rank there are zero eigenvalues, this feature should be revealed by the fact that the smallest eigenvalues have a lot of probability mass on values close to zero. The computation can be made easily by simulating values of Π from its posterior distribution which is a matricvariate Student distribution under a non-informative prior (this follows from Theorem 9.1). For the examples of the previous subsection, Bauwens and Lubrano (1996) concluded in favour of one cointegrating relation in the first case (money demand), and two in the second one (import demand and prices).

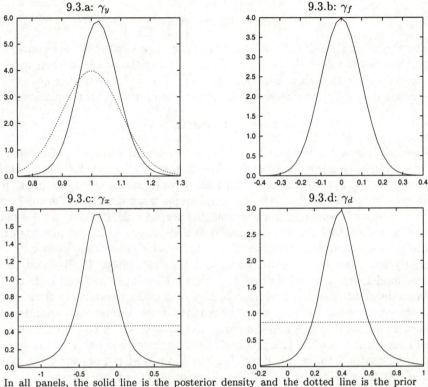

In all panels, the solid line is the posterior density and the dotted line is the prior
density (in panel b, they are almost the same).

FIG. 9.3. Import demand and prices: prior and posterior densities

9.4 Simultaneous Equation Models

This section contains a brief guide to the literature on the Bayesian approach to
simultaneous equation systems. Bayesian inference for this model started to be
developed in the 1960s, with unpublished papers by Drèze (1962), Rothenberg
(1963), and Zellner (1965), because this model was considered as a highly relevant
tool for applied structural economic modelling. Classical estimation methods
had been developed in the 1950s at the Cowles Foundation, but these methods
rely on precise identification restrictions and their justification was in terms of
asymptotic results. The unpublished paper of Drèze (1962) gave birth to a series
of papers, in particular Drèze (1976) for the limited information approach, and
Drèze and Morales (1976) for the full information one. Drèze and Richard (1983)
provide a comprehensive survey of this work and some extensions.

9.4.1 *Limited Information Analysis*

Drèze (1976) develops the Bayesian limited information approach to the estimation of a single structural equation as

$$y_1 = Y_2\beta + Z_1\gamma + u, \tag{9.36}$$

where y_1 $(T \times 1)$ and Y_2 $(T \times n)$ contain the observations on the endogenous variables of the model, Z_1 $(T \times k_1)$ is the matrix of the predetermined variables included in the structural equation, and u $(T \times 1)$ is the vector of errors. This equation is usually completed by the unrestricted reduced form equations:

$$Y_2 = Z_1\Pi_1 + Z_2\Pi_2 + V_2, \tag{9.37}$$

where Z_2 $(T \times k_2)$ is the matrix of the predetermined variables not included in the structural equation, and V_2 $(T \times n)$ is the matrix of errors. It is assumed that $(u_t\, v_{2t}')' \sim N_{1+n}(0, \Sigma)$. Drèze's (1976) main contribution was to define a 'non-informative' prior and to derive the marginal posterior density of the coefficients of the structural equation. In particular, the posterior density of β is a 1-1 poly-t density, see (A.130) for a definition. It is non-integrable in the just identified case $(n = k_2)$, and it is integrable if $n < k_2$, in which case its moments of order strictly less than $k_2 - n$ exist. Chao and Phillips (1998a, 1998b) analyse the same model with Jeffreys' prior (proposed by Kleibergen and van Dijk 1994b). Under Jeffreys' prior the posterior density of β is only known conditionally on Ω, the reduced form error covariance matrix. Its analytical expression is much more complicated than a poly-t density, and given that it is conditional on other parameters, it has to be marginalized. Despite this, Chao and Phillips are able to prove that it is integrable if $n \le k_2$, but that it does not possess finite integer moments (even if $k_2 - n > 0$). The difference between the results of Drèze and those of Chao and Phillips is due to the prior. Drèze's non-informative prior is

$$\varphi(\beta, \gamma, \Pi_1, \Pi_2, \Sigma) \propto |\Sigma|^{-(k+n+2)/2}, \tag{9.38}$$

where $k = k_1 + k_2$. It is based on an invariance argument such that the posterior density of β is invariant with respect to the parameterization of the equations that complete the structural equation; for more details see Drèze and Richard (1983: 545). Jeffreys' prior, proportional to the square root of the determinant of the information matrix, is given by

$$\varphi(\beta, \gamma, \Pi_1, \Pi_2, \Sigma) \propto (\sigma_{11})^{-(k_2-n)/2} |\Sigma|^{-(k+n+2)/2} |\Pi_2'Z_2'M_{Z_1}Z_2\Pi_2|^{1/2}, \tag{9.39}$$

where $M_{Z_1} = I_T - Z_1'(Z_1'Z_1)^{-1}Z_1$. It is equal to zero if the matrix Π_2 in (9.37) is not of full rank n, i.e. when the rank condition for identification fails. Thus it gives zero weight to the region of the parameter space where the rank condition fails, and low weight where it nearly fails. Under Drèze's flat prior, this does not occur. Indeed, Maddala (1976) criticized the sharpness of the posterior density of β obtained by Drèze in the overidentified case as being spurious.

Bauwens and van Dijk (1990) propose two additional parameterizations for the limited information system (9.36)–(9.37). They are obtained by decomposing the joint density of y_1 and Y_2 in marginal and conditional densities. This can obviously be done in two ways. The model is still formed by two equations, but the two error terms are independent (by the properties of the normal distribution). This gives the possibility of defining other priors (including non-informative and Jeffreys' priors), by considering each part of the model separately, and to derive relevant posterior densities.

9.4.2 Full Information Analysis

Full information analysis of a system of simultaneous equations is more difficult than limited information analysis. Essentially, there are no analytical results providing the marginal posterior densities of any parameter, except in the case of a system of two equations. The treatment of the model requires heavy numerical integrations. The pathbreaking paper in this respect is that of Kloek and van Dijk (1978), who proposed applying importance sampling for the first time in this context. Let us write the ith equation of a system of $m = n + 1$ equations as

$$y_i = X_i \delta_i + u_i. \tag{9.40}$$

In this notation, the matrix X_i contains the endogenous and predetermined variables included in the equation; for example, if the first equation is given by (9.36), $X_1 = (Y_2 \, Z_1)$. Drèze and Morales (1976) proposed an informative prior density, called the extended natural conjugate prior, such that prior information is easy to introduce on the vectors δ_i through a prior mean and covariance matrix. There is a non-informative limit of this prior, which is

$$\varphi(\delta, \Sigma) \propto |\Sigma|^{-(k+n+2)/2}, \tag{9.41}$$

where $\delta = (\delta_1' \, \delta_2' \ldots \delta_m')'$, and Σ is the covariance matrix of the error vector $(u_1 \, u_2 \ldots u_m)'$ supposed to be $N_m(0, \Sigma)$. For this class of priors, the posterior densities $\varphi(\delta_i | \delta_I, \text{data})$ are all 1-1 poly-t densities, where δ_I is the vector obtained by deleting δ_i from δ. This immediately suggests computation of the marginal posterior results by a Gibbs sampling algorithm, since it is feasible to simulate a 1-1 poly-t density (see Bauwens and Richard 1985). As far as we know, this has not yet been tried. Bauwens (1984) used importance sampling, since Gibbs sampling was not yet known to econometricians at that time. In particular, he used the exact conditional density $\varphi(\delta_i | \delta_I, \text{data})$ as part of an importance function for δ, which was completed for δ_I by another density. Other importance functions he used rely on knowledge of these conditional densities. Van Dijk's (1984) thesis also contains several proposals of importance functions for the numerical integration of the posterior density of δ, in particular a mixed integration method which combines a univariate deterministic integration rule with importance sampling; see also van Dijk, Kloek, and Boender (1985).

In the particular case of a system of two equations, Drèze and Morales (1976) prove that the marginal posterior density of δ_1 (and thus also of δ_2) is a 2-1 poly-t density. As implied by Theorem A.22, it is possible to obtain the moments of such a density by unidimensional numerical integration (irrespective of the dimension of δ_i). A different approach to the two-equation system can be found in Richard (1973). He manages to treat the model analytically with respect to all the parameters except the three 'simultaneity' parameters (the two coefficients of the endogenous variables and the correlation coefficient of the error terms), which are treated by numerical integration using Gauss rules (see Section 3.3).

APPENDIX A

PROBABILITY DISTRIBUTIONS

A number of probability distributions together with their density are used in the course of the book. For ease of reference we regroup their definitions in this appendix, together with a short discussion of their key properties. Additional references of interest are, among others, Johnson and Kotz (1972), Johnson, Kotz, and Balakrishnan (1994, 1995) for an extensive discussion of a broad range of distributions, and Drèze and Richard (1983) for additional details or some matricvariate distributions. In Appendix B, we present sampling algorithms for most of the distributions reviewed in this appendix.

In line with the way in which they are used in the text, density functions are given in the form of density kernels times their integrating constants. We have included a number of auxiliary results that can facilitate derivations based upon density functions often by eliminating direct (and tedious) algebraic manipulations of the densities themselves. Random variables are denoted by capital letters. The symbol $\sim$ reads as 'is distributed as'; the symbol μ_r denotes rth-order moments centred on the origin.

A.1 Univariate Distributions

A.1.1 The Uniform Distribution

A random variable $a \leq X \leq b$ has a uniform distribution on $[a, b]$, i.e. $X \sim U(a, b)$, if its density function is given by

$$f_u(x|a, b) = C_u^{-1}(a, b) \times 1, \tag{A.1}$$

with

$$C_u(a, b) = \frac{1}{b - a}. \tag{A.2}$$

Its moments are given by

$$\mu_r = \frac{1}{r + 1} \frac{b^{r+1} - a^{r+1}}{b - a} \qquad \text{for } r > -1. \tag{A.3}$$

Its mean and variance are

$$\mu_1 = \frac{1}{2}(a + b), \qquad \text{Var}(X) = \frac{1}{12}(b - a)^2. \tag{A.4}$$

A key property of the uniform distribution is given by the following 'inversion' theorem.

Theorem A.1 *Let F denote a strictly increasing (invertible) distribution function. If $X \sim U(0,1)$ and $Y = F^{-1}(X)$, then Y has distribution function F.*

Proof $\Pr[Y \leq a] = \Pr[F^{-1}(X) \leq a] = \Pr[X \leq F(a)] = F(a)$. $\qquad\qquad\square$

Remark: Theorem A.1 is very useful to construct random number generators for arbitrary (univariate) probability distributions: given a random uniform number u between 0 and 1, $F^{-1}(u)$ is a realization of the random variable distributed as F. When the analytical expression of $F^{-1}(.)$ is not known, a numerical solution of the equation $F^{-1}(u) = y$ is needed. For most distributions, however, there exist faster algorithms, all of which use a uniform random number generator (see Appendix B for details). Theorem A.1 can be extended to the case where F is constant on non-zero measure subsets of $\mathbb{R}$.

A.1.2 *The Gamma, Chi-squared, and Beta Distributions*

A.1.2.1 *The Gamma Function*
The gamma function is defined by the following integral identity:

$$\Gamma(\alpha) = \int_0^\infty x^{\alpha-1} \exp(-x)dx \qquad \text{for } x > 0. \tag{A.5}$$

Integration by parts produces the gamma recursion

$$\Gamma(\alpha) = (\alpha - 1)\Gamma(\alpha - 1) \qquad \text{for } \alpha > 1, \tag{A.6}$$

whence for $\alpha = n$, a strictly positive integer, $\Gamma(\alpha) = (n - 1)!$. As we mostly use integer or half-integer values of α, the following values are useful in conjunction with (A.6):

$$\Gamma(1) = 1, \qquad \Gamma(1/2) = \sqrt{\pi}. \tag{A.7}$$

A proof of the latter result proceeds as follows. Following (A.5) we find that

$$[\Gamma(1/2)]^2 = \int_0^\infty \int_0^\infty (x_1 x_2)^{-1/2} \exp(-x_1 - x_2)dx_1 dx_2.$$

The transformation $x_1 = z \sin^2 \theta$ and $x_2 = z \cos^2 \theta$ is one to one for $x_i > 0$ and leads to the following expression:

$$[\Gamma(1/2)]^2 = 2 \int_0^{\frac{\pi}{2}} \left[\int_0^\infty \exp(-z)dz \right] d\theta = \pi.$$

A.1.2.2 *The Gamma Distribution*
A random variable $X > 0$ has a gamma distribution with parameters $\alpha > 0$ and $\beta > 0$, i.e. $X \sim G(\alpha, \beta)$, if its density function is given by

$$f_g(x|\alpha, \beta) = C_g^{-1}(\alpha, \beta)x^{\alpha-1} \exp(-x/\beta), \tag{A.8}$$

where

$$C_g(\alpha, \beta) = \Gamma(\alpha)\beta^\alpha. \tag{A.9}$$

Clearly, if $X \sim G(\alpha, \beta)$ and $Y = X/\beta$, then $Y \sim G(\alpha, 1)$. Many useful properties of the gamma distribution follow from such a standardization, combined with the definition of the gamma function in eqn (A.5). In particular, the moments of X are given by

$$\mu_r = \frac{C_g(\alpha + r, \beta)}{C_g(\alpha, \beta)} = \beta^r \frac{C_g(\alpha + r, 1)}{C_g(\alpha, 1)} = \beta^r \frac{\Gamma(\alpha + r)}{\Gamma(\alpha)} \quad \text{for } \alpha + r > 0. \quad \text{(A.10)}$$

Its mean and variance are

$$\mu_1 = \alpha\beta, \qquad \text{Var}(X) = \alpha\beta^2. \quad \text{(A.11)}$$

The following theorem characterizes the convolution of independent gamma random variables with a common β parameter.

Theorem A.2 *Let $Y_i \sim G(\alpha_i, \beta)$ for $i : 1 \to n$ and Y_i independent of Y_j for all $i \neq j$. Let $Z = \sum_{i=1}^{n} Y_i$. Then*

$$Z \sim G(\alpha, \beta) \text{ with } \alpha = \sum_{i=1}^{n} \alpha_i. \quad \text{(A.12)}$$

Proof The proof proceeds by recursion on n. The proof for $n = 2$ is found in Theorem A.3 below. $\qquad\qquad\square$

A number of important distributions are derived from the gamma distribution by means of simple transformations and/or reparameterizations, among which are the chi-squared (χ^2), the gamma-1 and 2, the inverted gamma-1 and 2 distributions.

A.1.2.3 *The Chi-squared Distribution* The chi-squared distribution with ν degrees of freedom is obtained by a mere reparameterization of a specific gamma distribution, i.e.

$$X \sim \chi^2(\nu) \iff X \sim G\left(\frac{\nu}{2}, 2\right) \qquad \text{for } \nu > 0. \quad \text{(A.13)}$$

Following eqn (A.11), its mean and variance are given by

$$E(X) = \nu, \qquad \text{Var}(X) = 2\nu. \quad \text{(A.14)}$$

Theorem A.6 below provides an important characterization of the chi-squared distribution in terms of the standardized normal distribution.

A.1.2.4 *The Gamma-2 and Gamma-1 Distributions* The gamma-2 and gamma-1 distributions are defined as follows:

$$X \sim G_2(\nu, s) \iff Y = \sqrt{x} \sim G_1(\nu, s) \iff X \sim G\left(\frac{\nu}{2}, \frac{2}{s}\right) \quad \text{(A.15)}$$

for $s > 0$ and $\nu > 0$. Their respective means and variances follow from formula (A.10) and are given by

$$E(X) = \frac{\nu}{s}, \qquad \text{Var}(X) = \frac{2\nu}{s^2}, \qquad\qquad (A.16)$$

$$E(Y) = \sqrt{\frac{2}{s}} \frac{\Gamma(\frac{\nu+1}{2})}{\Gamma(\frac{\nu}{2})}, \qquad \text{Var}(Y) = \frac{\nu}{s} - [E(Y)]^2. \qquad (A.17)$$

A.1.2.5 *The Inverted Gamma-2 and Gamma-1 Distributions*   We define the inverted gamma-2 and gamma-1 distributions as follows:

$$X \sim IG_2(s,\nu) \iff Y = \sqrt{X} \sim IG_1(s,\nu) \iff Z = X^{-1} \sim G\left(\frac{\nu}{2},\frac{2}{s}\right), \quad (A.18)$$

for $\nu > 0$ and $s > 0$. Their respective means and variances are given by

$$E(X) = \frac{s}{\nu-2} \text{ for } \nu > 2, \quad \text{Var}(X) = \frac{2}{\nu-4}[E(X)]^2 \text{ for } \nu > 4, \qquad (A.19)$$

$$E(Y) = \sqrt{\frac{s}{2}} \frac{\Gamma(\frac{\nu-1}{2})}{\Gamma(\frac{\nu}{2})} \text{ for } \nu > 1, \quad \text{Var}(Y) = \frac{s}{\nu-2} - [E(Y)]^2 \text{ for } \nu > 2. \quad (A.20)$$

The inverted gamma-2 distribution is extensively used in connection with residual variances. For ease of reference, we reproduce here the density of a random variable $\sigma^2 > 0 \sim IG_2(s,\nu)$, as it follows from (A.8) and (A.9):

$$f_{Ig}(\sigma^2|\nu,s) = C_g^{-1}\left(\frac{\nu}{2},\frac{2}{s}\right)(\sigma^2)^{-\frac{1}{2}(\nu+2)} \exp\left(-\frac{s}{2\sigma^2}\right). \qquad (A.21)$$

A.1.2.6 *The Beta Distribution*   A random variable $0 < X < 1$ has a beta distribution with parameters $\alpha > 0$ and $\beta > 0$, i.e. $X \sim B(\alpha,\beta)$, if its density function is given by

$$f_b(x|\alpha,\beta) = C_b^{-1}(\alpha,\beta)x^{\alpha-1}(1-x)^{\beta-1}, \qquad (A.22)$$

with

$$C_b(\alpha,\beta) = \frac{\Gamma(\alpha)\Gamma(\beta)}{\Gamma(\alpha+\beta)}. \qquad (A.23)$$

Its moments are given by

$$\mu_r = \frac{C_b(\alpha+r,\beta)}{C_b(\alpha,\beta)} = \frac{\Gamma(\alpha+r)\Gamma(\alpha+\beta)}{\Gamma(\alpha)\Gamma(\alpha+\beta+r)} \text{ for } \alpha+r > 0. \qquad (A.24)$$

The following theorem provides an important characterization of the beta distribution and may serve, in particular, to construct a random number generator for beta distributions.

Theorem A.3 *Let Y_1 and Y_2 be independent gamma random variables: $Y_1 \sim G(\alpha,1)$ and $Y_2 \sim G(\beta,1)$. Let $Y = Y_1 + Y_2$ and $Z = Y_1/Y$. Then Y and Z are independent with $Y \sim G(\alpha+\beta,1)$ and $Z \sim B(\alpha,\beta)$.*

Proof The proof follows immediately from the expressions of the relevant densities as given in eqns (A.8) and (A.22). Note that the Jacobian of the transformation equals Y and, furthermore, that

$$C_b(\alpha, \beta) = \frac{C_g(\alpha, 1)C_g(\beta, 1)}{C_g(\alpha + \beta, 1)}.$$

□

A.1.3 *The Univariate Normal Distribution*

A random variable $X \in \mathbb{R}$ has a normal distribution with parameters μ and $\sigma^2 > 0$ (actually its mean and variance), i.e. $X \sim N(\mu, \sigma^2)$, if its density function is given by

$$f_N(x|\mu, \sigma^2) = C_N^{-1}(\sigma^2; 1) \exp\left[-\frac{1}{2\sigma^2}(x - \mu)^2\right], \qquad (A.25)$$

with

$$C_N(\sigma^2; 1) = \sigma\sqrt{2\pi} = \sigma\sqrt{2}\,\Gamma(1/2). \qquad (A.26)$$

The second argument of $C_N(.;.)$ is the dimension of X and is introduced for consistency of notation with the multivariate case, see (A.45).

A key property of the normal distribution is closeness with respect to linear transformations.

Theorem A.4 *If $X \sim N(\mu, \sigma^2)$ and $Y = aX + b$ with $a \neq 0$, then $Y \sim N(a\mu + b, a^2\sigma^2)$.*

Proof Replace x by $(y - b)/a$ in eqn (A.25) and account for the fact that the Jacobian is equal to $1/a$. □

An important practical implication of Theorem A.4, which extends to the multivariate case, is that as long as we restrict our attention to linear transformations of normal random variables, we have only to evaluate the first- and second-order moments since they fully characterize the underlying density function. The following corollary is important for random number generation as well as for deriving most properties of the normal distribution.

Corollary A.5 *If $Y \sim N(0, 1)$ and $X = \mu + \sigma Y$, then $X \sim N(\mu, \sigma^2)$.*

Furthermore, if $Y \sim N(0, 1)$, then the densities of $Y^2|Y \geq 0$, $Y^2|Y \leq 0$, and Y^2 all are $\chi^2(1)$. It follows that $C_N(1; 1) = C_g(\frac{1}{2}, 2) = \sqrt{2\pi}$, which validates eqn (A.26). Also,

$$E(Y^r|Y \geq 0) = (-1)^r E(Y^r|Y \leq 0) = 2^{\frac{r}{2}}\frac{\Gamma(\frac{r+1}{2})}{\Gamma(\frac{1}{2})}, \qquad (A.27)$$

whence, for integer k,

$$E(Y^{2k}) = 2^k\frac{\Gamma(k + \frac{1}{2})}{\Gamma(\frac{1}{2})}, \qquad E(Y^{2k+1}) = 0. \qquad (A.28)$$

The integer moments of X follow from Corollary A.1 together with the binomial expansion of $(\mu + \sigma y)^r$. In particular,

$$E(X) = \mu, \qquad \text{Var}(X) = \sigma^2, \qquad (A.29)$$

as stated above.

Theorem A.6 *If $Y_i \sim N(0,1)$ for $i : 1 \to n$ and Y_i independent of Y_j for all $i \neq j$, then*

$$Z = \sum_{i=1}^{n} Y_1^2 \sim \chi^2(n). \qquad (A.30)$$

Proof The proof is immediate for $n = 1$ (and has already been exploited above). The general result follows from Theorem A.2 together with formula (A.13).

$\square$

A.1.4 *Distributions Related to the Univariate Normal Distribution*

A.1.4.1 *The Univariate Student Distribution* A random variable $X \in \mathbb{R}$ has a Student (or t) distribution with parameters $\nu > 0$ (degrees of freedom) and $s > 0$ (scale factor), i.e. $X \sim t(\mu, s, m, \nu)$, if its density function is given by

$$f_t(x|\mu, s, m, \nu) = C_t^{-1}(s, m, \nu; 1)[s + m(x - \mu)^2]^{-\frac{1}{2}(\nu+1)}, \qquad (A.31)$$

with

$$C_t(s, m, \nu; 1) = C_b\left(\frac{1}{2}, \frac{\nu}{2}\right) s^{-\frac{1}{2}\nu} = \frac{\Gamma(\frac{\nu}{2})}{\Gamma(\frac{\nu+1}{2})} \pi^{1/2} s^{-\frac{1}{2}\nu} m^{-1/2}. \qquad (A.32)$$

Its (mean centred) moments are given by

$$E[(X - \mu)^{2k}] = \left(\frac{s}{m}\right)^k \frac{\Gamma(k + \frac{1}{2})\Gamma(\frac{\nu}{2} - k)}{\Gamma(\frac{1}{2})\Gamma(\frac{\nu}{2})} \qquad \text{for } \nu > 2k, \qquad (A.33)$$

$$E[(X - \mu)^{2k+1}] = 0 \qquad \text{for } \nu > 2k + 1. \qquad (A.34)$$

Its mean and variance are

$$E(X) = \mu \quad \text{for } \nu > 1, \qquad \text{Var}(X) = \frac{s}{\nu - 2} m^{-1} \quad \text{for } \nu > 2. \qquad (A.35)$$

The above parameterization is redundant as the density depends only on the ratio m/s. The usual normalizations are obtained either with $s = 1$ or $m = 1$. The standardized form of the distribution corresponds to $\mu = 0$, $s = \nu$, and $m = 1$.

Most properties of the (univariate) Student-t distribution follow from the following Bayesian and classical characterizations.

Theorem A.7 *(i) (Bayesian) If $X|\sigma^2 \sim N(\mu, \sigma^2)$ and $\sigma^2 \sim IG_2(s, \nu)$, then $X \sim t(\mu, s, 1, \nu)$.*

(ii) (Classical) If $X \sim N(\mu, \sigma^2)$, $Y/\sigma^2 \sim \chi^2(\nu)$, X is independent of Y, and $Z = \mu + \sqrt{s/Y}(X - \mu)$, then $Z \sim t(\mu, s, 1, \nu)$.

Proof (i) We multiply together the density functions of $X|\sigma^2$ and σ^2 as given in eqns (A.25) and (A.21) respectively. Integration w.r.t. σ^2 produces the following integral:

$$f(x) = \frac{1}{\sqrt{2\pi}} C_g^{-1} \left(\frac{\nu}{2}, \frac{2}{s} \right) \int_0^\infty (\sigma^2)^{-\frac{1}{2}(\nu+3)} \exp \left\{ -\frac{1}{2\sigma^2}[s + (x - \mu)^2] \right\} dx$$

$$= \frac{1}{\sqrt{2\pi}} C_g^{-1} \left(\frac{\nu}{2}, \frac{2}{s} \right) C_g \left(\frac{\nu+1}{2}, \frac{2}{s + (x - \mu)^2} \right).$$

whence (A.31) follows by using (A.21).

(ii) Consider the one-to-one bivariate transformation $W = \dfrac{1}{s} \cdot \dfrac{Y}{\sigma^2}$ and $Z = \mu + \sqrt{s/Y}(X - \mu)$ whose Jacobian is given by $s\sigma\sqrt{W}$. The joint density of (W, Z) is given by

$$f(w, z) = \frac{1}{\sqrt{2\pi}} C_g^{-1} \left(\frac{\nu}{2}, 2 \right) s^{\frac{1}{2}\nu} w^{\frac{1}{2}(\nu-1)} \exp \left\{ -\frac{1}{2} w[s + (z - \mu)^2] \right\}.$$

Integration with respect to W which has a $G \left(\dfrac{\nu+1}{2}, \dfrac{2}{s + (z - \mu)^2} \right)$ distribution produces the result.

□

Remarks:

1) The classical 't-test' statistic is standardized and is given by $T = \sqrt{\nu/Y}(X - \mu) = \sqrt{\nu/s}(Z - \mu)$. This corresponds to $\mu = 0$ and $s = \nu$ in part (ii) of Theorem A.7, which shows that the standardized Student variable with ν degrees of freedom is the ratio of a standard normal variable and the square root of an independent $\chi^2(\nu)/\nu$ variable.

2) The expressions of the moments on eqn (A.33) follow from the moment identity $E[(X - \mu)^r] = E_{\sigma^2}\{E_{X|\sigma^2}[(X - \mu)^r]\}$.

A.1.4.2 *The Hotelling and F-distributions*   A random variable $X > 0$ has a Hotelling distribution with parameters $\nu_1 > 0$ and $\nu_2 > 0$, i.e. $X \sim H(\nu_1, \nu_2)$, if its density function is given by

$$f_H(x|\nu_1, \nu_2) = C_b^{-1} \left(\frac{\nu_1}{2}, \frac{\nu_2}{2} \right) x^{\frac{1}{2}\nu_1 - 1} (1 + x)^{-\frac{1}{2}(\nu_1 + \nu_2)}. \tag{A.36}$$

The rescaled random variable $Y = \nu_2 X / \nu_1$ then has an F-distribution with degrees of freedom ν_1 and ν_2, i.e. $Y \sim F(\nu_1, \nu_2)$, and its density function is

$$f_F(y|\nu_1, \nu_2) = C_b^{-1} \left(\frac{\nu_1}{2}, \frac{\nu_2}{2} \right) \left(\frac{\nu_1}{\nu_2} \right)^{\frac{1}{2}\nu_1} y^{\frac{1}{2}\nu_1 - 1} \left(1 + \frac{\nu_1}{\nu_2} y \right)^{-\frac{1}{2}(\nu_1 + \nu_2)}. \tag{A.37}$$

The moments of X are given by

$$\mu_r = \frac{C_b(\frac{\nu_1}{2} + r, \frac{\nu_2}{2} - r)}{C_b(\frac{\nu_1}{2}, \frac{\nu_2}{2})} = \frac{\Gamma(\frac{\nu_1}{2} + r)\Gamma(\frac{\nu_2}{2} - r)}{\Gamma(\frac{\nu_1}{2})\Gamma(\frac{\nu_2}{2})}, \tag{A.38}$$

for $\nu_1 + 2r > 0$ and $\nu_2 - 2r > 0$. Its mean and variance are

$$\mu_1 = \frac{\nu_1}{\nu_2 - 2} \text{ for } \nu_2 > 2, \quad \text{Var}(X) = \frac{2\nu_1(\nu_1 + \nu_2 - 2)}{(\nu_2 - 2)^2(\nu_2 - 4)} \text{ for } \nu_2 > 4. \tag{A.39}$$

The moments of Y are

$$\text{E}(Y^r) = \left(\frac{\nu_2}{\nu_1} \right)^r \mu_r. \tag{A.40}$$

Theorem A.8   *(i) If $X \sim B(\frac{1}{2}\nu_1, \frac{1}{2}\nu_2)$, then $Y = X/(1 - X) \sim H(\nu_1, \nu_2)$.*
(ii) If $X \sim t(\mu, s, 1, \nu)$, then $Y = (X - \mu)^2/s \sim H(1, \nu)$.

Proof   The proof follows from the expression of the relevant density function, accounting for the relevant Jacobians which are $(1 - Y)^{-2}$ for (i) and $\frac{1}{2}\sqrt{s/Y}$ for (ii). Note that for (ii), the density function of X is symmetrical around μ and, furthermore, $Y > 0$ has two reciprocal images which are $\mu - s\sqrt{Y}$ and $\mu + s\sqrt{Y}$, so that the density of Y equals twice that of X constrained on $[\mu, \infty[$, times the appropriate Jacobian. $\square$

Remark: The chi-squared, Hotelling, and F-distributions we have defined are 'central' versions of more general families of distributions (of the same names). Central distributions are obtained by appropriate transformations of 'standardized' normal random variables (see Theorem A.7). Similar transformations of non-standardized normal random variables generate 'non-central' distributions. The latter are commonly used in classical statistics to evaluate the power functions of a broad range of test statistics. They are used far less frequently in Bayesian analysis, a context in which they would be reinterpreted as infinite mixtures of the corresponding central distributions. See Johnson, Kotz, and Balakrishnan (1994, 1995) for definitions and details.

A.2 Multivariate Distributions

A.2.1 *Preliminary: Choleski Decomposition*

Many key properties of multivariate distributions can be derived by means of linear transformations designed for (block) diagonalizing a positive definite symmetric (PDS) matrix of moments (means or covariances depending upon the distribution under consideration). In addition, transformations that can be written in fully recursive forms can be used efficiently to derive many results by recursion on the size of the random variables in question. The Choleski decomposition is exceptionally efficient on that account. For ease of reference let

$$C_n = \{\Sigma \mid \Sigma \text{ is } n \times n \text{ and PDS}\}. \tag{A.41}$$

Theorem A.9 *Let $\Sigma \in C_n$. There exists a (unique) lower triangular matrix L such that $\Sigma = LL'$. The condition $l_{ii} > 0$ for $i = 1, 2, \ldots, n$ is necessary and sufficient for the positivity of Σ.*

Proof The proof proceeds by recursion on n. Σ and L are partitioned conformably with each other. The Choleski decomposition of Σ is based on the following equation(s):

$$\begin{pmatrix} \Sigma_{11} & \Sigma_{12} \\ \Sigma_{21} & \Sigma_{22} \end{pmatrix} = \begin{pmatrix} L_{11} & 0 \\ L_{21} & L_{22} \end{pmatrix} \begin{pmatrix} L'_{11} & L'_{21} \\ 0 & L'_{22} \end{pmatrix} \tag{A.42}$$

or, equivalently,

$$\Sigma_{11} = L_{11} L'_{11} \in C_{n_1}, \qquad \Sigma_{21} = L_{21} L'_{11},$$

$$\Sigma_{22.1} = \Sigma_{22} - \Sigma_{21} \Sigma_{11}^{-1} \Sigma_{12} = L_{22} L'_{22} \in C_{n_2}. \tag{A.43}$$

The existence of L_{11} and L_{22} follows from the recursion on n and

$$L_{21} = \Sigma_{21} (L'_{11})^{-1},$$

since L_{11} is PDS. $\qquad \square$

Remarks:

1) The Choleski decomposition can be made fully recursive by starting from the upper left element of Σ and adding one dimension at a time (see Subsection A.2.2 for an important illustration of that principle). Clearly its unicity is relative to a specific ordering of the rows (and columns) of Σ. Conformable permutations of the rows and columns of Σ produce different factorizations.

2) Other decompositions of Σ are available such as the eigenroots–eigenvectors decomposition and are of interest in a variety of situations (e.g. to analyse the geometry of specific distributions or to isolate orthogonal directions of maximum variances). They are neither as operational nor as efficient as the Choleski decomposition for our purpose.

A.2.2   *The Multivariate Normal Distribution*

A random vector $X \in \mathbb{R}^p$ has a multivariate normal distribution with parameter $\mu \in \mathbb{R}^p$ and $\Sigma \in C_p$, i.e. $X \sim N_p(\mu, \Sigma)$, if its density function is given by

$$f_N^p(x|\mu, \Sigma) = C_N^{-1}(\Sigma; p) . \exp\left[-\frac{1}{2}(x - \mu)'\Sigma^{-1}(x - \mu)\right], \qquad (A.44)$$

with

$$C_N(\Sigma; p) = (2\pi)^{\frac{1}{2}p} |\Sigma|^{\frac{1}{2}}. \qquad (A.45)$$

As shown below, its mean vector and covariance matrix are given by μ and Σ respectively:

$$E(X) = \mu, \qquad \text{Var}(X) = \Sigma. \qquad (A.46)$$

Many important properties of the multivariate normal distribution follow from its following two key attributes: (i) it is stable under (non-singular) linear transformations, and (ii) independence in probability and linear independence are equivalent under (joint) normality.

Theorem A.10 *If $X \sim N_p(\mu, \Sigma)$ and $Y = AX + b$, when A is a square non-singular matrix of order p and $b \in \mathbb{R}^p$, then*

$$Y \sim N_p(A\mu + b, A\Sigma A'). \qquad (A.47)$$

Proof   (i) The quadratic form in formula (A.44) can be rewritten as

$$(x - \mu)'\Sigma^{-1}(x - \mu) = [A^{-1}(y - b) - \mu]'\Sigma^{-1}[A^{-1}(y - b) - \mu]$$
$$= [y - (A\mu + b)]'(A\Sigma A')^{-1}[y - (A\mu + b)].$$

(ii) The Jacobian of the transformation is given by $|A|^{-1}$ and $|A|.|\Sigma|^{-\frac{1}{2}} = |A\Sigma A'|^{\frac{1}{2}}$. $\square$

In the sequel of the discussion $X, \mu,$ and Σ are partitioned conformably with each other into

$$X = \begin{pmatrix} X_1, \\ X_2 \end{pmatrix} \quad \mu = \begin{pmatrix} \mu_1 \\ \mu_2 \end{pmatrix} \quad \Sigma = \begin{pmatrix} \Sigma_{11} & \Sigma_{12} \\ \Sigma_{21} & \Sigma_{22} \end{pmatrix}, \qquad (A.48)$$

where $X_i \in \mathbb{R}^{p_i} (p_1 + p_2 = p)$.

Theorem A.11 *Let $X \sim N_p(\mu, \Sigma)$ be partitioned according to (A.48). X_1 and X_2 are independent in probability if and only if they are linearly independent (i.e. $\Sigma_{12} = 0$).*

Proof If $\Sigma_{12} = 0$, then

(i) $|\Sigma| = |\Sigma_{11}|.|\Sigma_{22}|$ to the effect that $C_N(\Sigma, p) = \prod_{i=1}^{2} C_N(\Sigma_{ii}, p_i)$, and

(ii) $(x - \mu)'\Sigma^{-1}(x - \mu) = \Sigma_{i=1}^{2}(x_i - \mu_i)'\Sigma_{ii}^{-1}(x_i - \mu_i).$

It follows that $f(x)$, as given in formula (A.44), factorizes into the product of two marginal densities for X_1 and X_2 respectively. Conversely, the product of two (independent) marginal normal densities for X_1 and X_2 can be rewritten in the form of a joint normal density with $\Sigma_{12} = 0$. □

Important properties of the normal distribution immediately follow from Theorems A.10 and A.11.

Theorem A.12 *If $X \sim N_p(\mu, \Sigma)$, then*

$$X_1 \sim N_{p_1}(\mu_1, \Sigma_{11}), \tag{A.49}$$

$$X_2|X_1 \sim N_{p_2}(\mu_{2.1} + \Delta_{21}X_1, \Sigma_{22.1}), \tag{A.50}$$

with

$$\Delta_{21} = \Sigma_{21}\Sigma_{11}^{-1}, \; \mu_{2.1} = \mu_2 - \Delta_{21}\mu_1, \; \Sigma_{22.1} = \Sigma_{22} - \Sigma_{21}\Sigma_{11}^{-1}\Sigma_{12}, \tag{A.51}$$

and

$$((\mu_1, \Sigma_{11}), (\mu_{2.1}, \Delta_{21}, \Sigma_{22.1})) \in (\mathbb{R}^{p_1} \times C_{p_1}) \times (\mathbb{R}^{p_2} \times \mathbb{R}^{p_2 \times p_1} \times C_{p_2}). \tag{A.52}$$

Proof Consider the linear transformation $Y = AX$ with

$$A = \begin{pmatrix} I_{p_1} & 0 \\ -\Delta_{21} & I_{p_2} \end{pmatrix}.$$

It follows from Theorem A.10 that $Y \sim N_p(A\mu, A\Sigma A')$ with

$$A\mu = \begin{pmatrix} \mu_1 \\ \mu_{2.1} \end{pmatrix} \quad \text{and} \quad A\Sigma A' = \begin{pmatrix} \Sigma_{11} & 0 \\ 0 & \Sigma_{22.1} \end{pmatrix},$$

whence, by application of Theorem A.11,

$$Y_1 \equiv X_1 \sim N_{p_1}(\mu_1, \Sigma_{11}),$$

$$Y_2 \equiv Y_2|Y_1 \equiv Y_2|X_1 \sim N_{p_2}(\mu_{2.1}, \Sigma_{22.1}).$$

Formula (A.50) follows from the inverse transformation $X_2 = Y_2 + \Delta_{21}X_1$ which, conditionally on X_1, is linear in Y_2. Finally, the non-singularity of A implies that the condition $\Sigma \in C_p$ is equivalent to the conditions $\Sigma_{ii} \in C_{p_i}$ for $i = 1, 2$, independently of the value of Σ_{21} in $\mathbb{R}^{p_2 \times p_1}$. Also the transformation from μ to $(\mu_1, \mu_{2.1})$ is one to one for any given Σ in C_p. □

The conditional distribution of $X_2|X_1$, as given in formula (A.50), has two fundamental properties:

(i) its regression function is linear in X_1 and, therefore, coincides with the least squares approximation of X_2 by X_1;

(ii) its conditional covariance matrix $\Sigma_{22.1}$ is constant with respect to X_1 (homoscedasticity).

The following theorem links together the factorization of the multivariate normal distribution and the Choleski decomposition of its covariance matrix, as given in Theorems A.12 and A.9 respectively.

Theorem A.13 *If (i) $Y \sim N_p(0, I_k)$; (ii) L is the lower triangular matrix associated with the Choleski decomposition of $\Sigma \in C_p$; and (iii) $X = \mu + LY$, then*

$$(i) X \sim N_p(\mu, \Sigma), \text{ with } \Sigma = LL'; \tag{A.53}$$

$$(ii) X_1 \sim N_{p_1}(\mu_1, \Sigma_{11}), \text{ with } \Sigma_{11} = L_{11} L'_{11}; \tag{A.54}$$

$$(iii) X_2 | X_1 \equiv X_2 | Y_1 \sim N_{p_2}(\mu_2 + L_{21} Y_1, \Sigma_{22.1}) \text{ with } \Sigma_{22.1} = L_{22} L'_{22}. \tag{A.55}$$

Proof This follows from Theorems A.9 and A.12. □

Theorem A.13 leads to an efficient algorithm for the random generation of an arbitrary multivariate normal distribution by transformation of p independent random draws of a univariate standardized normal distribution. The recursive application of formulae (A.54) and (A.55) produces a complete factorization of a multivariate normal distribution into a conformable sequence of univariate marginal and conditional normal distributions.

Remark: Theorem A.13 provides a direct validation of formulae (A.45) and (A.46). The Jacobian of the transformation $X = \mu + LY$ is given by $|L|^{-1} = |\Sigma|^{-\frac{1}{2}}$, whence $C_N^{-1}(\Sigma, p) = |\Sigma|^{-\frac{1}{2}} . [C_N^{-1}(1)]^p$. We also have

$$\mathrm{E}_X(X) = \mathrm{E}_Y(\mu + LY) = \mu \text{ and } \mathrm{Var}_X(X) = \mathrm{Var}_Y(\mu + LY) = LL' = \Sigma.$$

Theorem A.12 admits a reciprocal which, for ease of reference, is formulated under its own set of notation.

Theorem A.14 *Let*

$$X \sim N_p(m, V), \tag{A.56}$$

$$Y | X \sim N_q(a + BX, \Omega), \tag{A.57}$$

where all vectors and matrices are dimensioned conformably with X and Y. Then

$$\begin{pmatrix} X \\ Y \end{pmatrix} \sim N_{p+q}(\mu, \Sigma), \tag{A.58}$$

with

$$\mu = \begin{pmatrix} m \\ a + Bm \end{pmatrix}, \quad \Sigma = \begin{pmatrix} V & VB' \\ BV & \Omega + BVB' \end{pmatrix}. \tag{A.59}$$

Proof We successively have

$$E_Y(Y) = E_X(a + BX) = a + Bm,$$
$$\text{Var}_Y(Y) = E_X(\Omega) + \text{Var}_X(a + BX) = \Omega + BVB',$$
$$\text{Cov}(X, Y) = \text{Cov}_X(X, BX) = VB'.$$

Normality follows from the fact that the joint distribution in (A.58) actually coincides with the product of the marginal distribution of X and the conditional distribution of $Y|X$, as given in formulae (A.56) and (A.57) respectively. □

A.2.3 *The Matricvariate Normal Distribution*

Let X and vec X denote a $p \times q$ random matrix and its pq-dimensional column expansion respectively.[4] X is said to have a matricvariate normal distribution with parameters $M \in \mathbb{R}^{p \times q}, P \in C_p$, and $Q \in C_q$, i.e. $X \sim MN_{p \times q}(\text{vec } M, Q \otimes P)$ if and only if vec $X \sim N_{pq}(\text{vec } M, Q \otimes P)$. Therefore, its density function is given by

$$f_{MN}^{p \times q}(X|M, Q \otimes P) = C_{MN}^{-1}(P, Q; p, q) \qquad \text{(A.60)}$$
$$\times \exp\{-\tfrac{1}{2}\text{tr}\,[Q^{-1}(X - M)'P^{-1}(X - M)]\},$$

with

$$C_{MN}(P, Q; p, q) = [(2\pi)^{pq} |P|^q |Q|^p]^{1/2}. \qquad \text{(A.61)}$$

The use of the trace operator in formula (A.60) originates from the following identity:

$$[\text{vec } (X - M)]'(Q \otimes P)^{-1}[\text{vec } (X - M)]$$
$$= \Sigma_{i=1}^q \Sigma_{j=1}^q q^{ij}(x_i - m_i)'P^{-1}(x_j - m_j)$$
$$= \text{tr}\,[Q^{-1}(X - M)'P^{-1}(X - M)],$$

where $(x_i - m_i)$ and q^{ij} denote the ith column of $X - M$ and the (i, j)th element of Q^{-1} respectively.

All the properties of the multivariate normal distribution apply to the matricvariate normal distribution through the vec operator. Naturally, only those partitionings of vec X which preserve the Kronecker product form of the corresponding covariance matrices apply to the matricvariate form of the distribution. In particular, this will be the case with the following partitionings of X:

$$X = (X_1\, X_2) = \begin{pmatrix} X_{(1)} \\ X_{(2)} \end{pmatrix}, \qquad \text{(A.62)}$$

where X_i and $X_{(i)}$ are $p \times q_i$ and $p_i \times q$ respectively ($p_1 + p_2 = p$ and $q_1 + q_2 = q$). The matrices M, P, and Q are partitioned conformably with X. The

---

[4]As usual, once we deal with random matrices, we do not distinguish between random variables and their realizations and use capital letters for both (which is which being determined by the context). A similar problem of notation arises with the column expansion of a random matrix (the column expansion of a $p \times q$ matrix A with columns $a_1, a_2, \ldots, a_q$ is defined as the pq-dimensional vector $(a_1', \ldots, a_q')'$).

following results are immediate matricvariate transpositions of the general results
in Theorem A.12:

$$X_1 \sim MN_{p \times q_1}(M_1, Q_{11} \otimes P), \tag{A.63}$$

$$X_2|X_1 \sim MN_{p \times q_2}(M_{2.1} + X_1 Q_{11}^{-1} Q_{12}, Q_{22.1} \otimes P), \tag{A.64}$$

$$X_{(1)} \sim MN_{p_1 \times q}(M_{(1)}, Q \otimes P_{11}), \tag{A.65}$$

$$X_{(2)}|X_{(1)} \sim MN_{p_2 \times q}(M_{(2.1)} + P_{21} P_{11}^{-1} X_{(1)}, Q \otimes P_{22.1}), \tag{A.66}$$

with

$$M_{2.1} = M_2 - M_1 Q_{11}^{-1} Q_{12} \text{ and } M_{(2.1)} = M_{(2)} - P_{21} P_{11}^{-1} M_{(1)}. \tag{A.67}$$

Bilinear transformations also preserve the Kronecker product form of covariance matrices. Let $X \sim MN_{p \times q}(M, Q \otimes P)$ and $Y = AXB + C$, where $A \in \mathbb{R}^{m \times p}$, rank $A = m \leq p, B \in \mathbb{R}^{q \times n}$, rank $B = n \leq q$, and $C \in \mathbb{R}^{m \times n}$. Then

$$Y \sim MN_{m \times n}(AMB + C, B'QB \otimes APA'). \tag{A.68}$$

Remarks:

1) Formula (A.68) can be obtained by application of the usual inverse transformation technique to formula (A.60). Alternatively we can use the following formula, which is found, for example, in Magnus and Neudecker (1988: 30):

$$\text{vec } (AXB) = (B' \otimes A) \text{ vec } X. \tag{A.69}$$

2) Formulae (A.63) to (A.67) can also be derived from formula (A.68) by selecting for A (or B) expressions that block-diagonalize P (or Q) along the lines of the proof of Theorem A.12.

3) Similar techniques can be applied to block partitions of X into (X_{ij}). See Richard (1973) for examples.

A.2.4 *The Normal–Inverted Gamma-2 Distribution*

The random variables $X \in \mathbb{R}^p$ and $\sigma^2 > 0$ have a joint normal–inverted gamma-2 distribution (often presented in the form of a 'normal–gamma' distribution in X and σ^{-2}) with parameters $\mu \in \mathbb{R}^p, M \in C_p, s > 0$, and $\nu > 0$, i.e. $(X, \sigma^2) \sim NIG(\mu, M, s, \nu)$, if and only if

$$\begin{align} &\text{(i)} \quad X|\sigma^2 \sim N_p(\mu, \sigma^2 M^{-1}), \\ &\text{(ii)} \quad \sigma^2 \sim IG_2(s, \nu). \end{align} \tag{A.70}$$

It follows from eqns (A.21) and (A.44) that the joint density of (X, σ^2) is given by

$$\begin{aligned} f_{NIg}(x, \sigma^2|\mu, M, s, \nu) = {} & C_{Ng}^{-1}(M, s, \nu; p) \\ & \times (\sigma^2)^{-\frac{1}{2}(\nu+p+2)} \exp\{-\tfrac{1}{2\sigma^2}[s + (x - \mu)'M(x - \mu)]\}, \end{aligned} \tag{A.71}$$

with

$$C_{NIg}(M, s, \nu; p) = \Gamma\left(\frac{\nu}{2}\right)\left(\frac{2}{s}\right)^{\frac{1}{2}\nu}(2\pi)^{\frac{1}{2}p}|M|^{-\frac{1}{2}}. \tag{A.72}$$

The first- and second-order moments of X and σ^2 are given by

$$\mathrm{E}(X) = \mathrm{E}_{\sigma^2}[\mathrm{E}_{X|\sigma^2}(X)] = \mu \quad \text{(for } \nu > 1\text{)}, \tag{A.73}$$

$$\mathrm{E}(\sigma^2) = \frac{s}{\nu - 2} \quad \text{(for } \nu > 2\text{)}, \tag{A.74}$$

$$\mathrm{Var}(X) = \mathrm{E}_{\sigma^2}[\mathrm{Var}_{X|\sigma^2}(X)] = \mathrm{E}(\sigma^2)\,M^{-1} \quad \text{(for } \nu > 2\text{)}, \tag{A.75}$$

$$\mathrm{Var}(\sigma^2) = \frac{2}{\nu - 4}[\mathrm{E}(\sigma^2)]^2 \quad \text{(for } \nu > 4\text{)}, \tag{A.76}$$

$$\mathrm{Cov}(X, \sigma^2) = \mathrm{Cov}_{\sigma^2}(\mu, \sigma^2) = 0 \quad \text{(for } \nu > 3\text{)}. \tag{A.77}$$

Note that, although X and σ^2 are clearly not independent of each other in probability, they are linearly independent. Implications of this special form of dependence between X and σ^2 are discussed in Section 4.4 in the context of the regression model.

A.2.5 The Multivariate Student Distribution

Though the (multivariate) Student distribution is a special case of the matric-variate Student distribution, which is discussed in Section A.2.7 below, we choose to discuss it on its own for ease of reference. A random variable $X \in \mathbb{R}^p$ has a multivariate Student distribution with parameters $\mu \in \mathbb{R}^p, P \in C_p$, and $\nu > 0$, i.e. $X \sim t_p(\mu, 1, P, \nu)$, if its density function is given by

$$f_t^p(x|\mu, P, \nu) = C_t^{-1}(P, 1, \nu; p)\,[1 + (x - \mu)'P(x - \mu)]^{-\frac{1}{2}(\nu+p)}, \tag{A.78}$$

with

$$C_t(P, 1, \nu; p) = \left[\Gamma\left(\frac{\nu}{2}\right)/\Gamma\left(\frac{\nu + p}{2}\right)\right]\pi^{\frac{1}{2}p}|P|^{-\frac{1}{2}}. \tag{A.79}$$

Its first- and second-order moments are given by

$$\mathrm{E}(X) = \mu \text{ (for } \nu > 1\text{)}, \qquad \mathrm{Var}(X) = \frac{1}{\nu - 2}P^{-1} \text{ (for } \nu > 2\text{)}. \tag{A.80}$$

Another parameterization of the Student distribution uses an extra scalar parameter and is given by

$$f_t^p(x|\mu, s, M, \nu) = C_t^{-1}(M, s, \nu; p)\,[s + (x - \mu)'M(x - \mu)]^{-\frac{1}{2}(\nu+p)}, \tag{A.81}$$

with

$$C_t(M, s, \nu; p) = \left[\Gamma\left(\frac{\nu}{2}\right)/\Gamma\left(\frac{\nu + p}{2}\right)\right]\pi^{\frac{1}{2}p}|M|^{-\frac{1}{2}}s^{-\nu/2}. \tag{A.82}$$

This is denoted briefly as $t_p(\mu, s, M, \nu)$. The two parameterizations are linked by $P = M/s$. The standardized form of the density corresponds to $\mu = 0, P = I_p/\nu$ in (A.78), and to $M = I_p$ with $s = \nu$ in (A.81).

Many important properties of the multivariate Student distribution can be derived from the following theorem.

Theorem A.15 *If*

$$X|\sigma^2 \sim N_p(\mu, \sigma^2 M^{-1}), \tag{A.83}$$

$$\sigma^2 \sim IG_2(s, \nu), \tag{A.84}$$

then

$$X \sim t_p(\mu, s, M, \nu), \tag{A.85}$$

$$\sigma^2|X \sim IG_2(s + (X - \mu)'M(X - \mu), \nu + p). \tag{A.86}$$

Proof We first have to integrate the joint density in formula (A.71) with respect to σ^2, given X. As we recognize a density kernel of an IG_2 distribution we find that

$$f(x|.) = C_{Ng}^{-1}(M, s, \nu; p) \, C_g(\nu + p, s + (x - \mu)'M(x - \mu)),$$

whence eqns (A.85) and (A.86) follow immediately. $\square$

The above theorem shows where the reparameterization with M and s comes from. Although s seems a redundant parameter, it arises naturally in the Bayesian analysis of the regression model.

Marginal and conditional distributions associated with the Student density as defined in eqn (A.78) are easily obtained by application of Theorem A.15.

Theorem A.16 *If*

$$X|\sigma^2 \sim N_p(\mu, \sigma^2 M^{-1}), \tag{A.87}$$

$$\sigma^2 \sim IG_2(s, \nu), \tag{A.88}$$

then

$$X_1 \sim t_{p_1}(\mu_1, s, M_{11.2}, \nu), \tag{A.89}$$

$$\sigma^2|X_1 \sim IG_2(s + (X_1 - \mu_1)'M_{11.2}(X_1 - \mu_1), \nu + p_1), \tag{A.90}$$

$$X_2|X_1 \sim t_{p_2}(\mu_2 - M_{22}^{-1}M_{21}(X_1 - \mu_1), q_2(X_1), M_{22}, \nu + p_1), \tag{A.91}$$

where

$$M_{11.2} = M_{11} - M_{12}M_{22}^{-1}M_{21}, \tag{A.92}$$

$$q_2(X_1) = s + (X_1 - \mu_1)'M_{11.2}(X_1 - \mu_1). \tag{A.93}$$

Proof Following formula (A.49) we have

$$X_1|\sigma^2 \sim N_{p_1}(\mu_1, \sigma^2 M_{11.2}^{-1}). \tag{A.94}$$

Formulae (A.89) and (A.90) follow by application of Theorem A.15. Next we apply formula (A.50), together with the matrix identity $M^{21}(M^{11})^{-1} = -M_{22}^{-1}M_{21}$, to obtain

$$X_2|X_1, \sigma^2 \sim N_{p_2}(\mu_2 - M_{22}^{-1}M_{21}(X_1 - \mu_1), \sigma^2 M_{22}^{-1}). \tag{A.95}$$

Formula (A.91) follows by application of Theorem A.15 to formulae (A.90) and (A.95). $\square$

A.2.6 *The Inverted Wishart Distribution*

A random matrix $\Sigma \in C_q$ has an inverted Wishart distribution with parameters $S \in C_q$ and $\nu > q - 1$, i.e. $\Sigma \sim IW_q(S, \nu)$, if its density function is given by

$$f_{IW}^q(\Sigma | S, \nu) = C_{IW}^{-1}(S, \nu; q) |\Sigma|^{-\frac{1}{2}(\nu+q+1)} \exp\left[-\frac{1}{2}\mathrm{tr}\,(\Sigma^{-1}S)\right], \qquad (A.96)$$

with

$$C_{IW}(S, \nu; q) = 2^{\frac{1}{2}\nu q} \pi^{\frac{1}{4}q(q-1)} \prod_{i=1}^{p} \Gamma\left(\frac{\nu+1-i}{2}\right) |S|^{-\frac{1}{2}\nu}. \qquad (A.97)$$

Recursion on the dimension q constitutes the key device for deriving many important properties of the inverted Wishart distribution, including the validation of its integrating constant. Assume for the moment that the expression of $C_{IW}(.)$, as given in formula (A.97) is correct. Let us partition Σ and S conformably with each other

$$\Sigma = \begin{pmatrix} \Sigma_{11} & \Sigma_{12} \\ \Sigma_{21} & \Sigma_{22} \end{pmatrix}, \qquad S = \begin{pmatrix} S_{11} & S_{12} \\ S_{21} & S_{22} \end{pmatrix}, \qquad (A.98)$$

where Σ_{ij} and S_{ij} are $q_i \times q_j$ matrices ($q_1 + q_2 = q$). The following theorem constitutes the cornerstone of a recursive analysis of the inverted Wishart density.

Theorem A.17 *If $\Sigma \sim IW_q(S, \nu)$, then*

$$\Sigma_{11} \text{ is independent of } (\Sigma_{11}^{-1}\Sigma_{12}, \Sigma_{22.1}), \qquad (A.99)$$

$$\Sigma_{11} \sim IW_{q_1}(S_{11}, \nu - q_2), \qquad (A.100)$$

$$\Sigma_{11}^{-1}\Sigma_{12} | \Sigma_{22.1} \sim MN_{q_1 \times q_2}(S_{11}^{-1}S_{12}, \Sigma_{22.1} \otimes S_{11}^{-1}), \qquad (A.101)$$

$$\Sigma_{22.1} \sim IW_{q_2}(S_{22.1}, \nu). \qquad (A.102)$$

Proof The proof consists of three steps.

(i) We first factorize $\mathrm{tr}\,(\Sigma^{-1}S)$, relying upon standard formulae for the inverse of a partitioned matrix:

$$\mathrm{tr}\,(\Sigma^{-1}S)$$
$$= \mathrm{tr}\left[\begin{pmatrix} \Sigma_{11}^{-1} + \Sigma_{11}^{-1}\Sigma_{12}\Sigma_{22.1}^{-1}\Sigma_{21}\Sigma_{11}^{-1} & -\Sigma_{11}^{-1}\Sigma_{12}\Sigma_{22.1}^{-1} \\ -\Sigma_{22.1}^{-1}\Sigma_{21}\Sigma_{11}^{-1} & \Sigma_{22.1}^{-1} \end{pmatrix}\begin{pmatrix} S_{11} & S_{12} \\ S_{21} & S_{22} \end{pmatrix}\right]$$
$$= \mathrm{tr}\,\{\Sigma_{11}^{-1}S_{11} + \Sigma_{22.1}^{-1}[(\Sigma_{21}\Sigma_{11}^{-1} - S_{21}S_{11}^{-1})S_{11}(S_{11}^{-1}S_{12} - \Sigma_{11}^{-1}\Sigma_{12}) + S_{22.1}]\}.$$

(ii) We also have

$$|\Sigma|^{-\frac{1}{2}(\nu+q+1)} = |\Sigma_{11}|^{-\frac{1}{2}(\nu+q+1)}\left[|\Sigma_{22.1}|^{-\frac{1}{2}(\nu+q_2+1)}|\Sigma_{22.1}|^{-\frac{1}{2}q_1}\right].$$

(iii) Finally, we verify by direct multiplication that

$$|\Sigma_{22.1}|^{\frac{1}{2}q_1} C_{IW}(S, \nu; q) = C_{IW}(S_{11}, \nu - q_2; q_1)$$
$$\times C_{MN}(S_{11}^{-1}, \Sigma_{22.1}; q_1, q_2) C_{IW}(S_{22.1}, \nu; q_2) \qquad (A.103)$$

□

Theorem A.18 *(i) Formula (A.97) is the integrating constant of the inverted Wishart density defined by (A.96).*

(ii) For $\nu > q + 1$, the expectation of Σ is given by

$$E(\Sigma) = \frac{1}{\nu - q - 1} S. \qquad (A.104)$$

Proof (i) $C_{IW}(s, \nu; 1)$ coincides with the integrating constant of the $IG_2(s, \nu)$ distribution, see (A.21) and (A.9). For $q > 1$, the validity of formula (A.97) immediately follows from formula (A.103) by recursion on q.

(ii) For $q = 1$ formula (A.104) coincides with formula (A.74). Assume it is correct for $q_1 < q$ and $q_2 < q$. Let us first compute expectations conditionally on Σ_{11} and $\Sigma_{22.1}$. We successively have

$$E(\Sigma_{12}|\Sigma_{11}, \Sigma_{22.1}) = \Sigma_{11} E(\Sigma_{11}^{-1}\Sigma_{12}|\Sigma_{11}, \Sigma_{22.1})$$
$$= \Sigma_{11} S_{11}^{-1} S_{12}, \qquad (A.105)$$

$$E(\Sigma_{22}|\Sigma_{11}, \Sigma_{22.1}) = \Sigma_{22.1} + E(\Sigma_{21}\Sigma_{11}^{-1}\Sigma_{12}|\Sigma_{11}, \Sigma_{22.1})$$
$$= \Sigma_{22.1} + S_{21} S_{11}^{-1} \Sigma_{11} S_{11}^{-1} S_{12}$$
$$+ E[(\Sigma_{21}\Sigma_{11}^{-1} - S_{21}S_{11}^{-1})\Sigma_{11}(\Sigma_{11}^{-1}\Sigma_{12} - S_{11}^{-1}S_{12})|\Sigma_{11}, \Sigma_{22.1}]$$

whence, following formula (A.101)[5],

$$E(\Sigma_{22}|\Sigma_{11}, \Sigma_{22.1}) = [1 + \text{tr} (S_{11}^{-1}\Sigma_{11})]\Sigma_{22.1} + S_{21}S_{11}^{-1}\Sigma_{11}S_{11}^{-1}S_{12}. \qquad (A.106)$$

Both formulae (A.105) and (A.106) are linear in Σ_{11} and $\Sigma_{22.1}$. The result follows from the fact that (by recurrence)

$$E(\Sigma_{11}) = \frac{1}{\nu - q - 1}S_{11}, \qquad E(\Sigma_{22.1}) = \frac{1}{\nu - q_2 - 1} S_{22.1}.$$

□

---

[5]We use the fact that if $X \sim MN_{p \times q}(M, Q \otimes P)$, then

$$E[(X - M)'B(X - M)] = \Sigma_{i=1}^{p}\Sigma_{j=1}^{q}E[(x_{(i)} - m_{(i)})b_{ij}(x_{(j)} - m_{(j)})]$$
$$= Q \Sigma_{i=1}^{p}\Sigma_{j=1}^{p}b_{ij}p_{ij} = Q\,\text{tr}\,(BP),$$

where $x'_{(i)} - m'_{(i)}$ is the ith row of $X - M$. Alternatively, we can restrict our attention to the case where $q_1 = 1$ in the proof of (A.104).

Remarks:

1) The following result, obtained from formulae (A.105) and (A.106), is used in the context of the limited information analysis of simultaneous equation systems—see e.g. Drèze and Richard (1983):

$$E(\Sigma|\Sigma_{11}) = \frac{1}{\nu - q_2 - 1}[1 + \text{tr } (S_{11}^{-1}\Sigma_{11})]\begin{pmatrix} 0 & 0 \\ 0 & S_{22.1} \end{pmatrix}$$
$$+ \begin{pmatrix} I_{q_1} \\ S_{21}S_{11}^{-1} \end{pmatrix} \Sigma_{11}(I_{q_1} \; S_{11}^{-1}S_{12}).$$

2) Higher order moments of Σ can also be obtained by recursion though their explicit derivation quickly becomes notationally 'heavy', to say the least.

3) If Σ has an inverted Wishart distribution, then $H = \Sigma^{-1}$ has a Wishart distribution, $H \sim W_q(S, \nu)$. The latter plays an important role in classical inference. Its analysis parallels that of the inverted Wishart distribution and similar recursive arguments apply.

A.2.7 *The Matricvariate Student Distribution*

A $p \times q$ random matrix X has a matricvariate Student distribution with parameters $M \in \mathbb{R}^{p \times q}, P \in C_p, Q \in C_q$, and $\nu > q - 1$, i.e. $X \sim Mt_{p \times q}(M, P, Q, \nu)$, if its density function is given by

$$f_{Mt}^{p \times q}(X|M, P, Q, \nu) = C_{Mt}^{-1}(P, Q, \nu; p, q)$$
$$\times [Q + (X - M)'P(X - M)]^{-\frac{1}{2}(\nu+p)}, \tag{A.107}$$

with

$$C_{Mt}(P, Q, \nu; p, q) = \pi^{\frac{1}{2}pq} |Q|^{-\frac{1}{2}\nu} |P|^{-\frac{1}{2}q} \prod_{i=1}^{q} \frac{\Gamma(\frac{\nu+1-i}{2})}{\Gamma(\frac{\nu+p+1-i}{2})}. \tag{A.108}$$

Its first- and second-order moments are given by

$$E(X) = M \text{ (for } \nu > q),$$
$$\text{Var(vec } X) = \frac{1}{\nu-q-1}Q \otimes P^{-1} \text{ (for } \nu > q + 1). \tag{A.109}$$

The following theorem provides a matricvariate generalization of Theorem A.15 (for $q = 1$, a matricvariate Student reduces to a p-dimensional multivariate Student).

Theorem A.19 *If*

$$X|\Sigma \sim MN_{p \times q}(M, \Sigma \otimes P^{-1}), \tag{A.110}$$
$$\Sigma \sim IW_q(Q, \nu), \tag{A.111}$$

then

$$X \sim Mt_{p \times q}(M, P, Q, \nu), \tag{A.112}$$
$$\Sigma|X \sim IW_q(Q + (X - M)'P(X - M), \nu + p). \tag{A.113}$$

Proof The joint density function of (X, Σ) is given by

$$f(X, \Sigma) = [|\Sigma|^{\frac{1}{2}p} C_{MN}^{-1}(P^{-1}, \Sigma; p, q) C_{IW}^{-1}(Q, \nu; q)]$$
$$\times |\Sigma|^{-\frac{1}{2}(\nu+p+q+1)} \exp\left(-\frac{1}{2}\{\text{tr } \Sigma^{-1}[Q + (X - M)'P(X - M)]\}\right).$$

Note that the first term between brackets no longer depends on $|\Sigma|$ thanks to the addition of the factor $|\Sigma|^{\frac{1}{2}p}$. We now treat this density as a function of Σ given X and recognize an inverted Wishart density kernel. It follows that

$$f(X) = |\Sigma|^{\frac{1}{2}p} C_{MN}^{-1}(P^{-1}, \Sigma; p, q) C_{IW}^{-1}(Q, \nu; q)$$
$$\times C_{IW}(Q + (X - M)'P(X - M), \nu + p; q),$$

whence eqn (A.112) and, by division, (A.113) follow immediately. □

Many useful properties of the matricvariate Student distribution can be derived by application of Theorem A.19 (including the validation of its integrating constant as given in formula (A.108)). In particular, we have

$$\text{Var}(\text{vec } X) = E_\Sigma[\text{Var}_{X|\Sigma}(\text{vec } X)] = E(\Sigma) \otimes P^{-1} = \frac{1}{\nu - q - 1} Q \otimes P^{-1},$$

as stated in formula (A.109). Next we partition X according to formula (A.62). The matrices M, P, and Q are partitioned conformably with X. Let

$$X_{2.1} = X_2 - X_1 \Sigma_{11}^{-1} \Sigma_{12}. \tag{A.114}$$

Theorem A.20 *If*

$$X|\Sigma \sim MN_{p\times q}(M, \Sigma \otimes P^{-1}), \tag{A.115}$$

$$\Sigma \sim IW_q(Q, \nu), \tag{A.116}$$

to the effect that $X \sim Mt_{p\times q}(M, P, Q, \nu)$, *then*

(i)

$$X_{(1)} \sim Mt_{p_1 \times q}(M_{(1)}, P_{11.2}, Q, \nu), \tag{A.117}$$

$$\Sigma|X_{(1)} \sim IW_{q_1}(Q + (X_{(1)} - M_{(1)})'P_{11.2}(X_{(1)} - M_{(1)}), \nu + p_1), \tag{A.118}$$

$$X_{(2)}|X_{(1)} \sim Mt_{p_2 \times q}(M_{(2)} - P_{22}^{-1}P_{21}(X_{(1)} - M_{(1)}), P_{22},$$
$$Q + (X_{(1)} - M_{(1)})'P_{11.2}(X_{(1)} - M_{(1)}), \nu + p_1); \tag{A.119}$$

(ii)

$$(X_1, \Sigma_{11}) \text{ is independent of } (X_{2.1}, \Sigma_{11}^1 \Sigma_{12}, \Sigma_{22.1}); \tag{A.120}$$

(iii)

$$X_1 \sim Mt_{p\times q_1}(M_1, P, Q_{11}, \nu - q_2), \tag{A.121}$$

$$X_2|X_1 \sim Mt_{p\times q_2}(M_2 + (X_1 - M_1)Q_{11}^{-1}Q_{12},$$
$$[P^{-1} + (X_1 - M_1)Q_{11}^{-1}(X_1 - M_1)']^{-1}, Q_{22.1}, \nu). \tag{A.122}$$

Proof (i) We first apply formulae (A.65) and (A.66) to the distribution of $X|\Sigma$, as given in formula (A.110), taking advantage of the (partitioned inverse) matrix identities $P^{21}(P^{11})^{-1} = -P_{22}^{-1}P_{21}$, $P^{11} = P_{11.2}^{-1}$, and $P^{22.1} = P_{22}^{-1}$. We find that

$$X_{(1)}|\Sigma \sim MN_{p_1 \times q}(M_{(1)}, \Sigma \otimes P_{11.2}^{-1}), \tag{A.123}$$

$$X_{(2)}|X_{(1)}, \Sigma \sim MN_{p_2 \times q}(M_{(2)} - P_{22}^{-1}P_{21}(X_{(1)} - M_{(1)}), \Sigma \otimes P_{22}^{-1}). \tag{A.124}$$

Formulae (A.117) and (A.118) follow by application of Theorem A.19 to formulae (A.116) and (A.123). Formula (A.119) then follows by application of Theorem A.19 to formulae (A.118) and (A.124).

(ii) We apply formulae (A.63) and (A.64) to the distribution of $X|\Sigma$ and find that

$$X_1|\Sigma \equiv X_1|\Sigma_{11} \sim MN_{p \times q_1}(M_1, \Sigma_{11} \otimes P^{-1}), \tag{A.125}$$

$$\begin{aligned} X_2|X_1, \Sigma &\equiv X_2|X_1, \Sigma_{11}^{-1}\Sigma_{12}, \Sigma_{22.1} \\ &\sim MN_{p \times q_2}(M_2 + (X_1 - M_1)\Sigma_{11}^{-1}\Sigma_{12}, \Sigma_{22.1} \otimes P^{-1}), \end{aligned} \tag{A.126}$$

whence (X_1 is independent of $X_{2.1}$) conditionally on Σ, which together with formulae (A.99), (A.125), and (A.126) implies formula (A.120).

(iii) Formula (A.121) follows from formulae (A.100) and (A.125) by application of Theorem A.19. Next we marginalize formula (A.126) with respect to $\Sigma_{11}^{-1}\Sigma_{12}|\Sigma_{22.1}$ whose distribution is given in formula (A.101). We find that[6]

$$\begin{aligned} X_2|X_1, \Sigma_{22.1} \sim MN_{p \times q_2}(M_2 + (X_1 - M_1)Q_{11}^{-1}Q_{12}, \\ \Sigma_{22.1} \otimes [P^{-1} + (X_1 - M_1)Q_{11}^{-1}(X_1 - M_1)']). \end{aligned} \tag{A.127}$$

Formula (A.122) follows by application of Theorem A.19 to formulae (A.102) and (A.127), accounting for the fact that X_1 is independent of $\Sigma_{22.1}$. □

A.2.8 *Poly-t Distributions*

Poly-t distributions are defined by the property that their density kernels are products, or products of ratios, of Student density kernels. Their analysis relies upon a pair of 'reduction' principles which are introduced below. Technical details are notationally tedious and are left out. They can be found in Richard and Tompa (1980) for analytical derivations and in Bauwens and Richard (1985) for Monte Carlo simulation.

---

[6]We take advantage of the matrix identity

$$\text{vec } [(X_1 - M_1)\Sigma_{11}^{-1}\Sigma_{12}] = [I_{q_2} \otimes (X_1 - M_1)].\text{vec } (\Sigma_{11}^{-1}\Sigma_{12}),$$

whence

$$\begin{aligned} V\{&\text{vec } [(X_1 - M_1)\Sigma_{11}^{-1}\Sigma_{12}]|X_1, \Sigma_{22.1}\} \\ &= [I_{q_2} \otimes (X_1 - M_1)].(\Sigma_{22.1} \otimes Q_{11}^{-1}).[I_{q_2} \otimes (X_1 - M_1)]' \\ &= \Sigma_{22.1} \otimes (X_1 - M_1)Q_{11}^{-1}(X_1 - M_1)'. \end{aligned}$$

Let $\overline{C}_p$ denote the set of $p \times p$ symmetric *semi*-positive definite matrices. A random variable $X \in \mathbb{R}^p$ has an m-0 poly-t distribution with parameter $S = \{(\mu_j, P_j, \nu_j); j : 1 \to m\}$ if a kernel of its density function is given by

$$\varphi_{m,0}(x|S) = \prod_{j=1}^{m} [1 + (x - \mu_j)' P_j (x - \mu_j)]^{-\frac{1}{2}\nu_j}. \tag{A.128}$$

Its parameters are subject to the following restrictions:

$$P_j \in \overline{C}_p, \ \sum_{j=1}^{m} P_j \in C_p, \ \nu_j > 0, \ \text{and} \ \sum_{j=1}^{m} \nu_j > p. \tag{A.129}$$

An m-n (ratio form) poly-t density kernel is defined as the ratio of an m-0 poly-t density kernel to an n-0 poly-t density kernel. We shall only consider here the case where $n = 1$. A random variable $X \in \mathbb{R}^p$ has an m-1 poly-t distribution with parameter S (as defined above) and $S_0 = (\mu_0, P_0, \nu_0)$ if a kernel of its density function is given by

$$\varphi_{m,1}(x|S, S_0) = \varphi_{m,0}(x|S) . [1 + (x - \mu_0)' P_0 (x - \mu_0)]^{\frac{1}{2}\nu_0}, \tag{A.130}$$

subject to the additional parameter constraint $\sum_{j=1}^{m} \nu_j > p + \nu_0$.

The next theorem expresses the m-0 poly-t distribution as the mixture of a conditional Student distribution by the distribution of $m - 1$ auxiliary random variables.

Theorem A.21 *The following identity holds:*

$$\varphi_{m,0}(x|S) = \int_0^1 \cdots \int_0^1 f_t^p(x|\mu_c, s_c, P_c, \nu) \, g(c_2, \ldots, c_m) \, dc_2 \ldots dc_m, \tag{A.131}$$

where

$$\nu = \sum_{i=1}^{m} \nu_i - k,$$

$$g(c_2, \ldots, c_m) = [|P_c| s_c^{\nu}]^{-1/2} \prod_{j=2}^{m} f_b \left(c_j | \tfrac{1}{2} \sum_{i=1}^{j-1} \nu_i, \tfrac{1}{2}\nu_j \right),$$

and μ_c, P_c, and s_c are derived by solving

$$S_c = \begin{pmatrix} P_c & -P_c \mu_c \\ -\mu_c' P_c & s_c + \mu_c' P_c \mu_c \end{pmatrix}.$$

S_c *is constructed recursively as follows:*

$$S(c; 1) = S_1,$$
$$S(c; j) = (1 - c_j) S_j + c_j S(c; j - 1), \quad 1 < j \le m,$$
$$S_c = S(c; m),$$

where S_j is defined like S_c from the parameters μ_j, P_j, and $s_j = 1$ of the m Student kernels constituting the m-0 poly-t kernel.

Proof The proof for the general case can be found in Richard and Tompa (1980: Theorem 2.1). For $m = 2$, the proof can be found in Subsection 4.5.1; see in particular formulae (4.70)–(4.76) where c corresponds to c_2 in the notation of this theorem. □

Theorem A.21 provides an algorithm for the Monte Carlo simulation of an m-0 poly-t random variable. A random draw of X is obtained by first drawing the $m - 1$ c_j from a density proportional to $g(c) = g(c_2, \ldots, c_m)$, followed by a random draw of $X|c$ from the Student density $t(\mu_c, s_c, M_c, \nu)$. The drawing of the c_j must be done numerically, which requires m to be small. When $m = 2$, the distribution function of c_2 can be tabulated by one-dimensional integration, and draws can easily be obtained by numerical inversion of the distribution function.

Theorem A.21 also applies to the numerator of an m-1 poly-t density kernel. It follows that m-1 poly-t density kernels can be reduced to integrals of (conditional) 1-1 poly-t density kernels, which is why our next theorem deals only with 1-1 poly-t density kernels.

Theorem A.22 *The following identity holds:*

$$
\int [1 + (x - \mu_0)' P_0 (x - \mu_0)]^{\frac{1}{2}\nu_0} [1 + (x - \mu_1)' P_1 (x - \mu_1)]^{-\frac{1}{2}\nu_1} dx
$$
$$
= |P_1|^{-\frac{1}{2}} \int [1 + (z - z_0)' \Lambda (z - z_0)]^{\frac{1}{2}\nu_0} [1 + z'z]^{-\frac{1}{2}\nu_1} dz, \tag{A.132}
$$

where $z = T^{-1}(x - \mu_1)$, T is a non-singular matrix that jointly diagonalizes P_0 and P_1, i.e. $T'P_1 T = I_p$ and $T'P_0 T = \Lambda = diag(\lambda_1 \ldots \lambda_p)$, and $z_0 = T^{-1}(\mu_0 - \mu_1)$.

Proof The proof follows from a standard theorem in linear algebra relative to the joint diagonalization of $P_1 \in C_p$ and $P_0 \in \overline{C}_p$ (see e.g. Gantmacher 1960: Chap. X). □

If, furthermore, $\frac{1}{2}\nu_0$ is an integer, then we can apply integration by parts in order to obtain recurrence formulae for the evaluation of the integrating constant and (first- and second-order) moments of X. See Richard and Tompa (1980) for details. Along similar lines, we can apply the usual multinomial expansion formula to the numerator under the integral in formula (A.132) in order to construct a random generator for 1-1 poly-t distributions in the form of a discrete mixture of continuous distributions. See Bauwens and Richard (1985) for details. Cases where $\frac{1}{2}\nu_0$ is not an integer can be analysed by means of (four points) Lagrangian interpolation between neighbouring integer values or by Monte Carlo importance sampling using as the importance function the 1-1 poly-t density when $\frac{1}{2}\nu_0$ is replaced by its (integer) ceil.

APPENDIX B

GENERATING RANDOM NUMBERS

In this appendix, we present some sampling techniques to generate random numbers from the distributions that are detailed in Appendix A. We do not intend to make a complete review of the best existing algorithms, but only to give one or two algorithms per distribution. The choices that have been made were dictated by a compromise between the ease and the efficiency of programming. More efficient, but more complicated, algorithms can be found for instance in Devroye (1986), Knuth (1981), or Rubinstein (1981).

All the non-uniform distributions are simulated using deterministic transformations of uniform random numbers. Consequently the disposal of a good uniform random number generator is of prime importance. We define below what we mean by good. Note first that, paradoxically, uniform random sequences are in fact fully deterministic and are therefore called pseudo-random. They can be obtained by the use of a linear congruential equation of the type:

$$X_t = (a X_{t-1} + c) \bmod m, \tag{B.1}$$

which produces a sequence of integers between 0 and m. The value of m is machine dependent. If integers are stored in words of 32 bits, then $m = 2^{31} - 1$. The starting value X_0 is called the seed. The maximum length of the period is given by m. The actual length depends on the choice of X_0, a, and c. The sequence is finally divided by m to obtain a sequence of rational numbers between zero and one. The advantage of such sequences is that they can be reproduced exactly. Marsaglia and Zaman (1993) have proposed a new generator which is an improvement over the usual congruential method; see Robert (1996: 20) for a textbook presentation.

A good generator produces a sequence of numbers with the following characteristics:

- the period is maximum;
- the empirical distribution is as close as possible to the uniform distribution;
- the generated sequence looks like an independent sequence.

Various examples and tests of usual uniform generators can be found in Knuth (1981).

B.1 General Methods for Univariate Distributions

Uniform pseudo-random numbers can be transformed into pseudo-random draws from a broad range of distributions following a small number of generic techniques we explain in this section for univariate distributions.

B.1.1 *Inverse Transform Method*

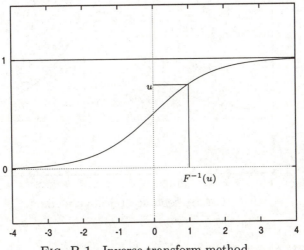

FIG. B.1. Inverse transform method

The (cumulative) distribution function $F(.)$ of a continuous random variable X is a monotonous increasing function between zero and one defined by

$$F(x) = \Pr(X \le x),\qquad\qquad(B.2)$$

and the random variable $U = F(X)$ has a uniform distribution. Since $F(.)$ is continuous and strictly increasing, its inverse exists. As shown in Theorem A.1, the random variable X defined by

$$X = F^{-1}(U)\qquad\qquad(B.3)$$

has F for its distribution function when U is uniform on [0,1]. When the analytical form of the distribution function is known, this property gives a very simple method for generating random numbers with distribution F. When such an analytical form is not known, it is in principle possible to compute it by numerical integration and invert the result by numerical interpolation as illustrated in Fig. B.1. This method is always available, but of course may be costly. It can, however, be very useful for quite complicated distributions when no other method exists. It is used for instance in the griddy-Gibbs algorithm documented in Chapter 3.

B.1.2 *Acceptance–Rejection Method*

Suppose we want to draw from a distribution $f(x)$ for which there is no available or efficient generator. We can choose a distribution $\mu(x|\alpha)$ from which it is easy to draw random numbers and which, multiplied by a constant c, envelops $f(x)$.

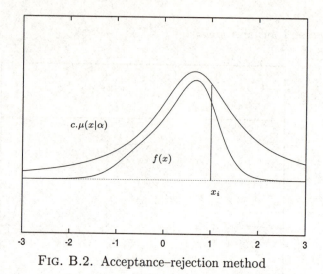

FIG. B.2. Acceptance–rejection method

We then draw a random number x_i from $\mu(x|\alpha)$ for which we have to decide if it can be accepted as a draw from $f(x)$. The draw is accepted if

$$f(x_i) \le c\,\mu(x_i|\alpha)\,U_i, \qquad (B.4)$$

where U_i is a random draw from the uniform distribution over $[0,1]$. Figure B.2 illustrates this condition. A uniform random number is drawn between 0 and $c\,\mu(x_i|\alpha)$, and x_i is accepted if the uniform draw is lower than $f(x_i)$. The expected probability of acceptance for a draw is given by

$$p = \frac{1}{c} \le 1. \qquad (B.5)$$

For the method to be efficient, $1 - p$ has to be kept to a minimum. This can be achieved by choosing an optimized envelope according to the following algorithm—see e.g. Devroye (1986):

$$\min_{\alpha} \sup_{x} \left[\log f(x) - \log \mu(x|\alpha)\right]. \qquad (B.6)$$

This algorithm looks for the value of α which indexes the envelope function which minimizes the maximum distance between the distribution from which to draw and its envelope.

The method is simplified if we can draw from the standardized version of $f(x)$ as an optimized envelope has to be found once for all. The desired draws are then obtained by a simple linear transformation of the standardized draws. A rejection algorithm for the standardized normal distribution is presented in Subsection B.2.6.

B.1.3 *Compound or Data Augmentation Method*

Suppose we want to draw from $f(x)$. It may be useful to define $f(x)$ as a marginal density of a bivariate density defined by

$$f(x) = \int g(x|y) \, h(y) \, dy, \qquad (B.7)$$

where $h(y)$ is a continuous density. A draw from $f(x)$ is obtained by drawing y_i from $h(y)$ and x_i from $g(x|y_i)$. This method is particularly attractive when it is simple to draw from $h(y)$ and $g(x|y)$. This technique can be applied for instance to the Student density which is a mixture of normal densities by an inverted gamma-2.

It is also possible to apply this method when $h(y)$ is discrete:

$$f(x) = \sum_i p_i \, g(x|y = i), \qquad (B.8)$$

with p_i being the weights of the mixture summing to one. This case is illustrated with an algorithm proposed by Bauwens and Richard (1985) for generating 1-1 poly-t densities.

B.2 Univariate Distributions

B.2.1 *Exponential Distribution*

The exponential distribution is a special case of the gamma distribution given in (A.8) where $\alpha = 1$. We note $X \sim \text{Expo}(\beta)$ when

$$f(x) = \beta^{-1} \exp(-x/\beta), \qquad (B.9)$$

with $\beta > 0$ and $x \geq 0$. As the distribution function is

$$F(x) = 1 - \exp(-x/\beta), \qquad (B.10)$$

the inverse transformation is

$$x = -\beta \log(1 - u), \qquad (B.11)$$

where u is a draw from the uniform distribution. As $1 - U$ has the same distribution as U, the simplest random generator for the exponential distribution is described in the following algorithm:

1) generate $u \sim U(0, 1)$
2) deliver $x = \beta \log u$ as $\text{Expo}(\beta)$

This algorithm is important for random number generation as it constitutes one of the bases for generating gamma, chi-squared, and beta distributions.

B.2.2 *Gamma Distribution*

Theorem A.2 states that the sum of n independent $G(\alpha_i, \beta)$ random variables is distributed as $G(\sum_{i=1}^n \alpha_i, \beta)$. As the exponential is a special case of the gamma for $\alpha = 1$, we can generate a $G(\alpha, \beta)$ as the sum of n identical $\text{Expo}(\beta)$, provided $n = \alpha$ is an integer. Consequently,

1) generate n variables $u_i \sim U(0,1)$
2) deliver $-\beta \sum_{i=1}^n \log u_i$ as $G(n, \beta)$

For large n, this algorithm can become relatively inefficient. If n exceeds 30, we can use a normal approximation to the $G(\alpha, 1)$ which is $N(0,1) \simeq \sqrt{4 G(\alpha, 1)} - \sqrt{4\alpha - 1}$:

1) draw $z \sim N(0,1)$
2) deliver $[z + \sqrt{4\alpha - 1}]^2/4$ as $G(\alpha, \beta)$

The combination of these two algorithms is very efficient. For non-integer α, other algorithms for the gamma distribution are based on the acceptance–rejection method. See some of the examples in the books of Rubinstein (1981) or Devroye (1986). The algorithm proposed by Ahrens and Dieter (1974) is based on a truncated Cauchy envelope and can be detailed as follows:

1) draw $u_1 \sim U(0,1)$
2) draw $y = \tan(\pi u_1)$
3) compute $x = y\sqrt{2\alpha - 1} + \alpha - 1$
4) if $x < 0$, redraw u_1
5) draw $u_2 \sim U(0,1)$
6) if $\log(u_2) > \log(1 + y^2) + (\alpha - 1)\log\left(\dfrac{x}{\alpha - 1}\right) - y\sqrt{2\alpha - 1}$, reject
7) deliver $x \times \beta$ as $G(\alpha, \beta)$

This algorithm is proposed by Knuth (1981) as a good compromise between execution time and complexity—see also Press (1992).

B.2.3 *Chi-squared Distribution*

The chi-squared distribution is a particular case of the gamma distribution with $\chi^2(\nu) \equiv G(\nu/2, 2)$. The algorithm we present now is an adaptation of one of the previous algorithms used for the gamma distribution. We must distinguish between even and odd values of ν. For even ν, the solution is simple:

1) generate $n = \nu/2$ variables $u_i \sim U(0,1)$
2) deliver $-2\sum_{i=1}^n \log u_i$ as $\chi^2(\nu)$

For odd values of ν, we proceed in two steps. For the integer part of $n = \nu/2$, we use the previous algorithm, which we complete for the last degree of freedom by the square of an $N(0,1)$ which is a $\chi^2(1)$:

1) generate $n - 0.5$ variables $u_i \sim U(0,1)$
2) generate $z \sim N(0,1)$

3) deliver $z^2 + 2\sum_{i=1}^{n-0.5} \log u_i$ as $\chi^2(\nu)$

For large ν, we can use the normal approximation which is $z \simeq \sqrt{2\chi^2(\nu)} - \sqrt{2\nu - 1}$:

1) generate $z \sim N(0,1)$
2) deliver $0.5\,[z + \sqrt{2\nu - 1}]^2$ as $\chi^2(\nu)$

Rubinstein (1981: 94) recommends it for $\nu > 30$.

B.2.4   *Inverted Gamma-2 Distribution*

The inverted gamma-2 $IG_2(s, \nu)$ is related to the $\chi^2(\nu)$ by a simple transformation. Let X be a random variable distributed as a $G_2(\nu, s)$ and let us consider the transformation $X \to \sigma^2$ defined by $X = s/\sigma^2$ of Jacobian $\partial X/\partial\sigma^2 = -s/\sigma^4$. Then $\sigma^2 = s/X$ is $IG_2(s, \nu)$. An algorithm to generate an $IG_2(s, \nu)$ is then

1) generate $x \sim \chi^2(\nu)$
2) deliver s/x as $IG_2(s, \nu)$

B.2.5   *Beta Distribution*

Sampling from the beta distribution $B(\alpha, \beta)$ results from the direct application of Theorem A.3 of Appendix A:

1) generate $y_1 \sim G(\alpha, 1)$
2) generate $y_2 \sim G(\beta, 1)$
3) deliver $y_1/(y_1 + y_2)$ as $B(\alpha, \beta)$

B.2.6   *Normal Distribution*

Many algorithms exist to generate random numbers from an $N(0,1)$. See the books cited in the references in the introduction. The best algorithms rely on the acceptance–rejection principle. We have selected a simple acceptance–rejection method which is called the polar method and which delivers two draws of the $N(0,1)$ each time. The method is due to Box and Muller (1958) and is documented in Knuth (1981: 104):

1) generate two uniforms u_1 and u_2 from $U(0,1)$
2) compute $A_i = 2\,u_i - 1$ and $A = A_1^2 + A_2^2$
3) if $A > 1$ restart at step 1
4) compute $D = \sqrt{-2\log(A)/A}$
5) deliver $z_i = 2\,A_i D$ as two independent $N(0,1)$

The rejection method is used to draw uniformly on the unit circle by rejecting from the square of length 2 all draws that do not belong to the circle of radius 1. So the rejection rate is $1 - \pi/4 \simeq 21$ per cent.

B.2.7   *Student Distribution*

The standardized density can be obtained by setting the scale factor s of (A.31) equal to ν, $m = 1$, and $\mu = 0$. The variance of the standardized density is

$\nu/(\nu - 2)$. The standardized Student density is given by the ratio between an $N(0, 1)$ and the square root of a $\chi^2(\nu)/\nu$. This property gives birth to the simple generator:

1) generate $z \sim N(0, 1)$ and $x \sim \chi^2(\nu)$
2) deliver $t = z/\sqrt{x/\nu}$ as $t(0, \nu, 1, \nu)$

If we want to impose a unit variance, we just have to multiply t by $\sqrt{(\nu - 2)/\nu}$, provided $\nu > 2$. If we want to generate a $t(\mu, s, m, \nu)$, the algorithm is

1) generate $z \sim N(0, 1)$ and $x \sim IG_2(s, \nu)$
2) deliver $\mu + z\sqrt{x/m}$ as $t(\mu, s, m, \nu)$

and is justified by part (i) of Theorem A.6.

B.2.8 *Cauchy Distribution*

The Cauchy distribution with scale parameter s and location parameter μ has the density

$$\pi^{-1}s^{1/2}[s + (x - \mu)^2]^{-1}. \tag{B.12}$$

This density is a particular case of the Student density with $\nu = 1$ and $m = 1$. However, contrary to the general Student density, its distribution function is known analytically to be

$$F(x) = 0.5 + \pi^{-1}\arctan[(x - \mu)/\sqrt{s}]. \tag{B.13}$$

Consequently the inverse transform method is easy to apply:

1) generate $u \sim U(0, 1)$
1) deliver $\mu - \sqrt{s}/\tan(\pi u)$ as Cauchy(μ, s).

B.3 General Methods for Multivariate Distributions

Dimensionality creates special problems. For instance, the acceptance–rejection method may quickly become inefficient in a multivariate context. This is well illustrated if one tries to draw random numbers in a hypersphere starting from a hypercube. When the dimension goes to infinity, Rubinstein (1981: 51) shows that the efficiency of the method goes to zero. Consequently the generation of multivariate distributions has to be discussed separately. A general principle is to break down the multi-dimensional aspect into a sequence of unidimensional steps.

B.3.1 *Multivariate Transformations*

Linear transformations are a useful tool for transforming a standardized random variable into a random variable with the same distribution but with a specified mean and variance. This applies to both the univariate and the multivariate case. As emphasized in Appendix A, the Choleski decomposition is particularly useful for that purpose. Consequently, in several cases, the problem of generating a general multivariate random variable reduces to the question of generating its standardized version which in turns boils down to generating independent univariate versions of it. This method is used for instance to generate the multivariate or the matricvariate normal.

B.3.2 *Factorization into Marginals and Conditionals*

If the marginal and conditional distributions are available in an analytical form and if it is easy to sample from these distributions, we can simulate a multivariate distribution using its decomposition. Let us consider the trivariate distribution $f(x, y, z)$. We always have

$$f(x, y, z) = f(x|y, z) f(y|z) f(z). \tag{B.14}$$

Consequently the trivariate distribution can be generated from three univariate dependent distributions. The multivariate normal can be generated in this way, but this is inefficient. On the contrary, it is an efficient method for the inverted Wishart density. This method is closely related to the data augmentation method of Section B.1.3.

B.3.3 *Markov Chains*

Let us once again consider the trivariate distribution $f(x, y, z)$. We suppose that it cannot be directly simulated, but that all its full conditionals have analytical expressions from which it is simple to draw random numbers. It is then possible to build a Markov chain with the conditional densities, which will converge finally to the joint distribution. This algorithm—known as the Gibbs sampler—works as follows:

$$x_{i+1} \sim f(x|y_i, z_i),$$
$$y_{i+1} \sim f(y|x_{i+1}, z_i),$$
$$z_{i+1} \sim f(z|x_{i+1}, y_{i+1}).$$

Another Markov chain algorithm is the Metropolis–Hastings algorithm. The Markov chain types of algorithm cannot reasonably be used for a single draw, as the chain needs a warm-up. This means that the chain must be initialized and the first ns draws have to be discarded. The value of ns depends on the rate of convergence of the chain towards a reasonable approximation of $f(x, y, z)$. An idea of the performance of the chain can be obtained by graphing the partial means of x, y, z. For more details, see Subsection 3.4.3 on MCMC (Markov chain Monte Carlo) methods.

B.4   Multivariate Distributions

B.4.1 *Multivariate Normal*

The application of Theorem A.9 provides a direct algorithm to generate random numbers from a normal distribution with mean μ and variance Σ. Denoting $\mathsf{Chol}(\Sigma)$ as the lower triangular matrix of the Choleski decomposition of Σ:

1) compute $C = \mathsf{Chol}(\Sigma)$
2) generate $z \sim N_k(0, I_k)$, i.e. k independent $N(0, 1)$
3) deliver $\mu + Cz$ as $N_k(\mu, \Sigma)$

B.4.2 *Multivariate Student*

We use the multivariate generalization of Theorem A.6. An algorithm to draw from a k-variate Student distribution with mean μ, variance–covariance Σ, and ν degrees of freedom works as follows:

1) compute $C = \mathsf{Chol}(\Sigma)$
2) generate $z \sim N_k(0, I_k)$
3) generate $x \sim \chi^2(\nu)$
4) deliver $\mu + Cz/\sqrt{x/(\nu - 2)}$ as $t_k(\mu, 1, \Sigma^{-1}\nu/(\nu - 2), \nu)$

This algorithm requires that $\nu > 2$ as its input is a variance–covariance matrix. For a $t(\mu, s, M, \nu)$, the algorithm is:

1) compute $C = \mathsf{Chol}(M^{-1})$
2) generate $z \sim N_k(0, I_k)$
3) generate $x \sim IG_2(s, \nu)$
4) deliver $\mu + Cz\sqrt{x}$ as $t_k(\mu, s, M, \nu)$

B.4.3 *Matricvariate Normal*

The matricvariate normal is a matricvariate generalization of the multivariate normal. It is thus easy to understand that its generator is not that different from what we have seen before. In the notation of Appendix A, let $Z \sim MN_{p \times q}(0, I_q \otimes I_p)$, see (A.60). Let us define $X = A'ZB + M$ with A, B, and M being rectangular matrices as specified in Appendix A. Then $X \sim MN_{m \times n}(M, B'B \otimes A'A)$, see (A.68). This property gives the key for defining a generator for X with mean M and variance–covariance $Q \otimes P$, starting from an $MN_{p \times q}(0, I_q \otimes I_p)$:

1) compute $A = \mathsf{Chol}(P)$
2) compute $B = \mathsf{Chol}(Q)$
3) generate $p \times q$ independent $N(0, 1)$ and store them in the $p \times q$ matrix Z
4) deliver $A'ZB + M$ as $MN_{p \times q}(M, Q \otimes P)$

B.4.4 *Inverted Wishart*

Let $\Sigma \sim IW_q(S, \nu)$ as defined in (A.96). We decompose S using the Choleski decomposition $S = CC'$. If $\Sigma \sim IW_q(S, \nu)$, then $\Omega = C\Sigma C' \sim IW_q(I_q, \nu)$. Consequently, we just have to define an algorithm to draw from a standardized inverted Wishart which is done by exploiting the decomposition of the distribution in marginals and conditionals as given in Theorem A.16.

The algorithm recursively computes a lower triangular matrix W starting from its bottom right element, such that $WW' = \Omega$. The diagonal elements of W elements are distributed as the square root of the inverted gamma-2 with appropriate degrees of freedom. Columns below the main diagonal are distributed as appropriate transformations of multivariate normal densities. The algorithm is

1) start decreasing loop on $i = [q, 1]$
2) generate $sw = \sqrt{IG_2(1, \nu + i - q)}$

3) $W[i,i] = sw$
4) if $i = q$, go to next i (step 9)
5) compute the vector of indices $e = [i+1, q-i]$
6) extract from W the matrix WLT of rows and columns indexed by e
7) generate $z \sim N_{q-i}(0,1)$
8) fill the elements of W as $W[e,i] = sw \times WLT \times z$
9) $i = i - 1$ (end of loop)
10) deliver $W \times W'$ as $IW(I_q, \nu)$

To draw an $IW(S, \nu)$, compute $C = \text{Chol}(S)$, deliver $C WW'C'$.

B.4.5 Matricvariate Student

Let X be a $p \times q$ random matrix distributed as an $Mt_{p \times q}(M, P, Q, \nu)$, see (A.107). From Theorem A.18, X can be sampled from a mixture of a matricvariate normal by an inverted Wishart. This leads to the following algorithm:

1) compute $S = \text{Chol}(Q)$ and $C = \text{Chol}(P^{-1})$
2) generate W such that $W W' \sim IW(I_q, \nu)$
3) generate $Z \sim MN_{p \times q}(I_q \otimes I_p)$
4) deliver $X = M + C Z W'S'$ as $Mt_{p \times q}(M, P, Q, \nu)$

Another description of the algorithm can be found in the appendix of Zellner, Bauwens, and van Dijk (1988).

B.4.6 Poly-t 2-0

The 2-0 poly-t distribution can be very useful as it provides a very flexible candidate for an importance function. In Theorem A.21, it is proved that a 2-0 poly-t is the mixture of a Student distribution by a random variable on the interval $[0,1]$. In the notation of (A.128) we have

$$f(x) \propto [1 + (x - \mu_1)'P_1(x - \mu_1)]^{-\nu_1/2}[1 + (x - \mu_2)'P_2(x - \mu_2)]^{-\nu_2/2}. \quad \text{(B.15)}$$

The following algorithm is based on Theorem A.21:

1) generate $c \sim g(c)$ by inverting numerically its distribution function
2) generate $h \sim G(\nu/2, 2/s_c)$
3) generate $z \sim N_k(0, I_k)$
4) compute $P_c = [cP_1 + (1-c)P_2]$
5) compute $\mu_c = P_c^{-1}[cP_1\mu_1 + (1-c)P_2\mu_2]$
6) compute $C = \text{Chol}(P_c^{-1})$
7) deliver $\mu_c + C z/\sqrt{h}$ as a draw of (B.15)

The explicit expression of the parameter s_c is

$$s_c = c(1 + \mu_1'P_1\mu_1) + (1-c)(1 + \mu_2'P_2\mu_2) - \mu_c'P_c\mu_c,$$

and that of the function $g(c)$ is

$$g(c) = [|P_c|s_c^\nu]^{-1/2} c^{\frac{1}{2}\nu_1 - 1}(1 - c)^{\frac{1}{2}\nu_2 - 1}.$$

B.4.7 *Poly-t 1-1*

A 1-1 poly-*t* is formed by the ratio of two Student kernels. In the notation of Appendix A, we have

$$f(x) \propto [1 + (x - \mu_1)' P_1 (x - \mu_1)]^{-\nu_1/2} [1 + (x - \mu_0)' P_0 (x - \mu_0)]^{\nu_0/2}. \quad \text{(B.16)}$$

In order to build a generator for this density, the 1-1 poly-*t* has first to be reduced to its canonical form by a change of variable and a simultaneous diagonalization of P_1 and P_0. Then the canonical form is expressed in the form of a rather complex mixture of continuous and discrete distributions when $\nu_0/2$ is an integer. For a complete description of the algorithm, see Bauwens and Richard (1985).

REFERENCES

Abramowitz, M. and Stegun, I.A. (1964). *Handbook of Mathematical Functions*. New York: Dover Publications.

Ahrens, J.H. and Dieter, U. (1974). Computer methods for sampling from gamma, beta, Poisson and binomial distributions. *Computing*, 12, 223–246.

Albert, J. and Chib, S. (1993). Bayesian inference of autoregressive time series with mean and variance subject to Markov jumps. *Journal of Business and Economic Statistics*, 11, 1–15.

Anderson, T.W. (1984). *An Introduction to Multivariate Statistical Analysis* (2nd edn). New York: Wiley.

Andrews, D.W.K. and Ploberger, W. (1994). Optimal tests when a nuisance parameter is present only under the alternative. *Econometrica*, 62, 1383–1414.

Ansley, C.F. (1979). An algorithm for the exact likelihood of a mixed autoregressive moving average process. *Biometrika*, 66, 59–65.

Aprahamian, F., Lubrano, M., and Marimoutou, V. (1994). A Bayesian approach to misspecification tests. GREQAM Discussion Paper 94A06. Marseilles.

Bacon, D.W. and Watts, D.G. (1971). Estimating the transition between two intersecting straight lines. *Biometrika*, 58, 525–534.

Balestra, P. (1980). A note on the exact transformation associated with the first order moving average process. *Journal of Econometrics*, 14, 381–394.

Bauwens, L. (1984). *Bayesian Full Information Analysis of Simultaneous Equation Models Using Integration by Monte Carlo*. Berlin: Springer Verlag.

Bauwens, L. (1991). The 'pathology' of the natural conjugate prior density in the regression model. *Annales d'Economie et de Statistique*, 23, 49–60.

Bauwens, L. and Giot, P. (1998). A Gibbs sampler approach to cointegration. *Computational Statistics*, 13, 339–368.

Bauwens, L. and Lubrano, M. (1991). Bayesian diagnostics for heterogeneity. *Annales d'Economie et de Statistique*, 20/21, 17–40.

Bauwens, L. and Lubrano, M. (1996). Identification restrictions and posterior densities in cointegrated Gaussian VAR systems. In: Fomby, T.B. (Ed.), *Advances in Econometrics, Vol. 11, Part B*, pp. 3–28. London: JAI Press.

Bauwens, L. and Lubrano, M. (1998). Bayesian inference on GARCH models using the Gibbs sampler. *The Econometrics Journal*, 1, C23–C46.

Bauwens, L. and Rasquero, A. (1993). Approximate HPD regions for testing residual autocorrelation using augmented regressions. In: Härdle, W. and Simar, L. (Eds.), *Computer Intensive Methods in Statistics*, pp. 47–61. Heidelberg: Physica Verlag.

Bauwens, L. and Richard, J.-F. (1985). A poly-t random variable generator, with application to Monte Carlo integration. *Journal of Econometrics*, 29, 19–46.

Bauwens, L. and van Dijk, H.K. (1990). Bayesian limited information analysis revisited. In: Gabszewicz, J.J., Richard, J.-F., and Wolsey, L. (Eds.), *Economic Decision-Making: Games, Econometrics and Optimisation*, Chap. 18. Amsterdam: North-Holland.

Bauwens, L., Bos, C.S., and van Dijk, H.K. (1998). Adaptive polar sampling. Discussion Paper TI 98–071/4, Tinbergen Institute. Amsterdam/Rotterdam.

Bauwens, L., Bulteau, J.-P., Gille, P., Longrée, L., Lubrano, M., and Tompa, H. (1981). *Bayesian Regression Programme (BRP) User's Manual.* CORE Computing Report 81-A-01. Université catholique de Louvain, Louvain-La-Neuve.

Bauwens, L., Fiebig, D., and Steel, M.F.J. (1994). Estimating end-use demand: a Bayesian approach. *Journal of Business and Economic Statistics*, 12, 221–231.

Bera, A.K. and Higgins, M.L. (1993). On ARCH models: properties, estimation and testing. *Journal of Economic Surveys*, 7, 305–366.

Berger, J.O. (1985a). *Statistical Decision Theory and Bayesian Analysis* (2nd edn). New York: Springer Verlag.

Berger, J.O. (1985b). In defense of the likelihood principle: axiomatics and coherence. In: Bernardo, J.M., DeGroot, M.H., Lindley, D.V., and Smith, A.F.M. (Eds.), *Bayesian Statistics 2*, pp. 33–65. Amsterdam: North-Holland.

Berger, J.O. and Bernardo, J.M. (1989). Estimating a product of means: Bayesian analysis with reference priors. *Journal of the American Statistical Association*, 84, 200-207.

Berger, J.O. and Bernardo, J.M. (1992). On the development of the reference prior method. In: Bernardo, J.M., Berger, J.O., Lindley, D.V., and Smith, A.F.M. (Eds.), *Bayesian Statistics 4*. London: Oxford University Press.

Berger, J.O. and Delampedy, M. (1987). Testing precise hypotheses. *Statistical Science*, 2, 317–352.

Berger, J.O. and Yang, R.Y. (1994). Non informative priors and Bayesian testing for the AR(1) model. *Econometric Theory*, 10, 461–482.

Bernardo, J.M. (1979). Reference prior distributions for Bayesian inference. *Journal of the Royal Statistical Society B*, 41, 113–147 (with discussion).

Bernardo, J.M. and Smith, A.F.M. (1994). *Bayesian Theory.* New-York: Wiley.

Blanchard, O.J. and Summers, L.H. (1986). Hysteresis and the European unemployment problem. In: Fisher, S. (Ed.), *NBER Macroeconomics Annual 1986*, pp. 15–77. Cambridge, MA: MIT Press.

Boldin, M.D. (1996). A check on the robustness of Hamilton's Markov switching model approach to the economic analysis of the business cycle. *Studies in Nonlinear Dynamics and Econometrics*, 1, 35–46.

Bollerslev, T. (1986). Generalized autoregressive conditional heteroscedasticity. *Journal of Econometrics*, 31, 307–327.

Bollerslev, T. (1987). A conditionally heteroscedastic time series model for speculative prices and rates of return. *Review of Economics and Statistics*, 69, 542–547.

Bollerslev, T., Chou, R.Y., and Kroner, K.F. (1992). ARCH modelling in finance: a review of the theory and empirical evidence. *Journal of Econometrics*, 52, 5–59.

Bollerslev, T., Engle, R.F., and Nelson, D.B. (1994). ARCH models. In: Engle, R.F. and McFadden, D.L. (Eds.), *Handbook of Econometrics, Vol. IV*, Chap. 49. Amsterdam: North-Holland.

Box, G.E.P. and Muller, M.E. (1958). A note on the generation of random normal deviates. *Annals of Mathematical Statistics*, 29, 610–611.

Breusch, T.S. and Pagan, A.R. (1979). A simple test for heteroscedasticity and random coefficient variation. *Econometrica*, 47, 1287–1294.

Campbell, J.Y., Lo, A.W., and MacKinley, A.C. (1997). *The Econometrics of Financial Markets*. Princeton, NJ: Princeton University Press.

Carnap, R. (1962). *Logical Foundations of Probability* (2nd edn). Chicago: University of Chicago Press.

Carruth, A. and Henley, A. (1990). Can existing consumption functions forecast consumer spending in the late 1980's? *Oxford Bulletin of Economics and Statistics*, 52, 211–222.

Casella, G. and George, E.I. (1992). Explaining the Gibbs sampler. *The American Statistician*, 46, 167–174.

Casella, G. and Robert, C.P. (1996). Rao–Blackwellisation of sampling schemes. *Biometrika*, 83, 81–94.

Chao, J.C. and Phillips, P.C.B. (1998a). Posterior distributions in limited information analysis of the simultaneous equations model using the Jeffreys prior. *Journal of Econometrics*, 87, 49–86.

Chao, J.C. and Phillips, P.C.B. (1998b). Jeffreys prior analysis of the simultaneous equations model in the case of $n+1$ endogenous variables. Cowles Foundation for Research in Economics, Yale University.

Chen, C.W.S. and Lee, J.C. (1995). Bayesian inference of threshold autoregressive models. *Journal of Time Series Analysis*, 16, 483–492.

Chib, S. (1993). Bayes regression with autocorrelated errors. *Journal of Econometrics*, 58, 275–294.

Chib, S. (1996). Inference in panel data models via Gibbs sampling. In: Matyas, L. and Sevestre, P. (Eds.), *The Econometrics of Panel Data* (2nd edn), Chap. 26. Dordrecht: Kluwer Academic Publishers.

Chib, S. and Greenberg, E. (1994). Bayes inference in regression models with ARMA(p,q) errors. *Journal of Econometrics*, 64, 183–206.

Chib, S. and Greenberg, E. (1995). Understanding the Metropolis–Hastings algorithm. *The American Statistician*, 49, 327–335.

Chib, S. and Greenberg, E. (1996). Markov Chain Monte Carlo simulation methods in econometrics. *Econometric Theory*, 12, 409–431.

Cook, P. and Broemeling, L.D. (1996). Analysing threshold autoregressions with a Bayesian approach. In: Fomby, T.B. (Ed.), *Advances in Econometrics: Bayesian Methods Applied to Time Series Data, Vol. 11, Part B*, pp. 89–107. Greenwich, CT: JAI Press.

Danielson, J. and Richard, J.-F. (1993). Accelerated Gaussian importance sampler with application to dynamic latent variable models. *Journal of Applied Econometrics*, 8, 153–173.

Davidson, J.E.H., Hendry, D.F., Sbra, F., and Yeo, S. (1978). Econometric modelling of the aggregate time-series relationship between consumers expenditure and income in the United Kingdom. *Economic Journal*, 88, 661–692.

Davies, R.B. (1977). Hypothesis testing when a nuisance parameter is present only under the alternative. *Biometrika*, 74, 33–43.

Davis, P.J. and Rabinowitz, P. (1975). *Methods of Numerical Integration.* New York: Academic Press.

De Finetti, B. (1937). Foresight: its logical laws, its subjective sources. Reprinted in: Kyburg, H.E. and Smokler, H. (Eds.), *Studies in Subjective Probability,* (1964), pp. 93–158. New York: Wiley.

De Finetti, B. (1974). *Theory of Probability, Vol. 1.* New York: Wiley.

De Finetti, B. (1975). *Theory of Probability. Vol. 2.* New York: Wiley.

DeGroot, M.H. (1970). *Optimal Statistical Decisions.* New York: McGraw-Hill.

DeJong, D.N. (1996). A Bayesian search for structural breaks in U.S. GNP. In: Fomby, T.B. (Ed.), *Advances in Econometrics: Bayesian Methods Applied to Time Series Data, Vol. 11, Part B*, pp. 109–146. Greenwich, CT: JAI Press.

DeJong, D.N. and Whiteman, C.H. (1989). Trends and cycles as unobserved components in US real GNP: a Bayesian perspective. *Journal of the American Statistical Association Papers and Proceedings*, 63–70.

DeJong, D.N. and Whiteman, C.H. (1991a). Reconsidering 'Trends and random walks in macroeconomic time series'. *Journal of Monetary Economics*, 28, 221–254.

DeJong, D.N. and Whiteman, C.H. (1991b). The temporal stability of dividends and stock prices: evidence from the likelihood function. *American Economic Review*, 81, 600–617.

DeJong, D.N. and Whiteman, C.H. (1991c). The case for trend stationarity is stronger than we thought. *Journal of Applied Econometrics*, 6, 413–421.

DeJong, D.N. and Whiteman, C.H. (1993). Estimating moving average parameters: classical pile-ups and Bayesian posteriors. *Journal of Business and Economic Statistics*, 11, 311–317.

Devroye, L. (1986). *Non uniform Random Variate Generation.* New York: Springer Verlag.

Dickey, D.A. and Fuller, W.A. (1978). Distribution of the estimator for autoregressive time series with a unit root. *Journal of the American Statistical Association*, 74, 427–431.

Doan, T., Litterman, R.B., and Sims, C.A. (1984). Forecasting and conditional projection under realistic prior distributions. *Econometric Reviews*, 3, 1–

100.

Drèze, J.H. (1962). The Bayesian approach to simultaneous equations estimation. *ONR Research Memorandum* 67, The Technological Institute, Northwestern University.

Drèze, J.H. (1975). Axiomatic theories of choice, cardinal utility and subjective probability: a review. In: Drèze, J.H. (Ed.), *Allocation under Uncertainty*. London: Macmillan.

Drèze, J.H. (1976). Bayesian limited information analysis of the simultaneous equations model. *Econometrica*, 44, 1045–1075.

Drèze, J.H. (1978). Bayesian regression analysis using poly-t densities. *Journal of Econometrics*, 6, 329–354.

Drèze J.H. (1980). Réduction progressive des heures et partage du travail. *Rapport pour la 3ième Commission du 4ième Congrès des Economistes Belges de Langue Française*, 1–29.

Drèze, J.H. and Modigliani, F. (1981). The trade-off between real wages and unemployment in an open economy (Belgium). *European Economic Review*, 15, 1–40.

Drèze, J.H. and Morales, J.A. (1976). Bayesian full information analysis of simultaneous equations. *Journal of the American Statistical Association*, 71, 919–923.

Drèze, J.H. and Richard, J.-F. (1983). Bayesian analysis of simultaneous equation systems. In: Griliches, Z. and Intriligator, M.D. (Eds.), *Handbook of Econometrics, Vol. I*, Chap. 9. Amsterdam: North-Holland.

Durbin, J. and Watson, G.S. (1950). Testing for serial correlation in least squares regression. *Biometrika*, 37, 409–428.

Edwards, W., Lindman, H., and Savage, L.J. (1963). Bayesian statistical inference for psychological research. *Psychological Review*, 70, 193–242.

Engle, R.F. (1982). Autoregressive conditional heteroscedasticity with estimates of the variance of United Kingdom inflation. *Econometrica*, 50, 987–1008.

Engle, R.F. and Bollerslev, T. (1986). Modelling the persistence of conditional variances. *Econometric Reviews*, 5, 1–50.

Engle, R.F. and Granger, C.W.J. (1987). Co-integration and error correction: representation, estimation and testing. *Econometrica*, 55, 251–276.

Engle, R.F. and Mustafa, C. (1992). Implied ARCH models for option prices. *Journal of Econometrics*, 52, 289–311.

Engle, R.F., Hendry, D.F., and Richard, J.-F. (1983). Exogeneity. *Econometrica*, 51, 277–304.

Fair, R.C. and Jaffee, D.M. (1972). Methods of estimation for markets in disequilibrium. *Econometrica*, 40, 497–514.

Ferreira, P.E. (1975). A Bayesian analysis of a switching regression model: known number of regimes. *Journal of the American Statistical Association*, 70, 370–374.

Fisher, R.A. (1956). *Statistical Methods and Scientific Inference*. Edinburgh: Oliver and Boyd.

Florens, J.-P. and Mouchart, M. (1982). A note on noncausality. *Econometrica*, 50, 583–591.

Florens, J.-P. and Mouchart, M. (1985a). Conditioning in dynamic models. *Journal of Time Series Analysis*, 53, 15–35.

Florens, J.-P. and Mouchart, M. (1985b). A linear theory for noncausality. *Econometrica*, 53, 157–175.

Florens, J.-P., Mouchart, M., and Richard, J.-F. (1974). Bayesian inference in error-in-variables models. *Journal of Multivariate Analysis*, 4, 419–452.

Forbes, C.S., Kalb, G.R.J., and Kofman, P. (1997). Bayesian arbitrage threshold analysis. Monash Discussion Paper.

Franses, P.-H., Hoek, H., and Paap, R. (1997). Bayesian analysis of seasonal unit roots and mean shifts. *Journal of Econometrics*, 78, 359–380.

Gantmacher, F. (1960). *Matrix Theory*. New York: Chelsea.

Gelman, A. and Rubin, D. (1994). A single series from the Gibbs sampler provides a false sense of security. In: Bernardo, J.M., Berger, J.O., Dawid, A.P., and Smith, A.F.M. (Eds.), *Bayesian Statistics 4*. Oxford: Oxford University Press.

Geweke, J. (1986a). Exact inference in the inequality constrained normal linear regression model. *Journal of Applied Econometrics*, 1, 127–141.

Geweke, J. (1986b). Modelling the persistence of conditional variances: a comment. *Econometric Reviews*, 5, 57–61.

Geweke, J. (1988a). Antithetic acceleration of Monte Carlo integration in Bayesian inference. *Journal of Econometrics*, 38, 73–89.

Geweke, J. (1988b). Exact inference in models with autoregressive conditional heteroscedasticity. In: Barnett, W.A., Berndt, E.R., and White, H. (Eds.), *Dynamic Econometric Modeling*, pp. 73–104. Cambridge: Cambridge University Press.

Geweke, J. (1989a). Bayesian inference in econometric models using Monte Carlo integration. *Econometrica*, 57, 1317–1339.

Geweke, J. (1989b). Exact predictive densities in linear models with ARCH disturbances. *Journal of Econometrics*, 40, 63–86.

Geweke, J. (1992). Evaluating the accuracy of sampling-based approaches to the calculation of posterior moments. In: Bernardo, J.M., Berger, J.O., Dawid, A.P., and Smith, A.F.M. (Eds.), *Bayesian Statistics 4*. Oxford: Oxford University Press.

Geweke, J. (1993). Bayesian treatment of the independent Student-t linear model. *Journal of Applied Econometrics*, 8, S19–S40.

Geweke, J. (1994). Bayesian comparison of econometric models. Working Paper 532. Research Department, Federal Reserve Bank of Minneapolis.

Geweke, J. (1995). Posterior simulators in econometrics. Working Paper 555. Research Department, Federal Reserve Bank of Minneapolis.

Geweke, J. (1996). Bayesian reduced rank regression in econometrics. *Journal of Econometrics*, 75, 121–146.

Geweke, J. and Terui, N. (1993). Bayesian threshold autoregressive models for nonlinear time series. *Journal of Time Series Analysis*, 14, 441–454.

Ghysels, E., Harvey, A.C., and Renault, E. (1995). Stochastic volatility. In: Maddala, G.S. and Rao, C.R. (Eds.), *Handbook of Statistics, Vol. 14: Statistical Methods in Finance*, Chap. 5. Amsterdam: North-Holland.

Ghysels, E., McCulloch, R.E., and Tsay, R.S. (1998). Bayesian inference for periodic regime-switching models. *Journal of Applied Econometrics*, 13, 129–143.

Ginsburgh, V., Tishler, A., and Zang, I. (1980). Alternative estimation methods for two regime models. *European Economic Review*, 13, 207–228.

Glosten, L.R., Jagannathan, R., and Runkle, D.E. (1993). On the relation between the expected value and the volatility of the nominal excess return on stocks. *Journal of Finance*, 48, 1779–1801.

Granger, C.W.J. (1969). Investigating causal relations by econometric models and cross-spectral methods. *Econometrica*, 37, 424–438.

Granger, C.W.J. and Newbold, P. (1986). *Forecasting Economic Time Series*. London: Academic Press.

Granger, C.W.J. and Teräsvirta, T. (1993). *Modeling Nonlinear Economic Relationships*. Oxford: Oxford University Press.

Gregory, A.W. and Hansen, B.E. (1996). Tests for cointegration in models with regime and trend shifts. *Oxford Bulletin of Economics and Statistics*, 58, 555–560.

Griffiths, W.E., Drynan, R.G., and Prakash, S. (1979). Bayesian estimation of a random coefficient model. *Journal of Econometrics*, 10, 201–220.

Hall, R.E. (1978). Stochastic implication of the life cycle-permanent income hypothesis: theory and evidence. *Journal of Political Economy*, 86, 971–987.

Hamilton, J.D. (1989). A new approach to the economic analysis of non stationary time series and the business cycle. *Econometrica*, 57, 357–384.

Hamilton, J.D. (1994). *Time Series Analysis*. Princeton, NJ: Princeton University Press.

Hammersley, J.M. and Handscomb, D.C. (1964). *Monte Carlo Methods*. London: Chapman and Hall.

Hansen, B.E. (1996). Inference when a nuisance parameter is not identified under the null hypothesis. *Econometrica*, 64, 413–430.

Harvey, A.C. (1990). *The Econometric Analysis of Time Series* (2nd edn). London: Philip Allan.

Hastings, W.K. (1970). Monte Carlo sampling methods using Markov chains and their applications. *Biometrika*, 57, 97–109.

Hendry, D.F. and Mizon, G.E. (1978). Serial correlation as a convenient simplification, not a nuisance: a comment on a study of the demand for money by the Bank of England. *The Economic Journal*, 88, 549–563.

Hendry, D.F. and Richard, J.-F. (1982). On the formulation of empirical models in dynamic econometrics. *Journal of Econometrics*, 20, 3–33.

Hendry, D.F. and von Ungern-Sternberg, T. (1981). Liquidity and inflation effects on consumers' expenditure. In: Deaton, A. (Ed.), *Essays in the Theory and Measurement of Consumer Behaviour*. Cambridge: Cambridge University Press.

Hendry, D.F., Pagan, A.R., and Sargan, J.D. (1984). Dynamic specification. In: Griliches, Z. and Intriligator, M.D. (Eds.), *Handbook of Econometrics*, Chap. 18. Amsterdam: North-Holland.

Hesterberg, T. (1991). Importance sampling for Bayesian estimation. In: Buja, A. and Tukey, P. (Eds.), *Computing and Graphics in Statistics*, Vol. 36 of the IMA Volumes in Mathematics and Its Applications, pp. 63–75.

Heston, S. (1993). A closed form solution for options with stochastic volatility with applications to bond and currency options. *Review of Financial Studies*, 6, 327–343.

Hoek, H., Lucas, A., and van Dijk, H.K. (1995). Classical and Bayesian aspects of robust unit root inference. *Journal of Econometrics*, 69, 27–59.

Hoover, K.D. (1988). On the pitfalls of untested common factor restrictions: the case of the inverted Fisher hypothesis. *Oxford Bulletin of Economics and Statistics*, 50, 125–138.

Hurwicz, L. (1950). Least squares bias in time series. In: Koopmans, T.C. (Ed.), *Statistical Inference in Dynamic Economic Models*. Cowles Commission Monograph 10, pp. 365–383. New York: Wiley.

Jacquier, E., Polson, N.G., and Rossi, P.E. (1994). Bayesian analysis of stochastic volatility models. *Journal of Economic and Business Statistics*, 12, 371–389.

Jansen, E.S. and Teräsvirta, T. (1996). Testing parameter constancy and super exogeneity in econometric equations. *Oxford Bulletin of Economics and Statistics*, 58, 735–763.

Jeffreys, H. (1961). *The Theory of Probability* (3rd edn). Oxford: Clarendon Press.

Johansen, S. (1991). Estimation and hypothesis testing of cointegration vectors in Gaussian autoregressive models. *Econometrica*, 59, 1551–1580.

Johansen, S. (1995). Identifying restrictions of linear equations. *Journal of Econometrics*, 69, 111–132.

Johansen, S. and Juselius, K. (1994). Identification of the long run and short run structure. An application to the ISLM model. *Journal of Econometrics*, 63, 7–36.

Johnson, N.L. and Kotz, S. (1972). *Distributions in Statistics: Continuous Multivariate Distributions*. New York: Wiley.

Johnson, N.L., Kotz, S., and Balakrishnan, N. (1994). *Continuous Univariate Distributions, Vol. 1* (2nd edn). New York: Wiley.

Johnson, N.L., Kotz, S., and Balakrishnan, N. (1995). *Continuous Univariate Distributions, Vol. 2* (2nd edn). New York: Wiley.

Judge, G.G., Griffiths, W.E., Carter Hill, R., Lütkepohl, H., and Lee, T.-C. (1985). *The Theory and Practice of Econometrics* (2nd edn). New York:

Wiley.

Kadane, J. (1974). The role of identification in Bayesian theory. In: Fienberg, S.E. and Zellner, A. (Eds.), *Studies in Bayesian Econometrics and Statistics: in honour of Leonard J. Savage*, pp. 175–191. Amsterdam: North-Holland.

Kadane, J.B. (1980). Predictive and structural methods for eliciting prior distributions. In: Zellner, A. (Ed.), *Bayesian Analysis in Econometrics and Statistics*, pp. 89–109. Amsterdam: North-Holland.

Kadane, J.B., Chan, N.H., and Wolfson, L.J. (1996). Priors for unit root models. *Journal of Econometrics*, 75, 99–111.

Kadane, J.B., Dickey, J.M., Winkler, R.L., Smith, W.S., and Peters, S.C. (1980). Interactive elicitation of opinion for a normal linear model. *Journal of the American Statistical Association*, 75, 845–854.

Kadiyala, K.R. and Karlsson, S. (1997). Numerical methods for estimation and inference in Bayesian VAR models. *Journal of Applied Econometrics*, 12, 99–132.

Kass, R.E., Tierney, L., and Kadane, J.B. (1990). The validity of posterior expansions based on Laplace's method. In: Geisser, S., Hodges, S.J., Press, S.J., and Zellner, A. (Eds.), *Bayesian and Likelihood Methods in Statistics and Econometrics*, pp. 473–488. New York: North-Holland.

Kendall, M.G. and Stuart, A. (1967). *The Advanced Theory of Statistics, Vol. 2* (3rd edn). London: Griffin.

Keynes, J.M. (1921). *A Treatise on Probability*. London: Macmillan. Reprinted by Harper, New York, 1962.

Kiefer, N.M. and Richard, J.-F. (1979). A Bayesian approach to hypothesis testing and evaluating estimation strategies. CORE Discussion Paper 7927. Louvain-La-Neuve.

King, R.G., Plosser, C.I., and Rebelo, S.T. (1988). Production, growth and business cycles: I. The basic neoclassical model. *Journal of Monetary Economics*, 21, 195–232.

Kleibergen, F. and Hoek, H. (1995). Bayesian analysis of ARMA models using uninformative priors. Econometric Institute Technical Report No. 9553/A. Rotterdam.

Kleibergen, F. and Paap, R. (1997). Priors, posterior odds and Lagrange multiplier statistics in Bayesian analyses of cointegration. Mimeo.

Kleibergen, F. and van Dijk, H.K. (1993). Non-stationarity in GARCH models: a Bayesian analysis. *Journal of Applied Econometrics*, 8 (Supplement), 41–61.

Kleibergen, F. and van Dijk, H.K. (1994a). On the shape of the likelihood/ posterior in cointegration models. *Econometric Theory*, 10, 514–551.

Kleibergen, F. and van Dijk, H.K. (1994b). Bayesian analysis of simultaneous equation models using noninformative priors. Discussion Paper TI 94–134, Tinbergen Institute. Amsterdam/Rotterdam.

Kloek, T. and van Dijk, H.K. (1978). Bayesian estimates of equation system parameters: an application of integration by Monte Carlo. *Econometrica*,

46, 1–19.

Knuth, D.E. (1981). *The Art of Computer Programming, Vol. 2.* Reading, MA: Addison-Wesley.

Kolmogorov, A.N. (1950). *Foundations of the Theory of Probability.* New York: Chelsea.

Koop, G. (1991). Intertemporal properties of real output: a Bayesian approach. *Journal of Business and Economic Statistics,* 9, 253–265.

Koop, G. (1998). Bayesian inference in models based on equilibrium search theory. University of Edinburgh, Dept. of Economics.

Koop, G. and Potter, S.M. (1995). Bayesian analysis of endogenous delay threshold models using the Gibbs sampler. Mimeo.

Koop, G. and Potter, S.M. (1999). Bayes factors and nonlinearity: evidence from economic time series. *Journal of Econometrics,* 88, 251–281.

Koop, G. and Steel, M.F.J. (1991). To criticize the critics: an objective Bayesian analysis of stochastic trends: a comment. *Journal of Applied Econometrics,* 6, 365–370.

Koop, G., Ley, E., Osiewalski, J., and Steel, M.F.J. (1997). Bayesian analysis of long memory and persistence using ARFIMA models. *Journal of Econometrics,* 76, 149–169.

Koop, G., Osiewalski, J., and Steel, M.F.J. (1995). Bayesian long run prediction in time series models. *Journal of Econometrics,* 69, 61–80.

Koop, G., Steel, M.F.J., and Osiewalski, J. (1995). Posterior analysis of stochastic frontier models using Gibbs sampling. *Computational Statistics,* 10, 353–373.

Kyburg, H.E. (1970). *Probability and Inductive Logic.* London: Macmillan.

Leamer, E.E. (1982). *Specification Searches: ad hoc Inference with Non Experimental Data.* New York: Wiley.

Lin, C.F. and Teräsvirta, T. (1994). Testing the constancy of regression parameters against continuous change. *Journal of Econometrics,* 62, 211–228.

Lindgren, G. (1978). Markov regime models for mixed distributions and switching regressions. *Scandinavian Journal of Statistics,* 5, 81–91.

Lindley, D.V. (1957). A statistical paradox. *Biometrika,* 44, 187–192.

Lindley, D.V. (1972). *Bayesian Statistics: a Review.* Philadelphia: SIAM.

Lindley, D.V. and Smith, A.F.M. (1972). Bayes estimates for the linear model. *Journal of the Royal Statistical Society B,* 34, 1–41.

Lindley, D.V., Tversky, A., and Brown, R.V. (1979). On the reconciliation of probability assessments. *Journal of the Royal Statistical Society A,* 142, 146–180.

Litterman, R.B. (1986). Forecasting with Bayesian vector autoregressions—five years of experience. *Journal of Business and Economic Statistics,* 4, 25–38.

Lubrano, M. (1985). Bayesian analysis of switching regression models. *Journal of Econometrics,* 29, 69–95.

Lubrano, M. (1986). *Contributions à l'Inférence Bayesienne dans les Modèles de Déséquilibre: Applications au Marché du Travail.* Unpublished Ph.D. Dissertation, University of Toulouse.

Lubrano, M. (1993). Bayesian unit root tests with endogenous break point: an application to the analysis of persistence in European unemployment rate series. Mimeo.

Lubrano, M. (1995a). Testing for unit roots in a Bayesian framework. *Journal of Econometrics*, 69, 81–109.

Lubrano, M. (1995b). Bayesian tests for cointegration in the case of structural breaks: an application to the analysis of wage moderation in France. *Recherches Economiques de Louvain*, 61, 479–507.

Lubrano, M. (1999). Bayesian analysis of nonlinear time series models with a threshold. In: Barnett, W.A., Hendry, D.F., Hylleberg, S., Teräsvirta, T., Tjøstheim, ans D. and Würtz, A. (Eds.), *Nonlinear Econometric Modelling*. Cambridge: Cambridge University Press.

Lubrano, M., Pierse, R.G., and Richard, J.-F. (1986). Stability of a UK money demand equation: a Bayesian approach to testing exogeneity. *Review of Economic Studies*, 53, 603–634.

Luukkonen, R., Saikkonen, P., and Teräsvirta, T. (1988). Testing linearity against smooth transition autoregression. *Biometrika*, 75, 491–499.

MacEachern, S.N. and Berliner, L.M. (1994). Subsampling the Gibbs sampler. *The American Statistician*, 48, 188–190.

Maddala, G.S. (1976). Weak priors and sharp posteriors in simultaneous equation models. *Econometrica*, 44; 345–351.

Maddala, G.S. and Nelson, F.D. (1974). Maximum likelihood methods for models of markets in disequilibrium. *Econometrica*, 42, 1013–1030.

Magnus, J.R. and Neudecker, H. (1988). *Matrix Differential Calculus with Applications in Statistics and Econometrics*. New York: Wiley.

Marsaglia, G. and Zaman, A. (1993). The KISS generator. Technical Report, University of Florida.

Marshall, R.C., Richard, J.-F., and Zarkin, G.A. (1992). Posterior probabilities of the independence axiom with nonexperimental data (or buckle up and fan out). *Journal of Business and Economic Statistics*, 10, 31–44.

McCulloch, R.E. and Tsay, R.S. (1993). Bayesian inference and prediction for mean and variance shifts. *Journal of the American Statistical Association*, 88, 968–978.

Metropolis, N., Rosenbluth, A.W., Rosenbluth, M.N., Teller, A.H., and Teller, E. (1953). Equations of state calculations by fast computing machines. *Journal of Chemical Physics*, 21, 1087–1091.

Mizon, G.E. (1995). A simple message for autocorrelation correctors: don't. *Journal of Econometrics*, 69, 267–288.

Monahan, J.F. (1983). Fully Bayesian analysis of ARMA time series models. *Journal of Econometrics*, 21, 307–331.

Morales, J.A. (1971). *Bayesian Full Information Structural Analysis*. Berlin: Springer Verlag.

Nelson, D.B. (1990). Stationarity and persistence in the GARCH(1,1) model. *Econometric Theory*, 6, 318–334.

Nelson, D.B. (1991). Conditional heteroscedasticity in asset returns: a new approach. *Econometrica*, 59, 347–370.

Nelson, C. R. and Plosser, C.I. (1982). Trends and random walks in macroeconomic time series: some evidence and implications. *Journal of Monetary Economics*, 10, 139–162.

Neyman, J. (1952). *Lectures and Conferences on Mathematical Statistics and Probability*. Washington, DC: Dept. of Agriculture.

Noh, J., Engle, R.F., and Kane, A. (1994). Forecasting volatility and option prices of the S & P 500 index. *Journal of Derivatives*, 17–30. Reprinted in: Engle, R.F. (Ed.), *ARCH: Selected Readings*, (1995), Chap. 15. Oxford: Oxford University Press.

Novick, M. (1969). Multiparameter Bayesian indifference procedures. *Journal of the Royal Statistical Society B*, 31, 29–51.

O'Brien, R.J. (1970). Serial correlation in econometric models. In: Hilton, K. and Heathfield, D.F. (Eds.), *The Econometric Study of the United Kingdom*, pp. 375–437. London: Macmillan.

Osiewalski, J. and Welfe, A. (1998). The price–wage mechanism: an endogenous switching model. *European Economic Review*, 42, 365–374.

Pagan, A.R. (1978). Detecting autocorrelation after Bayesian regression. CORE Discussion Paper 7825. Louvain-La-Neuve.

Pagan, A.R. (1984). Model evaluation by variable addition. In: Hendry, D.F. and Wallis, K.F. (Eds.), *Econometrics and Quantitative Economics*, pp. 103–133. Oxford: Blackwell.

Pagan, A.R. (1996). The Econometrics of Financial Markets. *Journal of Empirical Finance*, 3, 15–102.

Peguin-Feisolle, A. (1994). Bayesian estimation and forecasting in nonlinear models: application to a LSTAR model. *Economic Letters*, 46, 187–194.

Percy, D.F. (1992). Prediction for seemingly unrelated regressions. *Journal of the Royal Statistical Society B*, 54, 243–252.

Perron, P. (1989). The great crash, the oil price shock, and the unit root hypothesis. *Econometrica*, 57, 1361–1401.

Perron, P. and Vogelsang, T.J. (1992). Nonstationarity and level shifts with an application to purchasing power parity. *Journal of Business and Economic Statistics*, 10, 301–320.

Pfann, G.A., Schotman, P.C., and Tschernig, R. (1996). Nonlinear interest rate dynamics and the implications for the term structure. *Journal of Econometrics*, 74, 149–176.

Phillips, P.C.B. (1991a). To criticize the critics: an objective Bayesian analysis of stochastic trends. *Journal of Applied Econometrics*, 6, 333–364.

Phillips, P.C.B. (1991b). Bayesian routes and unit roots: de rebus prioribus semper est disputandum. *Journal of Applied Econometrics*, 6, 435–474.

Phillips, P.C.B. (1998). Posterior distributions in limited information analysis of the simultaneous equations model using the Jeffreys prior. *Journal of Econometrics*, 87, 49–86.

Pole, A.M. and Smith, A.F.M. (1985). A Bayesian analysis of some threshold switching models. *Journal of Econometrics*, 29, 97–119.

Potter, S.M. (1995). A nonlinear approach to US GNP. *Journal of Applied Econometrics*, 10, 109–125.

Pratt, J.W. (1965). Bayesian interpretation of standard inference statements (with discussion). *Journal of the Royal Statistical Society B*, 27, 169–203.

Press, W.H. (1992). *Numerical Recipes C Book (The Art of Scientific Computing)*. Cambridge: Cambridge University Press.

Quandt, R.E. (1958). The estimation of parameters of a linear regression system obeying two separate regimes. *Journal of the American Statistical Association*, 53, 873–880.

Raiffa, H. and Schlaifer, R. (1961). *Applied Statistical Decision Theory*. Cambridge, MA: MIT Press.

Richard, J.-F. (1973). *Posterior and Predictive Densities for Simultaneous Equation Models*. Berlin: Springer Verlag.

Richard, J.-F. (1975). A note on the information matrix of the multivariate normal distribution. *Journal of Econometrics*, 3, 57–60.

Richard, J.-F. (1977). Bayesian analysis of the regression model when the disturbances are generated by an autoregressive process. In: Aykac, A. and Brumat, C. (Eds.), *New Developments in the Application of Bayesian Methods*, pp. 185–209. Amsterdam: North-Holland.

Richard, J.-F. (1980). C-type distributions and disequilibrium models. Mimeo.

Richard, J.-F. (1996). Simulation techniques. In: Matyas, L. and Sevestre, P. (Eds.), *The Econometrics of Panel Data* (2nd edn), pp. 613–638. Dordrecht: Kluwer Academic Publishers.

Richard, J.-F. and Steel, M.F.J. (1988). Bayesian analysis of systems of seemingly unrelated regression equations under a recursive extended natural conjugate prior density. *Journal of Econometrics*, 38, 7–37.

Richard, J.-F., and Tompa, H. (1980). On the evaluation of poly-*t* density functions. *Journal of Econometrics*, 12, 335–351.

Richard, J.-F. and Zhang, W. (1997). Accelerated Monte Carlo integration: an application to dynamic latent variable models. In: Mariano, R., Weeks, M., and Schuermann, T. (Eds.), *Simulation Based Inference in Econometrics: Methods and Applications*. Cambridge: Cambridge University Press.

Ritter, C. and Tanner, M.A. (1992). Facilitating the Gibbs sampler: the Gibbs stopper and the griddy-Gibbs sampler. *Journal of the American Statistical Association*, 87, 861–868.

Robert, C.P. (1996). *Méthodes de Monte Carlo par Chaînes de Markov*. Paris: Economica.

Rothenberg, T. (1963). A Bayesian analysis of simultaneous equation systems. Econometric Institute Report 6315, Erasmus University, Rotterdam.

Rubin, H. (1950). Consistency of maximum likelihood estimates in the explosive case. In: Koopmans, T.C. (Ed.), *Statistical Inference in Dynamic Economic Models*. Cowles Commission Monograph 10, pp. 356–364. New York: Wiley.

Rubinstein, R.Y. (1981). *Simulation and the Monte Carlo Method*. New York: Wiley.

Sargan, J.D. (1961). The maximum likelihood estimation of economic relationships with autoregressive residuals. *Econometrica*, 29, 414–426.

Sargan, J.D. (1964). Wages and prices in the United Kingdom: a study in econometric methodology. Reprinted in: Hendry, D.F. and Wallis, K.F. (1984), *Economics and Quantitative Economics*, pp. 275–314. Oxford: Blackwell.

Savage, L.J. (1954). *The Foundations of Statistics*. New York: Wiley.

Savage, L.J. (1962). Subjective probability and statistical practice. In: Savage, L.J. *et al.*, *The Foundations of Statistical Inference*. London: Methuen.

Savage, L.J. (1971). Elicitation of personal probabilities and expectations. *Journal of the American Statistical Association*, 66, 783–801.

Schotman, P.C. (1994). Priors for the AR(1) model, parameterisation issues and time series considerations. *Econometric Theory*, 10, 579–595.

Schotman, P.C. (1996). A Bayesian approach to the empirical valuation of bond options. *Journal of Econometrics*, 75, 183–215.

Schotman, P.C. and van Dijk, H.K. (1991a). A Bayesian analysis of the unit root hypothesis in real exchange rates. *Journal of Econometrics*, 49, 195–238.

Schotman, P.C. and van Dijk, H.K. (1991b). On Bayesian routes to unit roots. *Journal of Applied Econometrics*, 49, 387–401.

Schotman, P.C. and van Dijk, H.K. (1993). Posterior analysis of possibly integrated time series with an application to real GNP. In: Caines, P., Geweke, J., and Taqqu, M. (Eds.), *New Directions in Time Series Analysis, Part II*. New York: Springer Verlag.

Schwarz, G. (1978). Estimating the dimension of a model. *Annals of Statistics*, 6, 461–464.

Shephard, N. (1996). Statistical aspects of ARCH and stochastic volatility. In: Cox, D.R., Hinkley, D.V., and Barndorff-Nielsen, O.E. (Eds.), *Time Series Models in Econometrics, Finance and Other Fields*, pp. 1–67. London: Chapman and Hall.

Shephard, N. and Pitt, M.K. (1997). Likelihood analysis of non-Gaussian measurement time series. *Biometrika*, 84, 653–667.

Sims, C.A. (1980). Macroeconomics and Reality. *Econometrica*, 48, 1–48.

Sims, C.A. (1988). Bayesian skepticism on unit root econometrics. *Journal of Economic Dynamics and Control*, 12, 463–474.

Sims, C.A. (1991). To criticize the critics: comment. *Journal of Applied Econometrics*, 6, 423–434.

Sims, C.A. and Uhlig, H. (1991). Understanding unit rooters: a helicopter tour. *Econometrica*, 59, 1591–1600.

Smith, A.F.M., Skene, A.M., Shaw, J.E.H., and Naylor, J.C. (1987). Progress with numerical and graphical methods for practical Bayesian statistics. *The Statistician*, 36, 75–82.

Sneessens, H. (1985). Two alternative stochastic specifications and estimation methods for quantity rationing models: a Monte Carlo comparison. *European Economic Review*, 29, 111–136.

Steel, M.F.J. (1998). Posterior analysis of stochastic volatility models with flexible tails. *Econometric Reviews*, 17, 109–143.

Stein, C. (1956). Inadmissibility of the usual estimator of the mean of a multivariate normal distribution. In: Neyman, J. and Scott, E.L. (Eds.), *Proceedings of the Third Berkeley Symposium*, pp. 197–206. Berkeley, University of California.

Stein, E.M. and Stein, J.C. (1991). Stock price distributions with stochastic volatility: an analytic approach. *Review of Financial Studies*, 4, 727–752.

Stigler, S.M. (1982). Thomas Bayes's Bayesian Inference. *Journal of the Royal Statistical Society A*, 142, 250–258.

Teräsvirta, T. (1994). Specification, estimation and evaluation of smooth transition autoregressive models. *Journal of the American Statistical Association*, 89, 208–218.

Teräsvirta, T. (1996). Two stylized facts and the GARCH(1,1) model. Working paper No. 96, Stockholm School of Economics.

Teräsvirta, T. and Anderson, H.M. (1992). Modeling nonlinearities in business cycles using smooth transition autoregressive models. *Journal of Applied Econometrics*, 7, S119–S136.

Thornber, H. (1967). Finite sample Monte Carlo studies: an autoregressive illustration. *Journal of the American Statistical Association*, 62, 801–818.

Tiao, G.C. and Tsay, R.S. (1994). Some advances in nonlinear and adaptive modelling in time series. *Journal of Forecasting*, 13, 109–131.

Tierney, L. (1994). Markov chains for exploring posterior distributions. *Annals of Statistics*, 22, 1701–1762.

Tierney, L. and Kadane, J.B. (1986). Accurate approximations for posterior moments and marginal densities. *Journal of the American Statistical Association*, 81, 82–86.

Tierney, L., Kass, R.E., and Kadane, J.B. (1989a). Fully exponential Laplace approximations to expectations and variances of nonpositive functions. *Journal of the American Statistical Association*, 84, 710–716.

Tierney, L., Kass, R.E., and Kadane, J.B. (1989b). Approximate marginal densities of nonlinear functions. *Biometrika*, 76, 425–433.

Tishler, A. and Zang, I. (1981). A new maximum likelihood algorithm for piecewise regression. *Journal of the American Statistical Association*, 76, 980–987.

Tompa, H. (1973). The iterative Simpson method of numerical integration. CORE Discussion Paper 7336, Université catholique de Louvain, Louvain-La-Neuve.

Tong, H. and Lim, K.S. (1980). Threshold autoregression, limit cycles and cyclical data. *Journal of the Royal Statistical Society B*, 42, 245–292.

Tsay, R.S. (1989). Testing and modeling threshold autoregressive processes. *Journal of the American Statistical Association*, 84, 231–240.

Uhlig, H. (1994a). What macroeconomists should know about unit roots. *Econometric Theory*, 10, 645–671.

Uhlig, H. (1994b). On Jeffreys' prior when using the exact likelihood function. *Econometric Theory*, 10, 633–644.

Uhlig, H. (1997). Bayesian vector autoregressions with stochastic volatility. *Econometrica*, 65, 59–73.

Urbain, J.-P. (1992). On weak exogeneity in error correction models. *Oxford Bulletin of Economics and Statistics*, 54, 187–208.

Urbain, J.-P. (1995). Partial versus full system modelling of cointegrated systems: an empirical illustration. *Journal of Econometrics*, 63, 177–210.

van Dijk, H.K. (1984). *Posterior analysis of econometric models using Monte Carlo integration*. Unpublished Dissertation, Erasmus University Rotterdam.

van Dijk, H.K., Kloek, T., and Boender, C.G. (1985). Posterior moments computed by mixed integration. *Journal of Econometrics*, 29, 3–18.

Venn, J. (1886). *The Logic of Chance*. London: Macmillan. Reprinted by Chelsea, New York, 1963.

Villa, P. (1996). La fonction de consommation sur longue période en France. *Revue Economique*, 47, 111–142.

Von Mises, R. (1928). *Wahrscheinlichkeit, Statistik, und Warheit*. Wien: J. Springer. English translation, *Probability, Statistics and Truth* (2nd edn). New York: Macmillan, 1954.

White, J.S. (1958). The limiting distribution of the serial correlation coefficient in the explosive case. *Annals of Mathematical Statistics*, 29, 1188–1197.

Winkler, R.L. (1967). The assessment of prior distributions in Bayesian analysis. *Journal of the American Statistical Association*, 62, 776–800.

Winkler, R.L. (1972). *Introduction to Bayesian Inference and Decision*. New York: Holt, Rinehart and Winston.

Yu, B. and Mykland, P. (1994). Looking at Markov samplers through CUMSUM path plots: a simple diagnostic idea. Technical Report 413. Department of Statistics, University of California at Berkeley.

Zakoian, J.-M. (1994). Threshold heteroscedastic models. *Journal of Economic Dynamics and Control*, 18, 931–955.

Zellner, A. (1965). Bayesian and non-Bayesian analysis of simultaneous equation models. Paper presented at the First World Congress of the Econometric Society, Rome.

Zellner, A. (1971). *An Introduction to Bayesian Inference in Econometrics*. New York: Wiley.

Zellner, A. (1985). Bayesian Statistics in Econometrics. In: Bernardo, J.M., De-Groot, M.H., Lindley, D.V., and Smith, A.F.M. (Eds.), *Bayesian Statistics*, pp. 571–581. Amsterdam: North-Holland.

Zellner, A. (1986a). Bayesian estimation and prediction using asymmetric loss functions. *Journal of the American Statistical Association*, 81, 446–494.

Zellner, A. (1986b). On assessing prior distributions and Bayesian regression analysis with *g*-prior distributions. In: Goel, P. and Zellner, A., *Bayesian Inference and Decision Techniques*. Amsterdam: Elsevier Science Publishers.

Zellner, A. and Min, C. (1995). Gibbs sampler convergence criteria. *Journal of the American Statistical Association*, 90, 921–927.

Zellner, A. and Tiao, G.C. (1964). Bayesian analysis of the regression model with autocorrelated errors. *Journal of the American Statistical Association*, 59, 763–778.

Zellner A., Bauwens, L., and van Dijk, H.K. (1988). Bayesian specification analysis and estimation of simultaneous equation models using Monte Carlo methods. *Journal of Econometrics*, 38, 39–72.

Zivot, E. (1994). A Bayesian analysis of the unit root hypothesis within an unobserved components model. *Econometric Theory*, 10, 552–578.

SUBJECT INDEX

AUTHOR INDEX